MTEL General
03 Curriculum
Teacher Certification Exam

By: Sharon Wynne, M.S.

XAMonline, INC.
Boston

XAMonline, Inc.
21 Orient Avenue
Melrose, MA 02176
Toll Free 1-800-301-4647
Email: info@xamonline.com
Web: www.xamonline.com
Fax: 1-617-583-5552

Library of Congress Cataloging-in-Publication Data

Wynne, Sharon A.
    General Curriculum: Teacher Certification / Sharon A. Wynne.
    ISBN 978-1-60787-403-4
    1. General Curriculum.
    2. Study Guides.
    3. MTEL
    4. Teachers' Certification & Licensure.
    5. Careers

Disclaimer:
The opinions expressed in this publication are the sole works of XAMonline and were created independently from the National Education Association, Educational Testing Service, or any State Department of Education, National Evaluation Systems or other testing affiliates.

Between the time of publication and printing, state specific standards as well as testing formats and website information may change that is not included in part or in whole within this product. Sample test questions are developed by XAMonline and reflect similar content as on real tests; however, they are not former tests. XAMonline assembles content that aligns with state standards but makes no claims nor guarantees teacher candidates a passing score. Numerical scores are determined by testing companies such as NES or ETS and then are compared with individual state standards. A passing score varies from state to state.

Printed in the United States of America œ-1

MTEL General Curriculum 03
ISBN 978-1-60787-403-4

Project Manager:	Sharon Wynne, MS
Project Coordinator:	Victoria Anderson, MS
Content Coordinators/Authors:	Rennell Brunclik, BS
	Susan Andres, MS
	Frances Stanford, MS
	Natalie Arnett, BS
	Janis Petersen, PhD
	David White, MS
	Ted Purinton, PhD
	Christina Forsyth, MS
	Barbara Casey, PhD
	Kelley Eldredge, MS
	Vickie Pittard, MS
	James Stark, MS
	Don Rogerson, BS
	Michele Di Amico, BS
Sample test:	Shelley Wake, MS
	Deborah Harbin, MS
	Christina Godard, BS
	Kim Putney, BS
	Carol Moore, BS
	Vickie Pittard, MS
Editors: Managing	Dr. Harte Weiner, PhD
Proof reader	Heather Sugioka, MS
	Cathi Evans, AA
	Beth Anderson, PhD
	Donna Quesinberry; MS
	Paul Giacomelli, MS
	Vickie Pittard, MS
	Mary Arena, BS
	Christina Forsyth, MS
	Don Rogerson, BS
	Bonnie Snyder, PhD
	Jane Carter, MS
	Deborah Harbin, MS
Copy editor	Zakia Hyder, MS
Sample test	Christina Forsyth, MS
Pre-Flight	Mary Collins, BS
Production	David Aronson
Graphic Artist	Jenna Hamilton

Table of Contents

COMPETENCY 6.0   **UNDERSTAND AND APPLY NUMBER PROPERTIES AND NUMBER REPRESENTATIONS**

COMPETENCY 7.0   **UNDERSTAND AND APPLY NUMBER OPERATIONS TO REPRESENT AND SOLVE PROBLEMS**

COMPETENCY 8.0   UNDERSTAND AND APPLY PATTERNS, RELATIONS, ALGEBRA, AND PRINCIPLES OF GEOMETRY

Great Study and Testing Tips!

What to study in order to prepare for the subject assessments is the focus of this study guide, but equally important is *how* you study.

You can increase your chances of truly mastering the information by taking some simple, but effective steps.

Study Tips:

1. Eat foods that aid the learning process. Foods such as milk, nuts, seeds, rice, and oats help your study efforts by releasing natural memory enhancers called CCKs (cholecystokinin), composed of tryptophan, choline, and phenylalanine. All of these chemicals enhance the neurotransmitters associated with memory. Before studying, try a light, protein-rich meal of eggs, turkey, and fish. These foods release memory-enhancing chemicals. The better the connections, the more you comprehend.

Likewise, before you take a test, stick to a light snack of energy-boosting and relaxing foods. A glass of milk, a piece of fruit, or some peanuts all release various memory-boosting chemicals and help you to relax and focus.

2. Learn to take great notes. A byproduct of our modern culture is that we have grown accustomed to getting our information in short doses (i.e. TV news sound bites or *USA Today* style newspaper articles). We've subconsciously trained ourselves to assimilate information in neat little packages. If your notes are scrawled all over the paper, it fragments the flow of the information.

Strive for clarity. Newspapers use a standard format to achieve clarity. Your notes can be much clearer through use of proper formatting. A very effective format is called the "Cornell Method."

> Take a sheet of loose-leaf, lined notebook paper and draw a line all the way down the paper about 1-2" from the left-hand edge.

> Draw another line across the width of the paper about 1-2" up from the bottom. Repeat this process on the reverse side of the page.

Look at the highly effective result. You have ample room for notes, a left-hand margin for special-emphasis items or inserting supplementary data from the textbook, a large area at the bottom for a brief summary, and a little rectangular space for just about anything you want.

3. Get the concept, then the details. Too often we focus on the details and don't gather an understanding of the concept. However, if you memorize only dates, places, or names, you may well miss the whole point of the subject.

A key way to understand things is to put them in your own words. If you are working from a textbook, automatically summarize each paragraph in your mind. If you are outlining text, don't simply copy the author's words.

Rephrase the text in your own words. You remember your own thoughts and words much better than someone else's, and subconsciously tend to associate the important details to the core concepts.

4. Ask Why? Pull apart written material paragraph by paragraph and don't forget the captions under the illustrations.

Example: If the heading is "stream erosion," flip it around to read: "Why do streams erode?" Then answer the questions.

Training your mind to think in a series of questions and answers will not only help you learn more, it will lessen your test anxiety because you are now used to answering questions.

5. Read for reinforcement and future needs. Even if you have only 10 minutes, take your notes or book in your hand. Your mind is similar to a computer; you have to input data in order to have it processed. By reading, you are creating the neural connections for future retrieval. The more times you read something, the more you reinforce the learning of ideas.

Even if you don't fully understand something on the first pass, your mind stores much of the material for later recall.

6. Relax to learn. Our bodies respond to an inner clock called biorhythms. Burning the midnight oil works well for some people, but not for everyone.

If possible, set aside a particular place to study that is free of distractions. Shut off the television, cell phone, and pager and exile your friends and family during your study period.

If silence really bothers you, try background music. Light classical music at a low volume has been shown to aid in concentration. Music that evokes pleasant emotions without lyrics is highly suggested. Try just about anything by Mozart. It relaxes you.

7. Use arrows, not highlighters. At best, it's difficult to read a page full of yellow, pink, blue, and green streaks. Try staring at a neon sign for a while and you'll soon see how the horde of colors obscures the message.

A quick note, a brief dash of color, an underline, and an arrow pointing to a particular passage are much clearer than a horde of highlighted words.

8. Budget your study time. Although you shouldn't ignore any of the material, allocate your available study time in the same ratio that topics may appear on the test.

Testing Tips:

1. Get smart, play dumb. Don't read anything into the question. Don't make an assumption that the test writer is looking for something else than what is asked. Stick to the question as written and don't read extra things into it.

2. Read the question and all the choices _twice_ before answering the question. You may miss something by not carefully reading, and then rereading, both the question and the answers.

If you really don't have a clue as to the right answer, leave it blank on the first attempt. Go on to the other questions; they may provide clues as to how to answer the skipped questions.

If later on, you still can't answer the skipped ones . . . _guess._ The only penalty for guessing is that you _might_ get it wrong. Only one thing is certain; if you don't put anything down, you _will_ get it wrong!

3. Turn the question into a statement. Look at the way the questions are worded. The syntax of the question usually provides a clue. Does it seem more familiar as a statement rather than as a question? Does it sound strange?

By turning a question into a statement, you may be able to spot if an answer sounds right, and it may also trigger memories of material you have read.

4. Look for hidden clues. It's actually very difficult to compose multiple-foil (choice) questions without giving away part of the answer in the options presented.

In most multiple-choice questions, you can often readily eliminate one or two of the potential answers. This leaves you with only two real possibilities, and your odds automatically go to fifty-fifty for very little work.

5. Trust your instincts. For every fact that you have read, you subconsciously retain something of that knowledge. On questions that you aren't really certain about, go with your basic instincts. Your first impression on how to answer a question is usually correct.

6. Mark your answers directly on the test booklet. Don't bother trying to fill in the optical scan sheet on the first pass through the test.

7. Watch the clock! You have a set amount of time to answer the questions. Don't get bogged down trying to answer a single question at the expense of 10 questions you can more readily answer.

DOMAIN I.	LANGUAGE ARTS

COMPETENCY 1.0   UNDERSTAND THE HISTORY AND STRUCTURE OF THE ENGLISH LANGUAGE

Early printing presses, such as this, created an avenue for mass production of the written language.

Skill 1.1   Major developments in the history of the English language (e.g., invention of the printing press, standardization of written language, development of dictionaries)

The major developments in the history of the English language include the emergence of standard written and oral English and the development of the printing press and standard dictionaries. A pioneer in the study of how English was standardized is John H. Fisher, a Medievalist and author, who researched and wrote many books on the subject – including *The Emergence of Standard English* and *The Importance of Chaucer*. Fisher was a professor of English at the University of Tennessee before he retired in 1996 to further his research in the standardization of the English language.

According to Fisher, the standardization of English began in the 1400s during the Old English period. During this time, people who spoke English used the Latin alphabet to write out and pronounce sounds.

 Johannes Gutenberg invented the printing press in 1440. The printing press created an avenue for mass production of the written language. The ability to transfer images and words to paper repeatedly and consistently allowed for the widespread distribution of standardized written language.

Skill 1.2   Major linguistic origins of the English language (e.g., Anglo-Saxon roots, Celtic influences, Greek and Roman elements)

Figure 1 English Family Tree

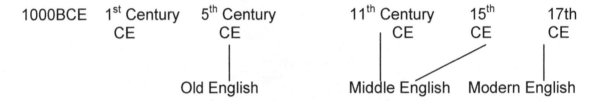

The English language has Germanic roots tracing back to tribes living in the British Isles in the 5th Century. The Angles, Saxons and Jutes were Germanic tribes who had crossed the North Sea from Denmark and Germany. The Celtics were the original habitants of Britain who spoke a Celtic language, which was quickly displaced along with the inhabitants to Wales and Scotland as the Germanic tribes took over the land and the language.

The land of origin for the Angles was Engle, and the language was Englisc – later changed to English. During the 5th century, written Old English included a West Saxon dialect derived from Scandinavian languages. The writing system of English comes from Latin origins brought over from Ireland. English words derived from Latin include the following:

- Street
- Kettle
- Cheese
- Angel
- Candle

The Viking influence contributed Norse words to the English language, some of which coexisted with English words:

- Anger-wrath
- Nay-no
- Dike-ditch
- Skip-shift
- Sky
- Egg
- Skin

English is the second most spoken language in the world, with an estimated 300 million people who speak English as a second language and another 100 million who speak it as a foreign language. English provides a global connection of communication in over 45 countries. Some examples of countries where English is a major secondary language include the following:

- Australia
- Bahamas

- Belize
- Bermuda
- Canada
- Grenada
- Ireland
- Jamaica

- New Zealand
- St. Vincent
- South Africa
- United Kingdom
- United States of America

Many languages have contributed to the English language worldwide. Borrowed words from Latin, Greek, French, German and Spanish create an enormous spoken and written English vocabulary base. The English vocabulary is considered one of the largest in the world. The core of the English language remains Anglo-Saxon, based in Old English.

Skill 1.3   Derivatives and borrowings

Borrowed words

A borrowed word (or a loanword) is a word that has been adopted from another language (the source language) directly into the native language with little or no change. Borrowing is a result of cultural interactions between two language communities.

A newly borrowed word gradually adopts the characteristics and sound of the adopted language. Eventually, the borrowed word begins to resemble the words of the native language. With time, people in the borrowing community do not perceive the word as a loanword at all. It has become a part of our American cultural history to adopt loanwords from the languages of the various cultures with which we have come in contact.

Some examples of words borrowed from other languages are:

French: jail, duchess, poultry, clarinet, diamond
Latin: abdomen, anatomy, physician, insane, janitor, notorious
Greek (many of these via Latin): atmosphere, comedy, history, pneumonia, skeleton
Spanish: alligator, armadillo, guitar, mosquito, tornado
Italian: broccoli, macaroni, piano, umbrella, violin
German: loafer, noodle, poodle, pretzel, sauerkraut
Yiddish: bagel, Hanukkah, kosher, klutz, matzo

Derived words

Derived words are words that have been formed by joining two words together.. The original words usually have two separate meanings. When combined, they produce a completely new word. Examples of derived words are:

Jet-black: very dark black in color

Jet lag: the feeling of being very tired due to traveling on a plane

Many of the root words that define our native language have Greek and Latin origins. It would be extremely beneficial to early readers to learn as many Greek and Latin root words as possible, in order to comprehend larger words.

Skill 1.4   Differences between oral and written English (e.g., level of formality, diversity of oral dialects, and uniformity of written language)

Often, people assume that written language is simply a codified oral language (in other words, it is oral language put into symbols on a page). This is far from the truth. Consider, first, how children can speak fluently before they can communicate fluently in writing. Consider also how it is very easy for most adults to orally discuss issues, but how often adults struggle when putting words on paper.

A significant difference between oral and written language is the level of formality. Oral language tends to be informal, while written language is more formal. Highly formalized oral language may sound unnatural to listeners. Similarly, it is not easy for some readers to accept highly informal styles of writing

Another difference between oral and written language is that written language is not easily influenced by the diversity of oral dialects. Oral language, on the other hand, can be strongly influenced by the country's regions, local culture, and other factors. Generally, accent, word choice, tone, and other elements distinguish oral language from written language.

Finally, written language is more uniform than oral language. While speaking out loud, people regularly use run-on and fragment sentences or make other grammatical errors that typically go unnoticed by listeners. People also add emphasis in oral speech through repeated phrases, volume, tone, and other elements unavailable in written language.

Understanding the difference between oral and written language is important for teachers because both skills need to be developed in students separately. Often teachers assume that oral language develops naturally and that no specific work needs to be done in the classroom to enhance it. This is not true. Although informality and unevenness are accepted more readily in oral language, students must learn and practice the skills needed to express themselves competently in oral language (both in formal presentations and informal discussions).

By modeling good oral language and having students practice it through classroom discussions, oral presentations, and group discussions, teachers can provide students good outlets to improve their oral language skills. To teach writing skills, on the other hand, instructors need a different set of tools. Writing skills begin with basic language development and progressively move through improvement in vocabulary, research skills, topic selection, content organization, content revision, and more. (These tools are discussed later in this domain.)

Skill 1.5   Fundamental language structures (i.e., phonology, morphology, syntax, and semantics)

Phonics

As opposed to phonemic awareness, the study of phonics must be done with the eyes open to make the connection between the sounds and letters on a page. Students learning phonics might see the word "bad" and sound each letter out slowly until they recognize that they just said the word.

Phonological awareness means the ability of the reader to recognize the sound of spoken language. This recognition includes how these sounds can be blended together, segmented (divided up), and manipulated (switched around). This awareness then leads to phonics, a method for teaching children to read. It helps them "sound out words."

Development of phonological skills may begin during pre-K years. Indeed, by the age of 5, a child who has been exposed to rhyme can recognize a rhyme. Such a child can demonstrate phonological awareness by filling in the missing rhyming word in a familiar rhyme or rhymed picture book.

Children gain phonological awareness when they are taught the sounds made by letters, the sounds made by various combinations of letters, and how to recognize individual sounds in words.

Phonological awareness skills include:

1. Rhyming and syllabification
2. Blending sounds into words, such as pic-ture-boo-k
3. Identifying the beginning or starting sounds of words and the ending or closing sounds of words
4. Breaking words down into sounds, also called "segmenting" words
5. Recognizing other smaller words in a big word by removing starting sounds, such as "hear" to "ear"

Phonemic Awareness
Phonemic awareness is the acknowledgement of sounds and words, such as a child's realization that some words rhyme. Onset and rhyme, for example, are skills that might help students learn that the sound of the first letter "b" in the word "bad" can be changed with the sound "d" to make it "dad." The key in

phonemic awareness is that it can be taught with the students' eyes closed. In other words, it's all about sounds, not about ascribing written letters to sounds.

To be phonemically aware means that the reader and listener can recognize and manipulate specific sounds in spoken words. Phonemic awareness deals with sounds in words that are spoken. The majority of phonemic awareness tasks, activities, and exercises are oral.

Since distinguishing between individual sounds – phonemes – within words is a prerequisite to associating sounds with letters and manipulating sounds to blend words (in order to read), the teaching of phonemic awareness is crucial to emergent reading. For phonics instruction to be effective, children need a strong background in phonemic awareness.

Morphology, Syntax and Semantics

Morphology is the study of word structure. When readers develop morphemic skills, they are developing an understanding of patterns they see in words. For example, English speakers realize that cat, cats, and caterpillar share some similarities in structure. This understanding helps readers to recognize words at a faster and easier rate, since each word doesn't need individual decoding.

Syntax refers to the rules or patterned relationships that correctly produce phrases and sentences from words. When readers develop an understanding of syntax, they begin to understand the structure of how sentences are built and eventually how grammar is used.

Example: "I am going to the movies."
             This statement is syntactically and grammatically correct.

Example: "They am going to the movies:
             This statement is syntactically correct since all the words are in their correct place. However, it is is grammatically incorrect with the use of the word "they" rather than "I," the use of a colon instead of a period at the end of the sentence, and the lack of end quotes.

Semantics refers to the meaning expressed when words are arranged in a specific way. This is where connotation and denotation of words play a role in reading.

All of these skill sets are important in developing effective word-recognition skills and helping emerging readers develop fluency.

Pragmatics

Pragmatics deals with the difference between the writer's intended meaning and the sentence meaning (the literal meaning of the sentence) based on social context. Those who are competent in pragmatics are able to understand the writer's intended meaning or what the writer is trying to convey. In a simpler sense, pragmatics can be considered the social rules of language.

For example, a child sitting beside her mother at a fancy restaurant after her great-grandmother's funeral looks over to the table next to them. She sees a very elderly woman eating her dessert. "Mom?" she asks, patiently waiting for response. When her mother addresses her, she states loudly, "That woman is old like Grandma. Is she going to die soon too?" Of course embarrassed, the mother hushes her child. However, this is a simple example of immature pragmatics. The child has the vocabulary, the patience to wait her turn, and some knowledge of conversational rules; however, she is not aware that certain topics are socially inappropriate and does not adapt her language to the situation.

Skill 1.6   Parts of speech (e.g., noun, verb, adjective, adverb, conjunction, preposition)

A verb agrees in number with its subject. To make the verb and subject agree, one must properly identify the subject.

- <u>One</u> of the boys <u>was playing</u> too rough.
- <u>No one</u> in the class, neither the teacher nor the students, <u>was listening</u> to the message from the intercom.
- The <u>candidates,</u> including a grandmother and a teenager, <u>are debating</u> some controversial issues.

If two singular subjects are connected by *and,* the verb must be plural.

- A <u>man and</u> his <u>dog were jogging</u> on the beach.

If two singular subjects are connected by *or* or *nor,* a singular verb is required.

- Neither <u>Dot nor Joyce has missed</u> a day of school this year.
- Either <u>Fran or Paul is missing</u>.

If one singular subject and one plural subject are connected by *or* or *nor,* the verb agrees with the subject nearest to the verb.

- Neither the <u>coach nor the players were able to sleep</u> on the bus.

If the subject is a collective noun, its sense of number in the sentence determines the verb: singular if the noun represents a group or unit and plural if the noun represents individuals.

- The House of Representatives has adjourned for the holidays.
- The House of Representatives have failed to reach agreement on the subject of adjournment.

Use of verbs (tense)

Present tense is used to express that which is currently happening or is always true.

- Randy is playing the piano.
- Randy plays the piano like a pro.

Past tense is used to express action that occurred in a past time.

- Randy learned to play the piano when he was six years old.

Future tense is used to express action or a condition of future time.

- Randy will probably earn a music scholarship.

Present perfect tense is used to express action or a condition that started in the past and is continued to or completed in the present.

- Randy has practiced piano every day for the last ten years.
- Randy has never been bored with practice.

Past perfect tense expresses action or a condition that occurred as a precedent to some other action or condition.

- Randy had considered playing clarinet before he discovered the piano.

Future perfect tense expresses action that started in the past or the present and will conclude at some time in the future.

- By the time he goes to college, Randy will have been an accomplished pianist for more than half of his life.

Use of verbs (mood) Indicative mood is used to make unconditional statements; subjunctive mood is used for conditional clauses or wish statements that pose conditions that are untrue. Verbs in subjunctive mood are plural with both singular and plural subjects.

- If I were a bird, I would fly.

- I wish I were as rich as Donald Trump.

Verb conjugation The conjugation of verbs follows the patterns used in the discussion of tense above. However, the most frequent problems in verb use stem from the improper formation of past and past participial forms.

Regular verb: believe, believed, (have) believed

Irregular verbs: run, ran, run; sit, sat, sat; teach, taught, taught

Other problems stem from the use of verbs that are the same in some tense but have different forms and different meanings in other tenses.

- I lie on the ground.
- I lay on the ground yesterday.
- I have lain down.

- I lay the blanket on the bed.
- I laid the blanket there yesterday.
- I have laid the blanket every night.

- The sun rises.
- The sun rose.
- The sun has risen.

- He raises the flag.
- He raised the flag.
- He had raised the flag.

- I sit on the porch.
- I sat on the porch.
- I have sat on the porch swing.

- I set the plate on the table.
- I set the plate there yesterday.
- I had set the table before dinner.

Two other verb problems stem from misusing the preposition *of* for the verb auxiliary *have* and misusing the verb *ought* (now rare).

Incorrect:	I should of gone to bed.
Correct:	I should have gone to bed.

Incorrect:	He hadn't ought to get so angry.
Correct:	He ought not to get so angry.

Use of pronouns

A pronoun used as a subject of predicate nominative is in nominative case.

- She was the drum majorette.
- The lead trombonists were Joe and he.
- The band director accepted whoever could march in step.

A pronoun used as a direct object, indirect object or object of a preposition is in objective case.

- The teacher praised him.
- She gave him an A on the test.
- Her praise of him was appreciated.
- The students whom she did not praise will work harder next time.

Common pronoun errors occur from misuse of reflexive pronouns:

Singular: *myself, yourself, herself, himself, itself*
Plural: *ourselves, yourselves, themselves.*
Incorrect: Jack cut hisself shaving.
Correct: Jack cut himself shaving.

Incorrect: They backed theirselves into a corner.
Correct: They backed themselves into a corner.

Use of adjectives

An adjective should agree with its antecedent in number.

- Those apples are rotten.
- This one is ripe.
- These peaches are hard.

Comparative adjectives end in -er and superlatives in -est, with some exceptions like *worse* and *worst.* Some adjectives that cannot easily make comparative inflections are preceded by *more* and *most.*

- Mrs. Carmichael is the better of the two basketball coaches.
- That is the hastiest excuse you have ever contrived.

As shown below, avoid double comparisons.

Incorrect: This is the worstest headache I ever had.
Correct: This is the worst headache I ever had.

When comparing one thing to others in a group, exclude the thing under comparison from the rest of the group.

Incorrect: Joey is larger than any baby I have ever seen. (Since you have seen him, he cannot be larger than himself.)
Correct: Joey is larger than <u>any other</u> baby I have ever seen.

Include all necessary words to make a comparison clear in meaning.

I am as tall as my mother. I am as tall as she (is).
My cats are better behaved than those of my neighbor.

Plurals

The multiplicity and complexity of spelling rules based on phonics, letter doubling, etc., and the exceptions to these make a good dictionary an essential tool.

Most plurals of nouns that end in hard consonants or hard consonant sounds followed by a silent *e* are made by adding *s*. Some words ending in vowels only add *s* (fingers, numerals, banks, bugs, riots, homes, gates, radios, bananas.).

Nouns that end in soft consonant sounds *s, j, x, z, ch,* and *sh,* add *es*. Some nouns ending in *o* add es (dresses, waxes, churches, brushes, tomatoes).

Nouns ending in *y* preceded by a vowel just add *s* (boys, alleys).

Nouns ending in *y* preceded by a consonant change the *y* to *i* and add *es* (babies, corollaries, frugalities, poppies).

Some nouns' plurals are formed irregularly or remain the same (sheep, deer, children, leaves, oxen).

Some nouns derived from foreign words, especially Latin, may make their plurals in two different ways – one of them Anglicized. Sometimes, the meanings are the same; other times, the two plurals are used in slightly different contexts. It is always wise to consult the dictionary.

appendices, appendixes criterion, criteria
indexes, indices   crisis, crises

Make the plurals of closed (solid) compound words in the usual way.

timelines, hairpins, cupfuls

Make the plurals of open or hyphenated compounds by adding the change in inflection to the words that change in number.

fathers-in-law, courts-martial, masters of art, doctors of medicine

Make the plurals of letters, numbers, and abbreviations by adding *s*.

fives and tens, IBMs, 1990s, *p*s and *q*s (Note that letters are italicized.)

Possessives

Make the possessives of singular nouns by adding an apostrophe followed by the letter *s* (*'s*).

baby's bottle, father's job, elephant's eye, teacher's desk, sympathizer's protests, week's postponement

Make the possessive of singular nouns ending in *s* by adding either an apostrophe or an (*'s*) depending upon common usage or sound. When making the possessive causes difficulty, use a prepositional phrase instead. Even with the sibilant ending, with a few exceptions, it is advisable to use the (*'s*) construction.

dress's color, species' characteristics or characteristics of the species, James' hat or James's hat, Delores's shirt

Make the possessive of plural nouns ending in *s* by adding the apostrophe after the *s*.

horses' coats, jockeys' times, four days' time

Make possessives of plural nouns that do not end in *s* the same way as singular nouns, by adding's.

children's shoes, deer's antlers, cattle's horns

Make possessives of compound nouns by adding the inflection at the end of the word or phrase.

the mayor of Los Angeles' campaign, the mailman's new truck, the mailmen's new trucks, my father-in-law's first wife, the keepsakes' values, several daughters-in-law's husbands

Skill 1.7   Sentence types (e.g., simple, compound, complex) and sentence purposes (e.g., declarative, imperative, interrogative)

Clauses
Clauses are connected word groups that are composed of *at least* one subject and one verb. A *subject* is the doer of an action or the element that is being joined. A verb conveys either the action or the link.

Students are waiting for the start of the assembly.
 subject   verb

At the end of the play, students wait for the curtain to come down.
                   subject   verb

Clauses can be independent or dependent.

Independent clauses can stand alone or can be joined to other clauses.

Independent clause

- for
- and
- nor
- but

- or
- yet
- so

(Independent clause)   ;   (Independent clause)
(Dependent clause)   ,   (Independent clause)
(Independent clause)   ;   (Dependent clause)

Dependent clauses, by definition, contain at least one subject and one verb. However, they cannot stand alone as a complete sentence. They are structurally dependent on the main clause.

There are two types of dependent clauses:

1. those with a subordinating conjunction
2. those with a relative pronoun

Sample subordinating conjunctions:

- Although
- When
- If   (dependent clause)   ,   (independent clause)
- Unless
- Because

Example:
> Unless a cure is discovered, many more people will die of the disease.

Sample relative pronouns:

	who	
	whom	
Independent clause	which	relative dependent clause
	that	

Example:
> The White House has an official website, which features press releases, news updates, and biographies of the President and Vice-President.

Sentences
Sentences are made up of two parts: the subject and the predicate. The subject (like in the clause section above) is the doer of an action or the element that is being joined. In addition, any adjectives describing this doer or element are also part of the subject. The predicate is made up of the verb and any other adverbs, adjectives, pronouns or clauses that describe the action of the sentence.

Sentence structure
Recognize simple, compound, complex, and compound-complex sentences. Use dependent (subordinate) and independent clauses correctly to create these sentence structures.

- **Simple**   Joyce wrote a letter.
- **Compound**   Joyce wrote a letter, and Dot drew a picture.
- **Complex**   While Joyce wrote a letter, Dot drew a picture.

Compound/Complex

> When Mother asked the girls to demonstrate their newfound skills, Joyce wrote a letter, and Dot drew a picture.

Note: Do **not** confuse compound sentence elements with compound sentences.

Simple sentence with compound subject:

> <u>Joyce</u> <u>and Dot</u> wrote letters.
> <u>The girl</u> in row three <u>and the boy</u> next to her were passing notes across the aisle.

Simple sentence with compound predicate:

> Joyce <u>wrote letters</u> and <u>drew pictures.</u>
> The captain of the high school debate team <u>graduated with honors</u> and <u>studied broadcast journalism in college.</u>

Simple sentence with compound object of preposition:

Colleen graded the students' essays for <u>style</u> and <u>mechanical accuracy.</u>

A simple sentence contains one independent clause which contains one subject, one verb, and one predicate.

In the following examples, the subject is underlined once and the predicate is underlined twice:

<u>The dancer</u> <u><u>bowed.</u></u>
<u>Nathan</u> <u><u>skied down the hill</u></u>.

A compound sentence is made up of two independent clauses joined by a conjunction, a correlative conjunction (i.e., either-or, neither-nor) or a semicolon. Each of these independent clauses could stand on its own, but for sentence variety, authors will often combine them. In the following examples, the subjects of each independent clause are underlined once, the predicates of each independent clause are underlined twice, and the conjunction is in bold:

<u>Samantha</u> <u><u>ate the cookie</u></u>, **and** <u>she</u> <u><u>drank her milk</u></u>.

<u>Mark</u> <u><u>is excellent with computers</u></u>; <u>he</u> <u><u>has worked with them for years</u></u>.

Either <u>Terry</u> <u><u>runs the project</u></u> **or** <u>I</u> <u><u>will not participate</u></u>.

A complex sentence is made up of one independent clause and at least one dependent clause. In the following examples, the subjects of each clause are underlined once, the predicates are underlined twice, the independent clause is in plain text, and the dependent clause is in italics:

When <u>Jody</u> <u><u>saw</u></u> how clean the house was, <u>she</u> <u><u>was</u></u> happy.
<u>Brian</u> <u><u>loves</u></u> taking diving lessons, *which <u>he</u> <u><u>has done</u></u> for years*.

Sentence completeness

Avoid fragments and run-on sentences. Recognition of sentence elements necessary to make a complete thought, proper use of independent and dependent clauses, and proper punctuation will correct such errors.

Skill 1.8   Rules of English grammar and conventions of edited American English

Commas indicate a brief pause. They are used to set off dependent clauses and long introductory word groups. They are also used to separate words in a series.

They are used to set off unimportant material that interrupts the flow of the sentence, and they separate independent clauses joined by conjunctions.

Error: After I finish my master's thesis I plan to work in Chicago.

Problem: A comma is needed after an introductory dependent word-group containing a subject and verb.

Correction: *After I finish my master's thesis, I plan to work in Chicago.*

Error: I washed waxed and vacuumed my car today.

Problem: Words in a series should be separated by commas. Although the word *and* is sometimes considered optional, it is often necessary to clarify the meaning.

Correction: *I washed, waxed, and vacuumed my car today.*

Error: She was a talented dancer but she is mostly remembered for her singing ability.

Problem: A comma is needed before a conjunction that joins two independent clauses (complete sentences).

Correction: *She was a talented dancer, but she is mostly remembered for her singing ability.*

Error: This incident is I think typical of what can happen when the community remains so divided.

Problem: Commas are needed to set apart nonessential words or words that interrupt the main clause.

Correction: *This incident is, I think, typical of what can happen when the community remains so divided.*

Semicolons and colons

Semicolons are needed to divide two or more closely related independent sentences. They are also needed to separate items in a series containing commas. Colons are used to introduce lists and to emphasize what follows.

Error: I climbed to the top of the mountain, it took me three hours.

Problem: A comma alone cannot separate two independent clauses. Instead a semicolon is needed to separate two related sentences.

Correction: *I climbed to the top of the mountain; it took me three hours.*

Error: In the movie, asteroids destroyed Dallas, Texas, Kansas City, Missouri, and Boston, Massachusetts.

Problem: Semicolons are needed to separate items in a series that already contains commas.

Correction: *In the movie, asteroids destroyed Dallas, Texas; Kansas City, Missouri; and Boston, Massachusetts.*

Error: Essays will receive the following grades, A for excellent, B for good, C for average, and D for unsatisfactory.

Problem: A colon is needed to emphasize the information or list that follows.

Correction: *Essays will receive the following grades: A for excellent, B for good, C for average, and D for unsatisfactory.*

Error: The school carnival included: amusement rides, clowns, food booths, and a variety of games.

Problem: The material preceding the colon and the list that follows are not complete sentences. Do not separate a verb (or preposition) from the object.

Correction: *The school carnival included amusement rides, clowns, food booths, and a variety of games.*

Apostrophes

Apostrophes are used to show either contractions or possession.

Error: She shouldnt be permitted to smoke cigarettes in the building.

Problem: An apostrophe is needed in a contraction in place of the missing letter.

Correction: *She shouldn't be permitted to smoke cigarettes in the building.*

Error: My cousins motorcycle was stolen from his driveway.

Problem: An apostrophe is needed to show possession.

Correction: *My cousin's motorcycle was stolen from his driveway.*
(Note: The use of the apostrophe before the letter "s" means that there is just one cousin. The plural form would read the following way: My cousins' motorcycle was stolen from their driveway.)

Error: Children screams could be heard for miles.

Problem: An apostrophe and the letter s are needed in the sentence to show whose screams it is.

Correction: *Children's screams could he heard for miles.*
(Note: Because the word children is already plural, the apostrophe and s must be added afterward to show ownership.)

Quotation marks

Use double quotation marks to enclose a direct quotation and to enclose the title of an article, a song, an essay, or a short story.

Error: Franklin Roosevelt once said, There is nothing to fear but fear itself.

Problem: Double quotation marks are needed to set off the quotation.

Correction: *Franklin Roosevelt once said, "There is nothing to fear but fear itself."*

Error: In the song Streets of Philadelphia, Bruce Springsteen pays tribute to a man dying from AIDS.

Problem: Use double quotations to set off the title of a song.

Correction: *In the song "Streets of Philadelphia," Bruce Springsteen pays tribute to a man dying from AIDS.*

Capitalization

Capital letters are used to indicate specific names of people, places, buildings, companies, courses, products, holidays, days of the week, months, and major sections of the country and the world. Capital letters are also used to signal the start of a sentence and of a direct quotation.

Error: Emma went to Dr. Peters for treatment since her own Doctor was on vacation.

Problem: The use of capital letters with Emma and Dr .Peters is correct since they are specific (proper) names; the title Dr. is also capitalized. However, the word doctor is not a specific name and should not be capitalized.

Correction: *Emma went to Dr. Peters for treatment since her own doctor was on vacation.*

Error: Our Winter Break does not start until next wednesday.

Problem: Days of the week are capitalized, but seasons are not capitalized.

Correction: *Our winter break does not start until next Wednesday.*

Error: The exchange student from israel who came to study biochemistry spoke spanish very well.

Problem: Languages and the names of countries are always capitalized. Courses are also capitalized when they refer to a specific course; they are not capitalized when they refer to courses in general.

Correction: *The exchange student from Israel who came to study Biochemistry spoke Spanish very well.*

Parallelism

Recognize parallel structures using phrases (prepositional, gerund, participial, and infinitive) and omissions from sentences that create the lack of parallelism.

Prepositional phrase/single modifier

Incorrect: Colleen ate the ice cream with enthusiasm and hurriedly.
Correct: Colleen ate the ice cream with enthusiasm and in a hurry.
Correct: Colleen ate the ice cream enthusiastically and hurriedly.

Participial phrase/infinitive phrase

Incorrect: After hiking for hours and to sweat profusely, Joe sat down to rest and drinking water.
Correct: After hiking for hours and sweating profusely, Joe sat down to rest and drink water.

Recognition of dangling modifiers

Dangling phrases are attached to sentence parts in such a way that they create ambiguity and incorrectness of meaning.

Participial phrase

Incorrect:	Hanging from her skirt, Dot tugged at a loose thread.
Correct:	Dot tugged at a loose thread hanging from her skirt.
Incorrect:	Relaxing in the bathtub, the telephone rang.
Correct:	While I was relaxing in the bathtub, the telephone rang.

Infinitive phrase

Incorrect:	To improve his behavior, the dean warned Fred.
Correct:	The dean warned Fred to improve his behavior.

Prepositional phrase

Incorrect:	On the floor, Father saw the dog eating table scraps.
Correct:	Father saw the dog eating table scraps on the floor.

Recognition of syntactical redundancy or omission
These errors occur when superfluous words have been added to a sentence or key words have been omitted from it.

Redundancy

Incorrect:	Joyce made sure that when her plane arrived that she retrieved all of her luggage.
Correct:	Joyce made sure that when her plane arrived she retrieved all of her luggage.
Incorrect:	He was a mere skeleton of his former self.
Correct:	He was a skeleton of his former self.

Omission

Incorrect:	Sue opened her book, recited her textbook, and answered the teacher's subsequent question.
Correct:	Sue opened her book, recited from the textbook, and answered the teacher's subsequent question.

Avoidance of double negatives

This error occurs from positioning two negatives that, in fact, cancel each other in meaning.

Incorrect: Dot didn't have no double negatives in her paper.
Correct: Dot didn't have any double negatives in her paper.

Correct use of coordination and subordination

Connect independent clauses with the coordinating conjunctions – *and, but, or, for,* or *nor* – when their content is of equal importance. Use subordinating conjunctions – although, because, before, if, since, though, until, when, whenever, wherever – and relative pronouns – that, who, whom, which – to introduce clauses that express ideas that are subordinate to main ideas expressed in independent clauses. (See *Sentence Structure* above.)

Be sure to place the conjunctions so that they express the proper relationship between ideas (cause/effect, condition, time, space).

Incorrect: Because mother scolded me, I was late.
Correct: Mother scolded me because I was late.

Incorrect: The sun rose after the fog lifted.
Correct: The fog lifted after the sun rose.

Notice that placement of the conjunction can completely change the meaning of the sentence. Main emphasis is shifted by the change.

- Although Jenny was pleased, the teacher was disappointed.
- Although the teacher was disappointed, Jenny was pleased.

- The boys who wrote the essay won the contest.
- The boys who won the contest wrote the essay.

Note: While not syntactically incorrect, the second sentence makes it appear that the boys won the contest for something else before they wrote the essay.

Revisions involving punctuation and capitalization in a given text

The candidate should be cognizant of proper rules and conventions of punctuation, capitalization, and spelling. Competency exams will generally test the ability to apply more advanced skills; thus, a limited number of more challenging rules are presented here. Rules should be applied according to the American style of English, i.e. spelling *theater* instead of *theatre* and placing terminal marks of punctuation almost exclusively within other marks of punctuation.

Punctuation

Using terminal punctuation in relation to quotation marks

In a quoted statement that is either declarative or imperative, place the period inside the closing quotation marks.

- "The airplane crashed on the runway during takeoff."

If the quotation is followed by other words in the sentence, place a comma inside the closing quotations marks and a period at the end of the sentence.

- "The airplane crashed on the runway during takeoff," said the announcer.

In most instances in which a quoted title or expression occurs at the end of a sentence, the period is placed before either the single or double quotation marks.

- "The middle school readers were unprepared to understand Bryant's poem, 'Thanatopsis.'"
- Early book length adventure stories like *Don Quixote* and *The Three Musketeers* were known as "picaresque novels."

There is an instance in which the final quotation mark would precede the period – if the content of the sentence were about a speech or quote so that the understanding of the meaning would be confused by the placement of the period.

- The first thing out of his mouth was "Hi, I'm home."
  but
- The first line of his speech began "I arrived home to an empty house".

In sentences that are interrogatory or exclamatory, the question mark or exclamation point should be positioned **outside** the closing quotation marks if the quote itself is a statement or command or cited title.

- Who decided to lead us in the recitation of the "Pledge of Allegiance"?
- Why was Tillie shaking as she began her recitation, "Once upon a midnight dreary..."?
- I was embarrassed when Mrs. White said, "Your slip is showing"!

In sentences that are declarative but the quotation is a question or an exclamation, place the question mark or exclamation point **inside** the quotation marks.

- The hall monitor yelled, "Fire! Fire!" "Fire! Fire!"
- Cory shrieked, "Is there a mouse in the room?" (In this instance, the question supersedes the exclamation.)

Using periods with parentheses or brackets

Place the period inside the parentheses or brackets if they enclose a complete sentence, independent of the other sentences around it.

- Stephen Crane was a confirmed alcohol and drug addict. (He admitted as much to other journalists in Cuba.)

If the parenthetical expression is a statement inserted within another statement, the period in the enclosure is omitted.

- Mark Twain used the character Injun Joe (He also appeared in *The Adventures of Tom Sawyer*) as a foil for Jim in *The Adventures of Huckleberry Finn*.

When enclosed matter comes at the end of a sentence requiring quotation marks, place the period outside the parentheses or brackets.

- "The secretary of state consulted with the ambassador [Powell]."

Using commas

Separate two or more coordinate adjectives, modifying the same word and three or more nouns, phrases, or clauses in a list.

- Maggie's hair was dull, dirty, and lice-ridden.
- Dickens portrayed the Artful Dodger as a skillful pickpocket, loyal follower of Fagin, and defendant of Oliver Twist.
- Ellen daydreamed about getting out of the rain, taking a shower, and eating a hot dinner.
- In Elizabethan England, Ben Jonson wrote comedies, Christopher Marlowe wrote tragedies, and William Shakespeare composed both.

Use commas to separate antithetical or complimentary expressions from the rest of the sentence.

- The veterinarian, not his assistant, would perform the delicate surgery.
- The more he knew about her, the less he wished he knew.
- Randy hopes to, and probably will, get an appointment to the Naval Academy.

- His thorough, though esoteric, scientific research could not easily be understood by high school students.

Using double quotation marks with other punctuation

Quotations – whether words, phrases, or clauses – should be punctuated according to the rules of the grammatical function they serve in the sentence.

- The works of Shakespeare, "the bard of Avon," have been contested as originating with other authors.
- "You'll get my money," the old man warned, "when 'Hell freezes over'"
- Sheila cited the passage that began "Four score and seven years ago...." (Note the ellipsis followed by an enclosed period.)
- "Old Ironsides" inspired the preservation of the U.S.S. Constitution.

Use quotation marks to enclose the titles of shorter works: songs, short poems, short stories, essays, and chapters of books. (See "Using Italics" for punctuating longer titles.)

- "The Tell-Tale Heart"
- "Casey at the Bat"
- "America the Beautiful"

Using semicolons

Use semicolons to separate independent clauses when the second clause is introduced by a transitional adverb. (These clauses may also be written as separate sentences, preferably by placing the adverb within the second sentence.)

- The Elizabethans modified the rhyme scheme of the sonnet; thus, it was called the English sonnet.

Or

- The Elizabethans modified the rhyme scheme of the sonnet. It thus was called the English sonnet.

Use semicolons to separate items in a series that are long and complex or have internal punctuation.

- The Italian Renaissance produced masters in the fine arts: Dante Alighieri, author of the *Divine Comedy;* Leonardo da Vinci, painter of *The Last Supper;* and Donatello, sculptor of the *Quattro Coronati,* the four saints.
- The leading scorers in the WNBA were Haizhaw Zheng, averaging 23.9 points per game; Lisa Leslie, 22; and Cynthia Cooper, 19.5.

Using colons

Place a colon at the beginning of a list of items. (Note its use in the sentence about Renaissance Italians on the previous page.)

- The teacher directed us to compare Faulkner's three symbolic novels: *Absalom, Absalom!, As I Lay Dying,* and *Light in August.*

Do **not** use a colon if the list is preceded by a verb, such as the verb "are" in the following sentence.

- Three of Faulkner's symbolic novels are *Absalom, Absalom!, As I Lay Dying,* and *Light in August.*

Using dashes

Place dashes to denote sudden breaks in thought.

- Some periods in literature – the Romantic Age, for example – spanned different time periods in different countries.

For amplification or explanation, use dashes instead of commas if commas are already used elsewhere in the sentence.

- The Fireside Poets included the three Brahmins – James Russell Lowell, Henry Wadsworth Longfellow, Oliver Wendell Holmes – as well as John Greenleaf Whittier.

Use italics to punctuate the titles of long works of literature, names of periodicals, musical scores, works of art, motion pictures, television shows, and radio programs.. (When unable to write in italics, students should be instructed to underline in their own writing where italics would be appropriate.)

Idylls of the King	*Hiawatha*	*The Sound and the Fury*
Mary Poppins	*Newsweek*	*The Nutcracker Suite*

Capitalization

Capitalize all proper names of persons (including specific organizations or agencies of government); places (countries, states, cities, parks, and specific geographical areas); and things (political parties, structures, historical and cultural terms, and calendar and time designations); and religious terms (any deity, revered person or group, and sacred writings).

- Percy Bysshe Shelley, Argentina, Mount Rainier National Park, Grand Canyon, League of Nations, the Sears Towers, Birmingham, Lyric Theater,

Americans, Midwesterners, Democrats, Renaissance, Boy Scouts of America, Easter, God, Bible, Dead Sea Scrolls, Koran

Capitalize proper adjectives and titles used with proper names.

- California Gold Rush, President John Adams, French fries, Homeric epic, Romanesque architecture, Senator John Glenn

Learn more about:
John H. Fisher and his research on the standardization of English:
http://www.childrenofthecode.org/interviews/fisher.htm
Johannes Gutenberg and the invention of the printing press:
http://www.ideafinder.com/history/inventors/gutenberg.htm
Phonemic awareness and phonics instruction:
http://content.scholastic.com/browse/article.jsp?id=4497
Conventions of edited American English:
http://www.pbs.org/standarddeviantstv/episode_res_grammar.html

COMPETENCY 2.0   **UNDERSTAND AMERICAN LITERATURE AND SELECTED LITERATURE FROM CLASSICAL AND CONTEMPORARY PERIODS**

Skill 2.1   **Historically or culturally significant works, authors, and themes of U.S. literature; selected literature from classical and contemporary periods**

American Literature is defined by a number of clearly identifiable periods.

The Colonial Period
William Bradford's excerpts from *The Mayflower Compact* relate vividly the hardships of crossing the Atlantic in such a tiny vessel, the misery and suffering of the first winter, the approaches of the American Indians, the decimation of their ranks, and the establishment of the Bay Colony of Massachusetts.

Anne Bradstreet's poetry relates much concerning colonial New England life. From her journals, modern readers learn of the everyday life of the early settlers, the hardships of travel, and the responsibilities of different groups and individuals in the community., Early American literature also reveals the commercial and political adventures of the Cavaliers who came to the New World with King George's blessing.

William Byrd's journal, *History of the Dividing Line,* concerning his trek into the Dismal Swamp separating the Carolinian territories from Virginia and Maryland makes quite lively reading. A privileged insider to the English Royal Court, Byrd, like other Southern Cavaliers, was given grants to pursue business ventures.

The Revolutionary Period
This period saw great orations, such as Patrick Henry's *Speech to the Virginia House of Burgesses* – the "Give me liberty or give me death" speech – and George Washington's *Farewell to the Army of the Potomac.* Less memorable and thought rambling by modern readers are Washington's inaugural addresses.

The *Declaration of Independence*, the brainchild predominantly of Thomas Jefferson, with some prudent editing by Ben Franklin, is a prime example of neoclassical writing – balanced, well crafted, and focused.

Epistles include the exquisitely written, moving correspondence between John Adams and Abigail Adams. The poignancy of their separation – she in Boston, he in Philadelphia – is palpable and real.

The Romantic Period
Early American folktales – the emergence of a distinctly American writing, not just a stepchild to English forms – constitute this period. Washington Irving's characters, Icabod Crane and Rip Van Winkle, create a uniquely American

folklore devoid of English influences. The characters are indelibly marked by their environment and the superstitions of the New Englander. The early American writings of James Fenimore Cooper and his Leatherstocking Tales – with their stirring accounts of drums along the Mohawk, the French and Indian Wars, the futile British defense of Fort William Henry, and the brutalities of this time frame – provide readers a window to their uniquely American world. Natty Bumppo, Chingachgook, Uncas, and Magua are unforgettable characters that reflect the American spirit in thought and action.

The poetry of the Fireside Poets – James Russell Lowell, Oliver Wendell Holmes, Henry Wadsworth Longfellow, and John Greenleaf Whittier – was - was recited by American families and read in the long New England winters. In "The Courtin'," Lowell used Yankee dialect to tell a narrative. Spellbinding epics by Longfellow such as *Hiawatha*, *The Courtship of Miles Standish*, and *Evangeline* told of adversity, sorrow, and ultimate happiness in a uniquely American warp. "Snowbound" by Whittier relates the story of a captive family isolated by a blizzard, stressing family closeness. Holmes' "The Chambered Nautilus" and his famous line, "Fired the shot heard round the world," put American poets on a firm footing with other world writers.

Nathaniel Hawthorne and Herman Melville are the preeminent early American novelists, writing on subjects definitely regional, specific and American, yet sharing insights about human foibles, fears, loves, doubts, and triumphs. Hawthorne's writings range from children's stories, such as *Little Daffydowndilly*, to his adult fare of dark, brooding short stories such as "Dr. Heidegger's Experiment" and "Rapuccini's Daughter." His masterpiece, *The Scarlet Letter*, takes on the society of hypocritical Puritan New Englanders who ostensibly left England to establish religious freedom, but became entrenched in judgmental finger wagging. They ostracize Hester and condemn her child, Pearl, as a child of Satan. Great love, sacrifice, loyalty, suffering, and related epiphanies add universality to this tale. *The House of the Seven Gables* also deals with kept secrets, loneliness, societal pariahs, and love ultimately triumphing over horrible wrong. Herman Melville's great opus, *Moby Dick*, follows a crazed Captain Ahab on his Homeric odyssey to conquer the great white whale that has outwitted him and his whaling crews time and again. The whale has even taken Ahab's leg and, according to Ahab, wants all of him. Melville recreates in painstaking detail, and with insider knowledge of the harsh life of a whaler out of New Bedford, by way of Nantucket.

For those who don't want to learn about every guy rope or all parts of the whaler's rigging, Melville offers up the succinct tale of Billy Budd and his Christ-like sacrifice to the black-and- white maritime laws on the high seas. An accident results in the death of one of the ship's officers, a slug of a fellow, who had taken a dislike to the young, affable, shy Billy. Captain Vere must hang Billy for the death of Claggert, but knows that this is not right. However, an example must be given to the rest of the crew so that discipline can be maintained.

Edgar Allan Poe creates a distinctly American version of romanticism with his 16-syllable line in "The Raven," the classical "To Helen," and his Gothic "Annabelle Lee." The horror short story can be said to originate from Poe's pen. "The Tell - Tale Heart," "The Cask of Amontillado," "The Fall of the House of Usher," and "The Masque of the Red Death" are exemplary short stories. The new genre of detective story also emerges with Poe's "Murders in the Rue Morgue."

American Romanticism has its own offshoot in the Transcendentalism of Ralph Waldo Emerson and Henry David Thoreau. One wrote about transcending the complexities of life; the other, who wanted to get to the marrow of life, pitted himself against nature at Walden Pond and wrote an inspiring autobiographical account of his sojourn, aptly titled *On Walden Pond.* He also wrote passionately on his objections to the interference of government on the individual in "On the Duty of Civil Disobedience." Emerson's elegantly crafted essays and war poetry still give validation to several important universal truths. Probably most remembered for his address to Thoreau's Harvard graduating class, "The American Scholar," he defined the qualities of hard work and intellectual spirit required of Americans in their growing nation.

The Transition between Romanticism and Realism
The Civil War period ushers in the poignant poetry of Walt Whitman and his homage to all who suffer from the ripple effects of war and presidential assassination. His "Come up from the Fields, Father" about a Civil War soldier's death and his family's reaction and "When Lilacs Last in the Courtyard Bloom'd" about the effects of Abraham Lincoln's death on the poet and the nation should be required readings in any American literature course. Further, his *Leaves of Grass* gave America its first poetry truly unique in form, structure, and subject matter.

Emily Dickinson, like Walt Whitman, leaves her literary fingerprints on a vast array of poems, all but three of which were never published in her lifetime. Her themes of introspection and attention to nature's details and wonders are, by any measurement, world-class works. Her posthumous recognition reveals the timeliness of her work. American writing had most certainly arrived!

During this period, such legendary figures as Paul Bunyan and Pecos Bill rose from the oral tradition. Anonymous storytellers around campfires told tales of a huge lumberman and his giant blue ox, Babe, whose adventures were explanations of natural phenomena – like those of footprints filled with rainwater becoming the Great Lakes. Similarly, the whirling-dervish speed of Pecos Bill explained the tornadoes of the Southwest. Like ancient peoples, finding reasons for the happenings in their lives, these American pioneer storytellers created a mythology appropriate to the vast reaches of the unsettled frontier.

Mark Twain also left giant footprints with his unique blend of tall tale and fable. "The Celebrated Jumping Frog of Calaveras County" and "The Man that

Corrupted Hadleyburg" are epitomes of short story writing. Move to novel creation, and Twain again rises head and shoulders above others with his bold, still disputed, oft-banned *The Adventures of Huckleberry Finn*, which examines such taboo subjects as a white person's love of a slave, the issue of leaving children with abusive parents, and the outcomes of family feuds. Written partly in dialect and southern vernacular, *The Adventures of Huckleberry Finn* is touted by some as the greatest American novel.

The Realistic Period

The late nineteenth century saw a reaction against the tendency of romantic writers to look at the world through rose-colored glasses. Writers like Frank Norris (*The* Pit) and Upton Sinclair (*The Jungle*) used their novels to decry conditions for workers in slaughterhouses and wheat mills. In *The Red Badge of Courage*, Stephen Crane wrote of the daily sufferings of the common soldier in the Civil War. Realistic writers wrote of common, ordinary people and events using detail that would reveal the harsh realities of life. They broached taboos by creating protagonists whose environments often destroyed them. Romantic writers would have only protagonists whose indomitable wills helped them rise above adversity. Crane's *Maggie: A Girl of the Streets* deals with a young woman forced into prostitution to survive. In *An Occurrence at Owl Creek Bridge* Ambrose Bierce relates the unfortunate hanging of a Confederate soldier.

Short stories, like Bret Harte's "The Outcasts of Poker Flat" and Jack London's "To Build a Fire," deal with unfortunate people whose luck in life has run out. Many writers, sub-classified as naturalists, believed that man was subject to a fate over which he had no control.

Skill 2.2	Literature of other cultures; elements of literary analysis (e.g., analyzing story elements, interpreting figurative language); and varied focuses of literary criticism (e.g., the author, the context of the work, the text, the response of the reader)

Central America/Caribbean

Central America and the Caribbean encompass a wide variety of cultures that reflect colonial influence by England, Spain, Portugal, France, and The Netherlands. Caribbean writers include Samuel Selvon from Trinidad and Armando Valladares from Cuba. Central American authors include the novelist Gabriel Garcia Marquez *(One Hundred Years of Solitude)* from Colombia, as well as the 1990 Nobel Prize winning poet Octavia Paz *(The Labyrinth of Solitude)* from Mexico and Mexican feminist Rosario Castellanos *(The Nine Guardians)*. Carlos Solorzano, a dramatist whose plays include *Dona Beatriz*, *The Hapless*, *The Magician*, and *The Hands of God*, represents Guatemala.

South America

Chilean Gabriela Mistral was the first Latin American writer to win the Nobel Prize for literature. She is best known for her collections of poetry, *Desolation* and

Tenderness. Chile was also home to Pablo Neruda who, in 1971, won the Nobel Prize for literature for his poetry. His 29 volumes of poetry have been translated into more than 60 languages attesting to his universal appeal. *Twenty Love Poems* and *A Song of Despair* are justly famous.

Isabel Allende is carrying on the Chilean literary standards with her acclaimed novel, *The House of the Spirits.* Argentinean Jorge Luis Borges is considered by many literary critics to be the most important writer of this century from South America. His collections of short stories, *Ficciones,* brought him universal recognition.

Also from Argentina, Silvina Ocampo, a collaborator with Borges on a collection of poetry, is famed for her poetry and short story collections, which include *The Fury* and *the Days of the Night.*

English Literature
The Anglo-Saxon period spanned six centuries but produced only a smattering of literature. The first English epic is *Beowulf,* anonymously transcribed by Christian monks from oral traditions many years after the events in the narrative supposedly occurred. This Teutonic saga relates the three triumphs of the hero, Beowulf, over legendary monsters. "The Seafarer," a shorter poem, some history, and some riddles are the rest of the Anglo-Saxon canon.

The Medieval period includes Geoffrey Chaucer, the father of English literature, whose *Canterbury Tales* are written in the vernacular or common language of England, not in Latin. Thomas Malory's *Le Morte d'Arthur* calls together the tales from Europe as well as England concerning the legendary King Arthur, Merlin, Guinevere, and the Knights of the Round Table. This generative work set down the many Arthurian legends that stir the chivalric imagination. William Shakespeare, the Bard of Avon, wrote 154 sonnets, 39 plays, and two long narrative poems. His sonnets are justifiably called the greatest sonnet sequence in all of literature. Shakespeare dispensed with the octave/sestet format of the Italian sonnet and invented his three quatrains, one heroic couplet format. His plays are divided into comedies, history plays, and tragedies. Lines from these plays are quoted more often than from any other author. The tragedies *Hamlet, Macbeth, Othello,* and *King Lear* are acknowledged to be the most brilliant examples of this genre.

John Milton's devout Puritanism was the wellspring of his creative genius that closes the remarkable productivity of the English Renaissance. His social commentary in such works as *Areopagitica, Samson Agonistes,* and his elegant sonnets would be enough to solidify his stature as a great writer. It is his masterpiece based in part on the Book of Genesis that places Milton very near the top rung of a handful of the most renowned of all writers. *Paradise Lost,* written in balanced, elegant neoclassic form, truly does justify the ways of God to man.

The greatest allegory about man's journey to the Celestial City (Heaven) was written at the end of the English Renaissance, as was John Bunyan's *The Pilgrim's Progress,* which describes virtues and vices personified. This work is, or was for a long time, second only to the *Bible* in numbers of copies printed and sold.

The Jacobean Age gave us the marvelously witty and cleverly constructed conceits of John Donne's metaphysical sonnets, as well as his insightful meditations, his version of sermons or homilies. "Ask not for whom the bell tolls" and "no man is an island unto himself" are famous epigrams from Donne's *Meditations.* His most famous metaphysical conceit is that which compares lovers to a footed compass traveling seemingly separately, but always leaning towards one another and conjoined in "A Valediction Forbidding Mourning."

Ben Jonson, author of the wickedly droll play *Volpone,* and the Cavalier *carpe diem* poets Robert Herrick, Sir John Suckling, and Richard Lovelace also wrote during King James I's reign.

The Restoration and Enlightenment reflect the political turmoil of the regicide of Charles I, the interregnum puritan government of Oliver Cromwell, and the restoring of the monarchy to England by the coronation of Charles II, who had been given refuge by the French King Louis. Neoclassicism became the preferred writing style, especially for Alexander Pope. New genres, such as *The Diary of Samuel Pepys,* the novels of Daniel Defoe, the periodical essays and editorials of Joseph Addison and Richard Steele, and Alexander Pope's mock epic, *The Rape of the Lock,* demonstrate the diversity of expression during this time.

Writers who followed were contemporaries such as Dr. Samuel Johnson, the lexicographer of *The Dictionary of the English Language.* Fittingly, this Age of Johnson, which encompasses James Boswell's biography of Dr. Johnson, Robert Burns' evocative regional poetry in Scottish dialect, and the mystical pre-Romantic poetry of William Blake usher in the Romantic Age and its revolution against neoclassicism.

The Romantic Age features writers known as the First Generation Romantics, William Wordsworth and Samuel Taylor Coleridge, who collaborated on *Lyrical Ballads,* which defines and exemplifies the tenets of this style of Romantic writing. The Second Generation includes George Gordon, Lord Byron, Percy Bysshe Shelley, and John Keats. These poets wrote sonnets, odes, epics, and narrative poems, most paying homage to nature. Wordsworth's best known works are "Intimations on Immortality" and "The Prelude." Byron's satirical epic, *Don Juan,* and his autobiographical *Childe Harold's Pilgrimage* are irreverent, witty, self-deprecating and, in part, cuttingly critical of other writers and critics. Shelley's odes and sonnets are remarkable for their sensory imagery. Keats' sonnets, odes, and longer narrative poem, *The Eve of St. Agnes,* are remarkable for their introspection and the tender age of the poet, who died when he was only twenty-five.

Others who wrote during the Romantic Age are the essayist, Charles Lamb, and the novelist, Jane Austin. The Bronte sisters, Charlotte and Emily, wrote one novel each, which are noted as two of the finest ever written, *Jane Eyre* and *Wuthering Heights*. Marianne Evans, also known as George Eliot, wrote several important novels: *Middlemarch, Silas Marner, Adam Bede,* and *The Mill on the Floss.*

The Victorian Period is remarkable for the diversity and proliferation of work in three major areas. Poets who are typified as Victorians include Alfred Lord Tennyson who wrote *Idylls of the King,* twelve narrative poems about the Arthurian legend; and Robert Browning who wrote chilling dramatic monologues such as "My Last Duchess," as well as long poetic narratives such as *The Pied Piper of Hamelin.* Browning's wife Elizabeth wrote two major works, the epic feminist poem, *Aurora Leigh,* and her deeply moving and provocative *Sonnets from the Portuguese* in which she details her deep love for Gerard Manley Hopkins, a Catholic priest. She wrote poetry with sprung rhythm (see Glossary of Literary Terms in 4.2). A. E. Housman, Matthew Arnold, and the Pre-Raphaelites, especially the brother and sister duo, Dante Gabriel and Christina Rossetti, contributed much to round out the Victorian poetic era. The Pre-Raphaelites, a group of 19th-century English painters, poets, and critics, reacted against Victorian materialism and the neoclassical conventions of academic art by producing earnest, quasi-religious works. Medieval and early Renaissance painters up to the time of the Italian painter Raphael inspired the group. Robert Louis Stevenson, the great Scottish novelist, wrote his adventures for young adults.

Victorian prose ranges from the, keenly woven plot structures of Charles Dickens to the deeply moving Dorset/Wessex novels of Thomas Hardy, in which women are repressed and life is more struggle than euphoria. Rudyard Kipling wrote about colonialism in India in works like *Kim* and *The Jungle Book* that evoke exotic locales. Victorian drama is primarily represented by Oscar Wilde, whose satirical masterpiece, *The Importance of Being Earnest,* farcically details and lampoons Victorian social mores.

The early twentieth century is represented by George Bernard Shaw's dramas: *St. Joan, Man and Superman, Major Barbara*, and *Arms and the Man.* Joseph Conrad, E. M. Forster, Virginia Woolf, James Joyce, Graham Greene, George Orwell, and D. H. Lawrence comprise some of the century's very best novelists. Twentieth century poets of renown include W. H. Auden, Robert Graves, T. S. Eliot, Edith Sitwell, Stephen Spender, Dylan Thomas, Philip Larkin, Ted Hughes, and Hugh MacDiarmid.

Continental European Literature

Germany

German poet and playwright, Friedrich von Schiller, is best known for his history plays, *William Tell* and *The Maid of Orleans.* He is a leading literary figure in Germany's Golden Age of Literature. Also from Germany, Rainer Maria Rilke, the great lyric poet, is one of the poets of the unconscious or stream of consciousness. Germany also has given the world Herman Hesse *(Siddhartha),* Gunter Grass *(The Tin Drum),* and the greatest of all German writers, Johann Wofgang von Goethe.

Scandinavia

Scandinavia has produced the work of the Danish writer Hans Christian Andersen who advanced the fairy tale genre with such wistful tales as "The Little Mermaid" and "Thumbelina." The social commentary of Henrik Ibsen in Norway startled the world of drama with such issues as feminism *(A Doll's House* and *Hedda Gabler)* and the effects of sexually transmitted diseases *(The Wild Duck* and *Ghosts).* Sweden's Selma Lagerlof is the first woman to ever win the Nobel Prize for literature. Her novels include *Gosta Berling's Saga* and the world-renowned children's work, *The Wonderful Adventures of Nils..*

Russia

Russian literature is vast and monumental, marked by Fyodor Dostoyevsky's *Crime and Punishment* and *The Brothers Karamazov.* These are examples of psychological realism. Dostoyevsky's influence on modern writers cannot be overly stressed. LeoTolstoy's *War and Peace* is the sweeping account of the invasion of Russia and Napoleon's taking of Moscow. This novel is called the national novel of Russia. Further advancing Tolstoy's greatness is his ability to create believable, unforgettable female characters, especially Natasha in *War and Peace* and the heroine of *Anna Karenina .* Alexander Pushkin is famous for his poetry; Anton Chekhov for drama *(Uncle Vanya, The Three Sisters, The Cherry Orchard);* Yevgeny Yevtushenko for poetry *(Babi Yar).* Boris Pasternak won the Nobel Prize *(Dr. Zhivago).* Aleksandr Solzhenitsyn *(The Gulag Archipelago)* returned to Russia in 1994 after years of expatriation in Vermont. Ilya Varshavsky who creates fictional societies that are dystopias – the opposite of utopias – represents science fiction.

France

The multifaceted French literature is universal in scope, almost always championing some social cause: the poignant short stories of Guy de Maupassant; the fantastic poetry of Charles Baudelaire *(Les Fleurs de Mal);* the groundbreaking lyrical poetry of Arthur Rimbaud and Paul Verlaine; and the existentialism of Jean-Paul Sartre *(No Exit, The Flies, Nausea),* Andre Malraux, *(The Conquerors),* and Albert Camus *(The Stranger* and *The Plague).* Drama in France is best represented by Edmond Rostand's *Cyrano de Bergerac* and the neo-classical dramas of Jean Racine and Pierre Corneille *(El Cid).* Feminist writings include those of Sidonie-Gabrielle Colette, known for her short stories and novels, as well as those of Simone de Beauvoir.

Great French novelists include Andre Gide, Honore de Balzac *(Cousin Bette),* Roger Gard Stendhal *(The Red and the Black),* and the father and son each named Alexandre Dumas *(The Three Musketeers* and *The Man in the Iron Mask).* Victor Hugo is the Charles Dickens of French literature, having penned two masterpieces: *The Hunchback of Notre Dame* and the French national novel, *Les Miserables.* The stream of consciousness of Marcel Proust's *Remembrance of Things Past,* along with the Absurdist theatre of Samuel Beckett and Eugene Ionesco *(The Rhinoceros),* attests to the genius of French writers.

Slavic nations

Austrian writer Franz Kafka *(The Metamorphosis, The Trial,* and *The Castle)* is considered by many to be the literary voice of the first-half of the twentieth century. Representing the Czech Republic is the poet Vaclav Havel. Slovakia has dramatist Karel Capek *(R.U.R).* Romania is represented by Elie Wiesel *(Night),* a Nobel Prize winner.

Spain

Spain's great writers include Miguel de Cervantes *(Don Quixote)* and Juan Ramon Jimenez. The anonymous national epic, *El Cid,* has been translated into many languages.

Italy

Italy's greatest writers include Virgil, who wrote the great epic (The Aeneid); Giovanni Boccaccio *(The Decameron);* Dante Alighieri *(The Divine Comedy);* and Alberto Moravia *(Contempt).*

Ancient Greece

Greece will always be foremost in literary assessments due to Homer's epics, *The Iliad* and *The Odyssey.* No one, except Shakespeare, is more often cited. Add to these the works of Plato and Aristotle for philosophy; the dramatists Aeschylus, Euripides, and Sophocles for tragedy, and Aristophanes for comedy. Greece is not only the cradle of democracy, but of literature as well.

Africa

African literary greats include South Africans Nadine Gordimer, a Nobel Prize winner, and Peter Abrahams, best known for his autobiography of life in Johannesburg *(Tell Freedom: Memories of Africa).* Chinua Achebe *(Things Fall Apart)* and the poet, Wole Soyinka, hail from Nigeria. Mark Mathabane wrote an autobiography, *Kaffir Boy,* about growing up in South Africa. Egyptian writer, Naguib Mahfouz, and Doris Lessing from Rhodesia, now Zimbabwe, write about race relations in their respective countries. Because of her radical politics, Lessing was banned from her homeland and the Union of South Africa, as was

Alan Paton whose simple story, *Cry, the Beloved Country,* brought the plight of blacks and the whites' fear of blacks under apartheid to the rest of the world.

Far East

Asia has many modern writers whose works are being translated for the western reading public. India's Krishan Chandar has authored more than 300 stories. Rabindranath Tagore won the Nobel Prize for literature in 1913 *(Song Offerings).* R.K. Narayan, one of India's most famous writers *(The Guide),* is highly interested in mythology and legends of India. Santha Rama Rau's work, *Gifts of Passage,* is her true story of life in a British school where she tries to preserve her Indian culture and traditional home.

Revered as Japan's most famous female author, Fumiko Hayashi *(Drifting Clouds)*, wrote more than 270 literary works in her lifetime. The classical age of Japanese literary achievement includes Kiyotsugu Kanami and his son Motokkiyo Zeami who developed the theatrical experience known as Noh drama to its highest aesthetic degree. The son is said to have authored over 200 plays, of which 100 are extant.

In 1968 the Nobel Prize for literature was awarded to Yasunari Kawabata *(The Sound of the Mountain, The Snow Country).*. His Palm-of-the-Hand Stories take the essentials of Haiku poetry and transform them into the short story genre.

Katai Tayama *(The Quilt)* is widely considered the father of the genre known as the Japanese confessional novel. The "slice of life" psychological writings of Ryunosuke Akutagawa gained him acclaim in the western world. His short stories, especially "Rashomon" and "In a Grove," are greatly praised for style as well as content.

China, too, has contributed to the literary world. Li Po, the T'ang dynasty poet from the Chinese Golden Age, preserves in writing the folk songs and mythology of China. Po further allows his reader to enter into the Chinese philosophy of Taoism and to know this feeling against expansionism during the T'ang dynastic rule. Jiang Fang wrote short pieces about love. Modern feminist and political concerns are written eloquently by Ting Ling, who used the pseudonym Chiang Ping-Chih. Her stories reflect her concerns about social injustice and her commitment to the women's movement.

Recognizing the author's purpose

An author may have more than one purpose in writing. An **author's purpose** may be to entertain, persuade, inform, describe, or narrate.

There are no tricks or rules to follow in attempting to determine an author's purpose. It is up to the reader to use his or her judgment.

Read the following paragraph:

> Charles Lindbergh had no intention of becoming a pilot. He was enrolled in the University of Wisconsin until a flying lesson changed the entire course of his life. He began his career as a pilot by performing daredevil stunts at fairs.

The author wrote this paragraph primarily to:

    A. Describe
    B. Inform
    C. Entertain
    D. Narrate

Since the author is simply telling us or informing us about the life of Charles Lindbergh, the correct answer here is (B).

Organizational pattern

The **organizational pattern** of a piece of writing is the way in which the author conveys the main idea and details. A list of organizational patterns commonly used on the test is given below:

- Addition - development of a subject point by point
- Cause and Effect - demonstration of how an event came about due to certain conditions or causes
- Classification - division of a subject into different categories or classes
- Comparison and Contrast - pointing out of similarities and/or differences
- Definition - explanation or clarification of the meaning of a word or term
- Explanation - explanation of something said earlier
- Generalization - making of a general statement, which includes the support of specific examples
- Order - listing in order of things or events; may be in order of time, importance or some other element
- Simple Listing - listing of items in no particular order
- Summary - summation of what has already been said in greater detail

Read the following paragraph:

> Rembrandt and Van Gogh were two Dutch painters. Both were from wealthy families. Both showed incredible talent at a young age. Van Gogh did not begin to paint seriously until he was twenty-seven. Rembrandt, on the other hand, had already completed many paintings by that age.

Which organizational pattern does the author use?

A. Comparison and Contrast
B. Simple Listing
C. Cause and Effect
D. Definition

Since the author is demonstrating how Rembrandt and Van Gogh were alike and how they were different, the correct answer is (A).

Learn more about:
American literature
http://www.wsu.edu/~campbelld/amlit/sites.htm
Literary analysis
www.stemstar.com/latarget.htm

COMPETENCY 3.0 UNDERSTAND LITERARY GENRES, ELEMENTS, AND TECHNIQUES

Skill 3.1 Basic literary terminology (e.g., flashback, foreshadowing)

See Skill 4.4

Skill 3.2 Characteristics of different genres and types of literature (e.g., myths, folk tales, fiction, nonfiction, drama, poetry)

The major literary genres include allegory, ballad, drama, epic, epistle, essay, fable, novel, poem, romance, and the short story. See also Skill 4.2 for more descriptions.

Allegory:
A story in verse or prose with characters representing virtues and vices. There are two meanings, symbolic and literal. John Bunyan's *The Pilgrim's Progress* is a well-known example of this genre.

Ballad:
A story told or sung, usually in verse and accompanied by music. Literary devices found in ballads include the refrain, or repeated section, and incremental repetition, or anaphora, for effect. Earliest forms were anonymous folk ballads. Later forms include Samuel Taylor Coleridge's Romantic masterpiece, "The Rime of the Ancient Mariner."

Drama:
Plays – comedy, modern, or tragedy – typically in five acts. Traditionalists and neoclassicists adhere to Aristotle's unities of time, place and action. Plot development is advanced via dialogue. Literary devices include asides, soliloquies and the chorus representing public opinion. Greatest of all dramatists/playwrights is William Shakespeare. Other dramaturges include Ibsen, Williams, Miller, Shaw, Stoppard, Racine, Moliere, Sophocles, Aeschylus, Euripides, and Aristophanes.

Epic:
Long poem, usually of book length, reflecting values inherent in the generative society. Epic devices include an invocation to a Muse for inspiration, purpose for writing, universal setting, protagonist and antagonist who possess supernatural strength and acumen, and interventions of a God or the gods. Understandably, there are very few epics: Homer's *Iliad* and *Odyssey*, Virgil's *Aeneid*, Milton's *Paradise Lost*, Spenser's *The Fairie Queene*, E.B. Browning's *Aurora Leigh*, and Pope's mock-epic, *The Rape of the Lock.*

Epistle:
A letter or other work written in the form of a letter.

Essay:
Typically, a prose work of limited length focusing on a topic and propounding a definite point of view in an authoritative tone. Great essayists include Carlyle, Lamb, DeQuincy, Emerson and Montaigne, who is credited with defining this genre.

Fable:
Terse tale offering up a moral or exemplum. Chaucer's "The Nun's Priest's Tale" is a fine example of a *bete fabliau* or beast fable in which animals speak and act characteristically human, illustrating human foibles. Aesop's fables have been adapted and repeated for centuries.

Legend:
A traditional narrative or collection of related narratives, popularly regarded as historically factual but usually a mixture of fact and fiction.

Myth:
Stories that are universally shared within a culture to explain its history and traditions.

Novel:
A long form of fictional prose containing a variety of characterizations, settings, local color and regionalism. Most have complex plots, expanded description, and attention to detail. Some of the great novelists include Austin, the Brontes, Twain, Tolstoy, Hugo, Hardy, Dickens, Hawthorne, Forster, and Flaubert.

Poem:
Rhythmic, often figurative works. Sub-genres include fixed types of literature such as the sonnet, elegy, ode, pastoral, and villanelle. Unfixed types of poetry include blank verse and dramatic monologue.

Romance:
A highly imaginative tale set in a fantastical realm dealing with the conflicts between heroes, villains, and/or monsters. "The Knight's Tale" from Chaucer's *Canterbury Tales, Sir Gawain and the Green Knight* and Keats' "The Eve of St. Agnes" are prime representatives.

Short Story:
Typically a terse narrative, with less development of characters. May include description, author's point of view, and tone. Poe emphasized that a successful short story should create one focused impact. Great short story writers include: Hemingway, Faulkner, Twain, Joyce, Shirley Jackson, Flannery O'Connor, de Maupassant, Saki, Edgar Allen Poe, and Pushkin.

Skill 3.3   Elements of fiction (e.g., plot, character, setting, theme, voice)

Most works of fiction contain a common set of elements that make them come alive to readers. Even though writers may not consciously think about each of these elements when they sit down to write, all stories essentially contain these "markers."

Let's look at a few of the most commonly discussed elements. The most commonly discussed story element in fiction is plot. Plot is the series of events in a story. Typically, but not always, a plot moves in a predictable fashion:

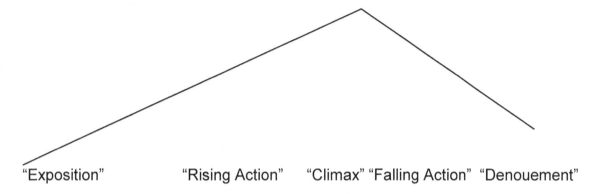

"Exposition"   "Rising Action"   "Climax" "Falling Action" "Denouement"

Exposition is where characters and their situations are introduced. *Rising action* is the point at which conflict starts to occur. *Climax* is the highest point of conflict, often a turning point. *Falling action* is the result of the climax. *Denouement* is the final resolution of the plot.

Character is another commonly studied story element. We will often find in stories heroes, villains, comedic characters, dark characters, etc. When we examine the characters of a story, we look to see who they are and how their traits contribute to the story. Often, because of their characteristics, plot elements become more interesting. For example, authors will pair unlikely characters together.

The setting of a story is the place or location where it occurs. Often, the specific place is not as important as some of the specifics about the setting. For example, the New York setting of *The Great Gatsby* is not as significant as the fact that it takes place amongst incredible wealth. Conversely, *The Grapes of Wrath*, although taking place in Oklahoma and California, has a more significant setting of poverty. In fact, as the story takes place *around* other migrant workers, the setting is even more significant. In a way, the setting serves as a reason for various conflicts to occur.

Themes of stories are the underlying messages, above and beyond all plot elements, that writers want to convey. Very rarely will one find that good literature is without a theme – or a lesson, message, or ideal. The best writers in the

English language all seem to want to convey something about human nature or the world, and they turn to literature in order to do that. Common themes in literature are jealousy, money, love, human against corporation or government, etc. These themes are never explicitly stated; rather, they are the result of the portrayal of characters, settings, and plots. Readers get the message even if the theme is not directly mentioned.

Finally, the mood of a story is the atmosphere or attitude the writer conveys through descriptive language. Often, mood fits in nicely with theme and setting. For example, in Edgar Allen Poe's stories, we often find a mood of horror and darkness. We get that from the descriptions of characters and the setting, as well as from specific plot elements. Mood simply helps us better understand the writer's theme and intentions through descriptive, stylistic language.

See also Skill 3.6

Skill 3.4   Types of poetry (e.g., lyric, narrative, haiku)

The sonnet is a fixed-verse form of Italian origin, which consists of 14 lines that are typically five-foot iambics rhyming according to a prescribed scheme. Popular since its creation in the thirteenth century in Sicily, it spread at first to Tuscany, where it was adopted by Petrarch. The Petrarchan sonnet generally has a two-part theme. The first eight lines, the octave, state a problem, ask a question, or express an emotional tension. The last six lines, the sestet, resolve the problem, answer the question, or relieve the tension. The rhyme scheme of the octave is abbaabba; that of the sestet varies.

Sir Thomas Wyatt and Henry Howard, Earl of Surrey, introduced this form into England in the sixteenth century. It played an important role in the development of Elizabethan lyric poetry, and a distinctive English sonnet developed, which was composed of three quatrains, each with an independent rhyme-scheme, and it ended with a rhymed couplet. A form of the English sonnet created by Edmond Spenser combines the English form and the Italian. The Spenserian sonnet follows the English quatrain and couplet pattern but resembles the Italian in its rhyme scheme, which is linked: abab bcbc cdcd ee. Many poets wrote sonnet sequences, where several sonnets were linked together, usually to tell a story. Considered to be the greatest of all sonnet sequences is one of Shakespeare's sonnets, addressed to a young man and a "dark lady," wherein the love story is overshadowed by the underlying reflections on time and art, growth and decay, and fame and fortune.

The sonnet continued to develop, more in topics than in form. When John Donne in the seventeenth century used the form for religious themes, some of which are almost sermons, or on personal reflections ("When I consider how my light is spent"), there were no longer any boundaries on the themes it could take.

The flexibility of the form is demonstrated in the wide range of themes and purposes it has been used for, from more frivolous concerns to serious statements about time and death. Wordsworth, Keats, and Elizabeth Barrett Browning used the Petrarchan form of the sonnet. A well-known example is Wordsworth's "The World Is Too Much With Us." Rainer Maria Rilke's Sonnets to Orpheus (1922) is a collection of well-known twentieth-century sonnets.

Analysis of a sonnet should focus on the form: Does it fit a traditional pattern or does it break from tradition? If it breaks, why did the poet choose to make that break? Does it reflect the purpose of the poem? What is the theme? What is the purpose? Is it narrative? If so, what story does it tell and is there an underlying meaning? Is the sonnet appropriate for the subject matter?

The limerick is a form of short, humorous verse, often nonsensical, and often ribald. Its five lines rhyme aabba with three feet in all lines except the third and fourth, which have only two. Rarely presented as serious poetry, this form is popular because almost anyone can write it.

Analysis of a limerick should focus on its form. Does it conform to a traditional pattern or does it break from the tradition? If it breaks, what impact does that have on the meaning? Is the poem serious or frivolous? Is it funny? Does it try to be funny but does not achieve its purpose? Is there a serious meaning underlying the frivolity?

A cinquain is a poem with a five-line stanza. Adelaide Crapsey (1878-1914) called a five-line verse form a cinquain and invented a particular meter for it. Similar to the haiku, there are two syllables in the first and last lines and four, six, and eight in the middle three lines. It has a mostly iambic cadence. Crapsey's poem, "November Night," is an example:

Listen…
With faint dry sound
Like steps of passing ghosts,
the leaves, frost-crisp'd, break from the trees
And fall.

Haiku is a very popular unrhymed form that is limited to seventeen syllables arranged in three lines thus: five, seven, and five syllables. This verse form originated in Japan in the seventeenth century. Accepted as serious poetry, it is Japan's most popular form. Originally, it was to deal with the season, the time of day, and the landscape although as it has come into more common use, the subjects have become less restricted. The imagist poets and other English writers used the form or imitated it. It's a form much used in classrooms to introduce students to poetry writing.

Analysis of a cinquain and a haiku poem should focus on form first. Does the haiku poem conform to the seventeen-syllable requirement and are they arranged in a five, seven, and five pattern? For a cinquain, does it have only five lines? Does the poem distill the words so as much meaning as possible can be conveyed? Does it treat a serious subject? Is the theme discernable? Short forms like these seem simple to dash off; however, they are not effective unless the words are chosen and pared so the meaning intended is conveyed. The impact should be forceful, and that often takes more effort, skill, and creativity than longer forms. This should be taken into account in their analysis.

Skill 3.5   Characteristics of poetry and poetic techniques (e.g., meter, rhyme, alliteration, figurative language)

People read poetry for many reasons, and they are often the very same reasons poets would give for writing it. Just the feel and sounds of the words that are turned by the artistic hands and mind of a poet into a satisfying and sometimes delightful experience is a good reason to read a poem. Good poetry constantly surprises.

However, the major purpose a writer of poetry has for creating his works of art is the sharing of an experience, a feeling, an emotion, and that is also the reason a reader turns to poetry rather than prose in his search for variety, joy, and satisfaction.

There is another important reason that poets create and that readers are drawn to their poems: They are interpreters of life. Poets feel deeply the things that others feel or even things that may be overlooked by others, and they have the skill and inspiration to recreate those feelings and interpret them in such a way that understanding and insight may come from the experience. They often bring understanding to life's big (or even not-so-big) questions.

Children can respond to poetry at very early stages. Elementary students are still at the stage where the sounds of unusual words intrigue and entertain them. They are also very open to emotional meanings of passages. Teaching poetry to 5th graders can be an important introduction to seeking meaning in literature. If a 5th grader enjoys reading poetry both silently and aloud, a habit may be formed that will last a lifetime.

When we speak of *structure* in poetry, we usually mean one of three things:

- The pattern of the sound and rhythm
- The visible shape it takes
- Rhyme or free verse

The pattern of the sound and rhythm

It helps to know the history of this peculiarity of poetry. Until the invention of the printing press, poetry was passed down in oral form and often set to music. A rhymed story is much easier to commit to memory, and adding a tune makes it even easier to remember. So it's not a surprise that much of the earliest literature, epics, odes, etc., is rhymed and was probably sung. When we speak of the pattern of sound and rhythm, we are referring to two things: verse form and stanza form.

The verse form is the rhythmic pattern of a single verse. An example would be any meter: Blank verse, for instance, is iambic pentameter. A stanza is a group of a certain number of verses (lines) having a rhyme scheme. If the poem is written, there is usually white space between the verses – although a short poem may be only one stanza. If the poem is spoken, there is a pause between stanzas.

The visible shape it takes

In the seventeenth century, some poets shaped their poems to reflect the theme. A good example is George Herbert's "Easter Wings." Since that time, poets have occasionally played with this device; it is, however, generally viewed as nothing more than a demonstration of ingenuity. The rhythm, effect, and meaning are often sacrificed to the forcing of the shape.

Rhyme and free verse

Poets also use devices to establish form that will underscore the meanings of their poems. A very common one is alliteration. When the poem is read aloud (which poetry is usually intended to be), the repetition of a sound may not only underscore the meaning, it may also add pleasure to the reading. Following a strict rhyming pattern can add intensity to the meaning of the poem in the hands of a skilled and creative poet. On the other hand, the meaning can be drowned out by the steady beat-beat-beat of it. Shakespeare very skillfully used the regularity of rhyme in his poetry, breaking the rhythm at certain points to very effectively underscore a point. For example, in Sonnet #130, "My mistress' eyes are nothing like the sun," the rhythm is primarily iambic pentameter. It lulls the reader (or listener) to accept that this poet is following the standard conventions for love poetry, which in that day reliably used rhyme and more often than not iambic pentameter to express feelings of romantic love along conventional lines.

However, in Sonnet #130, the last two lines sharply break from the monotonous pattern, forcing the reader or speaker to pause:

> And yet, by heaven, I think my love as rare
> As any she belied with false compare

Shakespeare's purpose is clear: He is not writing a conventional love poem; the object of his love is not the red-and-white conventional woman written about in other poems of the period. This is a good example where a poet uses form to underscore meaning.

Poets eventually began to feel constricted by rhyming conventions and began to break away and make new rules for poetry. When poetry was only rhymed, it was easy to define it. When free verse, or poetry written in a flexible form, came upon the scene in France in the 1880s, it quickly began to influence English-language poets such as T. S. Eliot, whose memorable poem, "The Wasteland," had an alarming but desolate message for the modern world. It's impossible to imagine that it could have been written in the soothing, lulling rhymed verse of previous periods. Those who first began writing in free verse in English were responding to the influence of the French *vers libre*. However, it should be noted that it could be loosely applied to the poetry of Walt Whitman, writing in the mid-nineteenth century, as can be seen in the first stanza of "Song of Myself":

> I celebrate myself, and sing myself,
> And what I assume you shall assume,
> For every atom belonging to me as good belongs to you.

When poetry was no longer defined as a piece of writing arranged in verses that had a rhyme-scheme of some sort, distinguishing poetry from prose became a point of discussion. Merriam Webster's *Encyclopedia of Literature* defines poetry as follows: "writing that formulates a concentrated imaginative awareness of experience in language chosen and arranged to create a specific emotional response through its meaning, sound and rhythm."

Poets choose the form of their poetry deliberately, based upon the emotional response they hope to evoke and the meaning they wish to convey. Robert Frost, a twentieth-century poet who chose to use conventional rhyming verse to make his point, is a memorable and often-quoted modern poet. Who can forget his closing lines in "Stopping by Woods on a Snowy Evening"?

> And miles to go before I sleep,
> And miles to go before I sleep.

Would they be as memorable if the poem had been written in free verse?

Slant Rhyme
This rhyme occurs when the final consonant sounds are the same, but the vowels are different. It occurs frequently in Irish, Welsh, and Icelandic verse. Examples include: green and gone, that and hit, ill and shell.

Alliteration
Alliteration occurs when the initial sounds of a word, beginning either with a consonant or a vowel, are repeated in close succession. Examples include: Athena and Apollo, Nate never knows, people who pen poetry.

Note that the words only have to be close to one another: Alliteration that repeats and attempts to connect a number of words is little more than a tongue-twister.

The function of alliteration, like rhyme, might be to accentuate the beauty of language in a given context, or to unite words or concepts through a kind of repetition. Alliteration, like rhyme, can follow specific patterns. Sometimes the consonants aren't always the initial ones, but they are generally the stressed syllables. Alliteration is less common than rhyme, but because it is less common, it can call our attention to a word or line in a poem that might not otherwise have the same emphasis.

Assonance

If alliteration occurs at the beginning of a word and rhyme at the end, assonance takes the middle territory. Assonance occurs when the vowel sound within a word matches the same sound in a nearby word, but the surrounding consonant sounds are different. "Tune" and "June" are rhymes; "tune" and "food" are assonant. The function of assonance is frequently the same as end rhyme or alliteration; all serve to give a sense of continuity or fluidity to the verse. Assonance might be especially effective when rhyme is absent: It gives the poet more flexibility, and it is not typically used as part of a predetermined pattern. Like alliteration, it does not so much determine the structure or form of a poem; rather, it is more ornamental.

Onomatopoeia

This is a word or group of words used to imitate the sounds being described. The early Batman series used *pow*, *zap*, *whop*, *zonk* and *eek* in an onomatopoetic way.

Rhythm

Rhythm in poetry refers to the recurrence of stresses at equal intervals. A stress (accent) is a greater amount of force given to one syllable in speaking than is given to another. For example, we put the stress on the first syllable of such words as father, mother, daughter, or child. The unstressed or unaccented syllable is sometimes called a slack syllable. All English words carry at least one stress – except articles and some prepositions such as by, from, at, etc. Indicating where stresses occur is to scan; doing this is called scansion. Very little is gained in understanding a poem or making a statement about it by merely scanning it. The pattern of the rhythm – the meter – should be analyzed in terms of its overall relationship to the message and impression of the poem.

Slack syllables, when they recur in pairs, cause rhythmic tripping and bouncing; on the other hand, recurrent pairs of stresses create a heavier rocking effect. The rhythm depends on words to convey meaning. Alone, they communicate nothing. When examining the rhythm and meaning of a poem, a good question to ask is whether the rhythm is appropriate to the theme. A bouncing rhythm, for example, might be dissonant in a solemn elegy.

Stops are those places in a poem where the punctuation requires a pause. An end-stopped line is one that *ends* in a pause. A line that has no punctuation at its end and is, therefore, read with only a slight pause after it is said to be run-on and the running on of its thought into the next line is called enjambment. These are used by a poet to underscore, intensify, or communicate meaning.

Rhythm, then, is a *pattern of recurrence* and in poetry is made up of stressed and relatively unstressed syllables. The poet can manipulate the rhythm by making the intervals between his stresses regular or varied, by making his lines short or long, by end-stopping his lines or running them over, by choosing words that are easier or less easy to say, by choosing polysyllabic words or monosyllables. The most important thing to remember about rhythm is that it conveys meaning.

The basic unit of rhythm is called a foot and is usually one stressed syllable with one or two unstressed ones or two stressed syllables with one unstressed one. A foot made up of one unstressed syllable and one stressed one is called an iamb. If a line is made of five iambs, it is iambic pentameter. A rhymed poem typically establishes a pattern such as iambic pentameter, and even though there will be occasional syllables that don't fit the pattern, the poem, nevertheless, will be said to be in iambic pentameter. In fact, a poem may be considered weak if the rhythm is too monotonous.

Skill 3.6   Types of drama (e.g., comedy, tragedy) and common dramatic devices (e.g., suspense, soliloquy)

In both drama and fiction, various dramatic events occur in a fairly predictable fashion. For example, all dramatic action begins with some sort of introductory scene where characters are introduced, basic premises are covered, and the plot is set so that action can occur. Rising action begins as the plot ramps up. It occurs as elements in the plot move toward some sort of problematic circumstance, whether comedic or tragic. If the plot is tragic, something bad will happen; if the plot is comedic, something good or humorous will happen. While there are many variations on these themes, most works fit into one of these two categories.

Back to the structure, as the rising action continues to move toward some ultimate fate, whether comedic or tragic, eventually it will hit a climax. The climax is the major turning point or significant event in the work. Everything that occurs after the climax is considered falling action, and the general idea is that once a work has hit the climax, the work is now moving toward conclusion. Falling action is generally the response to the climax (or the result of it). After the climax, most works like to allow the audience to imagine some of the consequences. Conclusion is the final event or the moment when the work entirely finishes. After that, everything else is left to the audience's imagination.

In drama, particularly, certain devices enhance the viewers' understanding of the plot. Three of these devices are:

Suspense

Suspense occurs at any moment where the audience knows something that a character on stage does not – and the "thing" the character does not know will cause him or her adverse affects.

Soliloquy

In essence, this is a speech to oneself. This is where a character possibly shares his or her feelings with the audience, almost as if the character is thinking out loud. This gives the audience clues as to what may happen, how the character is handling something, etc.

Aside

Usually, soliloquies occur in an aside, but not all asides contain soliloquies. An aside is any time where "real" time in the drama stops for a moment so that a character can address the audience or his or her thoughts so that the audience hears them (and the other characters do not).

Learn more about:
Literary genres and elements:
http://www.articleworld.org/index.php/Category:Literary_genres

COMPETENCY 4.0 UNDERSTAND LITERATURE FOR CHILDREN, INCLUDING GENRES, LITERARY ELEMENTS, AND LITERARY TECHNIQUES

Skill 4.1 Major works and authors of children's literature

A great example of a fantasy book that was propelled into a movie is Ronald Dahl's *Charlie and the Chocolate Factory*. Both book and movie use the fantasy of chocolate and living in a world of chocolate to show what would happen if that world suddenly changed. The theme for young readers is how to adapt to change when their world is altered.

Dick and Jane and *Winnie the Pooh* are early reader classics that have been on bookshelves for decades. They use human and animal characters to present morals and life lessons for readers who are beginning to conceptualize the dynamics of actions and consequences.

In the juvenile genre, Barbara Holland's *Prisoners at the Kitchen Table* (a mystery and suspense thriller about the kidnapping of a wealthy young girl and her best friend) creates a real problem needing real solutions. Readers are immediately drawn into a pressing issue and the need for a critical-thinking solution to resolve the issue.

There are many historical novels that have been translated into various media, from the big screen to DVD classics. Charles Dickens's classic, *A Christmas Carol,* presents its moral through its wealthy protagonist and his struggling worker who has a handicapped son. The protagonist has a lot to give, but is seasonally stingy to his workers until he is visited by ghosts who represent his past, present and future. When he sees the light of his actions, the protagonist becomes a transformed man.

There are many books on the market that inspire and transform young readers. The ability of authors to create literature that educates and informs is historical. Books and stories are about magic and fantasy that allow readers to escape and engage in imaginative activity that broadens cognitive thought and critical thinking development.

Book Types
Alphabet book—A book that utilizes letters of the alphabet in different ways that may or may not tell a story. These books often use rhyme and/or alliteration.

Wordless book—A picture book that tells a story or presents material through pictures with very little or no text.

Concept book—An informational book that introduces a single concept such as shape, color, size, or numbers.

Counting book—A picture book that focuses on numbers and counting.

Early chapter book—Transitional fiction that is longer than a standard picture book, with fewer pictures. This type of book is generally written for grades 1-3.

Easy reader—A book that is written for grade levels 1-2 in which phrases or sentences are repeated in the text in easily recognizable patterns.

Photo essay—A book that presents information on a concept or illustrates a story using photographs and text.

Picture book—A book in which the message depends upon pictures as much or more than text.

The following are examples of the book types described above:

Dr. Seuss (Theodor S. Geisel) - *The Cat In The Hat, Horton Hears A Who,; Dr. Seuss's ABC: An Amazing Alphabet Book*

Maurice Sendak - *Where the Wild Things Are*

Bill Martin and Eric Carle - *Brown Bear, Brown Bear, What Do You See?*

Lois Ehlert - *Fish Eyes: A Book You Can Count On*

Mary Pope Osborne - *The Magic Tree House* series

Stan and Jan Berenstain - *The Big Honey Hunt* and *it's All in the Family*

Dorling Kindersley - *My First Animal Book*

Margery Williams - *The Velveteen Rabbit*

Lucy Cousins - *Flower in the Garden (My Cloth Book)*

Skill 4.2   Genres of children's literature and their characteristics

Drama
Stories composed in verse or prose, usually for theatrical performance, where conflicts and emotion are expressed through dialogue and action.

Fable
Narration demonstrating a useful truth, especially in which animals speak as humans; legendary, supernatural tale.

Fairy Tale

Story about fairies or other magical creatures, usually for children.

Fantasy

Fiction with strange or other worldly settings or characters; fiction that invites suspension of reality.

Fiction

Narrative literary works whose content is produced by the imagination and is not necessarily based on fact.

Fiction in Verse

Full-length novels with plot, subplot(s), theme(s), major and minor characters, in which the narrative is presented in (usually blank) verse form.

Folklore

The songs, stories, myths, and proverbs of a people or "folk" as handed down by word of mouth.

Historical Fiction

Story with fictional characters and events in a historical setting.

Horror

Fiction in which events evoke a feeling of dread in both the characters and the reader.

Humor

Fiction full of fun, fancy, and excitement; meant to entertain. (Elements of humor may be found in all genres.)

Legend

Story, sometimes of a national or folk hero, which has a basis in fact but also includes imaginative material.

Mystery

Fiction dealing with the solution of a crime or the unraveling of secrets.

Mythology

Legend or traditional narrative, often partly based on historical events, that reveals human behavior and natural phenomena by its symbolism; often pertaining to the actions of the gods.

Poetry

Verse and rhythmic writing with imagery that creates emotional responses.

Realistic Fiction
Story that can actually happen and is true to life.

Science Fiction
Story based on impact of actual, imagined, or potential science, often set in the future or on other planets.

Short Story
Fiction of such brevity that it supports no subplots.

Tall Tale
Humorous story with blatant exaggerations and swaggering heroes who do the impossible with nonchalance.

NONFICTION

Nonfiction
Informational text dealing with an actual, real-life subject.

Biography/Autobiography
Narrative of a person's life; a true story about a real person.

Essay
A short literary composition that reflects the author's point or outlook.

Narrative Nonfiction
Factual information presented in a story format.

Speech
Public address or discourse.

Skill 4.3   Major themes associated with children's literature

In general, children's literature focuses on themes that pertain to choices, morals, and values. It is often intended to instruct students through entertaining stories, while also promoting an interest in reading.

Many cultures, including our own, use children's literature as a vehicle to instill proper values in children. It is not uncommon to find such themes as the victory of good over evil, acceptance of all races, sharing, or following advice given by parents or other adults. Themes are conveyed through the story and via a gradual transformation in the main characters' values.

Typically, the main characters encounter a situation that they must make a decision about. Their initial decisions – not the most moral – have various consequences. However, by the end of the story, the characters acknowledge their mistakes. By this point, they also change or grow in some way – leaving the reader with valuable lessons about making the right decisions and adopting proper values.

In contemporary multicultural literature, the pattern is not always as simple. The theme or moral is often made evident through more explicit characters, plot events, or situations. Some examples of contemporary, multicultural picture books are: *Nadia's Hands* by Karen English, *The Color of Home* by Mary Hoffman, *My Name was Hussein* by Hristo Kyuchukov, *Alias's Mission* by Mark Alan Stamaty, and *Chachaji's Cup* by Uma Krishnaswami.

Skill 4.4 Analysis of rhetorical and literary devices (e.g., analogies, metaphors, symbolism) in children's literature

Some essential terminology and literary devices are defined below:

Alliteration
The repetition of consonant sounds in two or more neighboring words or syllables. In its simplest form, it reinforces one or two consonant sounds. Example: Shakespeare's Sonnet #12:

   When I do count the clock that tells the time.

Some poets have used more complex patterns of alliteration by creating consonants both at the beginning of words and at the beginning of stressed syllables within words. Example: Shelley's "Stanzas Written in Dejection Near Naples":

   The City's voice itself is soft like solitude's

Allusion
Defined by Merriam Webster's *Encyclopedia of Literature* as "an implied reference to a person, event, thing, or a part of another text." Allusions are based on the assumption that there is a common body of knowledge shared by poet and reader and that a reference to that body of knowledge will be immediately understood. Allusions to the Bible and classical mythology are common in western literature on the assumption that they will be immediately understood.

Antithesis
Balanced writing about conflicting ideas, usually expressed in sentence form. Some examples are: expanding from the center, shedding old habits, and searching but never finding.

Aphorism
A focused, succinct expression about life from a sagacious viewpoint. Writings by Ben Franklin, Sir Francis Bacon, and Alexander Pope contain many

aphorisms. "Whatever is begun in anger ends in shame" is an aphorism.

Apostrophe
Literary device of addressing an absent or dead person, an abstract idea, or an inanimate object. Sonneteers, such as Sir Thomas Wyatt, John Keats, and William Wordsworth, address the moon, stars, and the dead Milton. For example, in William Shakespeare's *Julius Caesar*, Mark Antony addresses the corpse of Caesar in the speech that begins:

> "O, pardon me, thou bleeding piece of earth,
> That I am meek and gentle with these butchers!
> Thou art the ruins of the noblest man
> That ever lived in the tide of times.
> Woe to the hand that shed this costly blood!"

Blank Verse
Poetry written in iambic pentameter but unrhymed. Works by Shakespeare and Milton are epitomes of blank verse. Milton's "Paradise Lost" states, "Illumine, what is low raise and support, That to the highth of this great argument I may assert Eternal Providence And justify the ways of God to men."

Connotation
The ripple effect surrounding the implications and associations of a given word, distinct from the denotative or literal meaning. For example, "Good night, sweet prince, and flights of angels sing thee to thy rest," refers to a burial.

Consonance
The repeated usage of similar consonant sounds, most often used in poetry. "Sally sat sifting seashells by the seashore" is a familiar example.

Couplet
Two rhyming lines of poetry. Shakespeare's sonnets end in heroic couplets written in iambic pentameter. Pope is also a master of the couplet. His *Rape of the Lock* is written entirely in heroic couplets.

Denotation:
What a word literally means, as opposed to its connotative meaning. For example,

> "Good night, sweet prince, and flights of angels sing thee to thy *rest*"
> refers to sleep.

Diction
The right word in the right spot for the right purpose. The hallmark of a great writer is precise, unusual, and memorable diction.

Epiphany
The moment when the proverbial light bulb goes off in one's head and comprehension sets in.

Euphemism
The substitution of an agreeable or inoffensive term for one that might offend or suggest something unpleasant. Many euphemisms are used to refer to death to avoid using words, such as "passed away," "crossed over," or "passed."

Exposition
Fill-in or background information about characters meant to clarify and add to the narrative; the initial plot element which precedes the buildup of conflict.

Figurative language often uses one of English's many figures of speech. A few of these figures of speech are listed here:

- **Simile**: Direct comparison between two things. "My love is like a red-red rose."
- **Metaphor**: Indirect comparison between two things. The use of a word or phrase denoting one kind of object or action in place of another to suggest a comparison between them. While poets use them extensively, they are also integral to everyday speech. For example, chairs are said to have "legs" and "arms" although we know that it's humans and other animals that have these appendages.
- **Parallelism**: The arrangement of ideas in phrases, sentences, and paragraphs that balance one element with another of equal importance and similar wording. An example from Francis Bacon's *Of Studies:* "Reading maketh a full man, conference a ready man, and writing an exact man."

Flashback
Interruption of the chronological sequence of events by interjection of events or scenes of earlier occurrence, often in the form of reminiscence.

Foreshadowing
Inclusion of events or details that prepare the reader for what happens later. It can simply be an atmosphere or a specific scene or object that gives a clue to later development of plot.

Free Verse
Poetry that does not have any predictable meter or patterning. Margaret Atwood, E. E. Cummings, and Ted Hughes write in this form.

Hyperbole
Exaggeration for a specific effect. For example, "I'm so hungry that I could eat a million of these."

Iambic Pentameter

The two elements in a set five-foot line of poetry. An iamb is two syllables, unaccented and accented, per foot or measure. Pentameter means five feet of these iambs per line or ten syllables.

Imagery can be described as a word or sequence of words that refers to any sensory experience – that —that is, anything that can be seen, tasted, smelled, heard, or felt on the skin or fingers. While writers of prose may also use these devices, it is most distinctive of poetry. The poet intends to make an experience available to the reader. In order to do that, he must appeal to one of the senses, most frequently vision. The poet will deliberately paint a scene in such a way that the reader can see it. However, the purpose is not simply to stir visceral feeling but also to stir emotions. A good example is "The Piercing Chill I Feel" by Taniguchi Buson (1715-1783):

> The piercing chill I feel:
> My dead wife's comb, in our bedroom,
> Under my heel . . .

In only a few short words, the reader can feel many things: the shock that might come from touching the corpse, a literal sense of death, the contrast between her death and the memories he has of her when she was alive. Imagery might be defined as speaking of the abstract in concrete terms, a powerful device in the hands of a skillful poet.

Irony

An unexpected disparity between what is written or stated and what is really meant or implied by the author. The three types of literary irony are verbal, situational, and dramatic irony. Verbal irony is when an author says one thing and means something else. Dramatic irony is when an audience perceives something that a character in the literature does not know. Situational irony is a discrepancy between the expected result and actual results. Shakespeare's plays feature frequent and highly effective use of irony. O. Henry's short stories have ironic endings.

Motif

A key, oft-repeated phrase, name, or idea in a literary work. Dorset/Wessex in Hardy's novels and the moors and the harsh weather in the Bronte sisters' novels are effective use of motifs.

Onomatopoeia

Word used to evoke the sound in its meaning. The early Batman series used *pow*, *zap*, *whop*, *zonk* and *eek* in an onomatopoetic way.

Oxymoron

A contradiction in terms deliberately employed for effect. It is usually seen in a qualifying adjective whose meaning is contrary to that of the noun it modifies, such as "wise folly."

Paradox

Seemingly untrue statement, which when examined more closely proves to be true. John Donne's sonnet "Death Be Not Proud" postulates that death shall die and humans will triumph over death – at first thought not true, but ultimately explained in this sonnet.

Parallelism

A type of close repetition of clauses or phrases that emphasize key topics or ideas in writing. The psalms in the King James Version of the *Bible* contain many examples.

Personification

Human characteristics attributed to an inanimate object, an abstract quality, or animal. Examples: John Bunyan introduced characters named Death, Knowledge, Giant Despair, Sloth, and Piety in his *Pilgrim's Progress*. The metaphor of an arm of a chair is a form of personification.

Stream of Consciousness

A style of writing that reflects the mental processes of the characters expressing, at times, jumbled memories, feelings, and dreams. "Big time players" in this type of expression are James Joyce, Virginia Woolf, and William Faulkner.

A **symbol** is an object or action that can be observed with the senses in addition to its suggesting many other things. The lion is a symbol of courage; the cross a symbol of Christianity; the color green a symbol of envy. Symbols used in literature are usually of a different sort. They tend to be private and personal; their significance is only evident in the meaning(s) drawn. A good example is the huge pair of spectacles on a sign board in Fitzgerald's *The Great Gatsby*. They are interesting as a part of the landscape, but they also symbolize divine myopia. A symbol can certainly have more than one meaning, and the meaning may be as personal as the memories and experiences of the particular reader. In analyzing a poem or a story, it's important to identify the symbols and their possible meanings.

Looking for symbols is often challenging, especially for novice poetry readers. However, these suggestions may be useful: One strategy is to look for all the references to concrete objects such as a newspaper, black cats, etc. Note any that the poet emphasizes by describing in detail, by repeating, or by placing at the very beginning or ending of a poem. Ask yourself, what is the poem about? What does it add up to? Paraphrase the poem and determine whether or not the meaning depends upon certain concrete objects. Then ponder what the concrete object symbolizes in this particular poem. A symbol may be a part of a person's body – such as the eye of the murder victim in Poe's story "The Tell-Tale Heart" –or a look, a voice, or a mannerism.

Tone is the discernible attitude inherent in an author's work regarding the subject, readership, or characters. Swift's and Pope's tones are satirical. Boswell's tone toward Johnson is admiring.

Wit

A form of intellectual humor, delivered at the right time to make the audience laugh or feel amused. Quip and repartee are two types of wit. A quip is an intelligent observation that may develop into sarcasm. A repartee is a quick answer or comment. Mark Twain is famous for his use of this literary form.

At what stage should literary devices be taught to children and how soon should they be taught to apply such critical tools as metaphor, simile, analogy, etc? It's difficult to put an actual age on these curriculum decisions, but the importance of children's ability to identify analogies and comparisons has been known for some time. Critical thinking relies heavily on the ability to see and understand analogy and metaphor.

Even very young children understand comparison. They can point out something that looks like another, such as egg/ball. Analogy can be taught and forms an essential bridge to understanding metaphorical comparisons.

Skill 4.5   Comparison of different styles and communicative purposes in children's literature

Children's literature offers both children and adults a fresh perspective of reading and exploration. The communication style for connecting children to a story or idea must be age-appropriate and grade-level accessible for the young reader. The author must understand that children view the world differently and have a different sense of time and experience. Authors who write for children bring fresh and unbiased perspectives to the world of story and storytelling. Ideas are fresh and create a simple world of childhood experiences that are positive and written to incorporate a child's perspective.

Writers use the beauty of a child's imagination to create stories and books around contemporary issues. Children's books are created into two categories: fiction and nonfiction. However, varying age levels require different age-appropriate formats. For example, picture books might suit the primary ages while board books provide tutorial support to younger age readers. Board and picture books are generally hardcover-bound to lessen the wear and tear on the books. Books are written to share every imaginable life experience, societal experience and social experience that a child will encounter during each developmental and cognitive stage of life.

Certain coloring and activity books, often featuring characters and scenes from well-known children's stories, provide skill assessments for children. Interactive novelty books engage a child's imagination and cognitive skill. They include pop-ups or paper characters that can be removed and manipulated to create events and imaginary journeys.

Children's books address various morals, lessons, and world issues Age level books are written for preschoolers who are beginning to manipulate and understand words, as well as for juvenile readers who are looking for deeper meaning in their worlds.

Skill 4.6   Criteria for evaluating children's literature (e.g., reading level, literary quality, richness of vocabulary, appealing plot, interesting information, illustrations, gender preferences, variety of settings and characters)

Children's books can be nonfiction or fiction. Fiction books feature characters that are products of the author's mind and that engage in real-world drama and settings. Nonfiction books are based on factual information about real world events and persons. Autobiographical books depict true stories about the author's own life and experiences. *The Diary of Anne Frank* is an example of a autobiographical book written by a young girl experiencing the horrors of the Holocaust.

In writing children's literature, authors take into account the reading level of their readers, along with the age-appropriateness of the reading material. Children's books can be classified into the following categories:

Early readers: easy-to-read books from 5-50 pages for children ages 5-9 years old. Includes picture books, board books, activity books and stories that contain graphics. (Board books are also appropriate for ages younder than five, where adults may read to the children or help them recognize objects in the book.) Books from Dr. Seuss, Eric Carle, Margaret Wise Brown and Maurice Sendak are all good examples of early readers.

Middle grade readers: These books, written for ages 10-12, contain strong plots and relevant life lessons. The writing paints a picture of the world that middle graders see as modeling their struggles and concerns. The vocabulary becomes more complicated and the plots more complex. The reading tackles issues that are age-related and developmentally appropriate. E.B. White's *Charlotte's Web* is a popular example.

Young adult readers: The issues here are real and typical of the teenage world. They deal with relationships, politics, education and human nature. Dean Hughes' *Soldier Boys* (recommended for both middle graders and young adults) is a highly moving story of two young men who must face the disillusionment of hurrying into battle. It encompasses themes of human nature, politics, family values and relationships.

Word counts vary in each book category from 25 to 70,000. Each book has a major theme and relevancy. The plot and protagonist for middle and young adult readers are developed around an issue that is limited in viewpoint and sophistication. Themes about belonging and finding support amongst peers are common.

Skill 4.7 Analysis of excerpts of children's literature in relation to style, theme, or voice

Whether teachers use children's literature to introduce literary concepts or to give students fun, simple ways to enjoy literature, children's literature is a great way to get students to feel comfortable with literary analysis.

Let's take a fifth grade class, for example. The students are about to embark on the study of a complex novel. The teacher knows that students will need to understand the author's style, the theme of the work, and the author's voice. Does the teacher jump right into the novel? Or does the teacher use a simple piece of literature to first teach the concepts so that when they get into the more complex novel, for example, they will already know what the concepts mean?

Consider this: A novel involves a character telling the story of his friend. There is no doubt that if the author had the friend's mother tell the story, the novel would come across quite differently. So, the teacher presents *Goldilocks and the Three Bears*. This is a story that is told in third person. The teacher asks students to redesign the story as if Goldilocks had told the story. Then the teacher asks the students to redesign the story once more as if Papa Bear had told the story. Students will quickly see that while the plot does not change, the way the plot is presented changes slightly.

Children's literature can similarly enlighten students on the various aspects of theme and style, as well as many other literary elements. The more they learn literary elements through simple children's stories, the easier it will be for them to make connections to more complex literature.

Skill 4.8   Uses of children's literature (e.g., providing exposure to high-quality language, enhancing other areas of the curriculum, fostering cross-cultural understanding)

Children's literature uses age-appropriate language or vocabulary that is accessible for readers' cognitive levels. When language is approximated to a reader's level of understanding, it doesn't mean that the language is scaled down. For example, novels for middle-grade readers may have language that is accessible but also challenging. This makes the books both relevant and interesting to the reader.

Learn more about:
Children's literature, including genres, literary elements and literary analysis
http://www.lesley.edu/library/guides/research/literature_children.html
http://www.scils.rutgers.edu/~kvander/ChildrenLit/index.html

COMPETENCY 5.0   UNDERSTAND HOW TO APPLY WRITING SKILLS AND STRATEGIES FOR VARIOUS PURPOSES

Skill 5.1   Knowledge and use of prewriting strategies, including techniques for generating topics and developing ideas (e.g., brainstorming, semantic mapping, outlining, reading and researching)

Prewriting strategies assist students in a variety of ways. Listed below are the most common prewriting strategies students can use to explore, plan and write on a topic. It is important to remember when teaching these strategies that not all prewriting must eventually produce a finished piece of writing. In fact, in the initial lesson of teaching prewriting strategies, it might be more effective to have students practice prewriting strategies without the pressure of having to write a finished product. Remind students that they need to consider their audience when prewriting. .

Keep an idea book to jot down ideas that come to mind.

Write in a daily journal.

Write down whatever comes to mind. This is called free writing. Students do not stop to make corrections or interrupt the flow of ideas. A variation of this technique is focused free writing – writing on a specific topic – to prepare for an essay.

Make a list of all ideas connected with the chosen topic; this is called brainstorming. Make sure students know that this technique works best when they let their mind work freely. After completing the list, students should analyze the list for a pattern or way to group the ideas.
- Ask the questions who? what? when? where? why? and how? Help the writer approach the topic from several perspectives.
- Create a visual map on paper to gather ideas. Cluster circles and lines to show connections between ideas. Students should try to identify the relationship that exists between their ideas. If they cannot see the relationships, have them pair up, exchange papers, and have their partners look for some related ideas.
- Observe details of sight, hearing, taste, touch, and taste.
- Visualize by making mental images of something and write down the details in a list.

After students have practiced with each of these prewriting strategies, ask them to pick out the ones they prefer and to discuss how they might use the techniques with future writing assignments. It is important to remember that they can use more than one prewriting strategy at a time. They may also find that different writing situations may suggest certain techniques.

Skill 5.2 Formal elements of good writing (e.g., paragraphing, topic sentences, cohesive transitions)

Recognizing the main idea

A **topic** of a paragraph or story is what the paragraph or story is about. The **main idea** of a paragraph or story states the most important idea(s) that the author wants the reader to know about a topic. The topic and main idea of a paragraph or story are sometimes directly stated. There are times, however, that the topic and main idea are simply implied and not directly stated.

For example:

> Henry Ford was an inventor who developed the first affordable automobile. The cars that were being built before Mr. Ford created his Model-T were very expensive. Only rich people could afford to have cars.

The topic of this paragraph is Henry Ford. The main idea is that Henry Ford built the first affordable automobile.

Identifying supporting details

The **supporting details** are sentences that give more information about the topic and the main idea.

The supporting details in the above Henry Ford paragraph are that he was an inventor and that before he created his Model-T, only rich people could afford cars because they were too expensive.

Reading an essay should not take extraordinary effort. The ideas should be clear and straightforward. Anyone who has tried to write an essay knows that this sounds much easier than it really is! So, how do teachers actually help students to become proficient with writing multi-paragraph essays in ways that allow them to clearly communicate their ideas? The trick is to help them understand that various conventions of writing serve the purpose of making comprehension easier for their readers. Those conventions include good paragraphing; transitions between paragraphs, ideas, and sentences; topic sentences; concluding sentences; appropriate vocabulary; and sufficient context.

Good paragraphing entails dividing up ideas into chunks. A good paragraph typically includes a topic sentence that identifies the content of the paragraph. It also includes sufficient explanation of that topic sentence. For example, if a topic sentence suggests that the paragraph will be about the causes of the Civil War, the rest of the paragraph should actually explain specific causes of the Civil War.

As writers transition from one paragraph to another – or one sentence to another – they usually provide transitional phrases that give signposts to readers about what is coming next. Words like "however," "furthermore," "although," or "likewise" are good ways of communicating intention to readers. Even when writers choose more subtle transitions between paragraphs, their writing is structured in ways to make the reader follow the writer's thoughts seamlessly from one paragraph to the next. When ideas are thrown together on a page, it is hard to tell what the writer is actually doing with those ideas. Therefore, students need to become familiar with using transitional phrases.

Concluding sentences are not always necessary, but when appropriate, they provide a nice "farewell" or closing to a piece of writing. Students do not always need to use concluding sentences in paragraphs; however, they should be taught their potential benefits.

For writers to use appropriate vocabulary, they should be sensitive to the audience and purpose for their writing. For example, an essay on a scientific concept for a group of non-scientists should not use specialized vocabulary to explain concepts. However, writing for a group of scientists might contain jargon and professional terms not in common use outside of the field. Students need to learn that all writing has purpose and that good writers make conscious decisions about how to arrange their texts, which words to use, and which examples and metaphors to include.

Finally, when writers provide sufficient context, they ensure that readers do not have to extensively question the text to figure out what is going on. This requires knowing the audience. Using the scientific concept example from above, more context would be needed for an audience of non-scientists than for scientists.

Skill 5.3 Revising written texts to improve unity, coherence, and logical organization

Both teachers and students should be aware of the difference between revising and editing. Revising typically entails substantial changes to a written draft, and it is during this process that the ideas, content, and organization of a draft may be altered. Like revising, editing continues to make changes to a draft. However, the changes made during the editing process do more to enhance the ideas in the draft, rather than change or alter them. Finally, proofreading is the stage where grammatical and technical errors are addressed. Proofreading may also involve rechecking any factual information.

Effective teachers realize that revision and editing go hand-in-hand and that students often move back and forth between these stages during the course of one written work. These stages must be practiced individually as well as in pairs and small groups. Students must learn to analyze and improve their own work as well as the works of their peers. Some methods to use include:

- Students working in pairs analyze sentences for variety.
- Students work in pairs or groups to ask questions about unclear areas in the writing or to help students add details, information, etc.
- Students perform final edit.

Many teachers introduce writers' workshops to their students to maximize learning about the writing process. Writers' workshops vary across classrooms, but the main idea is for students to become comfortable with the writing process. A basic writers' workshop may include a block of classroom time committed to writing various projects (i.e., narratives, memoirs, book summaries, fiction, book reports, etc). Students use this time to write, meet with others to review/edit writing, make comments on writing, revise their own work, proofread, meet with the teacher, and publish their work.

Teachers who facilitate effective writers' workshops are able to meet with students one at a time to guide them in their individual writing needs. This approach allows the teacher to customize instruction for each student's writing level.

Students need to be trained to become effective at proofreading, revising and editing strategies. Listed below are some strategies to guide students through the final stages of the writing process. These can easily be incorporated into writers' workshops.

- Provide some guide sheets or forms for students to use during peer responses.
- Allow students to work in pairs and limit the agenda.
- Demonstrate the use of the guide sheet or form for the entire class.
- Give students a time limit or number of written pieces to be completed in a specific amount of time.
- Have the students read their partners' papers and ask at least three who, what, when, why, and how questions. The students answer the questions and use them as a place to begin discussing the piece.
- At this point in the writing process, a mini-lesson that focuses on some of the problems your students are having would be appropriate.

To help students revise, provide them with a series of questions that will assist them in revising their writing.

- Do the details give a clear picture? Add details that appeal to more than just the sense of sight.
- How effectively are the details organized? Reorder the details if needed.
- Are the thoughts and feelings of the writer included? Add personal thoughts and feelings about the subject.

Gone are the days when students engaged in skill practice with grammar worksheets. Grammar needs to be taught in the context of the students' own work. Listed below is a series of classroom practices that encourage meaningful context-based grammar instruction, combined with occasional mini-lessons and other language strategies that can be used on a daily basis. Connect grammar with students' own writing while emphasizing grammar as a significant aspect of effective writing. Emphasize the importance of editing and proofreading as an essential part of classroom activities.

- Provide students with an opportunity to practice editing and proofreading cooperatively.
- Give instruction in the form of 15- to 20-minute mini-lessons.
- Emphasize the sound of punctuation by connecting it to pitch, stress, and pause.
- Involve students in all facets of language learning, including reading, writing, listening, speaking and thinking. Good use of language comes from exploring all forms of it on a regular basis.

There are a number of approaches to grammar instruction in context of the writing.

- Sentence Combining: Try to use the student's own writing as much as possible. The theory behind combining ideas and the correct punctuation should be emphasized.
- Sentence and paragraph modeling: Provide students with the opportunity to practice imitating the style and syntax of professional writers.
- Sentence transforming: Give students an opportunity to change sentences from one form to another, such as from passive to active. Help them experiment with inverting the sentence order or changing forms of the words used.
- Daily Language Practice: Introduce or clarify common errors using daily language activities. Use actual student examples whenever possible. Correct and discuss the problems with grammar and usage.

Skill 5.4   Editing written work to ensure conformity to conventions of edited American English (e.g., grammar, punctuation, spelling, and proper use of easily confused words)

Teachers should be cognizant of proper rules and conventions of punctuation, capitalization, and spelling. They should apply these rules according to the American style of English, i.e. spelling "theater" instead of "theatre" and placing terminal marks of punctuation almost exclusively within other marks of punctuation. (See Skill 1.8.) Discussed below are some commonly misused words, along with explanations of word concepts such as homonyms, homophones, or heteronyms.

Students frequently encounter problems with **homonyms**, words that are spelled and pronounced the same as another but that have different meanings – such as mean, a verb, "to intend"; mean, an adjective, "unkind"; and mean, a noun or adjective, "average." These words are actually both homonyms and homographs (written the same way).

A similar phenomenon that causes trouble is heteronyms (also sometimes called heterophones), words that are spelled the same but have different pronunciations and meanings (in other words, they are homographs that differ in pronunciation or, technically, homographs that are not homophones). For example, the homographs desert (abandon) and desert (arid region) are heteronyms (pronounced differently); but mean (intend) and mean (average) are not. They are pronounced the same, or are homonyms.

Another similar occurrence in English is the capitonym, a word that is spelled the same but has different meanings when it is capitalized and may or may not have different pronunciations. Example: polish (to make shiny) and Polish (from Poland).

Some of the most troubling homonyms include its (third person, singular neuter pronoun) and it's ("it is"); there, their (third person plural pronoun), and they're ("they are"); and to, too, and two.

Some homonyms/homographs are particularly complicated. Fluke, for instance is a fish, a flatworm, the end parts of an anchor, the fins on a whale's tail, and a stroke of luck.

Commonly misused words:

Than is a conjunction used in comparisons; **then** is an adverb denoting time. One way to remember the difference is that *than* is used to *compare*; *then* tells *when*.
- That pizza is more <u>than</u> I can eat.
- Tom laughed, and <u>then</u> we recognized him.

There is an adverb specifying place; it is also an expletive.
- Adverb: Sylvia is lying <u>there</u> unconscious.
- Expletive: <u>There</u> are two plums left.

Their is a possessive pronoun. **They're** is a contraction of they are.
- Fred and Jane finally washed <u>their</u> car.
- <u>They're</u> later than usual today.

To is a preposition; **too** is an adverb; **two** is a number.
- Jane went to the market today.
- She went to school, too.
- She bought two books.

Your is a possessive pronoun; **you're** is a contraction of *you are*.
- You should do your homework.
- You're a good student.

See also Skill 1.8.

Skill 5.5   Techniques and stylistic requirements for writing for various purposes (e.g., to respond, inform, analyze, persuade, entertain), including factors related to the selection of topic and mode of written expression

To refine their communications, students must first understand the various structures of written communication. Here are some of them:

Basic expository writing simply gives information about a topic or is used to explain or define a topic. The writing is usually formal and uses facts, examples, and statistics. The tone is often direct, objective, and unemotional.

Descriptive writing centers on person, place, or object, using concrete and sensory words to create a mood or impression and arranging details in a chronological or spatial sequence.

Narrative writing is developed using an incident, anecdote or related series of events. Chronology, the five W's (who, what, when, why and where), topic sentence, and conclusion are essential ingredients.

Persuasive writing involves the writer's ability to select vocabulary and arrange facts and opinions in such a way as to direct the actions of the audience or, at the very least, to influence their mindset and opinions. Persuasive writing may incorporate exposition and narration to illustrate the main idea.

Skill 5.6   Clarifying intended audience; use of various techniques to convey meaning (e.g., precise vocabulary, figurative language, illustrations)

When students delve deep into a writing task, they can quickly forget that the writing has to convey meaning to a particular audience. Because they often feel that the teacher is their only audience, tailoring vocabulary, illustrations, and other writing elements to meet the needs of a particular audience may be ignored. Teachers, as much as possible, should specify other audiences for whom students are writing. These audiences could be real (sending letters to an elected official) or imaginary (pretending to write a newspaper article). This will give students By have practice in changing their language to meet specific needs.

Ask students to explain to a friend what they did last night. Have them include all the details. . Then, ask students to explain the same thing to their grandmother – tell all the details of what they did last night. Students will most likely note that they use different words, sentence structures, and details in the two explanations.

The basics of writing for a particular audience include the following:

- Precise Vocabulary: While students may not know all the best words that could summarize their thoughts, they should seek the most targeted vocabulary. Whenever one precise word can take the place of a variety of words, students should use that one precise word. Also, it is important that students realize that their vocabulary choice must truly convey the proper intention of the word meaning. Depending on audience, certain word changes can help relate more to the readers.
- Figurative language: Images, figures of speech, analogies, similes, and metaphors help to convey meaning to readers. Writers choose elements of figurative language depending on their audiences to help convey meaning that straightforward language may not.
- Illustrations: Detailed examples or illustrations can help make abstract ideas more concrete. The use of illustration depends on the audience.

In the past, teachers assigned reports, paragraphs and essays that focused on the teacher as the audience. However, for students to be meaningfully engaged in their writing, they must write for various reasons. Writing for different audiences and aims allows students to be involved in their writing. Listed below are suggestions that give students an opportunity to write in more creative and critical ways:

- Write audience-specific letters to the editor, a college, a friend, or a fellow student. Write stories to be read aloud to a group (the class, another group of students, or a group of elementary school students) or to be published in a literary magazine or class anthology.
- Write plays to be performed.
- Discuss the parallels between the different speech styles we use and writing styles for different readers or audiences.
- Allow students to write a particular piece for different audiences. Have them note how their vocabulary, tone, and content details might differ based on the audience.
- Make sure students consider the following when analyzing the needs of their audience:
  1. Why is the audience reading my writing? Do they expect to be informed, amused or persuaded?

2. What does my audience already know about my topic?
3. What does the audience want or need to know? What will interest them?
4. What type of language suits my readers?

- Expose students to writing that is on the same topic but with a different audience; have them identify the variations in sentence structure and style.
- As part of prewriting, have students clearly identify the audience.
- Remind your students that it is not necessary to identify all the specifics of the audience in the initial stage of the writing process. However, at some point, they must make some determinations about audience.

Learn more about:
American English and common errors
http://www.wsu.edu/%7Ebrians/errors/
Writing and editing skills
http://eolit.hrw.com/hlla/newmainlinks/writ.jsp
Organizing your writing
http://writing.colostate.edu/guides/processes/organize/list6.cfm

DOMAIN II.   **MATHEMATICS**

COMPETENCY 6.0   UNDERSTAND AND APPLY NUMBER PROPERTIES AND NUMBER REPRESENTATIONS

Skill 6.1   Number Sense

Rational numbers can be expressed as the ratio of two integers, $\frac{a}{b}$ where $b \neq 0$

<u>Example</u>:

$\frac{2}{3}$, $-\frac{4}{5}$, $5 = \frac{5}{1}$.

The rational numbers include integers, fractions and mixed numbers, terminating and repeating decimals. Every rational number can be expressed as a repeating or terminating decimal and can be shown on a number line.

Integers are positive and negative whole numbers and zero.

-6, -5, -4, -3, -2, -1, 0, 1, 2, 3, 4, 5, 6...

Whole numbers are natural numbers and zero.

0, 1, 2, 3, 4, 5, 6...

Natural numbers are the counting numbers.

1, 2, 3, 4, 5, 6...

Irrational numbers are real numbers that cannot be written as the ratio of two integers. These are infinite non-repeating decimals.

<u>Examples</u>:

$\sqrt{5} = 2.2360..$,   pi $= \prod = 3.1415927...$

A **fraction** is an expression of numbers in the form of x/y, where **x** is the numerator and **y** is the denominator, which cannot be zero.

<u>Example</u>:

$\frac{3}{7}$ 3 is the numerator; 7 is the denominator

If the fraction has common factors for the numerator and denominator, divide both by the common factor to reduce the fraction to its lowest form.

Example:

$$\frac{13}{39} = \frac{1 \times 13}{3 \times 13} = \frac{1}{3}$$ Divide by the common factor 13

A **mixed** number has an integer part and a fractional part.

Example:

$$2\frac{1}{4}, \ ^{-}5\frac{1}{6}, \ 7\frac{1}{3}$$

Percent = per 100 (written with the symbol %). Thus $10\% = \frac{10}{100} = \frac{1}{10}$.

Decimals = deci = part of ten. To find the decimal equivalent of a fraction, use the denominator to divide the numerator as shown in the following example.

Example:

Find the decimal equivalent of $\frac{7}{10}$.

- $$10\overline{)7.0}$$ with quotient $.7$, 70, 00

Since 10 cannot divide into 7 evenly, put a decimal point in the answer row on top; put a zero behind 7 to make it 70. Continue the division process. If a remainder occurs, put a zero by the last digit of the remainder and continue the division.

Thus $\frac{7}{10} = 0.7$

It is a good idea to write a zero before the decimal point so that the decimal point is emphasized.

Skill 6.2   Cardinal, ordinal, and negative numbers

Cardinal numbers are also known as "counting" numbers because they indicate quantity. Examples of cardinal numbers are 1, 2, and 10.

Ordinal numbers indicate the order of things in a set; for ex. 1st, 2nd, 10th. They do not show quantity, only position.

Negative numbers are numbers less than zero or to the left of zero on the number line.

Skill 6.3 Properties of real numbers (e.g., commutative, distributive)

Proper Properties are rules that apply for addition, subtraction, multiplication, or division of real numbers. These properties are:

Commutative: You can change the order of the terms or factors as follows.

For addition:
$$a + b = b + a$$

For multiplication:
$$ab = ba$$

Since addition is the inverse operation of subtraction and multiplication is the inverse operation of division, no separate laws are needed for subtraction and division.

Example:
$$5 + {}^-8 = {}^-8 + 5 = {}^-3$$

Example:
$${}^-2 \times 6 = 6 \times {}^-2 = {}^-12$$

Associative: You can regroup the terms as you like.

For addition:
$$a + (b + c) = (a + b) + c$$

For multiplication:
$$a(bc) = (ab)c$$

This rule does not apply for division and subtraction.

Example:
$$({}^-2 + 7) + 5 = {}^-2 + (7 + 5)$$
$$5 + 5 = {}^-2 + 12 = 10$$

Example:
$$(3 \times {}^-7) \times 5 = 3 \times ({}^-7 \times 5)$$
$${}^-21 \times 5 = 3 \times {}^-35 = {}^-105$$

Identity: Finding a number so that when added to a term results in that number (additive identity); finding a number such that when multiplied by a term results in that number (multiplicative identity).

For addition:

$a + 0 = a$ (zero is additive identity)

For multiplication:

$a \ 1 = a$ (one is multiplicative)

Example:

$17 + 0 = 17$

Example:

$^-34 \times 1 = \ ^-34$

The product of any number and one is that number.

Inverse: Finding a number such that when added to the number it results in zero; or when multiplied by the number results in 1.

For addition:

$a + (-a) = 0$

For multiplication:

$a \ (1/a) = 1$

($-a$) is the additive inverse of a; ($1/a$), also called the reciprocal, is the multiplicative inverse of a.

Example:

$25 + \ ^-25 = 0$

Example:

$5 \times \frac{1}{5} = 1$

The product of any number and its reciprocal is one.

Distributive: This technique allows us to operate on terms within parentheses without first performing operations within the parentheses. This is especially helpful when terms within the parentheses cannot be combined.

$a \ (b + c) = ab + ac$

Example:

$6 \times (\ ^-4 + 9) = (6 \times \ ^-4) + (6 \times 9)$

$6 \times 5 = \ ^-24 + 54 = 30$

To multiply a sum by a number, multiply each addend by the number, then add the products.

The order of real numbers

Symbol for inequality: For the symbols '$>$' (greater than) or '$<$' (less than), the big open side of the symbol always faces the larger of the two numbers and the point of the symbol always faces the smaller number.

Example:

Compare 15 and 20 on the number line.

Since 20 is further away from the zero than 15 is, then 20 is greater than 15, or $20 > 15$.

Example:

Compare $\dfrac{3}{7}$ and $\dfrac{5}{10}$.

To compare fractions, they should have the same least common denominator (LCD). The LCD in this example is 70.

$$\frac{3}{7} = \frac{3 \times 10}{7 \times 10} = \frac{30}{70} \qquad\qquad \frac{5}{10} = \frac{5 \times 7}{10 \times 7} = \frac{35}{70}$$

Since the denominators are equal, compare only the numerators.

$30 < 35$, so:

$$\frac{3}{7} < \frac{5}{10}$$

Skill 6.4 The structure of the base ten number system (e.g., place value, decimal expansions)

Decimals = deci = part of ten. To find the decimal equivalent of a fraction, use the denominator to divide the numerator as shown in the following example.

Example:

Find the decimal equivalent of $\dfrac{7}{10}$.

Since 10 cannot divide into 7 evenly $\dfrac{7}{10} = 0.7$

A number in standard form is represented by a number of digits separated by a decimal point. Each digit to the left of the decimal point increases progressively in powers of ten. Each digit to the right of the decimal point decreases progressively in powers of ten.

Example:

12345.6789 occupies the following powers of ten positions:

				10		0			
1	2	3	4	5	.	6	7	8	9

Names of power-of-ten positions:

= ones (note that any non-zero base raised to power zero is 1).

= tens   (number 1 and 1 zero or 10)

10 = hundred   (number 1 and 2 zeros or 100)

= thousand   (number 1 and 3 zeros or 1000)

= ten thousand   (number 1 and 4 zeros or 10000)

$= \dfrac{1}{10^1} = \dfrac{1}{10} =$ tenths   (1st digit after decimal point or 0.1)

$= \dfrac{1}{10^2} = \dfrac{1}{100} =$ hundredth   (2nd digit after decimal point or 0.01)

$= \dfrac{1}{10^3} = \dfrac{1}{1000} =$ thousandth   (3rd digit after decimal point or 0.001)

$= \dfrac{1}{10^4} = \dfrac{1}{10000} =$ ten thousandth   (4th digit after decimal point or 0.0001)

Example:

Write 73169.00537 in expanded form.

- We start by listing all the powers of ten positions.
- $10^4 \quad 10^3 \quad 10^2 \quad 10^1 \quad 10^0 \quad . \quad 10^{-1} \quad 10^{-2} \quad 10^{-3} \quad 10^{-4} \quad 10^{-5}$
- Multiply each digit by its power of ten. Add all the results.
- Thus $73169.00537 = (7 \times 10^4) + (3 \times 10^3) + (1 \times 10^2) + (6 \times 10^1)$

$$+ (9 \times 10^0) + (0 \times 10^{-1}) + (0 \times 10^{-2}) + (5 \times 10^{-3})$$

$$+ (3 \times 10^{-4}) + (7 \times 10^{-5})$$

Example:

Determine the place value associated with the underlined digit in 3.16$\underline{9}$5.

- $10^0 \quad . \quad 10^{-1} \quad 10^{-2} \quad 10^{-3} \quad 10^{-4}$
- 3   .   1   6   9   5
- The place value for the digit 9 is 10^{-3} or $\dfrac{1}{1000}$.

Example:

Find the number that is represented by

- $(7 \times 10^3) + (5 \times 10^0) + (3 \times 10^{-3})$.
- $= 7000 + 5 + 0.003$
- $= 7005.003$

Example:

Write 21×10^3 in standard form.
$= 21 \times 1000 = 21{,}000$

Example:

Write 739×10^{-4} in standard form.
$$= 739 \times 0.0001 = 0.0739$$

Skill 6.5   The expanded form of a number

See Skill 6.4

Skill 6.6   The application of number concepts to count, compare, sort, order, and round numbers

Whole Number Place Value
Consider the number 792. We can assign a place value to each digit.

Reading from left to right, the first digit (7) represents the hundreds' place. The hundreds' place tells us how many sets of one hundred the number contains. Thus, there are 7 sets of one hundred in the number 792.

The second digit (9) represents the tens' place. The tens' place tells us how many sets of ten the number contains. Thus, there are 9 sets of ten in the number 792.

The last digit (2) represents the ones' place. The ones' place tells us how many ones the number contains. Thus, there are 2 sets of one in the number 792.

Therefore, there are 7 sets of 100, plus 9 sets of 10, plus 2 ones in the number 792.

Decimal Place Value
More complex numbers have additional place values to both the left and right of the decimal point. Consider the number 374.8.

Reading from left to right, the first digit (3) is in the hundreds' place and tells us the number contains 3 sets of one hundred.

The second digit (7) is in the tens' place and tells us the number contains 7 sets of ten.

The third digit, 4, is in the ones' place and tells us the number contains 4 ones.

Finally, the number after the decimal (8) is in the tenths' place and tells us the number contains 8 tenths.

Place Value for Older Students
Each digit to the left of the decimal point increases progressively in powers of ten. Each digit to the right of the decimal point decreases progressively in powers of ten.

Example:
12345.6789 occupies the following powers of ten positions:

			10				0			
1	2	3	4	5	.	6	7	8	9	

Rounding numbers is a form of estimation that is very useful in many mathematical operations. For example, when estimating the sum of two three-digit numbers, it is helpful to round the two numbers to the nearest hundred prior to addition. We can round numbers to any place value.

Rounding Whole Numbers
To round whole numbers, first find the place value you want to round to (the rounding digit) and look at the digit directly to the right. If the digit is less than five, do not change the rounding digit and replace all numbers after the rounding digit with zeroes. If the digit is greater than or equal to five, increase the rounding digit by one and replace all numbers after the rounding digit with zeroes.

Example:
Round 517 to the nearest ten.

- 1 is the rounding digit because it occupies the tens' place.
- 517 rounded to the nearest ten = 520; because 7 > 5 we add one to the rounding digit.

Example:
Round 15,449 to the nearest hundred.

- The first 4 is the rounding digit because it occupies the hundreds' place.
- 15,449 rounded to the nearest hundred = 15,400; because 4 < 5 we do not add to the rounding digit.

Rounding Decimals

Rounding decimals is identical to rounding whole numbers except that you simply drop all the digits to the right of the rounding digit.

Example:
   Round 417.3621 to the nearest tenth.

- 3 is the rounding digit because it occupies the tenth place.
- 417.3621 rounded to the nearest tenth = 417.4; because 6 > 5 we add one to the rounding digit.

Skill 6.7   Equivalent forms of fractions, decimals, and percents

Percent = per 100 (written with the symbol %). Thus $10\% = \dfrac{10}{100} = \dfrac{1}{10}$.

Decimals = deci = part of ten. To find the decimal equivalent of a fraction, use the denominator to divide the numerator as shown in the following examples.

Example:
   Find the decimal equivalent of $\dfrac{7}{10}$.

$$
\begin{array}{r}
.7 \\
10\overline{)7.0} \\
\underline{70} \\
00
\end{array}
$$

Since 10 cannot divide into 7 evenly, put a decimal point in the answer row on top; put a zero behind 7 to make it 70. Continue the division process. If a remainder occurs, put a zero by the last digit of the remainder and continue the division.

$$\text{Thus } \frac{7}{10} = 0.7$$

It is a good idea to write a zero before the decimal point so that the decimal point is emphasized.

Example:

Find the decimal equivalent of $\dfrac{7}{125}$.

- $\begin{array}{r} .056 \\ 125\overline{)7.000} \\ \underline{625} \\ 750 \\ \underline{750} \\ 0 \end{array}$

Example:

Convert 0.056 to a fraction.

- Multiplying 0.056 by $\dfrac{1000}{1000}$ to get rid of the decimal point:

- $0.056 \times \dfrac{1000}{1000} = \dfrac{56}{1000} = \dfrac{7}{125}$

Example:

Find 23% of 1000.

- $= \dfrac{23}{100} \times \dfrac{1000}{1} = 23 \times 10 = 230$

Example:

Convert 6.25% to a fraction and to a mixed number.

- $6.25\% = 0.0625 = 0.0625 \times \dfrac{10000}{10000} = \dfrac{625}{10000} = \dfrac{1}{16}$

Operating with percent

Percent means per 100 (%).

Example:

- 10 percent $= \dfrac{10}{100} = \dfrac{1}{10} = 0.1$

Example:

- 10 percent of 150 means $\dfrac{10}{100} \times \dfrac{150}{1} = 15$

Example:
  Add 75% of 25 to 10% of 1000.

- $75\% \text{ of } 25 = \dfrac{75}{100} \times \dfrac{25}{1} = \dfrac{75}{4} \times \dfrac{1}{1} = \dfrac{75}{4} = 18\dfrac{3}{4}$ and

- $10\% \text{ of } 1000 = \dfrac{10}{100} \times \dfrac{1000}{1} = \dfrac{10}{1} \times \dfrac{10}{1} = 100$

Adding the two numbers gives:

- $18\dfrac{3}{4} + 100 = 118\dfrac{3}{4}$ or 118.75

Example:
  5 is what percent of 20?

- This is the same as converting $\dfrac{5}{20}$ to % form.

- $\dfrac{5}{20} \times \dfrac{100}{1} = \dfrac{5}{1} \times \dfrac{5}{1} = 25\%$

Example:
  An item on sale at 75% discount is now sold for $12.50. What was the selling price before the sale?

- $12.50 is 75% of the price. What was full price?
- $\dfrac{12.50}{75} \times \dfrac{100}{1} = \dfrac{50}{3} = \$16.667$ Then round to the nearest tenths place,

  equaling $16.67

Skill 6.8   Various equivalent symbolic representations of numbers (e.g., scientific notation, exponents)

See Skill 6.4.

Skill 6.9   Number theory concepts (e.g., prime and composite numbers)

The real number system includes all rational and irrational numbers.

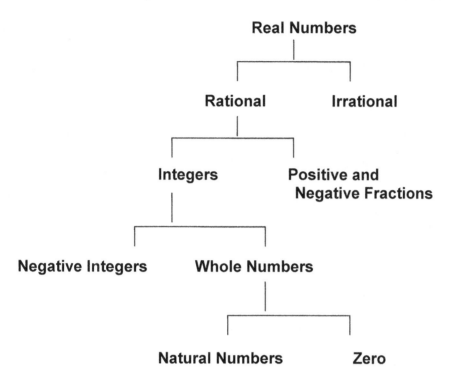

Rational numbers can be expressed as the ratio of two integers, $\frac{a}{b}$ where $b \neq 0$

Example:

$\frac{2}{3}$, $-\frac{4}{5}$, $5 = \frac{5}{1}$.

The rational numbers include integers, fractions and mixed numbers, terminating and repeating decimals. Every rational number can be expressed as a repeating or terminating decimal and can be shown on a number line.

Integers are positive and negative whole numbers and zero.
-6, -5, -4, -3, -2, -1, 0, 1, 2, 3, 4, 5, 6...

Whole numbers are natural numbers and zero.
0, 1, 2, 3, 4, 5, 6...

Natural numbers are the counting numbers.

Prime numbers are numbers that can only be factored into 1 and the number itself. When factoring into prime factors, all the factors must be numbers that cannot be factored again (without using 1). Initially numbers can be factored into any 2 factors. Check each resulting factor to see if it can be factored again.

Continue factoring until all remaining factors are prime. This is the list of prime factors. Regardless of what way the original number was factored, the final list of prime factors will always be the same.

Example:
Factor 30 into prime factors.

- Factor 30 into any 2 factors.
- $5 \cdot 6$ Now factor the 6.
- $5 \cdot 2 \cdot 3$ These are all prime factors.
- Factor 30 into any 2 factors.
- $3 \cdot 10$ Now factor the 10.
- $3 \cdot 2 \cdot 5$

These are the same prime factors even though the original factors were different.

Example:
Factor 240 into prime factors.

- Factor 240 into any 2 factors.
- $24 \cdot 10$ Now factor both 24 and 10.
- $4 \cdot 6 \cdot 2 \cdot 5$ Now factor both 4 and 6.
- $2 \cdot 2 \cdot 2 \cdot 3 \cdot 2 \cdot 5$ These are prime factors.

This can also be written as $2^4 \cdot 3 \cdot 5$.

Skill 6.10   The process of converting among graphic, numeric, symbolic, and verbal representations of numbers

Mathematical concepts and procedures can take many different forms. Students of mathematics must be able to recognize different forms of equivalent concepts.

For example, we can represent the slope of a line graphically, algebraically, verbally, and numerically. A line drawn on a coordinate plane will show the slope. In the equation of a line, y = mx + b, the term m represents the slope. We can define the slope of a line several different ways. The slope of a line is the change in the value of the y divided by the change in the value of x over a given interval. Alternatively, the slope of a line is the ratio of "rise" to "run" between two points. Finally, we can calculate the numeric value of the slope by using the verbal definitions and the algebraic representation of the line.

In order to understand mathematics and solve problems, one must know the definitions of basic mathematic terms and concepts. For a list of definitions and explanations of basic math terms, visit the following website:
http://home.blarg.net/~math/deflist.html

Additionally, one must use the language of mathematics correctly and precisely to accurately communicate concepts and ideas.

For example, the statement "minus ten times minus five equals plus fifty" is incorrect because minus and plus are arithmetic operations not numerical modifiers. The statement should read "negative ten times negative five equals positive 50".

Learn more about:
Properties of real numbers
http://www.purplemath.com/modules/numbprop.htm
Decimal expansion
http://planetmath.org/?op=getobj&from=objects&name=DecimalExpansion
The relationship among fractions, decimals and percents
http://www.mccc.edu/~kelld/CompFDP.htm

COMPETENCY 7.0 UNDERSTAND AND APPLY NUMBER OPERATIONS TO REPRESENT AND SOLVE PROBLEMS

Skill 7.1 Relationships among mathematical operations (e.g., multiplication and division as inverse operations)

Addition and Subtraction

These are the first mathematical operations that students are expected to learn. This requires not only an understanding of place value, but knowledge of the basic addition facts. Addition is conceptualized as the union of two sets.

Subtraction is more difficult because it has three different interpretations:

- *Taking away* a quantity from another. (Joy has 10 stickers. She gives 5 away to her friend Jamie. How many stickers does Joy have left?)
- *Comparison*: how much more one quantity is than another. (Tom and Matt are selling chocolate bars for the school band. In the first week, Tom sold 136 chocolate bars and Matt sold 97. How many more chocolate bars has Tom sold than Matt?)
- *Missing addend*: how much more of a quantity is needed. (Jeff is saving his money to buy a video game. The game costs $35.99 on sale. Jeff has $29.50 so far. How much more does he need to buy the video game?)

Multiplication and Division

There are different ways of interpreting these operations. Different students will find certain interpretations easier to understand than others. An understanding of the different ways of conceptualizing these operations will help the teacher adjust instruction for individual needs. Students need a mastery of addition and subtraction facts in order to do well in multiplication and division, which are extensions of these operations. The division algorithm is often the most difficult for students to learn.

Multiplication may be viewed in five different ways:

1. *Repeated addition*: 7×5 could be viewed as $7 + 7 + 7 + 7 + 7 = 35$
2. *Arrays*: 7×5 is depicted as 7 rows of 5 objects or 5 rows of 7 objects, like rows of seats in a classroom.
3. Cartesian product of two sets: This is the number of pairs that can be made with one member of each set, such as the number of combinations between card numbers and card suits (13 numbers times 4 suits = 52 cards.)
4. *Linear prototypes*: The problem 7×5 can be shown on a number line by starting with 0 and skipping 5 spaces 7 times, stopping on 35.
5. *Multiple sets*: 12×6 can be described in a problem like this: Jamal is buying pencils for school for himself and his two brothers. He buys 6 packages of pencils. Each package has 12 pencils. How many pencils did Jamal buy? ($12 \times 6 = 72$)

Division can be conceptualized in two ways, as in the example below of 32 divided by 8 = 4.

1. Measurement—the problem may be seen as 8 groups of 4. A sample problem could read, "Michelle has a 32-inch piece of yarn. She needs 8-inch pieces for her sting art project. How many pieces can she cut from the yarn?" (The yarn is measured into equal parts).
2. Partition—the problem may be seen as 8 dots in each of 4 groups. A sample problem could read "32 students go on a field trip to a museum. They are assigned to 4 tour guides for the guided tour. If the tour guides have an equal number of students in their groups, how many students are in each group?" (The total group of 32 students is broken up into 4 equal groups.)

Fractions

Fractions may be interpreted as:

- *A part of the whole* (probably the most familiar)—"Stacey is sharing a mushroom pizza with three friends. If everyone gets an equal share, what part of the pizza will each girl get?" Answer: 1/4.
- *A subset of a parent set*—"Josh's dog had eight puppies. Three puppies are white with spots. What fraction of the puppies are white with spots?" Answer: $\frac{3}{8}$
- $\frac{3}{8}$
- *A ratio*—Examples of rations could be two girls for every three boys in a class.

Decimal Fractions and Percents

Decimal fractions and percents are an extension of the place value system and common fractions. Students who have not mastered operations with common fractions will probably also have trouble with understanding decimal fractions and percents, as well as converting one to another.

Problem Solving

The skills of analysis and interpretation are necessary for problem solving. Skills necessary for successful problem solving include:

1. Identification of the main idea—what is the problem about?
2. Main question of the problem—what is the problem asking for?
3. Identifying important facts—what information is necessary to solve it?
4. Choose a strategy and an operation—how will the student solve the problem and with what operation?
5. Solve the problem—perform the computation
6. Check for accuracy of computation and compare the answer to the main question. Does it sound reasonable?
7. If solution is incorrect, repeat the steps.

Skill 7.2   Order of operations

When simplifying an algebraic expression, we must use the following order:

- Perform operations within parentheses.
- Evaluate exponents.
- Multiply and divide from left to right.
- Add and subtract when possible to produce a final answer.

Example:

$$3^3 - 5(b+2)$$

$$= 3^3 - 5b - 10$$

$$= 27 - 5b - 10 = 17 - 5b$$

Example:

$$2 - 4 \times 2^3 - 2(4 - 2 \times 3)$$

$$= 2 - 4 \times 2^3 - 2(4-6) = 2 - 4 \times 2^3 - 2(^-2)$$

$$= 2 - 4 \times 2^3 + 4 = 2 - 4 \times 8 + 4$$

$$= 2 - 32 + 4 = 6 - 32 = ^- 26$$

Skill 7.3   Procedures for enhancing computational fluency

Teachers must justify the procedures used in operational algorithms to ensure student understanding. Algorithms of the basic operations use number properties to simplify addition, subtraction, multiplication and division. The following are examples of operational algorithms, and their justifications and common errors in implementation.

Addition
The partial sums method of integer addition relies on the associative property of addition. Consider the partial sum algorithm of the addition of 125 and 89. We first sum the columns from left to right and then add the results.

$$\begin{array}{r} 125 \\ +\ \ 89 \\ \hline 100 \\ +\ 100 \\ +\ \ \ 14 \\ \hline 214 \end{array}$$

→ Hundreds column sum
→ Tens column sum
→ Ones column sum

The associative property of addition shows why this method works. We can rewrite 125 plus 89 as follows:

$$(100 + 20 + 5) + (80 + 9)$$

Using the associative property to group the terms:

$$(100) + (20 + 80) + (5 + 9) = 100 + 100 + 14 = 214$$

Note the final form is the same as the second step of the partial sums algorithm. When evaluating addition by partial sums, teachers should look for errors in assigning place values of the partial sums; for example, in the problem above, recording the sum of eight and two in the tens column as 10 instead of 100.

Rational number addition relies on the distributive property of multiplication over addition and the understanding that multiplication of any number by one yields the same number. Consider the addition of 1/4 to 1/3 by means of common denominator.

$$\frac{1}{4} + \frac{1}{3} = \frac{3}{3}(\frac{1}{4}) + \frac{4}{4}(\frac{1}{3}) = (\frac{3}{12}) + (\frac{4}{12}) = \frac{7}{12}$$

⟶ Recognize that $\frac{3}{3}$ and $\frac{4}{4}$ both equal 1.

Common errors in rational number addition are the failure to find a common denominator and adding both numerators and denominators.

Subtraction

The same change rule of substitution takes advantage of the property of addition of zero. The addition of zero does not change the value of a quantity.

$$289 - 97 = 292 - 100 \text{ because}$$
$$289 - 97 = (289 + 3) - (97 + 3) = (289 - 97) + (3 - 3) = 289 - 97 + 0$$

Note the use of the distributive property of multiplication over addition, the associative property of addition and the property of addition of zero in proving the accuracy of the same change algorithm. A common mistake when using the same change rule is adding from one number and subtracting from the other.

This is an error in reasoning resulting from misapplication of the distributive property (e.g. failing to distribute -1).

The same procedure, justification and error pattern applies to the subtraction of rational and real numbers.

$$13 - 2\frac{1}{3} = 13\frac{2}{3} - 3 \text{ because}$$

$$13 - 2\frac{1}{3} = (13 + \frac{2}{3}) - (2\frac{1}{3} + \frac{2}{3}) = (13 - 2\frac{1}{3}) + (\frac{2}{3} - \frac{2}{3}) = 13 - 2\frac{1}{3} + 0$$

or

$13 - 2.456 = 13.544 - 3$ because
$13 - 2.456 = (13 + 0.544) - (2.456 + 0.544) = (13 - 2.456) +$
$(0.544 - 0.544) = 13 - 2.456 + 0$

Multiplication

The partial products algorithm of multiplication decomposes each term into simpler numbers and sums the products of the simpler term

$$84 = 80 + 4$$
$$26 = 20 + 6$$

80 x 20	→	1600
80 x 6	→	480
20 x 4	→	80
6 x 4	→	24
		2184

We can justify this algorithm by using the "FOIL" method of binomial multiplication and the distributive property of multiplication over addition.

$$(80 + 4)(20 + 6) = (80)(20) + (4)(20) + (6)(80) + (6)(4)$$

Common errors in partial product multiplication result from mistakes in binomial multiplication and mistakes in pairing terms of the partial products (e.g. multiplying incorrect terms).

Division

We can justify the partial quotients algorithm for division by using the distributive property of multiplication over division. Because multiplication is the reverse of division, we check the result by multiplying the divisor by the partial sums.

```
18)   1440 |
     - 900 | 50
       540 |
     - 360 | 20
       180 |
     -  90 | 5
        90 |
     -  90 | 5
         0   80  ──→ final quotient = 80 with no remainder
```

Check:

$$18 (50 + 20 + 5 + 5) = (18)(50) + (18)(20) + (18)(5) + (18)(5) = 1440$$

Common errors in division often result from mistakes in translating words to symbols. For example, misinterpreting 10 divided by 5 as 5/10. In addition, when using the partial quotients algorithm, errors in subtraction and addition can produce incorrect results.

The main algorithm of rational number division is multiplication by the reciprocal. Thus,

$$\frac{\frac{1}{3}}{\frac{1}{4}} = (\frac{1}{3})(\frac{4}{1}) = \frac{4}{3} .$$

The definition of multiplication and division as inverse operations justifies the use of reciprocal multiplication.

See also Skill 7.6

Skill 7.4   Standard algorithms for basic arithmetic operations

The three basic number properties are distributive, commutative and associative. These number properties are the rules of number operations. The distributive property of multiplication over addition states that $x(y + z) = xy + xz$. The commutative property of multiplication and addition states that the order of numbers does not matter. In other words, $a + b = b + a$ and $ab = ba$. Finally, the associative property of addition and multiplication states that the grouping of numbers does not matter. In other words, $(a + b) + c = a + (b + c)$ and $a(bc) = (ab)c$.

Algorithms are methods or strategies for solving problems. There are several different algorithms for solving addition, subtraction, multiplication and division problems involving integers, rational numbers and real numbers.

See also Skill 7.3.

Rational and real number algorithms

Operations involving rational numbers represented as fractions require unique algorithms. For example, when adding or subtracting fractions we use the distributive property of multiplication over division to find common denominators.

When completing operations involving real numbers in decimal form we use similar algorithms to those used with integers. We use the associative, commutative and distributive properties of numbers to generate algorithms.

Skill 7.5   The use of number properties to analyze nonstandard computational algorithms

See Skill 8.2

Skill 7.6   Proving number facts and relationships

See Skill 7.3

Skill 7.7   Representing operations using concrete models

Concrete and visual representations can help demonstrate the logic behind operational algorithms. Blocks or other objects modeled on the base ten system are useful concrete tools. Base ten blocks represent ones, tens and hundreds. For example, modeling the partial sums algorithm with base ten blocks helps clarify the thought process. Consider the sum of 242 and 193. We represent 242 with two one hundred blocks, four ten blocks and 2 one blocks. We represent 193 with one one hundred block, nine ten blocks and 3 one blocks. In the partial sums algorithm, we manipulate each place value separately and total the results. Thus, we group the hundred blocks, ten blocks and one blocks and derive a total for each place value. We combine the place values to complete the sum.

An example of a visual representation of an operational algorithm is the modeling of a two-term multiplication as the area of a rectangle. For example, consider the product of 24 and 39. We can represent the product in geometric form. Note that the four sections of the rectangle equate to the four products of the partial products method.

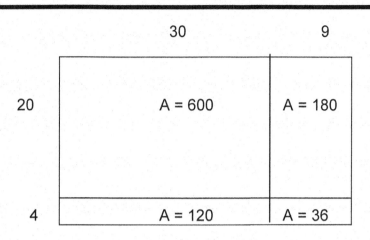

Thus, the final product is the sum of the areas or 600 + 180 + 120 + 36 = 936.

Mathematical operations can be shown using manipulatives or drawings. Multiplication can be shown using arrays.

Addition and subtraction can be demonstrated with symbols.

    ø ø ø î î î î   3 + 4 = 7   7 - 3 = 4

Fractions can be clarified using pattern blocks, fraction bars, or paper folding. Some examples of other manipulatives:

Example:
Using tiles to demonstrate both geometric ideas and number theory.

> Give each group of students 12 tiles and instruct them to build rectangles. Students draw their rectangles on paper.

    12 × 1

Encourage students to describe their reactions. Extend to 16 tiles. Ask students to form additional problems.

Skill 7.8   Multiple Solutions

See Skill 8.2

Skill 7.9   Solving problems involving integers, fractions, decimals, ratios and proportions, and percents

Two or more quantities can vary directly or inversely to each other. To convert the statements to equations, we introduce another quantity which is constant, called the constant of proportionality.

1. If x varies directly as y, then $x = ky$, where k is the constant of proportionality, or just a constant.
2. If x varies inversely as y, then $x = \dfrac{k}{y}$, where k is the constant.

Procedure to solve proportionality problems:

1. Translate the problem into a mathematical equation.
    Note: k is always in the numerator.
    - The variable that follows the word "directly" is also in the numerator.
    - The variable that follows the word "inversely" is in the denominator.
2. Substitute the given complete set of values in the equation to find k.
3. Since k is constant, it will stay the same for any values associated with the other variables.
4. Substitute the known values of the variables in the equation and solve for the missing variable.

<u>Example</u>:
    If x varies directly as y, and $x = 6$ when $y = 8$, find y when $x = 48$.
    x varies directly as $y \rightarrow x = ky$ (equation 1)

Substitute $x = 6$ and $y = 8$ into equation 1 to get
$$6 = 8k \rightarrow k = \frac{6}{8} \rightarrow k = \frac{3}{4}$$

Substitute $k = \dfrac{3}{4}$ into equation 1 for $x = 48$, we get:

$48 = \dfrac{3}{4}y$ Multiply both sides by $\dfrac{4}{3}$.

$\dfrac{4}{3}(48) = y$

$y = 64$

Example:

A varies inversely as the square of R. When A = 2, R = 4. Find A if R = 10.

A varies inversely as the square of R.

$$A = \frac{k}{R^2}$$ (equation 1), k is a constant.

Use equation 1 to find k when A = 2 and R = 4.

$$2 = \frac{k}{4^2} \rightarrow 2 = \frac{k}{16} \rightarrow k = 32.$$

Substituting k = 32 into equation 1 with R = 10, we get:

$$A = \frac{32}{10^2} \rightarrow A = \frac{32}{100} \rightarrow A = 0.32$$

Example:

x varies directly as the cube root of y and inversely as the square of z. When x = 2, y = 27 and z = 1. Find y when z = 2 and x = 1.

x varies directly as the cube root of y and inversely as the square of z.

$$x = k \cdot \frac{\sqrt[3]{y}}{z^2}$$ (equation 1), k is constant.

Substituting in equation 1 to solve for k when x = 2, y = 27 and z = 1 we get:

$$2 = k \cdot \frac{\sqrt[3]{27}}{1^2} \rightarrow 2 = k \cdot \frac{3}{1} \rightarrow 2 = 3k$$

$$k = \frac{2}{3}$$

To solve for y when z = 2 and x = 1, we substitute in equation 1 using the value we found for k to get:

$$1 = \frac{2}{3} \cdot \frac{\sqrt[3]{y}}{2^2} \rightarrow 1 = \frac{2 \cdot \sqrt[3]{y}}{3(4)} \rightarrow 1 = \frac{2 \cdot \sqrt[3]{y}}{12}$$

$$1 = \frac{\sqrt[3]{y}}{6} \rightarrow 6 = \sqrt[3]{y}$$ Cube both sides.

A **ratio** is a comparison of two numbers. A **proportion** is a statement that two ratios are equivalent. Proportions can be solved by using cross-products.

Example:

n *is to* 7 as 12 is to 14
written n:7::12:14 or

$$\frac{n}{7} = \frac{12}{14}$$

n × 14 = 7 × 12
Multiply to find the cross-product. 14 n = 84
14n 84=
Divide both sides of the equation by 14.
1414
n = 6

Proportions can be used to solve word problems whenever relationships are compared. Some situations include scale drawings and maps, similar polygons, speed, time and distance, cost, and comparison shopping.

Example:
Which is the better buy, 6 items for $1.29 or 8 items for $1.69?
Find the unit price.

$$\frac{6}{1} = \frac{1.29}{x}$$ $$\frac{8}{1} = \frac{1.69}{x}$$
6x = 1.29   8x = 1.69
x = 0.215   x = 0.21125

Thus, 8 items for $1.69 is the better buy.

Example:
A car travels 125 miles in 2.5 hours. How far will it go in 6 hours? Write a proportion comparing the distance and time.

$$\frac{125}{x} = \frac{2.5}{6}$$

$$2.5x = 750$$

$$\frac{2.5x}{2.5} = \frac{750}{2.5}$$

$$x = 300\,miles$$

Thus, the car can travel 300 miles in 6 hours. Word problems involving percents can be solved by writing the problem as an equation, then solving the equation. Keep in mind that "**of**" means "**multiplication**" and "**is**" means "**equals**."

<u>Example:</u>
The Ski Club has 85 members. 80% of the members are able to attend the meeting. How many members attend the meeting?

Restate the problem	What is 80% of 85?
Write an equation	$n = 0.8 \times 85$
Solve	$n = 68$

Sixty-eight members attend the meeting.

Skill 7.10 Strategies to estimate quantities (e.g., front end, rounding, regrouping)

ROUNDING

Rounding numbers is a form of estimation that is very useful in many mathematical operations. For example, when estimating the sum of two three-digit numbers, it is helpful to round the two numbers to the nearest hundred prior to addition. We can round numbers to any place value.

Rounding whole numbers

To round whole numbers, you first find the place value you want to round to (the rounding digit) and look at the digit directly to the right. If the digit is less than five, do not change the rounding digit and replace all numbers after the rounding digit with zeroes. If the digit is greater than or equal to five, increase the rounding digit by one and replace all numbers after the rounding digit with zeroes.

Example: Round 517 to the nearest ten.

1 is the rounding digit because it occupies the tens' place.

517 rounded to the nearest ten = 520; because 7 > 5 we add one to the rounding digit.

Example: Round 15,449 to the nearest hundred.

The first 4 is the rounding digit because it occupies the hundreds' place.

15,449 rounded to the nearest hundred = 15,400. Because 4 < 5, we do not add to the rounding digit.

Rounding decimals

Rounding decimals is identical to rounding whole numbers except that you simply drop all the digits to the right of the rounding digit.

Example: Round 417.3621 to the nearest tenth.

3 is the rounding digit because it occupies the tenth place.

417.3621 rounded to the nearest tenth = 417.4; because 6 > 5 we add one to the rounding digit.

REGROUPING TO ESTIMATE DIFFERENCES

We can estimate the difference of two numbers by first rounding the numbers and then subtracting the rounded numbers. When subtracting two rounded numbers, one rounded up and the other rounded down, we can improve our estimate by regrouping. For example, when estimating the difference of 540 and 355, we round 540 down to 500 and 355 up to 400. Thus, our estimated difference is 500 minus 400, or 100. Note that we rounded 540 down by 40 and 355 up by 45. Thus, the total amount of rounding is 85. Rounding 85 up to 100 and adding this rounded sum to 100 (our original estimate) gives us a final estimated difference of 200. This is closer to the actual difference of 185 (540 – 355). The regrouping method of estimation only works when we round the two numbers in opposite directions.

FRONT END ESTIMATION

While we can add or subtract rounded numbers to estimate sums and differences, another method, front-end estimation, is simpler and usually delivers results that are just as accurate. Front-end estimation is an elementary form of estimation of sums and differences. To estimate a sum or difference by front-end estimation, we add or subtract only the two highest place values and fill the remaining place values with zeroes.

Example: Estimate 4987 + 3512 by front-end estimation.

The estimated sum is 8400 (4900 + 3500).

Note that we do not round the numbers, but merely drop the digits after the two highest place values. In other words, we convert 4987 to 4900, not 5000.

Example: Estimate 3894 – 617 by front-end estimation.

The estimated difference is 3200 (3800 – 600).

Note that because 617 does not have a digit in the thousands place and 3894 does, we convert 617 to 600, not 610.

Skill 7.11   The relationships between number operations and algebra

An algebraic formula is an equation that describes a relationship among variables. While it is not often necessary to derive the formula, one must know how to rewrite a given formula in terms of a desired variable. **The Order of Operations** are to be followed when evaluating algebraic expressions. Follow these steps in order:

Simplify inside grouping characters such as parentheses, brackets, square root, fraction bar, etc.

1. Multiply out expressions with exponents.

2. Do multiplication or division, from left to right.

3. Do addition or subtraction, from left to right.

Example:
$$3^3 - 5(b + 2)$$

$$= 3^3 - 5b - 10$$

$$= 27 - 5b - 10 = 17 - 5b$$

Example:
$$2 - 4 \times 2^3 - 2(4 - 2 \times 3)$$
$$2 - 4 \times 2^3 - 8 + 4 - 6$$
$$2 - 4 \times 2^3 - 10$$
$$2 - 32 - 10$$
$$-30 - 10$$
$$= -40$$

Skill 7.12   The use of mathematical reasoning to solve problems involving numbers and number operations

This entails rewriting a given word problem into equivalent algebraic equations or inequalities.

Procedure:

- Assign variable labels to the major items being discussed.
- Use the description given to write the expression in algebraic terms.
- Translate the given problem into equation or inequality form.
- Use the appropriate procedure to find the final solution.

Example:

Find three consecutive numbers, such that the quotient of the largest number and 6 is $\frac{3}{2}$.

> Let the first number = x, the second number is $x + 1$, and the third number is $x + 2$ (since the numbers are in consecutive order).
>
> Quotient of the largest number and 6 is $\frac{3}{2}$ translates into $\frac{x+2}{6} = \frac{3}{2}$.
>
> Solving this by cross-multiplication, we get:

$$2(x + 2) = 3(6)$$
$$2x + 4 = 18 \rightarrow 2x = 14 \rightarrow x = 7$$

The first number is 7. 7 +1 = 8⊗8 is the second number. 7 + 2 = 9⊗9 is the third number. So, the three consecutive numbers are 7, 8, and 9.

Example:

A number divided by three times the number and 15 must be at least $\frac{1}{6}$. Find the least value for this number.

> Let the number = x.
> The number divided by three times the number and fifteen is
> $\frac{x}{3x+15}$. The number must be at least $\frac{1}{6}$, so the inequality is:

$$\frac{x}{3x+15} \geq \frac{1}{6}$$

> Cross multiply to solve for x.

$$6x \geq 3x + 15$$
$$3x \geq 15 \rightarrow x \geq 5$$

So the least value is $x = 5$.

Example:

The sum of a three-digit number is 14. If 4 times the hundredth digit is 13 less than 5 times the unit digit, and the tenth digit is twice the hundredth digit, find the three digit number.

Let the unit digit = U, the tenth digit = T, and the hundredth digit = H.

- The sum of the 3 digits is $14 \rightarrow H + T + U = 14$.   (equation 1)

- 4 times the hundredth digit is 13 less than 5 times the unit digit
  $5U - 4H = 13$.   (equation 2)

- The tenth digit is twice the hundredth digit $T = 2H$. (equation 3)

Solve simultaneously the three equations.

Substitute for $T = 2H$ from equation 3 into equation 1.

$H + 2H + U = 14$
$3H + U = 14$ (equation 4)

Add equation 4 and equation 2.

$3H + U = 14$

$^{-}4H + 5U = 13$

Multiply equation 4 by 4 to get
Multiply equation 2 by 3 to get

$12H + 4U = 56$

$+ \ ^{-}12H + 15U = 39$ $U = 5$

$0 + 19U = 95$

Back substitute $U = 5$ in equation 4 to get $3H + 5 = 14$.

$3H = 9$
$H = 3$

Back substitute $H = 3$ in equation 3 to get $T = 2(3)$.

$T = 6$

So the three-digit number is 365.

Note: Solving a system of 3 linear equations involves the following steps:

1. Eliminate one of the variables to reduce the system into two equations and two unknowns.

2. Reduce the two equations and two unknowns to a single equation with one variable. Use substitution or elimination method.

3. Solve the single equation to find the value of the variable.

4. Back substitute systematically in the appropriate equations to find the value of the other variables.

Learn more about:
Order of operations
http://www.regentsprep.org/Regents/math/orderop/Lorder.htm
Integers, fractions, decimals, ratios and proportions, and percents
http://edhelper.com/math_grade7.htm

COMPETENCY 8.0   UNDERSTAND AND APPLY PATTERNS, RELATIONS, ALGEBRA, AND PRINCIPLES OF GEOMETRY

Skill 8.1   Recognizing and extending patterns using a variety of representations (e.g., manipulatives, figures, numbers, algebraic expressions)

Example:
Conjecture about pattern presented in tabular form.

Kepler discovered a relationship between the average distance of a planet from the sun and the time it takes the planet to orbit the sun.

The following table shows the data for the six planets closest to the sun:

	Mercury	Venus	Earth	Mars	Jupiter	Saturn
Average distance, x	0.387	0.723	1	1.523	5.203	9.541
x^3	0.058	.378	1	3.533	140.852	868.524
Time, y	0.241	0.615	1	1.881	11.861	29.457
y^2	0.058	0.378	1	3.538	140.683	867.715

Looking at the data in the table, we can conjecture the following function for Kepler's relationship: $y = \sqrt{x^3}$

Representation of patterns using symbolic notation.

Example:
Find the recursive formula for the sequence 1, 3, 9, 27, 81…

We see that any term other than the first term is obtained by multiplying the preceding term by 3. Then, we may express the formula in symbolic notation as

$$a_n = 3a_{n-1},\ a_1 = 1$$

where a represents a term, the subscript n denotes the place of the term in the sequence and the subscript $n-1$ represents the preceding term.

Identification of patterns of change created by functions (e.g., linear, quadratic, exponential).

A **linear function** is a function defined by the equation $f(x) = mx + b$.

Example:
A model for the distance traveled by a migrating monarch butterfly looks like $f(t) = 80t$, where t represents time in days. We interpret this to mean that the average speed of the butterfly is 80 miles per day and distance traveled may be computed by substituting the number of days traveled for t. In a linear function, there is a **constant** rate of change.

The standard form of a **quadratic function** is $f(x) = ax^2 + bx + c$.

Example:
What patterns appear in a table for $y = x^2 - 5x + 6$?

x	y
0	6
1	2
2	0
3	0
4	2
5	6

We see that the values for y are **symmetrically** arranged.

An **exponential function** is a function defined by the equation $y = ab^x$, where a is the starting value, b is the growth factor, and x tells how many times to multiply by the growth factor.

Example: $y = 100(1.5)^x$

x	y
0	100
1	150
2	225
3	337.5
4	506.25

This is an **exponential** or multiplicative pattern of growth.

The **iterative process** involves repeated use of the same steps. A **recursive function** is an example of the iterative process. A recursive function is a function that requires the computation of all previous terms in order to find a subsequent term. Perhaps the most famous recursive function is the **Fibonacci sequence**. This is the sequence of numbers 1,1,2,3,5,8,13,21,34... for which the next term is found by adding the previous two terms.

Skill 8.2   Relationship between standard algorithms and fundamental concepts of algebra and geometry

Many algebraic procedures are similar to and rely upon number operations and algorithms. Two examples of this similarity are the adding of rational expressions and division of polynomials.

Addition of rational expressions is similar to fraction addition. The basic algorithm of addition for both fractions and rational expressions is the common denominator method. Consider an example of the addition of numerical fractions.

$$\frac{3}{5}+\frac{2}{3}=\frac{3(3)}{3(5)}+\frac{5(2)}{5(3)}=\frac{9}{15}+\frac{10}{15}=\frac{19}{15}$$

To complete the sum, we first find the least common denominator

Now, consider an example of rational expression addition.

$$\frac{(x+5)}{(x+1)}+\frac{2x}{(x+3)}=\frac{(x+3)(x+5)}{(x+3)(x+1)}+\frac{(x+1)2x}{(x+1)(x+3)}$$

$$=\frac{x^2+8x+15}{(x+3)(x+1)}+\frac{2x^2+2x}{(x+3)(x+1)}=\frac{3x^2+10x+15}{(x+3)(x+1)}$$

Note the similarity to fractional addition. The basic algorithm, finding a common denominator and adding numerators, is the same.

Division of polynomials follows the same algorithm as numerical long division. Consider an example of numerical long division.

$$
\begin{array}{r}
720 \\
6\overline{)4321} \\
\underline{42} \\
12 \\
\underline{12} \\
01
\end{array}
$$

720 1/6 = final quotient

Compare the process of numerical long division to polynomial division.

$$
\begin{array}{r}
x-9 \\
x+1\overline{)x^2-8x-9} \\
\underline{-x^2-x} \\
-9x-9 \\
\underline{+9x+9} \\
0+0
\end{array}
$$

x − 9 = final quotient

Note that the step-by-step process is identical in both cases.

Concrete and visual representations can help demonstrate the logic behind operational algorithms. Blocks or other objects modeled on the base ten system are useful concrete tools. Base ten blocks represent ones, tens and hundreds. For example, modeling the partial sums algorithm with base ten blocks helps clarify the thought process. Consider the sum of 242 and 193. We represent 242 with 2 one hundred blocks, 4 ten blocks and 2 one blocks. We represent 193 with 1 one hundred block, 9 ten blocks and 3 one blocks. In the partial sums algorithm, we manipulate each place value separately and total the results. Thus, we group the hundred blocks, ten blocks and one blocks and derive a total for each place value. We combine the place values to complete the sum.

An example of a visual representation of an operational algorithm is the modeling of a two-term multiplication as the area of a rectangle. For example, consider the product of 24 and 39. We can represent the product in geometric form. Note that the four sections of the rectangle equate to the four products of the partial products method.

	30	9
20	A = 600	A = 180
4	A = 120	A = 36

Thus, the final product is the sum of the areas or 600 + 180 + 120 + 36 = 936.

Skill 8.3 The application of concepts of variable, function, and equation to express relationships algebraically

Procedure for solving algebraic equations.

<u>Example</u>:

$3(x+3) = {}^- 2x + 4$ Solve for x.

Expand to eliminate all parentheses.

$3x + 9 = {}^- 2x + 4$

Multiply each term by the LCD to eliminate all denominators.
Combine like terms on each side when possible.
Use the properties to put all variables on one side and all constants on the other side.

$\rightarrow 3x + 9 - 9 = {}^- 2x + 4 - 9$ (subtract nine from both sides)

$\rightarrow 3x + 2x = {}^- 2x + 2x - 5$ (add $2x$ to both sides)

$\rightarrow 5x = {}^- 5$

$\rightarrow \dfrac{5x}{5} = \dfrac{{}^- 5}{5}$ (divide both sides by 5)

<u>Example</u>:

Solve: $3(2x + 5) - 4x = 5(x + 9)$

$6x + 15 - 4x = 5x + 45$

$2x + 15 = 5x + 45$

$^-3x + 15 = 45$

$^-3x = 30$

$x = {}^- 10$

Skill 8.4 Deriving algebraic expressions to represent real-world situations

Example:
Mark and Mike are twins. Three times Mark's age plus four equals four times Mike's age minus 14. How old are the boys?

Since the boys are twins, their ages are the same. "Translate" the English into Algebra.

Let x = their age

$$3x + 4 = 4x - 14$$
$$18 = x$$

The boys are each 18 years old.

Equations and inequalities

An equation consists of two statements linked by an equal sign (statement H1) = (statement H2).

Left Hand Side (LHS) = Right Hand Side (RHS)

If substituting a value for the variable results in LHS = RHS or a true statement, then the value is the solution for that equation.

Example:
$$2x = 6$$
(LHS) (RHS)
This statement is only true if we substitute 3 for x.
(True).

Therefore, 3 is a solution for the equation.

Example:
Is 2 a solution of $2x - 6 = 6x + 1$?

Substituting 2 for x:
$$2(2) - 6 = 6(2) + 1 \rightarrow 4 - 6 = 12 + 1 \rightarrow {}^- 2 = 13 \quad \text{(False)}$$

Therefore, 2 is not a solution.

An inequality has the same form as an equation, but the equal sign is replaced by one of the following inequality signs:

$$>$$
$$\geq$$

(LHS)   (RHS)

$$<$$

$$\leq$$

A solution to a given inequality is obtained by finding a reduced set equivalent to the given inequality.

Important facts about inequalities:

- Sense of inequality: This is the direction of the inequality. The larger number is always facing the open side.

$$25 > 3$$
$$3 < 25$$

- $\geq$ = "greater than OR equal to."
  $\leq$ = "less than OR equal to."

Thus, $25 \geq 3$ means $25 > 3$ or $25 = 3$. Since the first statement is true, but the second is false, we accept the total statement because of the "OR."

- When you divide or multiply by a negative number, you must change the direction of the inequality.

Example:

Dividing both sides by $^-3$ we get

$$\frac{^-3x}{^-3} < \frac{6}{^-3}$$ Note the change in direction.

Example:

$^-x \leq {}^- 4$

Multiplying both sides by -1 we get
$(^-1)(^-x) \geq (^-1)(^-4)$ Note the change in direction.

Properties of equations and inequalities:

- We can add or subtract any real number to both sides of the equation (or inequality).

$$3 = 3 \rightarrow 3 + 2 = 3 + 2 \rightarrow 5 = 5 \qquad \text{(still true)}$$

$$9 = 9 \rightarrow 9 - 3 = 9 - 3 \rightarrow 6 = 6 \qquad \text{(still true)}$$

$$x + 3 = 6 \rightarrow x + 3 - 3 = 6 - 3 \rightarrow x = 3$$

- We can multiply or divide both sides of an equation or an inequality by any real number except zero. Recall that when multiplying or dividing by a negative number we change the direction of the inequality.

$$3 = 3 \rightarrow 3 \times 2 = 3 \times 2 \rightarrow 6 = 6 \qquad \text{(still true)}$$

$$8 = 8 \rightarrow \frac{8}{4} = \frac{8}{4} \rightarrow 2 = 2 \qquad \text{(still true)}$$

$$^-2x = 6 \rightarrow \frac{^-2x}{^-2} = \frac{6}{^-2} \rightarrow x = ^-3$$

$$6 > 2 \rightarrow 6 \times 2 > 2 \times 2 \rightarrow 12 > 4 \qquad \text{(still true)}$$

$$^-3x \geq 5 \rightarrow \frac{^-3x}{^-3} \leq \frac{5}{^-3} \rightarrow x = \leq -\frac{5}{3}$$

$$^-2 < 6 \rightarrow \frac{^-2}{^-2} > \frac{6}{^-2} \rightarrow 1 > ^-3 \qquad \text{(still true)}$$

Procedure for solving linear equations:

<u>Example</u>:
$3(x + 3) = ^-2x + 4$ Solve for x.

- Expand to eliminate all parentheses.
- Multiply each term by the LCD to eliminate all denominators.
- Combine like terms on each side when possible.
- Use the properties to put all variables on one side and all constants on the other side.

$\rightarrow 3x + 9 = {}^- 2x + 4$

$\rightarrow 3x + 9 - 9 = {}^- 2x + 4 - 9$ (subtract nine from both sides)

$\rightarrow 3x + 2x = {}^- 2x + 2x - 5$ (add $2x$ to both sides)

$\rightarrow \dfrac{5x}{5} = \dfrac{{}^-5}{5}$ (divide both sides by 5)

$\rightarrow x = {}^- 1$

Example:

$\rightarrow {}^- x + 19 = 4x - 6$ (combine like terms on each side)

$\rightarrow {}^- x + 19 - 19 = 4x - 6 - 19$ (subtract 19 from both sides)

$\rightarrow {}^- x = 4x - 25$

$\rightarrow {}^- x - 4x = 4x - 4x - 25$ (subtract $4x$ from both sides)

$\rightarrow {}^- 5x = {}^- 25$

$\rightarrow \dfrac{{}^-5x}{{}^-5} = \dfrac{{}^-25}{{}^-5}$ (divide both sides by -5)

$\rightarrow x = 5$

Procedure for solving linear inequalities:

We use the same procedure used for solving linear equations, but the answer is represented in graphical form on the number line or in interval form.

Example:
Solve the inequality, show its solution using interval form, and graph the solution on the number line.

$$\dfrac{5x}{8} + 3 \geq 2x - 5$$

$$8\left(\dfrac{5x}{8}\right) + 8(3) \geq 8(2x) - 5(8) \qquad \text{Multiply by LCD = 8.}$$

$$5x + 24 \geq 16x - 40$$

Subtract 16x and 24 from both sides of the equation.

$$^-11x \geq ^- 64$$

$$\frac{^-11x}{^-11} \leq \frac{^-64}{^-11}$$

$$x \leq \frac{64}{11} \ ; \ x \leq 5\frac{9}{11}$$

Solution in interval form: $\left(^-\infty, 5\frac{9}{11}\right]$

Note: "] "means $5\frac{9}{11}$ is included in the solution.

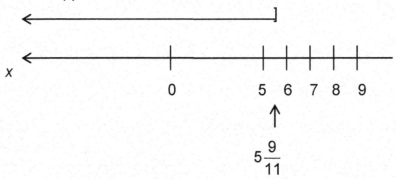

Note: Notation for expressing the final answer may vary with different authors.

1. [   ] means inclusion of numbers in the final answer. Also, a closed dot ($\bullet$) may be used in graphing.

2. (   ) means exclusion of the number in the final answer. Also, an open dot ($\circ$) may be used for graphing.

Example:
Solve the following inequality and express your answer in both interval and graphical form.

$$3x - 8 < 2(3x - 1)$$
$$3x - 8 < 6x - 2 \qquad \text{Distributive property.}$$
$$3x - 6x - 8 + 8 < 6x - 6x - 2 + 8$$

Add 8 and subtract $6x$ from both sides of the equation.

$$^-3x < 6$$

$$\frac{^-3x}{^-3} > \frac{6}{^-3} \qquad \text{Note the change in direction of the equality.}$$

Graphical form:

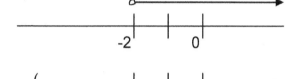

or

Interval form: $(^-2, \infty)$

Recall:
- Using a parentheses or an open circle implies the point is not included in the answer.
- Using a bracket or a closed circle implies the point is included in the answer.

Absolute value equations and equalities:

If a and b are real numbers, and k is a non-negative real number, the solution of $|ax + b| = k$ is $ax + b = k$ or $ax + b = ^- k$

Example:
$|2x + 3| = 9$ Solve for x.

$2x + 3 = 9$	or	$2x + 3 = ^- 9$
$2x + 3 - 3 = 9 - 3$	or	$2x + 3 - 3 = ^- 9 - 3$
$2x = 6$	or	$2x = ^- 12$
$\dfrac{2x}{2} = \dfrac{6}{2}$	or	$\dfrac{2x}{2} = \dfrac{^-12}{2}$
$x = 3$	or	$x = ^- 6$

Therefore, the solution is $x = \{3, {}^-6\}$

Example:

$|3x - 1| = {}^- 3$ Solve for x.

Since $k = -3$ is a negative number, and an absolute value cannot result in a negative, there is no solution.

If a and b are real numbers and k is a non-negative real number, the solution of $|ax + b| < k$ is ${}^-k < ax + b < k$

Example:
Solve $|7x + 3| < 25$

$${}^-25 < (7x + 3) < 25$$
$$({}^-25 - 3) < (7x) < (25 - 3)$$

Subtract 3 from all sides.

$${}^-28 < 7x < 22$$
$${}^-4 < x < \frac{22}{7}$$

Divide all terms by 7.

Solution in interval form is $\left({}^-4, \frac{22}{7}\right)$

Solution in graphical form:

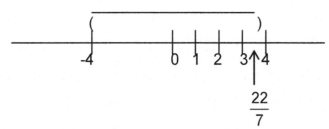

If a and b are real numbers and k is a non-negative real number, the solution of

$|ax + b| > k$ is $ax + b > k$ or $ax + b < {}^- k$

Example:
Solve $|2x - 7| > 5$

$(2x - 7) > 5$ or $(2x - 7) <^- 5$
$2x > 7 + 5$ or $2x < 7 - 5$ Add 7 to all sides.
$2x > 12$ or $2x < 2$ Divide all sides by 2.
$x > 6$ or $x < 1$

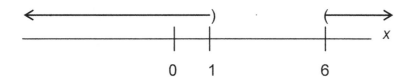

Solution: $(-\infty, 1) \cup (6, \infty)$

Skill 8.5   **The use of tables and graphs to explore patterns, relations, and functions**

A first degree equation can be written in the form $ax + by = c$. To graph this equation, find either one point and the slope of the line or find two points. To find a point and slope, solve the equation for y. This gets the equation in the **slope-intercept form,** $y = mx + b$. The point $(0,b)$ is the y-intercept and m is the line's slope.

To find two points, substitute any number for x, then solve for y. Repeat this with a different number. To find the intercepts, substitute 0 for x and then 0 for y.

Remember that graphs will go up as they go to the right when the slope is positive. Negative slopes make the lines go down as they go to the right.

If the equation solves to x = a constant, then the graph is a **vertical line.** It only has an x- intercept. Its slope is undefined.

If the equation solves to y = a constant, then the graph is a **horizontal line.** It only has a y-intercept. Its slope is 0 (zero).

When graphing a linear inequality, the line is dotted if the inequality sign is < or >. If the inequality signs are either ~ or ~ , the line on the graph is a solid line.
Shade above the line when the inequality sign is > or ~ . Shade below the line when the inequality sign is < or~ . For inequalities of the form $x > k$, $x \sim k$, $x < k$, or $x \sim k$, where k = any number, the graph will be a vertical line (solid or dotted.) Shade to the right for > or ~ . Shade to the left for < or ~ .

Remember: Dividing or multiplying by a negative number will reverse the direction of the inequality sign.

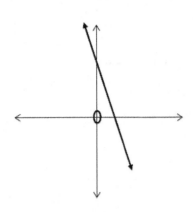

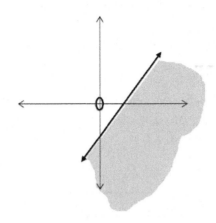

$5x + \dfrac{2y}{5} = 6$

$y = -x + 3\ 2$

$3x - 2y \sim 6$

$y \sim \dfrac{3x}{2} - 3$

Skill 8.6   Solving equations and inequalities

A **linear equation in one variable** can be written in the form **ax + b = 0,** where a and b are real numbers and a ~ 0.

An equation can be solved by performing the same operations on both sides of the equation.

Example:

$4x - 3 = {}^-5x + 6$

$(4x - 3) + 3 = ({}^-5x + 6) + 3$	Add 3.
$4x = {}^-5x + 9$	Simplify.
$4x + 5x = ({}^-5x + 9) + 5x$	Add 5x.
$9x = 9$	Simplify.
$\dfrac{9x}{9} = \dfrac{9}{9}$	Divide by 9.
$x = 1$	Simplify.

An **inequality** is a statement that orders two expressions. The symbols used are < (less than), > (greater than), ~ (less than or equal to), ~ (greater than or equal to) and ≠(not equal to). Most inequalities have an infinite number of solutions. Methods for solving inequalities are similar to those used for solving equations, with this exception--when both sides of an inequality are multiplied or divided by a <u>negative</u> real number, the inequality sign in reversed.

Example:

3x - 2 > 13

(3x - 2) + 2 > 13 + 2	Add 2.
3x > 15	Simplify.
3 3	Divide by 3.
x > 5	Simplify.

Thus the solution set is all real numbers greater than 5.

Example:

x + 11 ~ 5x + 3

(x + 11) - 11 ~ (5x + 3) - 11	Subtract 11.
x ~ 5x - 8	Simplify.
x - 5x ~ 5x - 8 - 5x	Subtract 5x. Simplify.
-4x ~ -8	Divide by -4.

Reverse the inequality sign.

Thus the solution set is all real numbers greater than or equal to 2.

Skill 8.7   Properties of lines and angles

Lines and angles are two fundamental concepts of geometry. There are several basic properties of lines and angles that students and prospective teachers should understand.

PROPERTIES OF LINES

A line is a one-dimensional figure extending to infinity in both directions. Two points on the line determine a line segment. The following is a list of several important properties of lines.

- **Parallel Lines** – Two lines in the same plane that do not intersect are parallel.
- **Skew Lines** – Two lines in different planes that do not intersect are skew.
- **Perpendicular Lines** – Two lines are perpendicular if they intersect in a right angle (90°).
- **Slope** – Given two points on a line (x_1, y_1) and (x_2, y_2), the slope of the line is the change in y $(y_2 - y_1)$ divided by change in x $(x_2 - x_1)$.

PROPERTIES OF ANGLES

Two lines diverging from a common point form an angle. We can measure angles (the distance between the two diverging lines) with two units, radians and degrees. The angle produced by two lines diverging in opposite directions (straight angle) measures 180° or π radians. A right angle produced by the intersection of perpendicular lines, measures 90° or π/2 radians. The following is a list of different classifications of angles:

- **Acute Angles** – Angles measuring between 0° and 90°.
- **Obtuse Angles** – Angles measuring between 90° and 180°.
- **Straight Angle** – The angle of a straight line measures 180°.
- **Reflex Angles** – Angles measuring between 180° and 360°.
- **Complementary Angles** – Two angles whose sum equals 90°.
- **Supplementary Angles** – Two angles whose sum equals 180°.
- **Congruent Angles** – Two angles with the same measure.

PROPERTIES OF ANGLES FORMED BY THE INTERSECTION OF PARALLEL LINES

Angles formed when a line intersects parallel lines have special properties. Consider the following diagram.

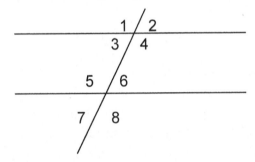

- **Vertical Angles are Congruent** – Angles 2 & 3, 1 & 4, 5 & 8, and 6 & 7 are vertical angles, which are congruent (even if the lines are not parallel).
- **Alternate Exterior and Alternate Interior Angles are Congruent** – Angles 3 & 6 and 4 & 5 are alternate interior angles. Angles 2 & 7 and 1 & 8 are alternate exterior angles. Alternate angles are congruent.
- **Corresponding Angles are Congruent** – Angles 2 & 6, 1 & 5, 3 & 7, and 4 & 8 are corresponding angles and are congruent.
- **Interior Angles on the Same Side of the Transversal are Supplementary** – Angles 3 & 5 and 4 & 6 are supplementary, the sum of these angles is 180°.
- **Exterior Angles on the Same Side of the Transversal are Supplementary** – Angles 1 & 7 and 2 & 8 are supplementary; the sum of these angles is 180°.

Skill 8.8   Attributes of two- and three-dimensional geometric figures

A **cylinder** has two congruent circular bases that are parallel.

A **sphere** is a space figure having all its points the same distance from the center.

A **cone** is a space figure having a circular base and a single vertex.

A **pyramid** is a space figure with a square base and 4 triangle-shaped sides.

A **tetrahedron** is a 4-sided space triangle. Each face is a triangle.

A **prism** is a space figure with two congruent, parallel bases that are polygons.

Skill 8.9 The application of the concepts of similarity and congruence to solve problems

Congruent figures have the same size and shape. If one is placed above the other, it will fit exactly. Congruent lines have the same length. Congruent angles have equal measures.

The symbol for congruent is $\cong$.

Polygons (pentagons) *ABCDE* and *VWXYZ* are congruent. They are exactly the same size and shape.

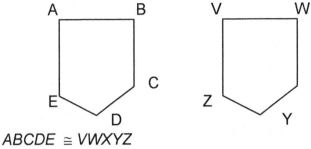

$ABCDE \cong VWXYZ$

The corresponding parts listed below show congruent angles or congruent sides:

corresponding angles	corresponding sides
$\angle A \leftrightarrow \angle V$	$AB \leftrightarrow VW$
$\angle B \leftrightarrow \angle W$	$BC \leftrightarrow WX$
$\angle C \leftrightarrow \angle X$	$CD \leftrightarrow XY$
$\angle D \leftrightarrow \angle Y$	$DE \leftrightarrow YZ$
$\angle E \leftrightarrow \angle Z$	$AE \leftrightarrow VZ$

<u>Example:</u> Given two similar quadrilaterals. Find the lengths of sides *x, y,* and *z.*

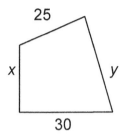

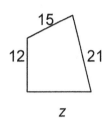

Since corresponding sides are proportional:
= so the scale is

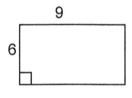

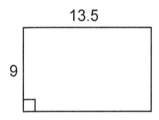

$3x = 60$	$3y = 105$	$5z = 90$
$x = 20$	$y = 35$	$z = 18$

Similarity

Two figures that have the same shape are **similar**. Polygons are similar if and only if corresponding angles are congruent and corresponding sides are in proportion. Corresponding parts of similar polygons are proportional.

Example: Given the rectangles below, compare the area and perimeter.

9	13.5

| 6 | | 9 | |

$A = LW$	$A = LW$	1. write formula
$A = (6)(9)$	$A = (9)(13.5)$	2. substitute
known values		
$A = 54$ sq. units	$A = 121.5$ sq. units	3. compute
$P = 2(L + W)$	$P = 2(L + W)$	1. write formula
$P = 2(6 + 9)$	$P = 2(9 + 13.5)$	2. substitute known values
$P = 30$ units	$P = 45$ units	3. compute

Notice that the areas relate to each other in the following manner:

Ratio of sides $\quad 9/13.5 = 2/3$

Multiply the first area by the square of the reciprocal $(3/2)^2$ to get the second area.

$$54 \times (3/2)^2 = 121.5$$

The perimeters relate to each other in the following manner:

Ratio of sides $\quad 9/13.5 = 2/3$

Multiply the perimeter of the first by the reciprocal of the ratio to get the perimeter of the second.

$$30 \times 3/2 = 45$$

Example: Tommy draws and cuts out 2 triangles for a school project. One of them has sides of 3, 6, and 9 inches. The other triangle has sides of 2, 4, and 6. Is there a relationship between the two triangles?

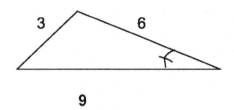

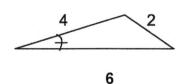

Take the proportion of the corresponding sides.

$$\frac{2}{3} \qquad \frac{4}{6} = \frac{2}{3} \qquad \frac{6}{9} = \frac{2}{3}$$

The smaller triangle is 2/3 the size of the large triangle.

Skill 8.10   Geometric transformations

<u>Example</u>:
Use the information given for each figure to find (S), the sum of the interior angles of an eight-sided polygon and a ten-sided polygon.

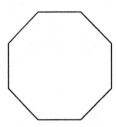

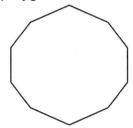

Listing the number of sides, number of triangles, and sum of interior angles, we have:

# of sides	# of triangles	sum of interior angles (S)
3	1	180 (=1(180°))
4	2	360 (=2(180°))

Following this pattern, the number of triangles is always 2 less than the number of sides and the sum of the interior angles is the number of triangles times 180 . Using the same pattern, we get the following:

# of sides	# of triangles	sum of interior angles (S)
6	4	4(180°)=720
8	6	6(180°)=1080
10	8	8(180°)=1440

Skill 8.11   The classification of figures according to symmetries

Symmetry is exact similarity between two parts or halves, as if one were a mirror image of the other.

A **Tessellation** is an arrangement of closed shapes that completely covers the plane without overlapping or leaving gaps. Unlike **tilings**, tessellations do not require the use of regular polygons. In art, the term is used to refer to pictures or tiles mostly in the form of animals and other life forms. These cover the surface of a plane in a symmetrical way without overlapping or leaving gaps. M. C. Escher is known as the "Father" of modern tessellations. Tessellations are used for tiling, mosaics, quilts, and other art forms.

If you look at a completed tessellation, you will see the original motif repeats in a pattern. There are 17 possible ways that a pattern can be used to tile a flat surface or "wallpaper."

There are four basic transformational symmetries that can be used in tessellations: **translation, rotation, reflection,** and **glide reflection**. The transformation of an object is called its image. If the original object was labeled with letters, such as $ABCD$, the image may be labeled with the same letters followed by a prime symbol,   .

A **translation** is a transformation that "slides" an object a fixed distance in a given direction. The original object and its translation have the same shape and size, and they face in the same direction.

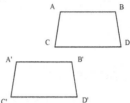

An example of a translation in architecture would be stadium seating. The seats are the same size and shape and face in the same direction.

A **rotation** is a transformation that turns a figure about a fixed point called the center of rotation. An object and its rotation are the same shape and size, but the figures may be turned in different directions. Rotations can occur in either a clockwise or a counterclockwise direction.

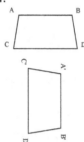

Rotations can be seen in wallpaper and art, and a Ferris wheel is an example of rotation.

An object and its **reflection** have the same shape and size, but the figures face in opposite directions.

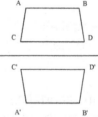

The line (where a mirror may be placed) is called the **line of reflection**. The distance from a point to the line of reflection is the same as the distance from the point's image to the line of reflection.

A **glide reflection** is a combination of a reflection and a translation.

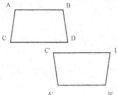

The tessellation below is a combination of the four types of transformational symmetry we have discussed:

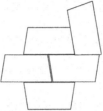

Skill 8.12   Connections between algebra and geometry (e.g., the use of coordinate systems)

A **function** is a relation in which different ordered pairs have different first coordinates. (No x values are repeated.)

A first-degree equation has an equation of the form ax + by = c. To find the slope of the line, solve the equation for y. This gets the equation into **slope-intercept form,** y = mx + b where m represents the slope of the line.

To find the y-intercept, substitute 0 for x and solve for y. This is the y-intercept. The y- intercept is also the value of b in y = mx + b.

To find the x- intercept, substitute 0 for y and solve for x. This is the x-intercept.

<u>Example 1</u>: Find the slope and y-intercept of $3x + 2y = 14$.

$$3x + 2y = 14$$
$$2y = -3x + 14$$

$$y = -\frac{2}{3}x + 7$$

The slope of the line is - , the value of m = -2/3
The y-intercept of the line is 7.

The intercepts can also be found by substituting 0 in place of the other variable in the equation.

Example 2:
Find the x- and y-intercepts of $3x + 2y = 14$.

To find the y-intercept, let $x = 0$
$3(0) + 2y = 14$
$0 + 2y = 14$
$2y = 14$
$y = 7$
$(0,7)$ is the y intercept.

To find the x- intercept: let $y = 0$
$3x + 2(0) = 14$
$3x + 0 = 14$
$3x = 14$
$(4.67, 0)$ is the x- intercept.

The y-intercept is the y-coordinate of the point where the line crosses the y-axis. The equation can be written in slope-intercept form, which is $y = mx + b$, where m is the slope and b is the y-intercept. To rewrite the equation into some other form, multiply each term by the common denominator of all the fractions. Then rearrange terms as necessary.

If the graph is a **vertical line,** then the equation solves to x = the x coordinate of any point on the line.

If the graph is a **horizontal line,** then the equation solves to y = the y coordinate of any point on the line.

Learn more about:
Variables, functions and equations
http://www.mathleague.com/help/algebra/algebra.htm
Solving linear inequalities
http://www.purplemath.com/modules/ineqlin.htm
Lines and angles
http://www.andrews.edu/~calkins/math/webtexts/geom03.htm
Basic geometry
http://www.andrews.edu/~calkins/math/webtexts/geom03.htm

COMPETENCY 9.0   UNDERSTAND AND APPLY CONCEPTS AND METHODS OF MEASUREMENT, DATA ANALYSIS, STATISTICS, AND PROBABILITY

Skill 9.1   **The use of both standard and nonstandard units of measurement to describe and compare phenomena**

Example:
Students are trying to determine the volume of a block.

Indirect measurement:
Students pour water into a graduated cylinder and note the volume of the cylinder. They then place the block in the cylinder and note the new volume. By deducting the first reading from the second reading, they can determine the volume of the block by displacement.

Direct measurement:
Students measure the length, height, and width of the block. They then determine the volume by multiplying the length times the width times the height.

Converting from larger units to smaller units (metric):
To convert larger units to smaller units, multiply.

Example:
If a packet of sugar weighs 0.5 grams, how many milligrams does it weigh?
     1 gram = 1000 milligrams
     0.5 grams x 1000 milligrams = 500 milligrams

Converting from smaller units to larger units (customary):
To convert smaller units to larger units, divide.

Example:
If an adult Kodiak bear weighs 1150 pounds, how many tons does it weigh?
     1 ton = 2000 pounds
     1150 pounds/2000 pounds = 0.575 tons

Skill 9.2   **Appropriate instruments, units, and procedures for solving various measurement problems (e.g., problems involving time, length, area, angles, volume, mass, temperature)**

Example
A class wants to take a field trip from New York City to Albany to visit the capital. The trip is approximately 160 miles. If they will be traveling at 50 miles per hour, how long will it take for them to get there (assuming they are traveling at a steady rate)?

Set up the equation as a proportion and solve: $\underline{50 \text{ miles}}$ mph for $\underline{160 \text{ miles}}$=
1 hours x hours

$(160 \text{ miles})(1 \text{ hour}) = (50 \text{ miles}) (x \text{ hours}) \; 160 = 50x, \; x \; = \; 3.2 \text{ hours}$

Example:
Students in a fourth grade class want to fill a 3-gallon jug using cups of water. How many cups of water are needed?

1 gallon = 16 cups of water
3 gallons x 16 cups = 48 cups of water are needed.

Skill 9.3   Estimation and conversion of measurements within the customary and metric system

Rounding measurements and conversions

Rounding a measurement to the nearest unit desired is a quick way of making a mathematical estimate or approximation of that measurement.

Measurements of length (English system)

12 inches (in)	=	1 foot (ft)
3 feet (ft)	=	1 yard (yd)
1760 yards (yd)	=	1 mile (mi)

Measurements of length (Metric system)

kilometer (km)	=	1000 meters (m)
hectometer (hm)	=	100 meters (m)
decameter (dam)	=	10 meters (m)
meter (m)	=	1 meter (m)
decimeter (dm)	=	1/10 meter (m)
centimeter (cm)	=	1/100 meter (m)
millimeter (mm)	=	1/1000 meter (m)

Conversion of length from English to Metric

1 inch	=	2.54 centimeters
1 foot	=	30.48 centimeters
1 yard	=	0.91 meters
1 mile	=	1.6 kilometers

Measurements of weight (English system)

28 grams (g)	=	1 ounce (oz)
16 ounces (oz)	=	1 pound (lb)
2000 pounds (lb)	=	1 ton (t) (short ton)

Measurements of weight (Metric system)

kilogram (kg)	=	1000 grams (g)
gram (g)	=	1 gram (g)
milligram (mg)	=	1/1000 gram (g)

Conversion of weight from English to metric

1 ounce	=	28 grams
1 pound	=	0.45 kilogram

Measurement of volume (English system)

8 fluid ounces (oz)	=	1 cup (c)
2 cups (c)	=	1 pint (pt)
2 pints (pt)	=	1 quart (qt)
4 quarts (qt)	=	1 gallon (gal)

Measurement of volume (Metric system)

kiloliter (kl)	=	1000 liters (l)
liter (l)	=	1 liter (l)
milliliter (ml)	=	1/1000 liters (ml)

Conversion of volume from English to metric

1 teaspoon (tsp)	=	5 milliliters
1 fluid ounce	=	15 milliliters
1 cup	=	0.24 liters
1 pint	=	0.47 liters
1 quart	=	0.95 liters
1 gallon	=	3.8 liters

Note: (') represents feet and (") represents inches.

Example:

The distance around a race course is exactly 1 mile, 17 feet, and $9\frac{1}{4}$ inches.

Approximate this distance to the nearest tenth of a foot.
Convert the distance to feet.
1 mile = 1760 yards = 1760   3 feet = 5280 feet.

$9\frac{1}{4}$ inches $= \frac{37}{4} \times \frac{1}{12} = \frac{37}{48} = 0.77083$ feet

So 1 mile, 17 feet and $9\frac{1}{4}$ inches = $5280 + 17 + 0.77083$ feet

$= 5297.\underline{7}7083$ feet.

Now, we need to round to the nearest tenth digit. The underlined 7 is in the tenth place. The digit in the hundredth place, also a 7, is greater than 5, the 7 in the tenths place needs to be rounded up to 8 to get a final answer of 5297.8 feet.

Example:
Round 2$\underline{7}$3,539.763 to the nearest ten thousand.
The underlined 7 is in the ten thousands position. The number in the thousands position is 3. Since 3 is less than 5, the number in the ten thousands position stays at 7 and all the digits to the right of the 7 are changed to zeros, to get this answer: 270,000.

Example:
Round 279.538 millimeters to the nearest centimeter.

We first convert 279.538 to centimeters.
Since 1 millimeter is 1/10 centimeter, we divide the number of millimeters by 10 to get the number of centimeters, which is 27.9538.

To round to the nearest centimeter, we must look at the number to the right of the decimal, which is 9. Since 9 is greater than 5, the seven becomes an 8 to get a final answer of 28 centimeters.

To estimate measurement of familiar objects, it is first necessary to determine the units to be used.

Examples:
Length/width/depth
- The coastline of Florida
- The width of a ribbon
- The thickness of a book
- The length of a football field
- The depth of water in a pool

Weight or mass
- A bag of sugar
- A school bus
- A dime

Capacity
- Paint needed to paint a bedroom
- Glass of milk
- Bottle of soda
- Medicine for child

Examples:
Estimate the measurements of the following objects.

Length of a dollar bill	6 in.
Weight of a baseball	1 pound
Distance from New York to Florida	1100 km
Amount of water to fill a medicine dropper	1 milliliter

| 16 ounces (oz.) = 1 pound (lb.) |
| 2,000 lb. = 1 ton (T.) |

| Length of a desk | 2 meters |

Depending on the degree of accuracy needed, an object may be measured to different units. For example, a pencil may be 6 inches to the nearest inch, or 6 3/8 inches to the nearest eighth of an inch. Similarly, it might be 15 cm to the nearest cm or 154 mm to the nearest mm.

The units of **length** in the customary system are inches, feet, yards and miles.

> 12 inches (in.) = 1 foot (ft.)
> 36 in. = 1 yard (yd.)
> 3 ft. = 1 yd.
> 5280 ft. = 1 mile (mi.)
> 1760 yd. = 1 mi.

To change from a **larger unit to a smaller unit, multiply.** To change from a **smaller unit to a larger unit, divide.**

Example:
4 mi. = ___yd.
> Since 1760 yd. = 1 mile, multiply 4 × 1760 = 7040 yd.

The units of **weight** are ounces, pounds and tons.

Example:

2.75 T. = _____ lb.

$2.75 \times 2{,}000 = 5{,}500$ lb.

The units of **capacity** are fluid ounces, cups, pints, quarts, and gallons.

```
8 fluid ounces (fl. oz.) = 1 cup (c.)
2 c. = 1 pint (pt.)
4 c. = 1 quart (qt.)
2 pt. = 1 qt.
4 qt. = 1 gallon (gal.)
```

Example1:

3 gal. = _____ qt.

$3 \times 4 = 12$ qt.

The metric system is based on multiples of ten. Conversions are made by simply moving the decimal point to the left or right.

kilo-	1000	thousands
hecto-	100	hundreds
deca-	10	tens
unit		
deci-	.1	tenths
centi-	.01	hundredths
milli-	.001	thousandths

The basic unit for **length** is the meter. One meter is approximately one yard.
The basic unit for **weight** or mass is the gram. A paper clip weighs about one gram.
The basic unit for **volume** is the liter. One liter is approximately a quart.

Skill 9.4 **The collection, organization, and communication of information using appropriate graphic and non-graphic representations (e.g., frequency distributions and percentiles)**

Percentiles divide data into 100 equal parts. A person whose score falls in the 65th percentile has outperformed 65 percent of all those who took the test. This does not mean that the score was 65 percent out of 100, nor does it mean that 65 percent of the questions answered were correct. It means that the grade was higher than 65 percent of all those who took the test.

Stanine "standard nine" scores combine the understandability of percentages with the properties of the normal curve of probability. Stanines divide the bell curve into nine sections. The largest of these stretches from the 40th to the 60th percentile and is called the "fifth stanine" (the average of taking into account error possibilities).

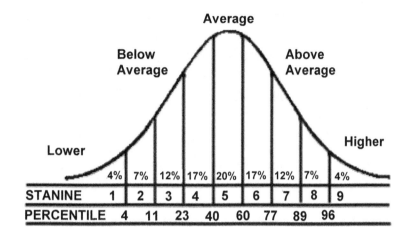

	Average

Quartiles divide the data into four parts. First find the median of the data set (Q2), then find the median of the upper (Q3) and lower (Q1) halves of the data set. If there are an odd number of values in the data set, include the median value in both halves when finding quartile values. For example, take the data set: {1, 4, 9, 16, 25, 36, 49, 64, 81}. First find the median value, which is 25. Since there are an odd number of values in the data set (nine), we include the median in both halves. To find the quartile values, we much find the medians of {1, 4, 9, 16, 25} and {25, 36, 49, 64, 81}.

Since each of these subsets had an odd number of elements (five), we use the middle value. Thus the first quartile value is 9 and the third quartile value is 49. If the data set had an even number of elements, you would average the middle two values. The quartile values are always either one of the data points, or exactly half way between two data points.

Example:
Given the following set of data, find the percentile of the score 104.
    70, 72, 82, 83, 84, 87, 100, 104, 108, 109, 110, 115
    Solution: Find the percentage of scores below 104.
    7/12 of the scores are less than 104. This is 58.333%; therefore, the score of 104 is in the 58th percentile.

Find the first, second and third quartile for the data listed.
    6, 7, 8, 9, 10, 12, 13, 14, 15, 16, 18, 23, 24, 25, 27, 29, 30, 33, 34, 37
    Quartile 1: The 1st Quartile is the median of the lower half of the data set, which is 11.
    Quartile 2: The median of the data set is the 2nd Quartile, which is 17.
    Quartile 3: The 3rd Quartile is the median of the upper half of the data set, which is 28.

Skill 9.5   The use of measures of central tendency and spread to analyze data; problems involving simple probabilities

Mean, median and mode are three measures of central tendency. The **mean** is the average of the data items. The **median** is found by putting the data items in order from smallest to largest and selecting the item in the middle (or the average of the two items in the middle). The **mode** is the most frequently occurring item. **Range** is a measure of variability. It is found by subtracting the smallest value from the largest value.

Example:
Find the mean, median, mode and range of the test scores listed below:

85	77	65
92	90	54
88	85	70
75	80	69
85	88	60
72	74	95

Mean (X) = sum of all scores ÷ number of scores = 78

Median = put numbers in order from smallest to largest. Pick middle number.
54, 60, 65, 69, 70, 72, 74, 75, <u>77</u>, <u>80</u>, 85, 85, 85, 88, 88, 90, 92, 95
both in middle
Therefore, median is average of two numbers in the middle or 78.5

Mode = most frequent number = 85

Range = largest number minus the smallest number = 95 – 54 = 41

Different situations require different information. If we examine the circumstances under which an ice cream store owner may use statistics collected in the store, we find different uses for different information.

Suppose, over a seven-day period, the store owner collects data on the ice cream flavors sold. He finds the mean number of scoops sold is 174 per day. The most frequently sold flavor is vanilla. This information is useful in determining how much ice cream to order in all and in what amounts for each flavor.

In the case of the ice cream store, the median and range have little business value for the owner.

Consider the set of test scores from a math class: 0, 16, 19, 65, 65, 65, 68, 69, 70, 72, 73, 73, 75, 78, 80, 85, 88, and 92. The mean is 64.06 and the median is 71. Since only three out of the total eighteen scores are less than the mean, the median (71) would be a more descriptive score.

If you take the example of a retail dress store, mode is what the owner would calculate to determine the most common dress size among shoppers and to order that size in a greater quantity for the store's inventory.

An understanding of the definitions is important in determining the validity and uses of statistical data. All definitions and applications in this section apply to ungrouped data.

- Data item: each piece of data is represented by the letter X.
- Mean: the average of all data represented by the symbol $\overline{X}$.
- Range: difference between the highest and lowest value of data items.
- Sum of the Squares: sum of the squares of the differences between each item and the mean. $Sx^2 = (X - \overline{X})^2$
- Variance: the sum of the squares quantity divided by the number of items. (The lower case Greek letter sigma squared (σ^2) represents variance.)

$$\frac{Sx^2}{N} = \sigma^2$$

The larger the value of the variance, the larger the spread.

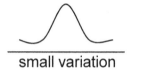

small variation   larger variation

Standard Deviation: the square root of the variance. The lower case Greek letter sigma (σ) is used to represent standard deviation. $\sigma = \sqrt{\sigma^2}$

Most statistical calculators have standard deviation keys on them and should be used when asked to calculate statistical functions. It is important to become familiar with the calculator and the location of the keys needed.

Example:
Given the ungrouped data below, calculate the mean, range, standard deviation and the variance.

| 15 | 22 | 28 | 25 | 34 | 38 |
| 18 | 25 | 30 | 33 | 19 | 23 |

Mean ($\overline{X}$) = 25.8333333
Range: $38 - 15 = 23$
Standard deviation (σ) = 6.6936952
Variance (σ^2) = 44.805556

Probability measures the chances of an event occurring. The probability of an event that *must* occur, a certain event, is **one**. When no outcome is favorable, the probability of an impossible event is **zero**.

P(event) = <u>number of favorable outcomes</u>
number of possible outcomes

<u>Example:</u>
Given one die with faces numbered 1 - 6, the probability of tossing an even number on one throw of the die is 3/6 or 1/2, since there are three favorable outcomes (even faces) and a total of six possible outcomes (faces).

If A and B are **independent** events, the probability that both A and B will occur is the product of their individual probabilities.

<u>Example:</u>
Given two dice, the probability of tossing a 3 on each of them simultaneously is the probability of a 3 on the first die, or 1/6, times the probability of tossing a 3 on the second die, also 1/6.

$$\frac{1}{6} \times \frac{1}{6} = \frac{1}{36}$$

<u>Example:</u>
Given a jar containing 10 marbles—three red, five black, and two white—what is the probability of drawing a red marble and then a white marble if the marble is returned to the jar after choosing?

$$\frac{3}{10} \times \frac{2}{10} = \frac{6}{100} = \frac{3}{50}$$

When the outcome of the first event affects the outcome of the second event, the events are **dependent.** Any two events that are not independent are dependent. This is also known as conditional probability.

Probability of (A and B) = P(A) × P(B given A)

<u>Example:</u>
Two cards are drawn from a deck of 52 cards, without replacement; that is, the first card is not returned to the deck before the second card is drawn. What is the probability of drawing a diamond?

A = drawing a diamond first
B = drawing a diamond second

P(A) = drawing a diamond first
P(B) = drawing a diamond second

P(A) = 13/52 = ¼   P(B) = 12/52 = 4/17

(PA+B) = ¼ X 14/17 = 1/17

Skill 9.6   Predictions based on simulations, theory, or data from the real world

Using graphic calculators to analyze and interpret data from a variety of disciplines (e.g., sciences, social sciences, technology).

<u>**Example – Life Science**</u>
Examine an animal population and vegetation density in a biome over time.
<u>**Example – Physical Science**</u>
Explore motions and forces by calculating speeds based on distance and time traveled and creating a graph to represent the data.
<u>**Example – Geography**</u>
Explore and illustrate knowledge of earth landforms.
<u>**Example – Economics/Finance**</u>
Compare car buying with car leasing by graphing comparisons and setting up monthly payment schedules based on available interest rates.

<u>**Learn more about simple probabilities:**</u>
http://math.youngzones.org/simple_prob.html

DOMAIN III.   HISTORY AND SOCIAL SCIENCE

COMPETENCY 10.0   UNDERSTAND MAJOR DEVELOPMENTS IN THE HISTORY OF THE UNITED STATES

Skill 10.1   Lives of indigenous peoples before the arrival of the Europeans

In North America, the landscape was hospitable to settlement and exploration. The North American continent, especially in what is now the United States, had a few mountain ranges and a handful of wide rivers – nothing like the dense jungles and staggeringly high mountains of South America. The area that is now Canada was cold but otherwise conducive to settlement. As a result, the Native Americans in the northern areas of the Americas were more spread out and their cultures more diverse than their South American counterparts.

The Pueblo, who lived in what is now the American Southwest, are perhaps best known for the villages they constructed from the sheer faces of cliffs and rocks and for *adobes*, mud-brick buildings that housed their living and meeting quarters. The Pueblos chose their own chiefs. This was perhaps one of the oldest representative governments in the world.

The Iroquois, who lived in the American Northeast, are noted for their organized government. The famous Five Nations of the Iroquois made treaties among themselves and shared leadership of their peoples.

For the North Americans, life was centered on finding and growing food. The people were proficient farmers and hunters. They grew such crops as *maize*, or corn, potatoes, squash, pumpkins and beans. They hunted all types of animals for food, including deer, bears, and buffalo. Despite the preponderance of crop-growing areas, many Native Americans did not domesticate animals other than dogs.

The Native Americans who lived in the wilds of Canada and in the Pacific Northwest lived off the land as well as the nearby water. Fishing was important in these places. The people used fish for food and for trade, exchanging the much-needed food for beads and other trinkets from neighboring tribes.

Religion was a personal affair for nearly all of these tribes, with beliefs in higher powers extending to Spirits in the sky and elsewhere in nature.

Skill 10.2   European exploration and settlement of North America

Columbus' first trans-Atlantic voyage was to test the theory that Asia could be reached by sailing west. This proved to be true, but could be done only after going around, across or through the landmass in between. After Spain dispatched explorers and conquistadors to gather wealth for Spanish monarchs, the British began searching for the "Northwest Passage," a land-sea route across North America and the eventual open sea to the wealth of Asia. However, this did not deter exploration and settlement. **Spain, France, and England** along with some participation by the **Dutch** led the way with expanding Western European civilization in the New World. These three nations had strong monarchial governments and were struggling for dominance and power in Europe. With the defeat of Spain's mighty Armada in 1588, England became the undisputed master of the seas. Spain lost its power and influence in Europe. France and England carried on their rivalry, leading to eventual British control in Asia.

Spain's influence was in Florida, from the Gulf Coast from Texas all the way west to California and south to the tip of South America and some of the islands of the West Indies. French control centered from New Orleans north to what is now northern Canada, including the entire Mississippi Valley, the St. Lawrence Valley, the Great Lakes, and the land that was part of the Louisiana Territory. A few West Indies islands were also part of France's empire. England settled the eastern seaboard of North America, including parts of Canada and from Maine to Georgia. Some West Indies islands also came under British control. The Dutch had New Amsterdam for a period but later ceded it to Britain.

One interesting aspect of all of this was that each of these nations, especially England, laid claim to land that extended partly or all the way across the continent, regardless of the fact that the others claimed the same land. The wars for dominance and control of power in Europe eventually extended to the Americas, especially North America.

The importance of the Age of Exploration was not only the discovery and colonization of the New World, but also the availability of better maps and charts; new accurate navigational instruments; increased knowledge; great wealth; and new and different foods and items not known in Europe. This new hemisphere offered refuge from poverty and persecution; it became a place to start a new and better life. The explorers found proof that Asia could be reached by sea and that the earth was round; ships and sailors would not sail off the edge of a flat earth and disappear forever into nothingness.

The part of North America claimed by **France** was called New France and consisted of the land west of the Appalachian Mountains. It included the St. Lawrence Valley, the Great Lakes, the Mississippi Valley, and the entire region of land westward to the Rockies. The French established the permanent settlements of Montreal and New Orleans, taking control of the two major gateways into the heart of North America. The St. Lawrence River, the Great Lakes, and the Mississippi River along with its tributaries made it possible for French explorers and traders to roam at will, unhindered in exploring, trapping, trading, and furthering the interests of France.

Most of the French settlements were in Canada along the St. Lawrence River. Only scattered forts and trading posts were found in the upper Mississippi Valley and Great Lakes region. The rulers of France originally intended New France to have vast estates owned by nobles and worked by peasants with the peasants living on the estates in compact farming villages – the New World version of the Old World's medieval system of feudalism. Each of the nobles wanted his estate to be on the river for ease of transportation. New France's settled areas were eventually established as a string of farmhouses stretching from Quebec to Montreal along the St. Lawrence and Richelieu Rivers.

In the non-settled areas of the interior were the French fur traders. They established contact with friendly Indian tribes, spending the winters with them to procure the furs needed for trade. In the spring, they would return to Montreal in time to trade their furs for the products brought by the cargo ships from France, which usually arrived at about the same time. Most of New France's wealth came from the fur trade, which provided a livelihood for many people. Manufacturers and workmen in France, ship owners, merchants, as well as the fur traders and their Indian allies all benefited.

Into the eighteenth century, French rivalry with the **British** grew stronger and stronger. New France was united under a single government and enjoyed the support of many Indian allies. The French traders were very diligent in preserving the forests and driving away game upon which the Indians depended for life. It was difficult for the French to defend all of their settlements as they were scattered over half of the continent. However, by the early 1750s, France was the most powerful nation in Western Europe. Its armies were superior to all others and its navy was giving the British stiff competition for control of the seas. The stage was set for confrontation in both Europe and America.

Spanish settlement had its beginnings in the Caribbean with the establishment of colonies on Hispaniola (at Santo Domingo which became the capital of the West Indies), Puerto Rico, and Cuba. There were a number of reasons for Spanish involvement in the Americas:

- The spirit of adventure
- The desire for land
- Expansion of Spanish power, influence, and empire
- The desire for great wealth
- Expansion of Roman Catholic influence and conversion of native peoples

The first permanent settlement in what is now the United States was in 1565 at **St. Augustine,** Florida. A later permanent settlement in the southwestern United States was in 1609 at Santa Fe, New Mexico. At the peak of Spanish power, the area in the United States claimed, settled, and controlled by Spain included Florida and all land west of the Mississippi River.

Although France and England lay claim to the same areas, Spain quickly built ranches and missions. It introduced the Indians to animals, plants and seeds from the Old World that they had never seen before. Spaniards brought in horses, cattle, donkeys, pigs, sheep, goats, and poultry. They cut barrels in half and filled them with earth to transport and transplant trees bearing apples, oranges, limes, cherries, pears, walnuts, olives, lemons, figs, apricots and almonds. Even sugar cane and flowers made it to America along with bags bringing seeds of wheat, barley, rye, flax, lentils, rice, and peas.

All Spanish colonies belonged to the king of Spain. Considered **an absolute monarch** with complete or absolute power, he claimed rule by divine right, the belief being God had given him the right to rule and he answered only to God for his actions. His word was final. The people had no voice in government. The land, the people, and the wealth all belonged to him to use as he pleased. He appointed personal representatives or viceroys, giving them complete authority to rule for him in his colonies. Since the majority of them were friends and advisers, they were richly rewarded with land grants, gold and silver, privileges of trading, and the right to operate the gold and silver mines.

By the 1750s in Europe, Spain was no longer the most powerful nation. The remaining rivalry was between Britain and France. For nearly 25 years, between 1689 and 1748, a series of armed conflicts involving these two powers took place. These conflicts spilled over into North America. The two nations fought for possession of colonies, especially in Asia and North America, and for control of the seas, but none of these conflicts was decisive.

The final conflict began in North America in 1754, in the Ohio River Valley. It was known in America as the French and Indian War and in Europe as the **Seven Years' War**. In America, both sides had advantages and disadvantages. The British colonies were well established and consolidated in a smaller area. British colonists outnumbered French colonists 23 to 1. Except for a small area in Canada, French settlements were scattered over a much larger area (roughly half of the continent) and were smaller. However, the French settlements were united under one government and were quick to act and cooperate when necessary. In addition, the French had many more Indian allies than the British. The British colonies had separate, individual governments and very seldom cooperated, even when necessary. In Europe, at that time, France was the more powerful of the two nations.

Both sides enjoyed victories and suffered defeats. If there was one person who could be given the credit for British victory, it is William Pitt. Pitt was a strong leader, enormously energetic, supremely self-confident, and determined on a complete British victory. Despite the advantages and military victories of the French, Pitt succeeded. He sent more troops to America, strengthened the British Navy, and gave to the officers of the colonial militia rank equal to the British officers. He saw to it that Britain took the offensive and kept it.

Of all the British victories, perhaps the most important was winning Canada.

The French depended on the St. Lawrence River for transporting supplies, soldiers, and messages – for maintaining the link between New France and the Mother Country. Tied into this waterway system were the connecting links of the Great Lakes and the Mississippi River and its tributaries, along which were scattered French forts, trading posts, and small settlements. When, in 1758, the British captured Louisburg on Cape Breton Island, New France was doomed. Louisburg gave the British navy a base of operations, preventing French reinforcements and supplies from getting to their troops. Other forts fell to the British: Frontenac, Duquesne, Crown Point, Ticonderoga, Niagara, those in the upper Ohio Valley, and, most importantly, Quebec and finally Montreal. Spain entered the war in 1762 to aid France, but it was too late. British victories occurred all around the world – in India, the Mediterranean, and Europe.

Spain, France and Britain met in Paris in 1763 to draw up the **Treaty of Paris**. Great Britain received most of India and all of North America east of the Mississippi River, except for New Orleans. Spain gave Britain control of Florida in return for Cuba and the islands of the Philippines, taken during the war. France lost nearly all of its possessions in America and India and was allowed to keep four islands: Guadeloupe, Martinique, Haiti on Hispaniola, and Miquelon and St. Pierre. France gave Spain New Orleans and the vast territory of Louisiana, west of the Mississippi River. Britain was now the most powerful nation.

Skill 10.3   The Revolutionary War and the formation of the national government; slavery

The colonies were divided generally into the three regions of New England, Middle Atlantic, and Southern. The distinct culture of each region affected attitudes, ideas towards politics, religion, and economic activities. The geography of each region also contributed to its unique characteristics.

The **New England** colonies consisted of Massachusetts, Rhode Island, Connecticut, and New Hampshire. Life in these colonies was centered on the towns. Each family farmed on its own plot of land. A short summer growing season and limited amount of good soil gave rise to other economic activities such as manufacturing, fishing, shipbuilding, and trade. The vast majority of the settlers shared similar origins, coming from England and Scotland. Towns were carefully planned and laid out the same way. The form of government was the town meeting, where all adult males met to make the laws. The legislative body, the General Court, consisted of an upper and lower house.

The **Middle or Middle Atlantic** colonies included New York, New Jersey, Pennsylvania, Delaware, and Maryland. New York and New Jersey were at one time the Dutch colony of New Netherland, and Delaware at one time was New Sweden. From their beginnings, these five colonies were considered "melting pots" that had settlers from many different nations and backgrounds. The main economic activity was farming, with the settlers scattered over the countryside cultivating rather large farms. The Indians were not as much of a threat as in New England, so they did not have to settle in small farming villages. The soil was very fertile, the land was gently rolling, and a milder climate provided a longer growing season. These farms produced a large surplus of food, not only for the colonists themselves but also for sale. This colonial region became known as the "breadbasket" of the New World. The New York and Philadelphia seaports were constantly filled with ships being loaded with meat, flour, and other foods for the West Indies and England.

There were other economic activities such as shipbuilding, iron mines, and factories producing paper, glass, and textiles. The legislative body in Pennsylvania was unicameral, consisting of one house. In the other four colonies, the legislative body had two houses. Counties and towns had units of local government.

The **Southern** colonies were Virginia, North and South Carolina, and Georgia. Virginia was the first permanent successful English colony and Georgia was the last. The year 1619 was a very important year in the history of Virginia and the United States with three very significant events. First, 60 women were sent to Virginia to marry and establish families. Second, 20 Africans – the first of thousands – arrived. Third, and most importantly, the Virginia colonists were granted the right to self-government. They began by electing representatives to the House of Burgesses, their legislative body.

Causes of the War for Independence

- With the end of the French and Indian War (The Seven Years' War), England reasserted control over the colonies in America. It particularly needed the revenue from the control of trade to pay for the recent war and to defend the new territory obtained as a result of the war.
- English leaders decided to impose a tax that would pay for the military defense of the American lands. The colonists rejected this idea for two reasons: (1) They were undergoing an economic recession, and (2) they believed it unjust to be taxed unless they had representation in the Parliament.
- England passed a series of laws that provoked fierce opposition:
  1. The Proclamation Act prohibited English settlement beyond the Appalachian Mountains to appease the Native Americans.
  2. The Sugar Act imposed a tax on foreign molasses, sugar, and other goods imported into the colonies.
  3. The Currency Act prohibited colonial governments from issuing paper money.

Opposition melded in Massachusetts. Leaders denounced "taxation without representation" and organized a boycott against imported English goods. The movement spread to other colonies rapidly.

The **Stamp Act** placed a tax on newspapers, legal documents, licenses, almanacs and playing cards. This was the first instance of an "internal" tax on the colonies. In response, the colonists formed secret groups called "the Sons of Liberty" and staged riots against the agents collecting the taxes and marking items with a special stamp. In October of 1765, representatives of nine colonies met in the Stamp Act Congress. They drafted resolutions stating their reasons for opposing the act and sent them to England. Merchants throughout the colonies applied pressure with a large boycott of imported English Goods. The Stamp Act was repealed three months later.

England then had a dual concern: to generate revenue and to regain control of the colonists. They passed the **Townshend Acts in 1767**. These acts placed taxes on lead, glass, paint, paper and tea, resulting in another very successful boycott of English goods. England responded by limiting the tax to tea. This ended the boycotts of everything except tea. The situation in the colonies between colonists and British troops was becoming increasingly strained. Despite a skirmish in New York and the **Boston Massacre** in 1770, tensions abated over the next few years.

The Tea Act of 1773 gave the British East India Company a monopoly on sales of tea. The colonists responded with the **Boston Tea Party**. England responded with the **Coercive Acts** (called the **Intolerable Acts** by the colonists) in 1774. This closed the port of Boston, changed the charter of the Massachusetts colony, and suppressed town meetings. Eleven colonies sent delegates to the first Continental Congress in 1774. The group issued the Declaration of Rights and Grievances, which vowed allegiance to the king but protested the right of Parliament to tax the colonies. The boycotts resumed at the same time.

Massachusetts mobilized its colonial militia in anticipation of difficulties with England. The British troops attempted to seize their weapons and ammunition. The result was two clashes with "minute men" at Lexington and Concord. The Second Continental Congress met a month later. Many of the delegates recommended a declaration of independence from Britain. The group established an army and commissioned George Washington as its commander.

British forces attacked patriot strongholds at **Breed's Hill** and **Bunker Hill.** Although the colonists withdrew, the loss of life for the British was nearly fifty percent of the army. The next month King George III declared the American colonies to be in a state of rebellion. The war quickly began in earnest. On July 3, 1776, British General Howe arrived in New York harbor with 10,000 troops to prepare for an attack on the city.

The following day, the Second Continental Congress accepted the final draft of the Declaration of Independence by unanimous vote.

Although the colonial army was quite small in comparison to the British army and lacked in formal military training, the colonists had learned a new method of warfare from the Indians. Many battles were fought in the traditional style of two lines of soldiers facing off and firing weapons. But the patriots had the advantage of understanding guerilla warfare – fighting from behind trees and other defenses.

When the war began, the colonies began to establish state governments. They intentionally designed a weak national government because they feared a centralized form of power. But the lack of continuity between the individual governments was confusing and economically damaging.

In 1787, the Constitutional Convention devised an entirely new form of government and outlined it in the Constitution of the United States. The Constitution was ratified quickly and took effect in 1789. Concerns that had been raised in or by the states regarding civil liberties and states' rights led to the immediate adoption of 12 amendments to the constitution, the first ten known as the Bill of Rights.

In regards to the American political system, it is important to realize that political parties are never mentioned in the United States Constitution. George Washington himself warned against the creation of "factions" in American politics that cause "jealousies and false alarms" and possibly damage the body politic. Thomas Jefferson echoed this warning, yet he came to lead a party himself.

Americans feared the emergence of political parties because they had witnessed how parties worked in Great Britain. British parties, called "factions," were made up of a few people interested in their own personal profit than in the public good. American leaders were very interested in keeping factions from forming in their new country. Ironically, disagreements between two of Washington's chief advisors – **Thomas Jefferson** and **Alexander Hamilton** – spurred the formation of the first political parties in the United States.

The two parties that developed through the early 1790s were led by Jefferson as the Secretary of State and Hamilton as the Secretary of the Treasury. Jefferson and Hamilton were different in many ways. They has separate views on what should be the proper form of government of the United States. This difference helped to shape the parties that formed around them.

Hamilton wanted the federal government to be stronger than the state governments. Jefferson believed that the state governments should be stronger. Hamilton supported the creation of the first Bank of the United States; Jefferson opposed it because he felt that it gave too much power to wealthy investors who would help run it. Jefferson interpreted the Constitution strictly; he argued that nowhere did the Constitution give the federal government the power to create a national bank.

Hamilton interpreted the Constitution much more loosely. He pointed out that the Constitution gave Congress the power to make all laws "necessary and proper" to carry out its duties. He reasoned that since Congress had the right to collect taxes, then Congress had the right to create the bank. Hamilton wanted the government to encourage economic growth. He favored the growth of trade, manufacturing, and the rise of cities as the necessary parts of economic growth. He favored the business leaders and mistrusted the common people. Jefferson believed that the common people, especially the farmers, were the backbone of the nation. He thought that the rise of big cities and manufacturing would corrupt American life.

Before long, leaders in other states began to organize support for either Jefferson or Hamilton. Jefferson's supporters called themselves **Democratic-Republicans** (often this was shortened just to Republicans, though in actuality it was the forerunner of today's Democratic Party). Hamilton and his supporters were known as **Federalists** because they favored a strong federal government. The Federalists had the support of the merchants and ship owners in the Northeast and some planters in the South. Small farmers, craft workers, and some of the wealthier landowners supported Jefferson and the Democratic-Republicans.

By the time Washington retired from office in 1796, the new political parties came to play an important role in choosing his successor. Each party put up its own candidates for office. The election of 1796 was the first one in which political parties played a role. By the beginning of the 1800s, the Federalist Party, torn by internal divisions, began declining. After Hamilton's bitter rival, Jefferson, was elected as president in 1800 and after Hamilton was killed in 1804 in a duel with Aaron Burr, the Federalist Party began to collapse. By 1816, after losing a string of important elections (Jefferson was re-elected in 1804, and James Madison, a Democratic-Republican, was elected in 1808), the Federalist Party ceased to be an effective political force and soon passed off the national stage.

By the late 1820s, new political parties had emerged. The **Democratic-Republican** Party, or simply the **Republican** Party, had been the major party for many years, but differences within it about the direction the country was to take caused a split after 1824. Those who favored strong national growth took the name **Whigs** after a similar party in Great Britain and united around then President John Quincy Adams. Many businesspeople in the Northeast as well as some wealthy planters in the South supported it.

Those who favored slower growth and were more supportive of workers and small farmers went on to form the new Democratic Party, with Andrew Jackson being its first leader as well as becoming the first president from it. It is the forerunner of today's party of the same name.

In the mid-1850s, the slavery issue was beginning to heat up. In 1854, the Whigs and some Northern Democrats opposed to slavery united to form the Republican Party. Before the Civil War, the Democratic Party was more heavily represented in the South and was thus pro-slavery for the most part.

Thus, by the time of the Civil War, the present structure of the major political parties had been formed. Though there were changes in ideology and platforms over the years, no other political parties would manage to gain enough strength to seriously challenge the "Big Two" parties.

Slavery

The trans-African slave trade refers to the movement of black African slaves over trade routes through the deserts of northern Africa to slave trading posts on the eastern and northern coasts of the continent. From these posts, slaves were transported to markets in Muslim cities such as Morocco, Cairo, Algiers and Tripoli. The practice began sometime in the ninth century and continued into the early years of the twentieth century, predating and outlasting the trans-Atlantic slave trade by Europeans.

The slaves themselves were sometimes captured by Arab traders on raiding missions, or were enslaved by other black groups as a result of war and subsequently traded into the slave market. These people came largely from sub-Saharan Africa, and once captured were moved across the deserts by caravan routes. These routes stretched from oasis to oasis from the interior to the coastal trading posts.

Slaves were exchanged for a variety of goods, including gold, horses, dye, jewels and cloth. They were sold mainly to become servants, or to join harems if they were female. Some male slaves were castrated and served as eunuchs who acted as guards for the harems of wealthy Muslims.

Arabs dominated the sea routes of the Red Sea and the Indian Ocean during the Middle Ages, and the slave trade expanded to bring laborers from posts on the eastern coast of Africa to the agricultural areas of India.

Little primary evidence remains of the Arab slave trade in Africa, and exact figures on the number of Africans who were sold into slavery are unknown. The trade was significant, however, not only in the widespread area it affected but also in the number of people upon which slavery was inflicted.

As the European nations grew their empires, seeking wealth and the raw materials and crops they were unable to produce at home, the need for cheap labor, particularly persons who would work under undesirable or even harmful circumstances of climate, hardship, and living condition, became acute. Several African nations on the Western coast of the continent quickly discovered a demand for African slaves. The people of these nations were themselves using slave labor by placing captives of war in slavery. As they discovered the demand for slaves, they moved into the interior of the continent and took captives for sale to European traders.

The trans-Atlantic slave trade refers to the purchase and transportation of people from West and Central Africa to the New World for slavery and other forms of bondage. The slaves were the middle element of a very prosperous three-part trade cycle referred to as **triangular trade**. The trade in slaves began in response to a labor shortage in the New World. There was a great need for cheap labor in mining and in agriculture. Particularly in the predominantly agricultural South, harvesting of many of the major cash crops – sugar, rice, tobacco, cotton – was labor-intensive. Seventy percent of the slaves brought to the U.S. were used in the production of sugar, which was the most labor-intensive crop.

Most estimates place the number of Africans involved in the slave trade in the area of 30 million. They were loaded into ships as tightly as they could be "packed in" and given minimal food and water. Most estimate the number who died on the ships from torture, disease and malnutrition at about three million. The ships delivered them to "seasoning camps" in the Caribbean where they were tortured into submission. Approximately two million more died there.

Agricultural economies developing in North and South America maintained a level of demand that enriched these slave-trading African nations. The slave trade became so lucrative that it became a critical point in the trade triangle that moved finished products from Europe to Africa, slaves from Africa to North and South America, and raw materials from North and South America to Europe. Many of the agricultural, mining, and related "industries" of the Americas depended heavily on a steady supply of cheap labor..

Although some religious leaders decried slavery from the beginning, most supported the slave trade by church teaching and by introducing the idea of the black man's and the white man's separate roles. Some taught that blacks should labor in exchange for the blessings of European civilization, including Christianity.

Skill 10.4   The Civil War and Reconstruction

The drafting, ratification and implementation of the Constitution united 13 different, independent states into a Union under one central government. The two crucial compromises of the convention delegates concerning slaves pacified Southerners, especially the slave owners, but the issue of slavery was not settled. From then on, **sectionalism** became stronger and more apparent each year putting the entire country on a collision course.

At the Constitutional Convention, one of the slavery compromises concerned counting slaves for deciding the number of representatives for the House and the amount of taxes to be paid. Southerners pushed for counting the slaves for representation but not for taxes. The Northerners pushed for the opposite. The resulting compromise, sometimes referred to as the **"three-fifths compromise,"** was that three-fifths of the slaves would be counted for both taxes and representation. The other compromise over slavery addressed the extent of the central government's control over commercial activities such as slave trade and trade with other nations. It was agreed that Congress would regulate commerce with other nations, including taxing imports. Southerners were worried about taxing slaves coming into the country and the possibility of Congress prohibiting the slave trade altogether. The agreement reached allowed the states to continue importation of slaves for the next 20 years, until 1808, at which time Congress would make the decision as to the future of the slave trade. During the 20-year period, no more than $10 per person could be levied on slaves coming into the country.

These two slavery compromises were a necessary concession to have Southern support and approval for the new document and new government. Many Americans felt that the system of slavery would eventually die out in the U.S., but by 1808, cotton was becoming increasingly important in the primarily agricultural South and the institution of slavery had become firmly entrenched in Southern culture. It is also evident that as early as the Constitutional Convention, anti-slavery feelings and opinions were very strong and lead to extremely active groups and societies.

The first serious clash between North and South occurred during 1819-1820 when James Monroe was in office as president. It concerned admitting Missouri as a state. In 1819, the U.S. consisted of 21 states: 11 free states and 10 slave states. The Missouri Territory allowed slavery and if admitted would cause an imbalance in the number of U.S. Senators. Alabama had already been admitted as a slave state, and that had balanced the Senate with the North and South each having 22 senators.

The first **Missouri Compromise** resolved the conflict by approving the admission of Maine as a free state along with Missouri as a slave state. The balance of power in the Senate continued with the same number of free and slave states.

In addition, the **Compromise of 1850** was a series of laws designed as a final solution to the issue. Concessions made to the North included the admission of California as a free state and the abolition of slave trading in Washington, D.C. The laws also provided for the creation of the New Mexico and Utah territories. As a concession to Southerners, the residents there would decide whether to permit slavery when these two territories became states. In addition, Congress authorized implementation of stricter measures to capture runaway slaves.

A few years after the compromises, Congress took up consideration of new territories between Missouri and present-day Idaho. Again, heated debate over permitting slavery in these areas flared up. Those opposed to slavery used the Missouri Compromise to prove their point, showing that the land being considered for territories was part of the area the Compromise had designated as banned to slavery. But on May 25, 1854, Congress passed the **Kansas-Nebraska Act,** which nullified this provision, created the territories of Kansas and Nebraska, and provided for the people of these two territories to decide for themselves whether or not to permit slavery. Feelings were so deep and divided that any further attempts to compromise would meet with little, if any, success. Political and social turmoil swirled everywhere. Kansas was called "Bleeding Kansas" because of the extreme violence and bloodshed throughout the area.

In 1857, the Supreme Court handed down an explosive decision. **Dred Scott** was a slave whose owner had taken him from slave state Missouri to free state Illinois, then into Minnesota territory, free under the provisions of the Missouri Compromise, and then finally back to slave state Missouri. Abolitionists presented a court case stating that since Scott had lived in a free state and free territory, he was in actuality a free man. Two lower courts had ruled before the Supreme Court became involved, one ruling in favor and one against.

The Supreme Court decided that residing in a free state and free territory did not make Scott a free man because Scott (and all other slaves) was not a U.S. citizen or a state citizen of Missouri. Therefore, he did not have the right to sue in state or federal courts. The Court went a step further and ruled that the old Missouri Compromise was now unconstitutional because Congress did not have the power to prohibit slavery in the territories.

Anti-slavery supporters were stunned. They had just formed the new Republican Party and one of its platforms was keeping slavery out of the territories. Now, according to the decision in the Dred Scott case, this basic party principle was unconstitutional. The only way to ban slavery in new areas was by a constitutional amendment, requiring ratification by three-fourths of all states. At this time, this was out of the question because the supporters would be unable to get a majority due to Southern opposition.

In 1859, abolitionist John Brown and his followers seized the federal arsenal at Harper's Ferry in what is now West Virginia. His purpose was to take the guns stored in the arsenal, give them to slaves nearby, and lead them in a widespread rebellion. Colonel Robert E. Lee of the United States Army captured him and his men, and after being found guilty at trial, he was hanged.

The issue of tariffs also was a divisive factor during this period, especially between 1829 and 1833. **The Embargo Act** of 1807 and the War of 1812 had completely cut off the source of manufactured goods for Americans, so it was necessary to build factories to produce what was needed. After 1815, when the war had ended, Great Britain proceeded to get rid of its industrial rivals by unloading its goods in America. To protect and encourage its own industries and their products, Congress passed the Tariff of 1816, which required high duties to be levied on manufactured goods coming into the United States. Southern leaders, such as John C. Calhoun of South Carolina, supported the tariff with the assumption that the South would develop its own industries.

The slavery issue was at the root of every problem, crisis, event, decision, and struggle from then on. The next crisis involved Texas. By 1836, Texas was an independent republic with its own constitution. During its fight for independence, Americans were sympathetic to and supportive of the Texans and some recruited volunteers who crossed into Texas to help the struggle.

Problems arose when the state petitioned Congress for statehood. Texas wanted to allow slavery, but Northerners in Congress opposed admission to the Union because it would disrupt the balance between free and slave states and give Southerners in Congress increased influence. There were others who believed that granting statehood to Texas would lead to a war with Mexico, which had refused to recognize Texas' independence. For the time being, statehood was put on hold.

In 1858, **Abraham Lincoln** and Stephen A. Douglas were running for the office of U.S. Senator from Illinois and participated in a series of debates, which directly affected the outcome of the 1860 Presidential Election. Douglas, a Democrat, was up for re-election and felt that if he won the race, he had a good chance of becoming president in 1860. Lincoln, a Republican, was not an abolitionist but believed that slavery was wrong. He firmly supported the Republican Party principle that slavery must not be allowed to extend any further.

Douglas, on the other hand, originated the doctrine of "popular sovereignty" and was responsible for supporting and getting through Congress the inflammatory Kansas-Nebraska Act. In the course of the debates, Lincoln challenged Douglas to show that popular sovereignty reconciled with the Dred Scott decision. Either way he answered Lincoln, Douglas would lose crucial support from one group or the other. If he supported the Dred Scott decision, Southerners would support him but he would lose Northern support. If he stayed with popular sovereignty, Northern support would be his but Southern support would be lost. His reply to Lincoln, stating that territorial legislatures could exclude slavery by refusing to pass laws supporting it, gave him enough support and approval to be re-elected to the Senate. But it cost him the Democratic nomination for president in 1860.

Southerners came to the realization that Douglas supported popular sovereignty but not necessarily the expansion of slavery. Two years later, Lincoln received the nomination of the Republican Party for president. The final straw came with the election of Lincoln to the presidency the next year. Due to a split in the Democratic Party, there were four candidates from four political parties. With Lincoln receiving a minority of the popular vote and a majority of electoral votes, the Southern states, one by one, voted to secede from the Union.

.By 1860, the nation had extended its borders north, south, and west. Industry and agriculture flourished. Although the U.S. was not actively involved in European affairs, its relationship with Great Britain improved. War, however, was unavoidable. The country was deeply divided along political lines concerning slavery and the election of Abraham Lincoln. Although the US had successfully emerged as a new and growing nation, the issue of human slavery had to be settled once and for all. One historian has stated that before 1865, the nation referred to itself as "the United States are ...," but after 1865 as "the United States is. ..." It took the Civil War to finally unify all states into one Union.

The nullification crisis of the mid-nineteenth century climaxed in 1828 over a new tariff levied by the Congress on imported manufactured goods. While this tariff protected the manufacturing and industrial interests of the North, it placed an additional burden of cost on the South, which was a higher consumer of manufactured goods. The North had become increasingly dependent on industry and manufacturing, while the South had become increasingly agricultural. Although the tariff was primarily intended to protect Northern manufacturing interests in the face of imports, the effect on the South was simply an increase in the prices of needed goods.

This disagreement reached its climax when John C. Calhoun, Jackson's vice president, led South Carolina to adopt the Ordinance of Nullification, declaring the tariff null and void within state borders. Although this issue came to the brink of military action, it was resolved by the enactment of a new tariff in 1832.

The question of a state's right to nullify any law of the nation which was contrary to local interests was based on the assumption that the United States was a union of independent commonwealths and that the general government was merely their agent. This was the Southern view. The North, however, assumed that the federal government was supreme and that the Union was inseparable.

When economic and slavery issues came to a head, the North declared slavery illegal. The South acted on the principles of the doctrine of nullification, declared the new laws null, and acted upon their presumed right as states to secede from the union and form their own government. The North saw secession as a violation of the national unity contract.

South Carolina was the first state to **secede** from the Union, and the first shots of the war were fired on Fort Sumter in Charleston Harbor. Both sides quickly prepared for war. The North had more in its favor: a larger population and superiority in finances, transportation facilities, and manufacturing, agricultural, and natural resources. It had about 92% of all industries and possessed most of the nation's gold and almost all known supplies of copper, coal, iron, and various other minerals. Since most of the nation's railroads were in the North and mid-West, men and supplies could be moved wherever needed; food could be transported from the farms of the mid-West to workers in the East and to soldiers on the battlefields. Overseas trade could go on as usual due to control of the navy and the merchant fleet. The Northern states numbered 24 and included western (California and Oregon) and border (Maryland, Delaware, Kentucky, Missouri, and West Virginia) states.

The Southern states numbered 11 and included South Carolina, Georgia, Florida, Alabama, Mississippi, Louisiana, Texas, Virginia, North Carolina, Tennessee, and Arkansas, making up the Confederacy. Although outnumbered in population, the South was completely confident of victory. They knew that all they had to do was fight a defensive war, protecting their own territory until the North, who had to invade and defeat an area almost the size of Western Europe, tired of the struggle and gave up. Another advantage of the South was that a number of its best officers had graduated from the U.S. Military Academy at West Point and had had long years of army experience, some even exercising varying degrees of command in the Indian wars and the war with Mexico. Men from the South were conditioned to living outdoors and were more familiar with horses and firearms than many men from northeastern cities. Since cotton was such an important crop, Southerners felt that British and French textile mills that depended on raw cotton would be forced to help the Confederacy in the war.

The South had specific reasons and goals for fighting the war, more so than the North. The major aims of the Confederacy never wavered: to win independence, to govern themselves as they wished, and to preserve slavery. The Northerners were not as clear in their reasons for conducting war. At the beginning, most believed, along with Lincoln, that preservation of the Union was paramount. Only a few extremely fanatical abolitionists looked on the war as a way to end slavery. However, by war's end, more and more Northerners had come to believe that freeing the slaves was just as important as restoring the Union.

The war strategies for both sides were relatively clear and simple. The South planned a defensive war, wearing down the North until it agreed to peace on

Southern terms. The exception was to gain control of Washington, D.C., go north through the Shenandoah Valley into Maryland and Pennsylvania in order to drive a wedge between the Northeast and mid-West, interrupt the lines of communication, and end the war quickly. The North had three basic strategies: blockade the Confederate coastline in order to cripple the South; seize control of the Mississippi River and interior railroad lines to split the Confederacy in two; and seize the Confederate capital of Richmond, Virginia, driving southward and joining up with Union forces coming east from the Mississippi Valley.

The South won decisively until the Battle of Gettysburg, July 1 - 3, 1863. Until Gettysburg, Lincoln's commanders, **McDowell, McClellan, Burnside and Hooker**, had only limited success. **Lee**, on the other hand, had many able officers, including **Jackson and Stuart** on whom he depended heavily. Jackson died at Chancellorsville and was replaced by **Longstreet**. Lee decided to invade the North, depending on **James Ewell Brown "Jeb" Stuart** and his cavalry to keep him informed of the location of Union troops and their strengths. Four things worked against Lee at Gettysburg:

- The Union troops gained the best positions and the best ground first, making it easier to make a stand there.
- Lee's move into Northern territory put him and his army a long way from food and supply lines. They were more or less on their own.
- Lee thought that his Army of Northern Virginia was invincible and could fight and win under any conditions or circumstances.
- Stuart and his men did not arrive at Gettysburg until the end of the second day of fighting. By then, it was a little too late. He and his men had to detour around Union soldiers and he was delayed getting the information Lee needed.

Lee made the mistake of failing to listen to Longstreet and following the strategy of regrouping back into Southern territory to the supply lines. He felt that regrouping was retreating and almost an admission of defeat. He was convinced the army would be victorious.

Longstreet was concerned about the Union troops occupying the best positions and felt that regrouping to a better position would be an advantage. He was also very concerned about the distance from supply lines. It was not the intention of either side to fight at Gettysburg, but the fighting began when a Confederate brigade stumbled into a unit of Union cavalry while looking for shoes. The third and last day, Lee launched the final attempt to break Union lines. **General George Pickett** sent his division of three brigades under Generals Garnet, Kemper, and Armistead against Union troops on Cemetery Ridge under command of General Winfield Scott Hancock. Union lines held and Lee and the defeated Army of Northern Virginia made their way back to Virginia. Although Lincoln's commander George Meade successfully turned back a Confederate charge, he and the Union troops failed to pursue Lee and the Confederates. This battle was the turning point for the North. After this, Lee never again had the troop strength to launch a major offensive.

The day after Gettysburg, on July 4, Vicksburg, Mississippi surrendered to Union **General Ulysses Grant**, thus severing the western Confederacy from the eastern part. In September 1863, the Confederacy won its last important victory at Chickamauga. In November, the Union victory at Chattanooga made it possible for Union troops to go into Alabama and Georgia, splitting the eastern Confederacy in two. Lincoln gave Grant command of all Northern armies in March of 1864. Grant led his armies into battles in Virginia, while Phil Sheridan and his cavalry did as much damage as possible.

In a skirmish at a place called Yellow Tavern, Virginia, Sheridan's and Stuart's forces met, with Stuart being fatally wounded. The Union won the Battle of Mobile Bay and in May 1864, **William Tecumseh Sherman** began his march to successfully demolish Atlanta, then on to Savannah. He and his troops turned northward through the Carolinas to Grant in Virginia. On April 9, 1865, Lee formally surrendered to Grant at Appomattox Courthouse, Virginia.

The Civil War took more American lives than any other war in history, the South losing one-third of its soldiers in battle compared to about one-sixth for the North. More than half of the total deaths were caused by disease and the horrendous conditions of field hospitals. Both sections paid a tremendous economic price, but the South suffered more severely from direct damages. Destruction was pervasive with towns, farms, trade, industry, homes, and lives of men, women, children all destroyed. An entire Southern way of life was lost. The deep resentment, bitterness, and hatred that remained for generations gradually lessened as the years went by, but legacies of it remain to this day. The South had no voice in the political, social, and cultural affairs of the nation, lessening to a great degree the influence of the more traditional Southern ideals. The Northern Yankee Protestant ideals of hard work, education, and economic freedom became the standard of the United States and helped influence the development of the nation into a modern, industrial power.

The effects of the Civil War were tremendous. Called the first modern war, it changed the methods of waging war. It introduced weapons and tactics that, when improved later, were used extensively in wars of the late 1800s and 1900s. Civil War soldiers were the first to fight in trenches, fight under a unified command, and wage a "major cordon defense" – a strategy of advance on all fronts. They were also the first to use repeating and breech-loading weapons. Observation balloons, submarines, ironclad ships, and mines, were used for the first time in war. So were telegraphy and railroads. This was not only a modern war, but "total war" – involving vast destruction and the use of all resources of the opposing sides. There was probably no way it could have ended other than total defeat and unconditional surrender of one side or the other.

By executive proclamation and constitutional amendment, slavery was officially ended, although deep prejudice and racism remained. The Union was preserved and the states were finally united. **Sectionalism**, especially in the area of politics, remained strong for another 100 years but not to the degree and with the violence as existed before 1861. It has been noted that the Civil War may have been American democracy's greatest failure for, from 1861 to 1865, calm reason – a basic characteristic of democracy – fell victim to human passion. Yet, democracy did survive.

Reconstruction

As the war dragged on to its bloody, destructive conclusion, Lincoln was very anxious to get the states restored to the Union. He showed flexibility in his thinking as he made changes to his Reconstruction program to make it as easy and painless as possible. Unfortunately, Lincoln was assassinated before Congress could approve many of his proposed changes. After Andrew Johnson became president and the Republicans gained control of Congress, harsh measures of radical Reconstruction were implemented.

The victory of the North established that no state has the right to end or leave the Union. Because of unity, the U.S. became a major global power. Lincoln never proposed to punish the South. He was most concerned with restoring the South to the Union in a program that was flexible and practical rather than rigid and unbending. In fact, he never really felt that the states had succeeded in leaving the Union but that they had left the 'family circle" for a short time. His plans consisted of two major steps:

First, all Southerners taking an oath of allegiance to the Union and promising to accept all federal laws and proclamations dealing with slavery would receive a full pardon. The only ones excluded from this were men who had resigned from civil and military positions in the federal government to serve in the Confederacy, those who were part of the Confederate government, those in the Confederate army above the rank of lieutenant, and Confederates who were guilty of mistreating prisoners of war and blacks. Second, a state would be able to write a new constitution, elect new officials, and return to the Union fully equal to all other states on a certain condition: A minimum number of persons (at least 10% of those who were qualified voters in their states before secession from the Union and who had voted in the 1860 election) had to take an oath of allegiance.

The South faced severe economic and social chaos after the war. Starvation and disease were rampant, especially in the cities. The U.S. Army provided some food and clothing for both whites and blacks, but the major responsibility fell to the Freedmen's Bureau. Though the bureau agents helped southern whites to a certain extent, their main responsibility was to the freed slaves. They were to protect the freedmen and assist them to become self-supporting. Northerners looked on it as a real, honest effort to help the South out of its chaos. Most white Southerners charged the bureau with causing racial friction, deliberately encouraging the freedmen to consider former owners as enemies.

As a result, as southern leaders began to be able to restore life as it had once been, they adopted a set of laws known as **black codes**, containing many of the provisions of the prewar "slave codes." White Southerners made every effort to keep the freedmen in a way of life subordinate to theirs.

Radicals in Congress pointed out these illegal actions by white Southerners as evidence that they were unwilling to support the complete freedom of black Americans and could not be trusted. Congress drafted its own program of Reconstruction, including laws that would protect and further the rights of blacks. Three amendments were added to the Constitution: The **13th Amendment** of 1865 outlawed slavery throughout the entire United States. The **14th Amendment** of 1868 made blacks American citizens. The **15th Amendment** of 1870 gave black Americans the right to vote and made it illegal to deny anyone the right to vote based on race.

Federal troops, stationed throughout the South, protected Republicans who took control of Southern governments. The bitterly resentful white Southerners fought the new political system by joining a secret society called the **Ku Klux Klan** and using violence to keep black Americans from voting and getting equality. However, before being allowed to rejoin the Union, the Confederate states were required to agree to all federal laws. Between 1866 and 1870, all of them had returned to the Union. Northern interest in Reconstruction was fading. Reconstruction officially ended when the last Federal troops left the South in 1877. It can be said that Reconstruction had a limited success. It set up public school systems and expanded legal rights of black Americans. Nevertheless, white "redeemer governments" rapidly worked to undo many of the changes from Reconstruction.

General Grant was elected president in 1868, serving two scandal-ridden terms. He was an honest and upright person, but greatly lacked political experience. His greatest weakness was a blind loyalty to his friends – dishonest people who used him to further their own interests. One of the sad results of the war was the rapid growth of business and industry, with large corporations controlled by unscrupulous men. However, after 1877, some degree of normalcy returned and there was time for rebuilding, expansion, and growth.

Skill 10.5   The settlement of the West

Westward expansion occurred for a number of reasons, most important being economic. Cotton had become important to most of the people who lived in the southern states. The effects of the Industrial Revolution, which began in England, were now being felt in the United States. With the invention of power-driven machines, the demand for cotton fiber greatly increased for the yarn needed in spinning and weaving. Eli Whitney's cotton gin made the separation of the seeds from the cotton more efficient and faster. This, in turn, increased the demand as more farmers became involved in growing and selling cotton.

The innovation and development of better methods of long-distance transportation moved the cotton in greater quantities to textile mills in England as well as the areas of New England and Middle Atlantic States in the U.S. As prices increased along with increased demand, southern farmers began expanding by clearing more land to grow more cotton. Movement, settlement, and farming headed west to utilize the fertile soils. This, in turn, increased need for a large supply of cheap labor. The system of slavery expanded, both in numbers and in the movement to lands "west" of the South.

The post-Reconstruction era represents a period of great transformation and expansion for the United States, both economically and geographically, particularly for the South, recovering from the Civil War and migrating west of the Mississippi River. Great numbers of former slaves moved west, away from their former masters and lured by the promise of land. White migration was also spurred by similar desires for land and resources, leading to boom economies of cotton, cattle and grain starting in Kansas and spreading westward.

Although industrial production grew fastest in the South during this period, the South was still predominantly agricultural. The South featured land tenancy and sharecropping, which did not really benefit the economic advancement of the remaining freed slaves. Most of the land was still owned by the large plantation landowners who retained their holdings from before the Civil War. The economic chasm dividing white landowners and black freedmen only widened as the tenants sank further into debt to their landlords.

Cotton farmers and slave owners were not the only ones heading west. Many people engaged in other economic endeavors also began migrating to seek their fortunes: trappers, miners, merchants, ranchers, and others. The Lewis and Clark expedition stimulated the westward push. Fur companies hired men, known as "Mountain Men," to go westward, searching for animal pelts to supply the market and meet the demands of the East and Europe. These men discovered the many passes and trails that would eventually be used by settlers in their trek to the west. The California gold rush, as well as missionaries who traveled west with the fur traders, encouraged increased settlement. By the 1840s, the population of Oregon country alone was increasing at a rate of about a thousand people a year.

It was the belief of many that the United States was destined to control all of the land between the two oceans – or as one newspaper editor termed it, **Manifest Destiny**. This mass migration westward put the U.S. government on a collision course with the Indians, Great Britain, Spain, and Mexico. The fur traders and missionaries ran up against the Indians in the northwest and the claims of Great

Britain for the Oregon country. The U.S. and Britain had shared the Oregon country. By the 1840s, however, the free and slave populations had increased and the settlers were demanding U.S. control of the government. This created tensions, but both nations reached a peaceful resolution. In a treaty they signed in 1846, Britain gave up its claims south of the 49th parallel.

In the American southwest, the results were exactly the opposite. Spain had claimed this area since the 1540s, spreading northward from Mexico City. In the 1700s, it had established missions, forts, villages, towns, and very large ranches. After the purchase of the Louisiana Territory in 1803, Americans began moving into Spanish territory. A few hundred American families in what is now Texas were allowed to live there, but had to agree to become loyal subjects to Spain. In 1821, Mexico successfully revolted against Spanish rule, won independence, and chose to be more tolerant towards the American settlers and traders. The Mexican government encouraged and allowed extensive trade and settlement, especially in Texas. Many of the new settlers were southerners and brought with them their slaves. Although slavery was outlawed in Mexico and was technically illegal in Texas, the Mexican government looked the other way.

The next acquisition, the Red River cession, came about as part of a treaty with Great Britain in 1818. It included parts of **North** and **South Dakota** and **Minnesota**. In 1819, east and west **Florida** was ceded to the U.S. by Spain along with parts of **Alabama, Mississippi, and Louisiana**. The U.S. then annexed **Texas** in 1845 and, after the war with Mexico in 1848, paid $15 million for what would become the states of **California, Utah, Nevada,** and parts of four other states. In 1846, the **Oregon Country** was ceded to the U.S., which extended the western border to the Pacific Ocean. The northern U.S. boundary was established at the 49th parallel. The states of **Idaho**, **Oregon** and **Washington** were formed from this territory. In 1853, the **Gadsden Purchase** rounded out the present boundary of the 48 conterminous states with payment to Mexico of $10 million for land that makes up the present states of **New Mexico and Arizona.**

Railroad expansion was another major factor that displaced natives and encouraged Americans to migrate to the West. The **transcontinental railroad** was completed in 1869, joining the West Coast with the existing rail infrastructure terminating at Omaha, Nebraska, its westernmost point. This not only enabled unprecedented movement of people and goods, it also hastened the near extinction of bison, which the Indians of the Great Plains, in particular, depended on for their survival.

By the 1880s, Secretary of State James G. Blaine pushed for expanding U.S. trade and influence to Central and South America. In the 1890s, when it looked like Great Britain was going to exert its influence and power in the Western Hemisphere, President Grover Cleveland invoked the **Monroe Doctrine** to intercede in Latin American affairs. In the Pacific, the United States lent its support to American sugar planters who overthrew the Kingdom of **Hawaii** and eventually annexed it as U.S. territory.

Once the American West was firmly under its control, the United States started looking beyond its shores. Overseas markets were becoming important as American industrial production became more efficient and manufacturing capacity grew. To protect its shipping, the U.S. modernized and built up the Navy, which by 1900 ranked third in the world, giving it the means to become an imperial power. **Midway Island** and **Alaska**, purchased in 1867, became the first overseas possessions.

During the 1890s, Spain controlled such overseas possessions as Puerto Rico, the Philippines, and Cuba. When the Cubans rebelled against Spanish rule, the U.S. government was besieged by demands from Americans to assist the Cubans in their revolt. This began the 1898 **Spanish-American War**, a turning point in American history. The U.S. used the explosion of the USS Maine as a pretext to invade Cuba, when the underlying reason was the United States' desire for empire and economic gain.

The U.S. war and victory against Spain then triggered the dispatch of the fleet under Admiral George Dewey to the Philippines. Army troops soon followed.
.

Victory over the Spanish proved fruitful for American territorial ambitions. Although Congress passed legislation renouncing claims to annex Cuba, the United States did gain control of the island of **Puerto Rico**, a permanent deep-water naval harbor at Guantanamo Bay, Cuba, the Philippines and various other Pacific islands formerly possessed by Spain. The decision to occupy the **Philippines** rather than grant it immediate independence led to the "Philippines Insurrection," a guerrilla war that lasted until 1902. U.S. rule over the Philippines lasted until 1942, but unlike the guerrilla war years, American rule was relatively benign. The peace treaty gave the U.S. possession of **Puerto Rico, the Philippines, Guam and Hawaii**, which was annexed during the war.

This success increased U.S. role in foreign affairs. The U.S. armed forces expanded and grew stronger under the administration of Theodore Roosevelt. His foreign policy – summed up in the slogan of "Speak softly and carry a big stick" – further supported efforts in diplomacy with a strong military. During the years before the outbreak of World War I, evidence of U.S. emergence as a world power could be seen in a number of actions.

Skill 10.6   **The transformation from an agrarian to an industrial economy (e.g., immigration, the rise of entrepreneurship, the development of science and technology)**

The **Agricultural Revolution** occurred first in England, marked by experimentation that resulted in increased crop production and a new and more technical approach to the management of agriculture. This revolution was hugely enhanced by the Industrial Revolution and the invention of the steam engine. Steam-powered tractors greatly increased crop production and significantly decreased labor costs. The Scientific Revolution, which encouraged learning from experimentation and led to philosophies of crop rotation and soil enrichment, also increased developments in agriculture. Improved irrigation and harvesting contributed to agricultural production.

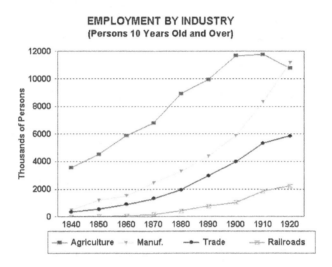

EMPLOYMENT BY INDUSTRY
(Persons 10 Years Old and Over)

There was a marked degree of industrialization before and during the Civil War, but at war's end, American industry was small. After the war, dramatic changes took place: machines replacing hand labor, extensive nationwide railroad service making possible the wider distribution of goods, invention of new products made available in large quantities, large amounts of money from bankers and investors for business expansion. American life was definitely affected by this phenomenal industrial growth. Cities became the centers of this new business activity and attracted mass population from elsewhere. Boom in business resulted in huge fortunes for some Americans and extreme poverty for many others. The discontent from this led to a number of new reform movements from which came measures to control the power and size of big business and to help the poor.

Of course, industry before, during, and after the Civil War was centered mainly in the North, especially the tremendous post-war industrial growth. The late 1800s and early 1900s saw the U.S. building its **military strength** and emerging as a world power.

The use of machines in **industry** enabled workers to produce a large quantity of goods much faster than by hand. With the increase in business, hundreds of workers were hired and assigned to perform specific jobs in the production process. This was a method of organization called **"division of labor."** By increasing production rate, it allowed businesses to lower their products' prices and make them affordable for more people. As a result, businesses were increasingly successful and profitable.

A great variety of new products or inventions became available, such as: the typewriter, the telephone, barbed wire, the electric light, the phonograph, and the gasoline automobile. From this list, the one that had the greatest effect on America's economy was the automobile. The country's many rich natural resources greatly affected the increase in business and industry. For example, the industrial machines were powered by the abundant water supply. The construction industry as well as products made from wood depended heavily on lumber from the forests. The steel industry depended on abundant supplies of coal and iron ore; it saw heavy profits from the use of steel in such things as skyscrapers, automobiles, bridges, railroad tracks, and machines. Other minerals such as silver, copper, and petroleum played a large role in industrial growth – especially petroleum, from which gasoline was refined as fuel for the increasingly popular automobile.

As business grew, methods of sales and promotion were developed. Salespersons went to all parts of the country, promoting the varied products, opening large department stores in the growing cities, offering the varied products at affordable prices. People who lived too far from the cities, making it impossible to shop there, had the advantage of using a mail-order service, buying what they needed from catalogs furnished by the companies. The development of communication services, such as the telephone and telegraph, increased the efficiency and prosperity of big business.

Business prosperity led to investments in corporate stocks and bonds. In their eager desire to share in the profits, individuals began investing heavily. Their investments made available the needed capital for companies to expand their operations. From this, banks increased in number throughout the country, making loans to businesses and significant contributions to economic growth. At the same time, during the 1880s, government made little effort to regulate businesses. This gave rise to monopolies where larger businesses were rid of their smaller competitors and assumed complete control of their industries.

Some owners in the same business would join or merge to form one company. Others formed what were called "**trusts**," a type of monopoly in which rival businesses were controlled but not formally owned. Monopolies had some good effects on the economy. Out of them grew large, efficient corporations that made important contributions to the nation's economic growth. Also, monopolies enabled businesses to keep their sales steady and avoid sharp fluctuations in price and production.

The downside of monopolies was the unfair business practices of the business leaders. Some acquired so much power that they took unfair advantage of others. Those who had little or no competition would require their suppliers to supply goods at a low cost, sell the finished products at high prices, and reduce the quality of the product to save money.

Between 1870 and 1916, more than 25 million immigrants came into the United States adding to the phenomenal population growth taking place. This aided business and industry in two ways: First, the number of consumers increased. This created a greater demand for products and enlarged the markets. Second, more workers were available to fill the new jobs created as a result of expanding business. The completion of the nation's transcontinental railroad in 1869 also contributed to the nation's economic and industrial growth. Mining companies were able to ship raw materials quickly, and finished products were now sent to all parts of the country. Many wealthy industrialists and railroad owners saw extensive and steadily increasing profits.

Technological innovations grew at a pace unmatched at any other time in American history. **Thomas Edison** was the most prolific inventor of the time, using a systematic and efficient method to invent and improve on technology in a profitable manner. The abundance of resources, together with growth of industry and the pace of capital investments, led to the growth of cities.

Populations were shifting from rural agricultural areas to urban industrial areas. By the early 1900s, a third of the nation's population lived in cities. Industry needed workers in its factories, mills and plants. Rural workers were being displaced by advances in farm machinery and by the increasing use of automation. Growing industries, more efficient transportation of goods and resources, and the availability of a labor force made up of foreign immigrants and displaced rural workers all fueled the dramatic growth in city population. Increased urban population, often packed into dense tenements, often without adequate sanitation or clean water. This led to public health challenges that required cities to establish sanitation, water and public health departments to cope with and prevent epidemics. Political organizations also saw the advantage of mobilizing the new industrial working class and created vast patronage programs that sometimes became notorious for corruption in big-city machine politics, like Tammany Hall in New York.

Skill 10.7 The Progressive Era and the New Deal; the emergence of the United States as a world power (e.g., the era of U.S. overseas expansion, World War I, World War II, the Cold War)

Populism is a philosophy concerned with the common sense needs of average people. It often finds expression as a reaction against perceived oppression of the average people by the wealthy elite in society. Often connected with religious fundamentalism, racism, or nationalism, populist movements claim to represent the majority of the people and call them to stand up to institutions or practices that seem detrimental to their well being.

Populism flourished in the late nineteenth and early twentieth centuries. Several political parties were formed out of this philosophy, including: the Greenback Party, the Populist Party, the Farmer-Labor Party, the Single Tax movement of Henry George, the Share Our Wealth movement of Huey Long, the Progressive Party, and the Union Party. In the 1890s, the People's Party won the support of millions of farmers and other working people. This party challenged the social ills of the monopolists of the "Gilded Age."

The tremendous change that resulted from the industrial revolution led to a demand for reform that would control the power of big corporations. The gap between the industrial moguls and the working people was growing. This disparity resulted in a public outcry for reform at the same time that there was an outcry for governmental reform that would end political corruption and elitism.

This fire was fueled by the writings of the "muckrakers" – investigative journalists who published scathing exposes of political and business wrongdoing The result was the rise of a group of politicians and reformers who supported a wide array of populist causes. The period 1900 to 1917 came to be known as the Progressive Era. Although these leaders came from many different backgrounds and were driven by different ideologies, they shared a fundamental belief that government should eradicate social ills and promote the common good and equality guaranteed by the Constitution.

The reforms initiated by these leaders and the spirit of **Progressivism** were far-reaching. Several states enacted legislation that would undermine the power of political machines. On a national level, the two most significant political changes were (1) the ratification of the 17th Amendment, which required that all U.S. Senators be chosen by popular election, and (2) the ratification of the 19th Amendment, which granted women the right to vote.

Major economic reforms of the period included the Sherman Antitrust Act, which was aggressively enforced; the Elkins Act and the Hepburn Act, which gave the Interstate Commerce Commission greater power to regulate the railroads; the Pure Food and Drug Act, which prohibited the use of harmful chemicals in food; and the Meat Inspection Act, which regulated the meat industry to protect the public against tainted meat. In addition, over two thirds of the states passed laws prohibiting child labor. Workmen's compensation was mandated, and the Department of Commerce and Labor was created.

Responding to concern over the environmental effects of the timber, ranching, and mining industries, Roosevelt set aside 238 million acres of federal lands to protect them from development. Wildlife preserves were established, the national park system was expanded, and the National Conservation Commission was created. The Newlands Reclamation Act also provided federal funding for the construction of irrigation projects and dams in semi-arid areas of the country.

The Wilson Administration carried out additional reforms. The **Federal Reserve Act** created a national banking system, providing a stable money supply. The Sherman Act and the Clayton Antitrust Act defined unfair competition, made corporate officers liable for the illegal actions of employees, and exempted labor unions from antitrust lawsuits. The Federal Trade Commission was established to enforce these measures. Finally, the 16th Amendment was ratified, establishing an income tax. This measure was designed to relieve the poor of a disproportionate burden in funding the federal government and make the wealthy pay a greater share of the nation's tax burden.

The **1929 Stock Market Crash** was the powerful event that is generally interpreted as the beginning of the Great Depression in America. Although the crash of the stock market was unexpected, it was not without identifiable causes. The 1920s had been a decade of social and economic growth and hope. But the attitudes and actions of the 1920s regarding wealth, production, and investment created several trends that quietly set the stage for the 1929 disaster.

The new president, Franklin D. Roosevelt, won the White House on his promise to the American people of a "new deal." Upon assuming the office, Roosevelt and his advisers immediately launched a massive program of innovation and experimentation to try to bring the Depression to an end and get the nation back on track. Congress gave the president unprecedented power to act to save the nation. During the next eight years, the most extensive and broadly based legislation in the nation's history was enacted. The legislation was intended to accomplish three goals: relief, recovery, and reform.

The first step in the **New Deal** was to relieve suffering. This was accomplished through a number of job-creation projects. The second step, the recovery aspect, was to stimulate the economy. The third step was to create social and economic change through innovative legislation. **The National Recovery Administration (NRA)** attempted to accomplish several goals:

- Restore employment
- Increase general purchasing power
- Provide character-building activity for unemployed youth
- Encourage decentralization of industry and thus divert population from crowded cities to rural or semi-rural communities
- Develop river resources in the interest of navigation, cheap power and light
- Complete flood control on a permanent basis
- Enlarge the national program of forest protection and develop forest resources
- Control farm production and improve farm prices
- Assist home builders and home owners
- Restore public faith in banking and trust operations

- Recapture the value of physical assets, whether in real property, securities, or other investments

These objectives and their accomplishment implied a restoration of public confidence and courage.

Among the "alphabet organizations" set up to work out the details of the recovery plan, the most prominent were:

- **Agricultural Adjustment Administration** (AAA), designed to re-adjust agricultural production and prices, thereby boosting farm income
- **Civilian Conservation Corps** (CCC), designed to give wholesome, useful activity in the forestry service to unemployed young men
- **Civil Works Administration** (CWA) and the **Public Works Administration** (PWA), designed to employ people in the construction and repair of public buildings, parks, and highways
- **Works Progress Administration** (WPA), designed to move individuals from relief rolls to work projects or private employment

To provide economic stability and prevent another market crash, Congress passed the **Glass-Steagall Act**, which separated banking and investing. The **Securities and Exchange** Commission was introduced to regulate dangerous speculative practices on Wall Street. **The Wagner Act** guaranteed a number of rights to workers and unions in an effort to improve worker-employer relations. The **Social Security Act of 1935** established pensions for the aged and infirm as well as a system of unemployment insurance.

Emergence of the United States as a world power

After taking full control of the American West, defeating Spain, and acquiring overseas possessions, the United States had undoubtedly begun to emerge as a nation of great power. Its manufacturing capacity and production had grown by leaps and bounds, and its navy had won the rank of third in the world. Midway Island and Alaska were now its own. (*See Skill 10.5, the settlement of the West.*) All of this together brought the country closer to becoming an imperial power.

By the 1880s, Secretary of State James G. Blaine pushed for expanding U.S. trade and influence to Central and South America. In the 1890s, when it looked like Great Britain was going to exert its influence and power in the western hemisphere, President Grover Cleveland invoked the **Monroe Doctrine** to intercede in Latin American affairs. In the Pacific, the United States lent its support to American sugar planters who overthrew the Kingdom of **Hawaii** and eventually annexed it as U.S. territory.

When the locals were revolting against the Spanish in Cuba, it aroused the interest and concern of Americans who were aware of what was happening "at their doorstep." In trying to put down the revolt, the Spanish were being cruel to women and children who were gathered into camps surrounded by armed guards and given little food. Much of the food that kept them alive came from supplies sent by the U.S. Americans were already concerned over years of anarchy and misrule by the Spanish. When reports of gross atrocities reached America, public sentiment clearly favored the Cuban people. President McKinley had refused to recognize the rebellion, but had affirmed the possibility of American intervention. Spain resented this attitude of the Americans. In February 1898, the American battleship *Maine* was blown up in Havana harbor. Although there was no incontrovertible evidence that the Spanish were responsible, popular sentiment accused Spanish agents and war became inevitable.

Two months later, Congress declared war on Spain and the U.S. quickly defeated them. The peace treaty gave the U.S. possession of Puerto Rico, the Philippines, Guam and Hawaii, which was annexed during the war. (*See Skill 10.5*)

Although the idea of a canal in Panama goes back to the early sixteenth century, work did not begin until 1880 by the French. The effort collapsed and the U.S. completed the task, opening the Panama Canal in 1914. Construction was an enormous task of complex engineering. The significance of the canal is that it connects the Gulf of Panama in the Pacific Ocean with the Caribbean Sea and the Atlantic Ocean. It eliminated the need for ships to skirt the southern boundary of South America, effectively reducing the sailing distance from New York to San Francisco by 8,000 miles (over half of the distance). The Canal results in a shorter and faster voyage, thus reducing shipping time and cost. The U.S. helped Panama win independence from Colombia in exchange for control of the Panama Canal Zone. A large investment was made in eliminating disease from the area, particularly yellow fever and malaria. After WWII, control of the canal became an issue of contention between the U.S. and Panama. Negotiations toward a settlement began in 1974, resulting in the Torrijos-Carter Treaties of 1977. Thus began the process of handing the canal over to Panama. On December 31, 1999, control of the canal was handed over to the Panama Canal Authority. Tolls for the use of the canal have ranged from $0.36, when Richard Halliburton swam the canal, to about $226,000.

World War I - 1914 to 1918
Causes: the surge of nationalism, increase in military strength and capabilities, massive colonization to acquire raw materials needed in industry and manufacturing, and military and diplomatic alliances. The initial spark, which started the conflagration, was the assassination of Austrian Archduke Francis Ferdinand and his wife in Sarajevo.

There were 28 nations involved in the war, not including colonies and territories. It began July 28, 1914 and ended November 11, 1918 with the signing of the Treaty of Versailles. Economically, the war cost a total of $337 billion; increased inflation; resulted in huge war debts; and caused a loss of markets, goods, jobs, and factories. Politically, old empires collapsed; many monarchies disappeared; smaller countries gained temporary independence; Communists seized power in Russia; and, in some cases, nationalism increased. Socially, total populations decreased because of war casualties and low birth rates. There were millions of displaced persons as villages and farms were destroyed. Cities grew while women made significant gains in the workforce and the ballot box. There was less social distinction and fewer classes. Attitudes completely changed and old beliefs and values were questioned. The peace settlement established the League of Nations to ensure peace, but it failed to do so.

World War II - 1939 to 1945
Causes: Ironically, the Treaty of Paris, the peace treaty ending World War I, ultimately led to the Second World War. Countries that fought in the first war were either dissatisfied over the "spoils" of war, or were punished so harshly that resentment continued building to an eruption twenty years later.

The economic problems of both winners and losers of the first war were never resolved, and the worldwide Great Depression of the 1930s dealt the final blow to any immediate recovery. Democratic governments in Europe were severely weakened, which in turn gave strength and encouragement to extreme political movements that promised to end the economic chaos in their countries.

Nationalism, which was a major cause of World War I, grew even stronger and seemed to feed the increasingly rampant feelings of discontent. Because of unstable economic conditions and political unrest, harsh dictatorships arose in several of the countries, especially where there was no history of experience in democratic government. Countries such as Germany, Japan, and Italy began to aggressively expand their borders and acquire additional territory.

In all, 59 nations became embroiled in World War II, which began September 1, 1939 and ended September 2, 1945. These dates include both the European and Pacific Theaters of war. The war resulted in more deaths and destruction than in any other armed conflict. It completely uprooted and displaced millions of people. The end of the war brought renewed power struggles, especially in Europe and China, with many Eastern European nations as well as China coming under complete control of the Communists, supported by the Soviet Union. With the development of and two-time deployment of an atomic bomb against two Japanese cities, the world found itself in the nuclear age. The peace settlement established the United Nations Organization, still existing and operating today.

Korean War - 1950 to 1953
Causes: Korea was under control of Japan from 1895 to the end of the Second World War in 1945. At war's end, the Soviet and U.S. military troops moved into Korea – with the U.S. troops in the southern half, the Soviet troops in the northern half, and the 38-degree North Latitude line as the boundary.

In 1947, the General Assembly of the UN ordered elections throughout all of Korea to select one government for the entire country. The Soviet Union would not allow the North Koreans to vote and set up a communist government there. The South Koreans set up a democratic government, but both groups claimed the entire country. There were clashes between the troops from 1948 to 1950. After the U.S. removed its remaining troops in 1949 and announced in early 1950 that Korea was not part of its defense line in Asia, the communists decided to act and invaded the south.

Participants of war were North and South Korea, United States of America, Australia, New Zealand, China, Canada. France, Great Britain, Turkey, Belgium, Ethiopia, Colombia, Greece, South Africa, Luxembourg, Thailand, the Netherlands, and the Philippines. It was the first war in which a world organization played a major military role and it presented a challenge to the UN, which had only been in existence five years.

The war began June 25, 1950 and ended July 27, 1953. A truce was drawn up and an armistice agreement was signed ending the fighting. A permanent treaty of peace has never been signed and the country remains divided between the communist North and the democratic South. It was a very costly and bloody war, destroying villages and homes and displacing and killing millions of people.

In the aftermath of the Second World War, with the Soviet Union having emerged as the *second* strongest power on Earth, the United States embarked on a policy known as "containment" of the communist menace. This involved what came to be known as the **Marshall Plan** and the **Truman Doctrine**. The Marshall Plan involved sending economic aid to Europe in the aftermath of the Second World War to try preventing the spread of communism. To that end, the US has devoted a larger and larger share of its foreign policy, diplomacy, and both economic and military might to combating it.

The Truman Doctrine offered military aid to countries that were in danger of communist upheaval. This led to the era known as the **Cold War** in which the United States took the lead along with the Western European nations against the Soviet Union and the Eastern Bloc countries. It was also at this time that the United States joined the **North Atlantic Treaty Organization** or NATO. This was formed in 1949 and comprised of the United States and several Western European nations for the purposes of opposing communist aggression.

The **United Nations** was formed in 1945 to replace the defunct League of Nations for the purposes of ensuring world peace. However, even with American support, peace wasn't easy to maintain. In the 1950s, the United States embarked on what was called the "Eisenhower Doctrine," after the then President Eisenhower. This aimed at trying to maintain peace in a troubled area of the world, the Middle East. However, unlike the Truman Doctrine in Europe, it would have little success.

By the 1980s, the United States embarked on what some saw as a renewal of the Cold War. This was because the U.S. was becoming more involved in trying to prevent communist insurgency in Central America. A massive expansion of its armed forces was undertaken at this time. As these events occurred, the Soviet Union, with a failing economic system and a foray into Afghanistan, was unable to compete. By 1989, events had come to a head, ending with the breakdown of the Communist Bloc, the virtual end of the monolithic Soviet Union, and the collapse of the communist system by the early 1990's.

Skill 10.8   The Civil Rights Movement

One of the earliest fighters for civil rights was a nineteenth century African American abolitionist named Frederick Douglass. Douglass was an escaped slave and captivating public speaker. His autobiography, *Narrative of the Life of Frederick Douglass*, relates the violence that was turned upon him because of his beliefs. In his later years, he was active in efforts to overturn Jim Crow laws.

The **Civil Rights Movement** generally refers to the nationwide effort made by black people and those who supported them to gain equal rights to whites and to eliminate segregation. Discussion of this movement is generally understood in terms of the period of the 1950s and 1960s.

The **key people** in the U.S. Civil Rights Movement are:

Rosa Parks – a black seamstress from Montgomery Alabama who, in 1955, refused to give up her seat on the bus to a white man. This event is generally understood as the spark that lit the fire of the Civil Rights Movement. She has been generally regarded as the "mother of the Civil Rights Movement."

Martin Luther King, Jr. – the most prominent member of the Civil Rights Movement. King promoted nonviolent methods of opposition to segregation. The "Letter from Birmingham Jail" explained the purpose of nonviolent action as a way to make people notice injustice. In 1963, he led the march on Washington and delivered the "I Have a Dream" speech. He received the 1968 Nobel Prize for Peace.

James Meredith – the first African American to enroll at the University of Mississippi.

Emmett Till – a teenage boy who was murdered in Mississippi while visiting from Chicago. The crime of which he was accused was "whistling at a white woman in a store." He was beaten and murdered, and his body was dumped in a river. His two white abductors were apprehended and tried. They were acquitted by an all-white jury. After the acquittal, they admitted their guilt, but remained free because of double jeopardy laws.

Ralph Abernathy – a major figure in the Civil Rights Movement who succeeded Martin Luther King, Jr. as head of the Southern Christian Leadership Conference

Malcolm X – a political leader and part of the Civil Rights Movement. He was a prominent Black Muslim.

Stokeley Carmichael – one of the leaders of the Black Power movement that called for independent development of political and social institutions for blacks. Carmichael called for black pride and maintenance of black culture. He was head of the Student Nonviolent Coordinating Committee.

Key events of the Civil Rights Movement include:

The murder of Emmett Till, 1955. (*See Till's story under "key people" in Civil Rights Movement.*)

Rosa Parks and the Montgomery Bus Boycott, 1955-56 – After refusing to give up her seat on a bus in Montgomery, Alabama, Parks was arrested, tried, and convicted of disorderly conduct and violating a local ordinance. When word reached the black community, a bus boycott was organized to protest the segregation of blacks and whites on public buses. The boycott lasted 381 days, until the ordinance was lifted.

Strategy shift to "direct action," 1955-1965 – nonviolent resistance and civil disobedience. This action consisted mostly of bus boycotts, sit-ins, and freedom rides.

Formation of the Southern Christian Leadership Conference, 1957 – This group was formed by Martin Luther King, Jr., John Duffy, Rev. C. D. Steele, Rev. T. J. Jemison, Rev. Fred Shuttlesworth, Ella Baker, A. Philip Randolph, Bayard Rustin and Stanley Levison. It provided training and assistance to local efforts to fight segregation. Nonviolence was its central doctrine and major method of fighting segregation and racism.

The Desegregation of Little Rock, 1957 – Following up on the decision of the Supreme Court in *Brown vs. Board of Education*, the Arkansas school board voted to integrate the school system. The NAACP chose Arkansas as the place to push integration because it was considered a relatively progressive Southern state. However, the governor called up the National Guard to prevent nine black students from attending Little Rock's Central High School.

Sit-ins – In 1960, students began to stage "sit-ins" at local lunch counters and stores as a means of protesting the refusal of those businesses to desegregate. The first was in Greensboro, North Carolina. This led to a rash of similar campaigns throughout the South. Demonstrators began to protest at parks, beaches, theaters, museums, and libraries. When arrested, the protesters made "jail-no-bail" pledges. This called attention to their cause and put the financial burden of providing jail space and food on the cities.

Freedom Rides – Activists traveled by bus throughout the Deep South to desegregate bus terminals (required by federal law). These protesters undertook extremely dangerous protests. Many buses were firebombed and attacked by the KKK, and protesters were beaten. They were crammed into small, airless jail cells and mistreated in many ways. Key figures in this effort included John Lewis, James Lawson, Diane Nash, Bob Moses, James Bevel, Charles McDew, Bernard Lafayette, Charles Jones, Lonnie King, Julian Bond, Hosea Williams, and Stokeley Carmichael.

The Birmingham Campaign, 1963-64 – A campaign was planned to use sit-ins, kneel-ins in churches, and a march to the county building to launch a voter registration campaign. Birmingham obtained an injunction forbidding all such protests. The protesters, including Martin Luther King, Jr., believed the injunction was unconstitutional and defied it. They were arrested. While in jail, King wrote his famous Letter from Birmingham Jail. When the campaign began to falter, the "Children's Crusade" called students to leave school and join the protests. The events became news when more than 600 students were jailed. The next day, more students joined the protest. The media was present; its vivid national broadcast showed children being knocked down with fire hoses and attacked by dogs sent after them. The resulting public outrage led the Kennedy administration to intervene. About a month later, a committee was formed to end hiring discrimination, arrange for the release of jailed protesters, and establish normative communication between blacks and whites. Four months later, the KKK bombed the Sixteenth Street Baptist Church, killing four girls.

The March on Washington, 1963 – This was a march on Washington for jobs and freedom. It was a combined effort of all major civil rights organizations. The goals of the march were: meaningful civil rights laws, a massive federal works program, full and fair employment, decent housing, the right to vote, and adequate integrated education. It was at this march that Martin Luther King, Jr. made the famous "I Have a Dream" speech.

Mississippi Freedom Summer, 1964 – Students were brought from other states to Mississippi to assist local activists in registering voters, teaching in "Freedom schools," and forming the Mississippi Freedom Democratic Party. Three of the workers disappeared – murdered by the KKK. It took six weeks to find their bodies. The national uproar forced President Johnson to send in the FBI. Johnson was able to use public sentiment to effect passage in Congress of the Civil Rights Act of 1964.

<u>Alabama, USA</u>

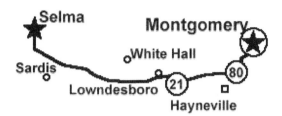

Selma to Montgomery marches, 1965 – Attempts to obtain voter registration in Selma, Alabama, had been largely unsuccessful due to opposition from the city's sheriff. M.L. King came to the city to lead a series of marches. He and over 200 demonstrators were arrested and jailed. Each successive march was met with violent resistance by police. In March, a group of over 600 intended to walk from Selma to Montgomery (54 miles). News media were on hand when, six blocks into the march, state and local law enforcement officials attacked the marchers with billy clubs, tear gas, rubber tubes wrapped in barbed wire, and bullwhips. Protesters were driven back to Selma. National broadcast of the footage provoked a nationwide response. President Johnson again used public sentiment to achieve passage of the Voting Rights Act of 1965. This law changed the political landscape of the South irrevocably.

Key policies, legislation and court cases included the following:

Brown v. Board of Education, 1954 – the Supreme Court declared that *Plessy v. Ferguson* was unconstitutional. This was the ruling that had established "Separate but Equal" as the basis for segregation. With this decision, the Court ordered immediate desegregation.

Civil Rights Act of 1964 – bars discrimination in public accommodations, employment and education.

Voting Rights Act of 1965 – suspended poll taxes, literacy tests and other voter tests for voter registration.

Skill 10.9   The Women's Rights Movement

The **women's rights movement** is concerned with the freedoms of women as differentiated from broader ideas of human rights. These issues are generally different from those that affect men and boys because of biological conditions or social constructs. The rights the movement has sought to protect throughout history include:

- The right to vote

- The right to work
- The right to fair wages
- The right to bodily integrity and autonomy
- The right to own property
- The right to an education
- The right to hold public office
- Marital rights
- Parental rights
- Religious rights
- The right to serve in the military
- The right to enter into legal contracts

The movement for women's rights has resulted in many social and political changes. Many of the ideas that seemed very radical merely 100 years ago are now normative. Some of the most famous leaders in the women's movement throughout American history are:

- Abigail Adams
- Susan B. Anthony
- Gloria E. Anzaldua
- Betty Friedan
- Olympe de Gouges
- Gloria Steinem
- Harriet Tubman
- Mary Wollstonecraft
- Virginia Woolf
- Germaine Greer

Many within the women's movement are primarily committed to justice and the natural rights of all people. This has led many members of the women's movement to be involved in the Black Civil Rights Movement, the gay rights movement, and the recent social movement to protect the rights of fathers.

Skill 10.10   The Vietnam War

The Vietnam War
U.S. Involvement - 1957 to 1973

Causes: U.S. involvement was the second phase of three in Vietnam's history. The first phase began in 1946 when the Vietnamese fought French troops for control of the country. Prior to 1946, Vietnam had been part of the French colony of Indochina (since 1861 along with Laos and Kampuchea or Cambodia). In 1954, the defeated French left and the country became divided into Communist North and Democratic South. U.S. aid and influence continued as part of the U.S. "Cold War" foreign policy to help any nation threatened by communism.

The second phase involved the U.S. commitment. The Communist Vietnamese considered the war one of national liberation, a struggle to avoid continual dominance and influence by a foreign power. A cease-fire was arranged in January, 1973, and a few months later U.S. troops left for good.

The third and final phase – fighting between the Vietnamese – ended on April 30, 1975, with the surrender of South Vietnam. The entire country was then united under communist leadership.

Participants in the Vietnam war were the United States of America, Australia, New Zealand, South and North Vietnam, South Korea, Thailand, and the Philippines. With active U.S. involvement from 1957 to 1973, it was the longest war participated in by the U.S. It was also tremendously destructive and completely divided the American public in their opinions and feelings about the war. Many were angered by the fact that it was the first war fought on foreign soil in which U.S. combat forces were totally unable to achieve their objectives.

Returning veterans had to not only readjust to normal civilian life, but also face bitterness, anger, and rejection. Many suffered severe physical and deep psychological problems. The war set a precedent with Congress and the American people actively challenging U.S. military and foreign policy. The emotional impact of the conflict, though tempered markedly by time, still exists.

Skill 10.11   The Persian Gulf War

The Persian Gulf War was fought in 1990-91 in Kuwait and Iraq and along the border of Saudi Arabia. The combatants were Iraq and a coalition of nations led by the United States. The immediate cause of the war was the invasion of Kuwait by Iraq on August 2, 1990. Iraqi leader Saddam Hussein justified the invasion by accusing Kuwait of slant drilling into Iraqi oil fields, and by renewing a former dispute over Kuwait's independence from Iraq. Prior to World War I, Kuwait was considered part of larger Iraq. Following the war, the British gained administrative control of Kuwait and treated it as an independent nation. Iraq did not recognize Kuwait's independence. Iraq also owed Kuwait a large debt for aid it received while fighting a war against Iran. Iraq claimed that because it acted as a buffer between Iran and Kuwait and Saudi Arabia, its war debts to these countries should be forgiven.

Immediately following Iraq's invasion of Kuwait, the United Nations imposed economic sanctions. Within a week, the United States, fearing that Iraq might next invade Saudi Arabia, began to send troops to that country in what was called Operation Desert Shield. Two naval battle groups were sent to the Persian Gulf as part of the operation.

As the U.S. amassed military resources in the region, it began to organize a coalition of other nations to give support in the case of conflict. The United

Nations passed a resolution in November, 1990, giving Iraq until January 15, 1991 to leave Kuwait. On January 12, the U.S. Congress authorized military action in Iraq. Iraq did not withdraw by the deadline, and the following day the U.S. began heavy aerial assaults on the country. Iraq responded with missile attacks and ground forces, but was quickly forced back into Iraq. The fighting was largely over in a matter of weeks, with the U.S. beginning to withdraw its forces from the area in early March, 1991.

Skill 10.12   The effects of the collapse of the Soviet Union and subsequent events on US leadership in world affairs

The Cold War was called such because no large-scale fighting took place directly between the two big protagonists, the United States and the Soviet Union.

Economics were a main cause of the Cold War, as well as political factors. A concern in both countries was that resources such as oil and food from other like-minded countries not be allowed to flow to "the other side."

The Soviet Union kept a tight leash on its supporting countries, including all of Eastern Europe, which made up a military organization called the **Warsaw Pact**. The Western nations responded by creating a military organization of their own, **the** North American Treaty Organization, or **NATO**. Another prime battleground was Asia, where the Soviet Union had allies in China, North Korea, and North Vietnam and the U.S. had allies in Japan, South Korea, Taiwan, and South Vietnam. The Korean War and Vietnam War were major conflicts in which both protagonists played big roles but didn't directly fight each other. The main symbol of the Cold War was the **arms race**, a continual buildup of missiles, tanks, and other weapons that became ever more technologically advanced and increasingly more deadly.

The ultimate weapon, which both sides had in abundance, was the nuclear bomb. Spending on weapons and defensive systems eventually occupied great percentages of the budgets of the U.S. and the USSR, and some historians argue that this high level of spending played a large part in the end of the latter.

The war was a cultural struggle as well. Adults brought up their children to hate "the Americans" or "the Communists." Cold War tensions spilled over into many parts of life in countries around the world. The ways of life in countries on either side of the divide were so different that they seemed entirely foreign to outside observers.

The Cold War continued to varying degrees from 1947 to 1991, when the Soviet Union collapsed. Other Eastern European countries had seen their communist governments overthrown by this time as well, marking the shredding of the "Iron Curtain." The "**Iron Curtain**" referred to the ideological, symbolic and physical separation of Europe between East and West.

The major thrust of U.S. foreign policy from the end of World War II to 1990 was the post-war struggle between non-communist nations, led by the United States, and the Soviet Union and the communist nations who were its allies. It was referred to as a "Cold War" because its conflicts did not lead to a major war of fighting, or a "hot war." Both the Soviet Union and the United States embarked on an arsenal buildup of atomic and hydrogen bombs as well as other nuclear weapons. Both nations had the capability of destroying each other but because of the continuous threat of nuclear war and accidents, extreme caution was practiced on both sides. The efforts of both sides to serve and protect their political philosophies and to support and assist their allies resulted in a number of events during this 45-year period.

Mikhail Gorbachev was elected leader by the Politburo in 1984, bringing with him a program of reform intended to bolster the flagging Soviet economy. As part of his plan, Gorbachev instituted a policy of economic freedoms called **perestroika**, which allowed private ownership of some businesses. He relaxed the government's control over the media in a policy of openness, called **glasnost**. He also instituted free, multi-party elections.

Gorbachev felt these new policies were required to apply pressure to more conservative members of the government, thereby increasing his support. The media seized upon their new freedom, however, and began reporting on the corruption and economic problems of the Soviet Union, which had been largely hidden from the public by the previous state-controlled news services. Meanwhile, the United States, under President Ronald Reagan, had rapidly increased its military spending, outpacing the Soviet Union and increasing economic pressure.

Faced with growing independence movements in many of the Eastern Bloc countries, the government under Gorbachev reversed Brezhnev's policies of tight control via the Communist Party. As the countries of Eastern Europe and Soviet states began pulling away from Russia, all these factors came together to cause the dissolution of the Soviet Union.

Skill 10.13   International terrorism

Modern global terrorism can trace its roots to 1967 when Israel defeated Arab forces in Palestine. Palestinian fighters, realizing they could not win a military battle against Israel, turned to urban terror tactics to attack Israel's population centers. Taking advantage of modern communications and technology, radical Palestinian organizations undertook a series of airline hijackings, bombings and kidnappings to draw attention to their demands and to terrorize and demoralize their enemies, specifically Israel. In 1972, at the Olympic Games in Munich, radical Palestinians kidnapped nine Israeli athletes who were all killed in a subsequent gun battle. Supported by some Arab states and criminal organizations, the radical Palestinians developed a network of connections through which their techniques and training could flow to other parts of the world. Terrorist activity continued throughout the 1970's. In 1979, the Soviet Union invaded Afghanistan and an Islamic revolution took place in Iran, two events that were to provide opportunities for terrorist tactics to advance as radical organizations gained valuable military experience and state support from the leadership in Iran.

During the 1980's, the use of suicide bombers became an effective technique to strike deeply. Anti-Israeli sentiments grew, as well as anti-US feelings over America's support of Israel. Radical terrorists began to choose western targets, as in the bombing of US Marine barracks in Lebanon in 1983 and the 1988 bombing of a Pan Am airliner over Scotland.

With the withdrawal of the Soviet Union from Afghanistan, and its subsequent collapse, the region of Afghanistan became a safe haven for radical groups to organize and train followers in terror tactics. The Taliban, a strict religious sect, took control in Afghanistan and harbored these groups, including Al-Qaeda.

Al-Qaeda is led by Saudi millionaire Osama Bin Laden and claims opposition to US military presence in Saudi Arabia and elsewhere in the Middle East. In 1993, Al-Qaeda operatives struck at the United States by bombing the World Trade Center in New York City. On September 11, 2001, Al-Qaeda followers hijacked four commercial airliners, flying two of them into the World Trade Center towers, and one into the Pentagon in Washington, D.C. The fourth airliner crashed in Pennsylvania. It was the largest single terrorist attack the world had seen, killing thousands of people. The United States reacted by launching an attack on Afghanistan, driving Bin Laden and his followers into the hills.

Since that attack, the prospect of global terrorism has become a reality in the modern world. Much of the world's foreign policy is now driven toward Middle Eastern states and domestic security policies.

Learn more about:
European exploration and colonial settlement
http://www.madison.k12.wi.us/tnl/detectives/History/U.S._History/I.___Age_of_Exploration_and__ Colonial_Settlement/
Causes of the Revolutionary War
http://www.historycentral.com/Revolt/causes.html
Slavery in the United States
http://www.pbs.org/wnet/slavery/
The Civil War
http://www.civil-war.net/
Heroes of the Civil Rights Movement
http://www.infoplease.com/spot/bhmheroes1.html

COMPETENCY 11.0   UNDERSTAND THE GOVERNMENTAL SYSTEM OF THE UNITED STATES; THE PRINCIPLES, IDEALS, RIGHTS, AND RESPONSIBILITIES OF U.S. CITIZENSHIP; AND THE FUNDAMENTAL PRINCIPLES AND CONCEPTS OF ECONOMICS

Skill 11.1   Purposes of government; functions of federal, state, and local government in the United States

The American nation was founded very much with the idea that the people would have a large degree of autonomy and liberty. The famous maxim "no taxation without representation" was a rallying cry for the Revolution – not only because the people didn't want to suffer the increasingly oppressive series of taxes imposed on them by the British Parliament, but also because the people could not in any way influence the lawmakers in Parliament in regard to those taxes. No American colonist had a seat in Parliament and no American colonist could vote for members of Parliament.

One of the crucial words in the Declaration of Independence is "liberty," the pursuit of which all should be free to attempt. That idea, that a people should be free to pursue their own course, even to the extent of making their own mistakes, has dominated political thought in the 200-plus years of the American republic.

Representation, the idea that a people can vote—or even replace—their lawmakers was not a new idea, except in America. Residents of other British colonies did not have these rights, of course, and America was only a colony, according to the conventional wisdom of the British Government at the time. What the Sons of Liberty and other revolutionaries were asking for was to stand on an equal footing with their fellow countrymen in England. Along with the idea of representation came the idea that key ideas and concepts can be deliberated and discussed, with theoretically everyone having a chance to voice their views. This applied to both lawmakers and the people who elected them. Lawmakers wouldn't just pass bills that became laws; rather, they would debate the strengths and weaknesses of proposed laws before voting on them. Members of both houses of Congress had the opportunity to speak out on the issues, as did the people at large, who could contact their lawmakers and express their views. The different branches of government were designed to serve as a mechanism of checks and balances on each other so that no one branch could become too powerful. They each have their own specific powers.

Another key concept in the American ideal is **equality**, the idea that every person has the same rights and responsibilities under the law. The Great Britain that the American colonists knew was one of a stratified society, with social classes firmly in place. It was clear that the more money and power a person had, the easier it was to avoid things like serving in the army or being charged with a crime. The goal of the Declaration of Independence and the Constitution was to provide equality for all who read those documents.

Due process under the law was also a primary concern of the founders. Various constitutional amendments protect the rights of people. Amendments five through eight protect citizens who are accused of crimes and are brought to trial. Every citizen has the right to due process of law, including the right to a trial by an impartial jury, the right to be defended by a lawyer, and the right to a speedy trial. The last two amendments limit the powers of the federal government to those that are expressly granted in the Constitution. Any rights not expressly mentioned in the Constitution, therefore, belong to the states or to the people.

The system is based on individual freedom of choice. The history of the country is filled with stories of people who ventured to America and made their fortunes.

Functions of federal, state and local government in the United States

Powers delegated to the federal government:

1. To tax
2. To borrow and coin money
3. To establish postal service
4. To grant patents and copyrights
5. To regulate interstate and foreign commerce
6. To establish courts
7. To declare war.
8. To raise and support the armed forces
9. To govern territories.
10. To define and punish felonies and piracy on the high seas
11. To fix standards of weights and measures
12. To conduct foreign affairs

Powers reserved to the states:

1. To regulate intrastate trade
2. To establish local governments
3. To protect general welfare
4. To protect life and property
5. To ratify amendments
6. To conduct elections
7. To make state and local laws

Concurrent powers of the federal government and states:

1. Both Congress and the states may tax.
2. Both may borrow money.
3. Both may charter banks and corporations.
4. Both may establish courts.
5. Both may make and enforce laws.
6. Both may take property for public purposes.
7. Both may spend money to provide for the public welfare.

Implied powers of the federal government:

1. To establish banks or other corporations, implied from delegated powers to tax, to borrow, and to regulate commerce
2. To spend money for roads, schools, health, insurance, etc., implied from powers to establish roads, to tax to provide for general welfare and defense, and to regulate commerce
3. To create military academies, implied from powers to raise and support an armed force
4. To locate and generate sources of power and sell surplus, implied from powers to dispose of government property, commerce, and war powers
5. To assist and regulate agriculture, implied from power to tax and spend for general welfare and to regulate commerce

Skill 11.2 The branches of government and their roles

Branches of Government Established by the U.S. Constitution

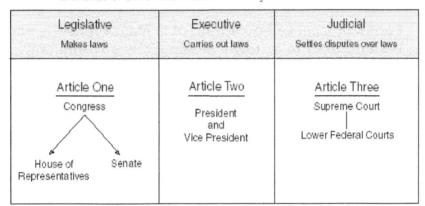

In the United States, the three branches of the federal government – the **Executive**, the **Legislative**, and the **Judicial** – divide their powers thus:

Legislative - Article I of the Constitution established the legislative or law-making branch of the government called the Congress. It is made up of two houses, the House of Representatives and the Senate. Voters in all states elect the members who serve in each house of Congress. The legislative branch is responsible for making laws, printing money, regulating trade, establishing the postal service and federal courts, approving the president's appointments, declaring war, and supporting the armed forces. The Congress also has the power to impeach (bring charges against) the president. Charges for impeachment are brought by the House and are tried in the Senate.

Executive – Article II of the Constitution created the executive branch of the government, headed by the president, who leads the country, recommends new laws, and can veto bills passed by the legislative branch. As the chief of state, the president carries out the laws of the country and the treaties and declarations of war passed by the legislative branch. The president also appoints federal judges and is commander in chief of the military when it is called into service. Other members of the executive branch include the vice-president, cabinet members, ambassadors, presidential advisers, members of the armed forces, and other appointed and civil servants of government agencies, departments and bureaus.

Judicial - Article III of the Constitution established the judicial branch of government headed by the Supreme Court. In an appeal capacity, citizens, businesses, and government officials can ask the Supreme Court to review a decision made in a lower court if someone believes that the ruling by a judge is unconstitutional. The Supreme Court has the power to rule that a law passed by the legislature, or an act of the executive branch, is illegal and unconstitutional (See *Judicial Review,* Section 1.2). The judicial branch also includes lower federal courts known as federal district courts that have been established by the Congress. The courts try lawbreakers and review cases referred from other courts.

Skill 11.3   Forms of local self-government in Massachusetts and the United States (e.g., town meeting, city government)

Massachusetts was originally settled by religious Puritans from England, and many of their traditions are evident in modern self-government in the state. One of the tenets of the Puritan sect was a congregational approach to church affairs, with no hierarchy of church leaders as in the English and Catholic churches.

Church decisions were settled at meetings of the church members themselves. This congregational approach was readily applied to civic matters, leading to the development of the town meeting as the basic body of local government. The town meeting is still used throughout New England to make local decisions. Even larger cities that have adopted a more representative government retain the terminology and some of the traditions of the town meeting.

The town meeting is an annual meeting of the residents of a town to act as a legislative body and to vote on town matters, including a budget for the upcoming year. In Massachusetts, smaller towns of less than 6,000 people hold open town meetings, where all registered voters can attend and vote. Larger towns can also hold open town meetings, but may opt for a representative town meeting, where voters elect representatives to attend the town meeting. An elected Board of Selectmen operates as an executive board in the period between town meetings to interpret the actions of the meeting.

The town meeting is particular to New England and is not a common form of government elsewhere. In other parts of the country, the town council is a common form of local government. Town or city councils are usually small, elected bodies of representatives with an elected or appointed leader or chairperson, or elected mayor. Forms vary across the country, but many cities also have an administrator or clerk who handles most of the day-to-day business of the city and receives approval on budgets and other actions from the council. Councils are often both legislative and executive in many forms and have authority to set local tax rates and pass budgets. Most states have local government at a county level as well, with an elected board of representatives often called supervisors or commissioners. County boards oversee county-wide issues and public matters in unincorporated areas outside of cities.

Skill 11.4   How laws are enacted and enforced

Federal laws are passed by the Congress, and can originate in either the House of Representatives or the Senate.

The first step in the passing of a law is for the proposed law to be introduced in one of the houses of Congress. A proposed law is called a **bill** while it is under consideration. It can be introduced or sponsored by a member of Congress by giving a copy to the clerk or by placing a copy in a special box called a hopper.

Once a bill is introduced, copies are printed and it is assigned to one of several standing committees of the house in which it was introduced. The committee studies the bill and performs research on the issues it would cover. Committees may call experts to testify on the bill and gather public comments. It may also revise the bill. Finally, it votes on whether to release the bill to be voted on by the full body. A committee may also lay aside a bill so that it cannot be voted on.

Once a bill is released, it can be debated and amended by the full body before being voted on. If it passes by a simple majority vote, the bill is sent to the other house of Congress, where the process begins again. When a bill has passed both the House and the Senate, it is assigned to a conference committee that is made up of members of both houses. This committee resolves differences between the House and Senate versions of a bill, if any, and then sends it back to both houses for final approval. Once a bill receives final approval, it is signed by the speaker of the House and the vice president, who is also the president of the Senate, and sent to the president. The president may sign the bill or veto it. If he vetoes the bill, his veto may be overruled if two-thirds of both the Senate and the House vote to do so. Once it is signed by the president, the bill becomes law.

Federal laws are enforced by the executive branch and its departments. The **Department of Justice**, led by the United States attorney general, is the primary law enforcement department of the federal government. It is aided by other investigative and enforcement departments such as the **Federal Bureau of Investigation** (FBI) and the **U.S. Postal Inspectors**.

Skill 11.5   The political process in the United States and the role of political parties

Political parties, as the term is now understood, did not exist during the colonial period. One issue that divided the colonists was the relation of the colonies to England. There was initially little difference of opinion on this question. About the middle of the eighteenth century, after England began to develop a harsher colonial policy, two factions arose in America. One favored home government and the other self-government. The former came to be known as **Tories**, the latter as **Whigs**. During the course of the American Revolution, a large number of Tories left the country either to return to England or move into Canada.

See also Skill 10.3.

Skill 11.6   Fundamental concepts and principles of capitalism (e.g., private property, wage labor, supply and demand, the global economy)

In a market economy the markets function on the basis of supply and demand and, if markets are free, the result is an efficient allocation of resources. **Private ownership** results in an efficient allocation of resources. Private property rights play an important role in resource allocation in our economy. If the pond next door to you is owned by your neighbor, you will not be using it as a garbage dump without compensating your neighbor in some way. Since the owner of a resource must be compensated in some way for that resource's use, private ownership results in prices being assigned to resources. These prices, based on scarcity (short supply), result in an efficient allocation of resources, whether the resources are renewable or non-renewable. Without private ownership of resources, there is no incentive to be efficient and to conserve scarce resources – as shown in examples of pollution. This is where government plays a role in somehow correcting the misallocation caused by the lack of ownership rights.

Markets functioning on the basis of **supply and demand** also result in efficiency. The seller's supply curve represents the different quantities of a good or service the seller is willing and able to bring to the market at different prices during a given period of time. The seller has to have the good and has to be willing to sell it. If either of these isn't true, then he/she isn't a part of the relevant market supply. The supply curve represents the selling and production decisions of the seller and is based on the costs of production. The costs of production of a product are based on the costs of the resources used in its production. The costs of resources are based on the **scarcity** of the resource. The scarcer a resource is, relatively speaking, the higher its price. A diamond costs more than paper because diamonds are scarcer than paper. All of these concepts are embodied in the seller's supply curve. The same thing is true on the buying side of the market. The buyer's preferences, tastes, income, etc. – all of his/her buying decisions – are embodied in the demand curve. The demand curve represents the various quantities of a good or a service the buyer is willing and able to buy at different prices during a given period of time.

If we compare the buying decisions of buyers with the selling decisions of sellers, the place where they coincide represents the market equilibrium. This is where the demand and supply curves intersect. At this one point of intersection, the buying decisions of buyers are equal to the selling decisions of sellers. The quantity that buyers want to buy at that particular price is equal to the quantity that sellers want to sell at that particular price. This is the market equilibrium. At this one point, the quantity demanded is equal to the quantity supplied. This price-quantity combination represents an efficient allocation of resources.

Consumers are basically voting for the goods and services that they want with their dollar spending. When a good accumulates enough dollar votes, the producer earns a profit. The existence of profits signals that consumers are satisfied with the way their society's scarce resources are being used. When consumers don't want a good or service, they don't purchase it and the producers doesn't accumulate enough dollar votes to have profits. Losses are the market's way of signaling that consumers don't want their scarce resources used in the production of that particular good or service. Firms that incur losses eventually go out of business. They either have a product that consumers don't want, or they have an inefficient production process that results in higher costs and therefore higher prices.

In today's world, markets are international. Nations are all part of a **global economy**. No nation exists in isolation or is totally independent of other nations. (Isolationism is referred to as autarky or a closed economy.) Membership in a global economy means that what one nation does affects other nations because economies are linked through international trade, commerce and finance. They all have open economies. International transactions affect the levels of income, employment and prices in each of the trading economies. The relative importance of trade is based on what percentage of Gross Domestic Product trade constitutes. In a country like the United States, trade represents only a few percent of GDP. In other nations, trade may represent over fifty percent of GDP. For those countries, changes in international transactions can cause many economic fluctuations and problems.

Skill 11.7   Democratic principles and values contained in the Declaration of Independence, the U.S. Constitution, and the Constitution of the Commonwealth of Massachusetts (e.g., the rule of law, due process, equal protection of the laws, majority rule, protection of minority rights)

Many of the core values in the U.S. democratic system can be found in the opening words of the **Declaration of Independence**, including the belief in equality and the rights of citizens to "life, liberty and the pursuit of happiness."

The Declaration emphasized the American colonists' belief that a government received its authority to rule from the people. The government's function should not be to suppress the governed, but to protect the rights of the governed, including protection from the government itself. These two ideals, popular sovereignty and the rule of law, are our core values.

Popular sovereignty grants citizens the ability to directly participate in their own government by voting and running for public office. This ideal – established in the **United States Constitution** – holds that all citizens have an equal right to engage in their own governance. The Constitution also contains a list of specific rights that citizens have, and which the government cannot infringe upon. Popular sovereignty also allows for citizens to change their government if they feel it is necessary

The rule of law is the ideal that the law applies not only to the governed, but to the government as well. The justice system protects citizens by requiring that any accusation of a crime be proved by the government before a person is punished. This is called due process and ensures that any accused person will have an opportunity to confront his accusers and provide a defense. Due process follows from the core value of a right to liberty. The government cannot take away a citizen's liberty without reason or proof. The correlating ideal is also a core value – that someone who does harm to another or breaks a law will receive justice under the democratic system. The punishment will fit the crime, and any citizen can appeal to the judicial system if he feels he has been wronged.

The **Constitution of the Commonwealth of Massachusetts** contains the same principles and values as the Declaration and the U.S. Constitution, preserving the rights of the citizens of that state and allowing them to participate directly in government. In addition to these core values, the Massachusetts Constitution makes specific mention of education and the encouragement of learning. It offers special protection to Harvard University and makes it a duty of public officials to "cherish the interests of literature and the sciences."

Skill 11.8   Responsibilities of U.S. citizens (e.g., respecting others' rights, obeying laws and rules, paying taxes, jury duty, voting)

A citizen of the United States may either be native-born or a **naturalized** citizen. **Naturalization** is the process by which one acquires citizenship. Upon a specialized occasion, one may also have dual-citizenship, which is citizenship in the United States as well as in another country. In order to become a citizen, several requirements must first be met.

A citizen in a democratic society is expected to do certain things in order to remain such a citizen. First and foremost, that person is expected to follow the laws of that society. The vast majority of the laws of a democratic society have been enacted to facilitate the continuance of that society. Many of these laws also have the rights of the citizens in mind. It is certainly easier to follow some of these laws than others. Throughout the history of democratic societies, however, laws have been passed that seem to violate the spirit of the rights of those citizens. In such cases, people work to overturn such laws, either directly by means of judicial solutions or indirectly by making sure that the lawmakers who create such laws are not re-elected.

This reinforces the idea that citizens have a responsibility to themselves; if the government is infringing on their basic rights, they have a natural right to speak up and do something about it. Related to this is the idea that the government of a democratic society exists in part to protect the rights of its citizens. People expect such protection, in both real and virtual terms. Real terms include civil and countrywide defense, and virtual terms include laws and the people who make them. If such protection standards are not being met, then the citizens have the right and even the duty to demand such protection and work to see that it is maintained or restored.

Citizens of a democratic society are also expected to participate in the political process, either directly or indirectly. In theory, anyone who is a citizen of a democratic society can run for election, be it at the local, state, or federal level. Other ways to participate in the political process include donating time and money to the political campaigns of others and speaking on behalf of or against certain issues. The most basic level of participation in the political process is to vote.

A democratic society is built on the theory of participatory government. Citizens of such a society expect that political debates on important issues will be public and ongoing, so that they can keep themselves informed on how their representatives view such issues. Information is meant to be shared, especially in a democratic society.

Bill Of Rights - The first ten amendments to the United States Constitution, dealing with civil liberties and civil rights. James Madison was credited with writing a majority of them. They are in brief:

1. Freedom of religion
2. Right to bear arms
3. Security from the quartering of troops in homes
4. Right against unreasonable search and seizures
5. Right against self-incrimination
6. Right to trial by jury and right to legal counsel
7. Right to jury trial for civil actions
8. No cruel or unusual punishment allowed
9. These rights shall not deny other rights the people enjoy
10. Powers not mentioned in the Constitution shall be retained by the states or the people

COMPETENCY 12.0   UNDERSTAND MAJOR DEVELOPMENTS IN WORLD HISTORY

Skill 12.1   Characteristics of early human civilizations

Although written records go back about 4,500 years, scientists have pieced together evidence that documents the existence of humans as much as 600,000 years ago. The first manlike creatures arose in many parts of the world about one million years ago. By slow stages, these creatures developed fire and tools. They had human-sized brains and inbred to produce *Cro-Magnon* type creatures (25,000 years ago), from which *homo sapiens* descended.

These primitive humans demonstrated wide behavior patterns and great adaptability. Although few details are available – including when language began to develop – they are believed to have lived in small communities that developed on the basis of the need to hunt. Cave paintings suggest a belief that pictures of animals might magically conjure up real ones. Some figurines seem to indicate belief in fertility gods and goddesses. Belief in some form of afterlife is indicated by burial formalities.

Fire and weapons were in use quite early. Archaeological evidence points to the use of hatchets, awls, needles and cutting tools in the Old Stone Age (1 million years ago). Artifacts of the New Stone Age (6,000-8,000 BCE) include indications of polished tools, domesticated animals, the wheel, and some agriculture. Pottery and textiles have been found dating to the end of the New Stone Age (Neolithic period). The discovery of metals in the Bronze Age (3,000 BCE) is concurrent with the establishment of what are believed to be the first civilizations. The Iron Age followed quickly on the heels of the Bronze Age.

By 4,000, humans lived in villages, engaged in animal husbandry, grew grains, sailed in boats, and practiced religions. Civilizations arose earliest in the fertile river valleys of the Nile, Mesopotamia, the Indus, and the Hwang Ho.

Ancient civilizations included the following:

The culture of Mesopotamia was autocratic in nature. The various civilizations that crisscrossed the Fertile Crescent usually had a single ruler at the head of the government and, in many cases, also the religion. The people were required to follow his strict instructions..

The civilizations of the Sumerians, Amorites, Hittites, Assyrians, Chaldeans, and Persians controlled various areas of the land we call Mesopotamia. With few exceptions, tyrants and military leaders controlled most aspects of society, including trade, religion, and the law. Each Sumerian city-state had its own god, with the city-state's leader doubling as its high priest. Trade was vastly important to these civilizations. Egypt and the Phoenician cities were powerful and regular trading partners of the various Mesopotamian cultures.

Legacies handed down to us from these people include:
- The first use of writing, the wheel, and banking (Sumeria)
- The first written set of laws (Code of Hammurabi)
- The first epic story (*Gilgamesh*)
- The first library dedicated to preserving knowledge (instituted by the Assyrian leader Ashurbanipal)
- The Hanging Gardens of Babylon (built by the Chaldean Nebuchadnezzar)

The ancient civilization of the **Sumerians** invented the wheel; developed irrigation through use of canals, dikes, and devices for raising water; devised the system of cuneiform writing; learned to divide time; and built large boats for trade. The Babylonians devised the **Code of Hammurabi**, a system of laws.

Egypt made numerous significant contributions, including construction of the great pyramids; development of hieroglyphic writing; preservation of bodies after death; making paper from papyrus; contributing to developments in arithmetic and geometry; the invention of the method of counting in groups of 1-10 (the decimal system); completion of a solar calendar; and laying the foundation for science and astronomy.

The earliest historical record of **Kush** is in Egyptian sources. They describe a region upstream from the first cataract of the Nile as "wretched." This civilization was characterized by a settled way of life in fortified mud-brick villages. They subsisted on hunting and fishing, herding cattle, and gathering grain. Skeletal remains suggest that the people were a blend of Negroid and Mediterranean peoples. This civilization appears to be the second-oldest in Africa (after Egypt). In what has been called "a magnificent irony of history," the Kushites conquered Egypt in the eighth century, creating the 25th dynasty. The dynasty ended in the seventh century when Egypt was defeated by the Assyrians. The Kushites were gradually pushed farther south by the Assyrians and later by the Persians. This essentially cut off contact with Egypt, the Middle East and Europe. They moved their capital to Meroe in about 591 BC, when Napata was conquered. Their attention then turned to sub-Saharan Africa. Free of Egyptian dominance, they developed innovations in government and other areas.

The ancient **Assyrians** had a highly organized military that used horse-drawn chariots.

The **Hebrews** or the ancient Israelites instituted "monotheism," the worship of one God.

The **Minoans** had a system of writing using symbols to represent syllables in words. They built palaces with multiple levels containing many rooms, bright paintings on the walls, water, and sewage systems with flush toilets, bathtubs, and hot and cold running water.

The **Mycenaeans** changed the Minoan writing system to suit their own language and used symbols to represent syllables.

The **Phoenicians** were sea traders well known for their manufacturing skills in glass and metals and the development of a widely used purple dye. They became proficient enough in the skill of navigation that they were able to sail by the stars at night. They devised an alphabet using symbols to represent single sounds, which was an extension of the Egyptian principle and writing system.

In **India**, the caste system was developed, the principle of zero in mathematics was discovered, and the major religion of Hinduism was founded.

China – considered by some historians to be the oldest, uninterrupted civilization in the world – was in existence around the same time as the ancient civilizations founded in **Egypt**, **Mesopotamia**, and the **Indus Valley**. The Chinese studied nature and weather; stressed the importance of education, family, and a strong central government; followed the religions of Buddhism, Confucianism, and Taoism; and invented such things as gunpowder, paper, printing, and the magnetic compass. China built the Great Wall, practiced crop rotation and terrace farming, established the silk industry, and developed caravan routes across Central Asia for extensive trade. It increased proficiency in rice cultivation and developed a written language based on drawings or pictographs.

The ancient **Persians** developed an alphabet; contributed the religions/philosophies of **Zoroastrianism**, **Mithraism**, and **Gnosticism**; and allowed conquered peoples to retain their own customs, laws, and religions.

Skill 12.2   Major eras, developments and turning points in Western civilization (e.g., ancient Israel, the emergence of Greek civilization, the rise and fall of the Roman Empire, the Middle Ages, the Renaissance and Reformation, the Age of Discovery, the scientific revolution, the Enlightenment, the age of revolution, World Wars I and II)

The ancient **Israelites** and **Christians** created a powerful legacy of political and philosophical traditions, much of which survives to this day. In law and religion, especially, we can draw a more or less straight line from then to now.

Israel was not the first ancient civilization to have a series of laws for its people to follow, but the **Ten Commandments** have maintained a central role in the laws of societies the world over. Such commandments as the ones that prohibit stealing and killing were revolutionary in their day because they applied to everyone, not just the disadvantaged. In many ancient cultures, the rich and powerful were above the law because the laws were not always clear and they could buy their way out of trouble. Echoing the Code of Hammurabi and preceding Rome's Twelve Tables, the Ten Commandments provided a written record of laws that everyone could follow.

The civilization of Israel is also known as the first to assume worship of just one god. Christian and Muslim communities built on this tradition. Rather than a series of gods, each of which was in charge of a different aspect of nature or society, the ancient Israelites, Christians, and Muslims believed in just one god.

The classical civilization of **Greece** built on the foundations laid by the Egyptians, Phoenicians, Minoans, and Mycenaeans. One of the most important contributions of Greece was the Greek alphabet – derived from the Phoenician letters – which formed the basis for the Roman alphabet and our present-day alphabet. Extensive trading and colonization helped spread the Greek civilization. The Greek love of sports, with emphasis on a sound body, led to the tradition of the Olympic Games. Greece developed a series of independent, strong city-states. The Greeks influenced the western traditions of drama, epic and lyric poetry. Greek fables and myths centered on the many gods and goddesses, and were later adopted by the Roman culture. Science, astronomy, medicine, mathematics, philosophy, art, architecture, and the practice of recording historical events were all important aspects of the Greek culture. The conquests of **Alexander the Great** spread Greek ideas to the areas he conquered. They also brought to the Greek world many ideas from Asia – mainly the value of ideas, wisdom, curiosity, and the desire to learn as much about the world as possible.

The ancient civilization of **Rome** lasted approximately 1,000 years, including the periods of republic and empire, although its history and its lasting influence on Europe was for a much longer period. There was a very sharp contrast between the curious, imaginative, inquisitive Greeks and the practical, simple, down-to-earth, no-nonsense Romans who spread and preserved the ideas of ancient Greece and other culture groups. The Romans' contributions and accomplishments are numerous, but the greatest of these included language, engineering, building, law, government, roads, trade, and the "**Pax Romana.**" Pax Romana was the long period of peace that enabled free travel and trade, spreading people, cultures, goods, and ideas over a vast area of the known world. In the end, Rome grew too big to manage and its enemies too many to turn back. The sprawling nature of the Empire made it too big to protect, and it dissolved into chaos and violence.

The end of the **Roman Empire** came when Germanic tribes took over most of Europe. The five major tribes were the Visigoths, Ostrogoths, Vandals, Saxons, and the Franks. In later years, the Franks successfully stopped the invasion of southern Europe by Muslims by defeating them under the leadership of Charles

Martel at the Battle of Tours in 732 AD. Thirty-six years later in 768 AD, the grandson of Charles Martel became King of the Franks and became known as Charlemagne. Although a man of war, Charlemagne was unique in his respect for and encouragement of learning. He made efforts to rule fairly and ensure just treatment of his people.

The **Reformation** period consisted of two phases: the **Protestant Revolution** and the **Catholic Reformation**.

The Protestant Revolution came about because of religious, political, and economic reasons. The religious reasons stemmed from abuses in the Catholic Church – including fraudulent clergy; the sale of religious offices, indulgences, and dispensations; different theologies within the Church; and frauds involving sacred relics.

The political reasons involved increase in the power of rulers who acted as "absolute monarchs" and wanted complete control, especially over the Church, and the growth of "nationalism" or patriotic pride in one's own country.

Economic reasons included the desire of ruling monarchs to possess and control all lands and wealth of the Church; deep animosity against the burdensome papal taxation; the rise of the affluent middle class and its clash with medieval Church ideals; and the growth of "intense" capitalism.

The Protestant Revolution began in Germany with **Martin Luther's** revolt against Church abuses. It spread to Switzerland where it was led by Calvin. It began in England with the efforts of King Henry VIII to have his marriage to Catherine of Aragon annulled so he could marry another and have a male heir. The results of the Revolution were split. It won increasing support from common people, as well as nobles and some rulers. The Church attempted to stop it.

The **Catholic Reformation** was undertaken by the Church in response to growing criticism, with the intent to slow or stop the Protestant Revolution. Major efforts to this end were made by the Council of Trent and the Jesuits. Six major results of the Reformation included:
- Religious freedom
- Religious tolerance
- More opportunities for education
- A limit put on rulers' power and control
- Increase in religious wars
- An increase in fanaticism and persecution

The **Scientific Revolution and the Enlightenment** are two of the most important turning points in the history of civilization, resulting in a new sense of self-examination and a wider view of the world than ever before.

The Scientific Revolution was, above all, a shift in focus from **belief** to **proof**. Scientists and philosophers wanted to see proof, not just believe what other people told them.

A Polish astronomer, **Nicolaus Copernicus,** crystallized a lifetime of observations into a book that was published about the time of his death. In this book, Copernicus argued that the sun, not the earth, was the center of a solar system and that other planets revolved around the sun, not the earth. This flew in the face of established church doctrine. The church still wielded tremendous power at this time, including the power to banish people or sentence them to prison or even death.

The Danish astronomer **Tycho Brahe** was the first to catalog his numerous observations of the night sky. Building on Brahe's data, German scientist Johannes Kepler instituted his theory of planetary movement, embodied in his famous laws of planetary movement. Using Brahe's data, Kepler also confirmed Copernicus's observations and argument that the earth revolved around the sun.

The most famous defender of this idea was **Galileo**, an Italian scientist who conducted many famous experiments in the pursuit of science. He is most well known, however, for his defense of the heliocentric (sun-centered) idea. He wrote a book comparing the two theories, but most readers could tell that he favored the new one. He was convinced of this mainly because of what he had seen with his own eyes. He had used the relatively new invention of the telescope to see four moons of Jupiter. They certainly did not revolve around the earth, so why should everything else? His ideas were not at all favored by the church, which was powerful enough in Italy to have Galileo placed under house arrest. Galileo died under house arrest, but his ideas survived. Picking up the baton was the English scientist **Isaac Newton**, best known as the discoverer of gravity and as a pioneering voice in the study of optics (light), calculus, and physics.

More than any other scientist, Newton argued for (and proved) the idea of a mechanistic world: one can see how the world works and prove it through observation.

The period from the 1700s to the 1800s was characterized in Western countries by opposing political ideas of democracy and nationalism. This resulted in strong nationalistic feelings and people of common cultures asserting their belief in the right to have a part in their government. The **American Revolution** was successful in helping the English colonists in America win their freedom from Great Britain. After more than one hundred years of mostly self-government, the colonists resented the increased British meddling and control. They declared their freedom, won the Revolutionary War with aid from France, and formed a new independent nation. In the **French Revolution**, middle and lower classes revolted against the gross political and economic excesses of the ruling class and the supporting nobility. It ended with the establishment of the first in a series of French Republics. Conditions leading to revolt included extreme taxation, inflation, lack of food, and total disregard for the degrading condition of the people on the part of the rulers, nobility, and the church.

The American and the French revolutions both liberated their people from unwanted government interference and installed a different kind of government. They were both fought for the liberty of the common people, and they both were built on writings and ideas that embraced such an outcome. Both revolutions proved that people could expect more from their government and that it was worth fighting for such rights as self-determination. However, several important differences should be emphasized:

The British colonists were striking back against unwanted taxation and other sorts of "government interference." The French people were starving and, in many cases, destitute and were striking back against an autocratic regime that cared more for high fashion and courtly love than bread and circuses.

- The American Revolution involved a years-long campaign of often bloody battles, skirmishes, and stalemates. The French Revolution was bloody to a degree but mainly an overthrow of society and its outdated traditions.

The American Revolution resulted in a representative government, which marketed itself as a beacon of democracy for the rest of the world. The French Revolution resulted in a consulship, a generalship, and then an emperor.

Skill 12.3 The impact of industrialization, nationalism, communism, and religion on modern world history

The last century and a half has been a time of rapid and extensive change on almost every front. Notably, there has been a growing concern for protecting human and civil rights. The end of imperialism and the liberation of former colonies and territorial holdings have created new nations and increased communication and respect among nations. Democracy has grown; Communism has risen and almost fallen. Nations are no longer ruled by distant mother countries or their resident governors. But both political and individual freedoms have been won through great struggle and loss of lives. Nationalism has risen and created new states, and nations have cultivated a national identity. Yet these individual nations have been brought into contact and cooperation in ways never before experienced in human history. Scientific and technological developments, new thinking in religion and philosophy, and new political and economic realities have combined to begin to create a global society that must now learn to define itself and understand how to cooperate and respect diversity in new ways.

The **Industrial Revolution**, which began in Great Britain and spread elsewhere, developed power-driven machinery (fueled by coal and steam) leading to the accelerated growth of industry. Large factories began to replace homes and small workshops as work centers. The lives of people changed drastically as a largely agricultural society changed to an industrial one. In Western Europe, the period of empire and colonialism began. The industrialized nations seized parts of Africa and Asia in an effort to control the raw materials the "mother country" needed to feed its industries and machines. Later developments included power based on electricity and internal combustion, replacing coal and steam.

During the eighteenth and especially the nineteenth centuries, **nationalism** – a belief in one's own nation or people – emerged as a powerful force in Europe and elsewhere in the world. Europeans began to think in terms of a nation of people who had similar beliefs, concerns, and needs. This was partly a reaction to a growing discontent with the autocratic governments of the day and also a general realization that there was more to life than the individual.

Nationalism precipitated several changes in government, most notably in France. It brought large groups of people together, as with the unifications of Germany and Italy. However, it failed to provide sufficient outlets for this sudden rise in national fervor. In the 1700s and 1800s, European powers and peoples began looking to Africa and Asia to find colonies – rich sources of goods, trade, and cheap labor. Africa, especially, suffered at the hands of European imperialists bent on expanding their reach outside the borders of Europe. Asia suffered colonial expansion, most notably in India and Southeast Asia.

Religion and philosophy saw great changes as well. Religious interpretation tended to swing like a pendulum between the liberal and the conservative. By the end of the twenty-first century, however, the struggle for meaning and identity had resulted in a generalized conservative trend. This tendency can be seen in most religions yet today. Religion and philosophy are, to be sure, the means of self-definition and the understanding of one's place in the universe. Recent conservative trends, however, have had a polarizing effect. Issues of the relationship of church and state have arisen and been resolved in most countries during this period. At the same time, there has been an increasing effort to understand the religious beliefs of others, either to create new ways to define one's religion over and against other religions, or as the basis of new attacks on the values and teachings of other religions. This struggle resulted in the philosophical movement known as existentialism, as seen in the writings of Soren Kierkegaard, Karl Jaspers, and Jean-Paul Sartre.

Learn more about:
Ancient civilizations
http://occawlonline.pearsoned.com/bookbind/pubbooks/stearns_awl/chapter2/objectives/deluxe-content.html
The Roman Empire
http://www.roman-empire.net/
The American and French Revolutions
http://www.theadvocates.org/freeman/8908pete.html
The Industrial Revolution
http://www.theadvocates.org/freeman/8908pete.html

COMPETENCY 13.0   UNDERSTAND BASIC GEOGRAPHIC CONCEPTS, PHENOMENA, AND PROCESSES, AND THE MAJOR GEOGRAPHIC FEATURES AND REGIONS OF THE UNITED STATES AND THE WORLD

Skill 13.1   Basic concepts of geography (e.g., location, place, movement)

GEOGRAPHY involves studying location and how living things and earth's features are distributed throughout the earth. It includes where animals, people, and plants live and the effects of their relationship with earth's physical features. Geographers explore the locations of earth's features, how they got there, and why it is so important.

What geographers study can be broken down into four areas:

Location: Being able to find the exact site of anything on the earth
Spatial relations: The relationships of earth's features, places, and groups of people with one another due to their location
Regional characteristics: Characteristics of a place, such as landform and climate, types of plants and animals, kinds of people who live there, and how they use the land
Forces that change the earth: Such as human activities and natural forces

Plate tectonics, is a geological theory that explains **continental drift**, the large movements of the solid portions of the Earth's crust floating on the molten mantle. There are 10 major tectonic plates, with several smaller plates. The surface of the earth can be drastically affected at the boundaries of these plates.

There are three types of plate boundaries: convergent, divergent, and transform. Convergent boundaries are where plates are moving toward one another. When this happens, the two plates collide and fold up against one another in what is called **continental collision**. In **subduction**, one plate slides under the other. Continental collision can create high mountain ranges, such as the Andes and Himalayas. Subduction often results in volcanic activity along the boundary, as in the "Ring of Fire" along the northern coasts of the Pacific Ocean.

Divergent boundaries occur where plates are moving away from one another, creating **rifts** in the surface. The Mid-Atlantic Ridge on the floor of the Atlantic Ocean, and the Great Rift Valley in east Africa are examples of rifts at divergent plate boundaries. Transform boundaries are where plates are moving in opposite directions along their boundary, grinding against one another. The tremendous pressures that build along these types of boundaries often lead to earthquake activity when this pressure is released. The San Andreas Fault along the West Coast of North America is an example of a transform boundary.

Erosion is the displacement of solid earth surfaces such as rock and soil. Erosion is often a result of wind, water or ice acting on surfaces with loose particles, such as sand, loose soils, or decomposing rock. Gravity can also cause erosion on loose surfaces. Factors such as slope, soil and rock composition, plant cover, and human activity all affect erosion.

Weathering is the natural decomposition of the earth's surface from contact with the atmosphere. It is not the same as erosion, but can be a factor in erosion. Heat, water, ice and pressure are all factors that can lead to weathering. Chemicals in the atmosphere can also contribute to weathering

Transportation is the movement of eroded material from one place to another by wind, water or ice. Examples of transportation include pebbles rolling down a streambed and boulders being carried by moving glaciers.

Deposition is the result of transportation, and occurs when the material being carried settles on the surface and is deposited. Sand dunes and moraines are formed by transportation and deposition of glacial material.

Skill 13.2 The use of globes, maps and other resources to access geographic information

We use **illustrations** of various sorts because it is often easier to demonstrate a given idea visually instead of orally. Sometimes it is even easier to do so with an illustration than a description. This is especially true in the areas of education and research because humans are visually stimulated. Among the more common illustrations used in political and social sciences are various types of **maps, graphs and charts**.

Although maps have advantages over globes and photographs, they do have a disadvantage that must be considered. Maps are flat and the earth is a sphere. When displayed on a map, the earth's features might appear stretched in some way. This stretching is called **distortion**. Distortion does not mean that maps are wrong; it simply means that they are not perfect representations of the earth or its parts. **Cartographers,** or mapmakers, try to design maps so that there is as little distortion as possible.

The process of putting the features of the earth onto a flat surface is called **projection**. All maps are really map projections. There are many different types. Each one deals in a different way with the problem of distortion. Map projections are made in a number of ways, and some use complicated mathematics.

The three most common map projections are:

(1) **Cylindrical Projections** - These are done by taking a cylinder of paper and wrapping it around a globe. A light is used to project the globe's features onto

the paper. Distortion is least where the paper touches the globe. For example, suppose that the paper was wrapped so that it touched the globe at the equator, the map from this projection would have just a little distortion near the equator. However, in moving north or south of the equator, the distortion would increase. The best known and most widely used cylindrical projection is the **Mercator Projection.** Gerard's Mercator, a Flemish mapmaker, first developed it in 1569.

(2) **Conical Projections** - The name for these maps comes from the fact that the projection is made onto a cone of paper. The cone is made so that it touches a globe at the base of the cone only. It can also be made so that it cuts through part of the globe in two different places. Again, there is the least distortion where the paper touches the globe. If the cone touches at two different points, there is some distortion at both of them. Conical projections are most often used to map areas in the **middle latitudes**. Maps of the United States are most often conical projections. This is because most of the country lies within these latitudes.

(3) **Flat-Plane Projections** - These are made with a flat piece of paper. It touches the globe at one point only. Areas near this point show little distortion. Flat-plane projections are often used to show the areas of the north and south poles. One such flat projection is called a **Gnomonic Projection**. On this kind of map, all meridians appear as straight lines. Gnomonic projections are useful because any straight line drawn between points on it forms a **Great-Circle Route**.

Great-Circle Routes can best be described by thinking of a globe, where the shortest route between two points can be found by simply stretching a string from one point to the other. If the string was extended in reality, so that it took into effect the globe's curvature, it would ascribe a great-circle. A great-circle is any circle that cuts a sphere, such as the globe, into two equal parts. Because of distortion, most maps do not show great-circle routes as straight lines. Gnomonic projections, however, do show the shortest distance between the two places as a straight line; that is why they are valuable for navigation. They are called **Great-Circle Sailing Maps.**

Libraries of all sorts are valuable when conducting research. Almost all have digitized search systems to assist in finding information on almost any subject. The **Internet** and **World Wide Web** make satellite imagery of nearly every point on the planet available to the public.

Conducting a research project once involved the use of punch cards, microfiche, and other manual means of storing the data in a retrievable fashion. Now, high-powered computers have made it easy for researchers to organize and retrieve information. Creating multilevel folders, copying and pasting into the folders, making ongoing additions to the bibliography as new sources are consulted, and using search-and-find functions make this stage of the research process faster and more productive. Serious research requires high-level analytical skills when it comes to processing and interpreting data. A degree in statistics or at least a graduate-level concentration is very useful. However, a team approach to a research project will often include a statistician in addition to members who are knowledgeable in the social sciences.

Skill 13.3   Global features (e.g., continents, hemispheres, latitude and longitude, poles)

Physical locations of the earth's surface features include the four major hemispheres and the parts of the earth's continents in them. Political locations are the political divisions within each continent. Both physical and political locations are precisely determined in two ways: (1) Surveying is done to determine boundary lines and distance from other features. (2) Exact locations are precisely determined by imaginary lines of latitude (parallels) and longitude (meridians). The intersection of these lines at right angles forms a grid, making it possible to pinpoint an exact location of any place using two grid coordinates.

The **Eastern Hemisphere**, located between the North and South Poles and between the Prime Meridian (0 degrees longitude) east to 180 degrees longitude, consists of most of Europe, all of Australia, most of Africa, and all of Asia, except for a tiny piece of the easternmost part of Russia that extends east of 180 degrees longitude.

The Western Hemisphere, located between the North and South Poles and between the Prime Meridian (0 degrees longitude) west to 180 degrees longitude, consists of all of North and South America, a tiny part of the easternmost part of Russia that extends east of 180 degrees longitude, and a part of Europe that extends west of the Prime Meridian (0 degrees longitude).

The **Northern Hemisphere**, located between the North Pole and the Equator, contains all of the continents of Europe and North America and parts of South America, Africa, and most of Asia.

The **Southern Hemisphere**, located between the South Pole and the Equator, contains all of Australia, a small part of Asia, about one-third of Africa, most of South America, and all of Antarctica.

The earth is divided into 24 wedge-shaped sections called **lunes** that are bordered by meridians 15° of longitude apart. Each lune represents a **time zone**. Each time zone is one hour apart. Greenwich Mean Time is located at the 0° longitude and is used as a point of reference for Coordinated Universal Time (UTC).

The earth's surface is made up of 70% water and 30% land. Physical features of the land surface include mountains, hills, plateaus, valleys, and plains. Other minor landforms include deserts, deltas, canyons, mesas, basins, foothills, marshes and swamps. Earth's water features include oceans, seas, lakes, rivers, and canals.

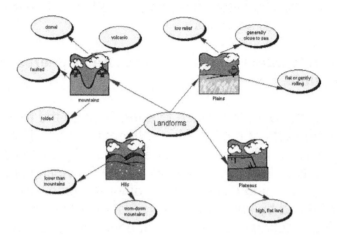

Mountains are landforms with steep slopes at least 2,000 feet or more above sea level. They are found in groups called mountain chains or mountain ranges. At least one range can be found on six of the earth's seven continents. North America has the Appalachian and Rocky Mountains; South America the Andes; Asia the Himalayas; Australia the Great Dividing Range; Europe the Alps; and Africa the Atlas, Ahaggar, and Drakensburg mountains. Mountains are commonly formed by volcanic activity, or when land is thrust upward where two tectonic plates collide.

Hills are elevated landforms rising to an elevation of about 500 to 2000 feet. They are found everywhere on earth, including Antarctica where they are covered by ice.

Plateaus are elevated landforms usually level on top. Depending on location, they range from being very cold to cool and healthful. Some plateaus are dry because they are surrounded by mountains that keep out any moisture. Some examples include the Kenya Plateau in East Africa, which is very cool. The plateau extending north from the Himalayas is extremely dry while those in Antarctica and Greenland are covered with ice and snow. Plateaus can be formed by underground volcanic activity, erosion, or colliding tectonic plates.

Plains are areas of flat or slightly rolling land, usually lower than the landforms next to them. Sometimes called lowlands (and sometimes located along **seacoasts)**, they support the majority of the world's people. Some are found inland. Many have been formed by large rivers, resulting in extremely fertile soil for successful cultivation of crops and numerous large settlements of people. In North America, the vast plains areas extend from the Gulf of Mexico north to the Arctic Ocean and between the Appalachian and Rocky Mountains. In Europe, rich plains extend east from Great Britain into central Europe on into the Siberian region of Russia. Plains in river valleys are found in China (the Yangtze River valley), India (the Ganges River valley), and Southeast Asia (the Mekong River valley).

Valleys are land areas that are found between hills and mountains. Some have gentle slopes containing trees and plants; others have very steep walls and are referred to as canyons. One notable example is Arizona's Grand Canyon of the Colorado River, which was formed by erosion.

Deserts are large dry areas of land receiving ten inches or less of rainfall each year. Among the larger deserts of the world are Africa's Sahara Desert, the Arabian Desert on the Arabian Peninsula, and the desert Outback that covers roughly one third of Australia. Deserts are found mainly in the tropical latitudes, and are formed when surrounding features such as mountain ranges extract most of the moisture from the prevailing winds.

Deltas are areas of lowlands formed by soil and sediment deposited at the mouths of rivers. The soil is generally very fertile, and most fertile river deltas are important crop-growing areas. One example is the delta of Egypt's Nile River, known for its production of cotton.

Mesas are the flat tops of hills or mountains – usually with steep sides. Mesas are similar to plateaus, but smaller.

Basins are considered to be low areas drained by rivers, or low spots in mountains.

Foothills are generally considered a low series of hills found between a plain and a mountain range.

Marshes and swamps are wet lowlands providing growth of such plants as rushes and reeds.

Oceans are the largest bodies of water on the planet. The four oceans of the earth are the **Atlantic Ocean**, one-half the size of the Pacific and separating North and South America from Africa and Europe; the **Pacific Ocean**, covering almost one-third of the entire surface of the earth and separating North and South America from Asia and Australia; the **Indian Ocean**, touching Africa, Asia, and Australia; and the ice-filled **Arctic Ocean,** extending from North America and Europe to the North Pole. The waters of the Atlantic, Pacific, and Indian Oceans also touch the shores of Antarctica.

Seas are smaller than oceans and are surrounded by land. Some examples include the Mediterranean Sea found between Europe, Asia, and Africa; and the Caribbean Sea, touching the West Indies, South and Central America. A **lake** is a body of water surrounded by land. The Great Lakes in North America are a good example.

Rivers, considered a nation's lifeblood, usually begin as very small streams, formed by melting snow and rainfall, flowing from higher to lower land, emptying into a larger body of water, usually a sea or an ocean. Examples of important rivers of the world include the Nile, Niger, and Zaire Rivers of Africa; the Rhine, Danube, and Thames Rivers of Europe; the Yangtze, Ganges, Mekong, Hwang He, and Irrawaddy Rivers of Asia; the Murray-Darling in Australia; and the Orinoco in South America. River systems are made up of large rivers and numerous smaller rivers or tributaries flowing into them. Examples include the vast Amazon River system in South America and the Mississippi River system in the United States.

Canals are man-made water passages constructed to connect two larger bodies of water. Famous examples include the **Panama Canal** across Panama's isthmus, connecting the Atlantic and Pacific Oceans, and the **Suez Canal** in the Middle East between Africa and the Arabian peninsulas, connecting the Red and Mediterranean Seas.

Skill 13.4   Major physical features and regions of Massachusetts, the United States and world areas

Massachusetts can be divided into six major geographic regions, each running north and south in bands.

The Taconic Mountains are a narrow group of hills that run along the western border of the state. To their east and running parallel to them is the Berkshire Valley, a 10-mile-wide strip of meadow lands. Between the Berkshire Valley and the Connecticut River is the Western New England Upland, which is where the Berkshire Hills are located. Mount Greylock, Massachusetts' highest point at 3,487 feet, is also located in this region. Bordering the western uplands on the east is the Connecticut Valley Lowland, a narrow region running north and south along the Connecticut River. Rich farmland is found along this valley.

The land rises again to the east of the Connecticut River, forming the Eastern New England Upland, then falls gradually into the Coastal Lowland. The Coastal Lowland is the largest single geographic region of the state and extends from 40-60 miles inland to the Atlantic Ocean.

The Massachusetts coast forms three major ocean areas. Massachusetts Bay is in the northern part of the state. The Charles River flows into the bay at Boston Harbor. South of Massachusetts Bay is Cape Cod, a long, curving hook of land that juts out into the Atlantic. Cape Cod Bay is enclosed within it. South of the cape is Nantucket Sound, formed by the southern coast of the cape and the islands of Nantucket and Martha's Vineyard.

The continental United States is bordered by the Pacific Ocean on the west and the Atlantic Ocean on the east. The country is divided into two main sections by the Rocky Mountains, which extend from New Mexico in the south through the Canadian border on the north. The western portion of the country contains forested, mountainous areas in the Pacific Northwest and Northern California, including Mt. St. Helens, an active volcano in the Cascade Range. Dryer, warmer regions in the south include the Mojave Desert in the Southwest. The Great Salt Lake is located in Utah, at the foot of the Wasatch Mountains, an extension of the Rockies.

The Rocky Mountains slope down in the east to the Great Plains, a large, grassy region drained by the Mississippi River, the nation's largest river, and one of the largest rivers in the world. The Great Plains gives way to hilly, forested regions in the east. The Appalachian Mountain chain runs along the eastern coast of the U.S. Along the border with Canada between Minnesota and New York are Lake Huron, Lake Ontario, Lake Michigan, Lake Erie and Lake Superior, known as the Great Lakes.

Alaska is located in northwestern North America and contains Mt. McKinley, also called Denali, which is the highest mountain on the continent. Hawaii is a series of volcanic islands in the South Pacific.

Of the seven continents, only one contains just one entire country and is the only island continent, Australia. Its political divisions consist of six states and one territory: Western Australia, South Australia, Tasmania, Victoria, New South Wales, Queensland, and Northern Territory.

Africa is made up of 54 separate countries, the major ones being Egypt, Nigeria, South Africa, Zaire, Kenya, Algeria, Morocco, and the large island of Madagascar.

Asia consists of 49 separate countries, including China, Japan, India, Turkey, Israel, Iraq, Iran, Indonesia, Jordan, Vietnam, Thailand, and the Philippines.

Europe's 43 separate nations include France, Russia, Malta, Denmark, Hungary, Greece, Bosnia and Herzegovina.

North America consists of Canada and the United States of America and the island nations of the West Indies and the "land bridge" of Middle America, including Cuba, Jamaica, Mexico, Panama, and others.

Thirteen separate nations together occupy the continent of South America, among them Brazil, Paraguay, Ecuador, and Suriname.

The continent of Antarctica has no political boundaries or divisions but is the location of a number of science and research stations managed by nations such as Russia, Japan, France, Australia, and India.

Skill 13.5   The relationship between geographic factors (e.g., climate, topography) and historical and current developments (e.g., human migrations, patterns of settlement, economic growth and decline)

Landforms are categorized by characteristics such as elevation, slope, orientation, stratification, rock exposure, and soil type. Landforms include berms, mounds, hills, cliffs, valleys, and others. Oceans and continents exemplify highest-order landforms. Landform elements are parts of a landform that can be further identified. The generic landform elements are pits, peaks, channels, ridges, passes, pools, planes etc., and can be often extracted from a digital elevation model using some automated or semi-automated techniques.

Elementary landforms (segments, facets, relief units) are the smallest homogeneous divisions of the land surface, at the given scale/resolution. A plateau or a hill can be observed at various scales, ranging from few hundred meters to hundreds of kilometers. Hence, the spatial distribution of landforms is often fuzzy and scale-dependent as is the case for soils and geological strata.

A number of factors, ranging from plate tectonics to erosion and deposition, can generate and affect landforms. Biological factors can also influence landforms – see for example, the role of plants in the development of dune systems and salt marshes, and the work of corals and algae in the formation of coral reefs.

Weather is the condition of the air at a particular place and time. When we speak of weather conditions, we might be referring to the temperature, air pressure, wind, moisture in the air, or precipitation (rain, snow, hail, or sleet).

Climate is average weather or daily weather conditions for a specific region or location over an extended period of time. Studying the climate of an area includes information gathered on the area's monthly and yearly temperatures and its monthly and yearly amounts of precipitation. The length of its growing season is another characteristic of an area's climate

In northern and central United States, northern China, south central and southeastern Canada, and the western and southeastern parts of the former Soviet Union is found the "climate of four seasons," the humid **continental climate** – spring, summer, fall, and winter. Cold winters, hot summers, and enough rainfall to grow a variety of crops are the major characteristics of this climate. In areas where the humid continental climate is found are some of the world's best farmlands as well as important activities such as trading and mining. Differences in temperatures throughout the year are determined by the distance a place is inland, away from the coasts.

The **steppe or prairie climate** is located in the interiors of the large continents like Asia and North America. These dry flatlands are far from ocean breezes and are called prairies or the Great Plains in Canada and the United States and steppes in Asia. Although the summers are hot and the winters are cold, the big difference is rainfall. In the steppe climate, rainfall is light and uncertain, 10 to 20 inches a year. Where rain is more plentiful, grass grows; in areas of less, the steppes or prairies gradually become deserts. These are found in the Gobi Desert of Asia, central and western Australia, southwestern United States, and in the smaller deserts found in Pakistan, Argentina, and Africa south of the Equator.

The two major climates found in the high latitudes are **tundra** and **taiga**. Tundra or marshy plain is a Russian word and aptly describes the climatic conditions in the northern areas of Russia, Europe, and Canada. Winters are extremely cold and very long. Surprisingly, less snow falls in the tundra area than in the eastern United States. However, due to the extreme cold, few people live there and no crops can be raised.

The taiga is the northern forest region and is located south of the tundra. The world's largest forestlands are found here along with vast mineral wealth and fur-bearing animals. Very few people live here because of an extremely short growing season in which to raise crops. The winter temperatures are colder and the summer temperatures are hotter than those in the tundra because the taiga climate region is farther from the waters of the Arctic Ocean. The taiga is found in the northern parts of Russia, Sweden, Norway, Finland, Canada, and Alaska with most of their lands covered with marshes and swamps.

The humid **subtropical climate** is found north and south of the tropics and is very moist. The areas with this type of climate are on the eastern side of continents and include Japan, Mainland China, Australia, Africa, South America, and the United States, where warm ocean currents are found. The winds that blow across these currents bring in warm moist air all year round. Long, warm summers; short, mild winters; and a long growing season allow for different crops to be grown several times a year. All contribute to the productivity of this climate type, which supports more people than any of the other climates.

The **marine climate** is found in Western Europe, the British Isles, the U.S. Pacific Northwest, the western coast of Canada and southern Chile, southern New Zealand, and southeastern Australia. A common characteristic of these lands is that they are either near water or surrounded by it. The ocean winds are wet and warm, bringing a mild rainy climate to these areas. In the summer, the daily temperatures average at or below 70 degrees F. During the winter, because of the warming effect of the ocean waters, the temperatures rarely fall below freezing.

In certain areas of the earth there exists a type of climate unique to areas with high mountains, usually different from their surroundings. This type of climate is called a "vertical climate" because the temperatures, crops, vegetation, and human activities change as one ascends the different levels of elevation. At the foot of the mountain, a hot and rainy climate is found with the cultivation of many lowland crops. As one climbs higher, the air becomes cooler, the climate changes sharply, and different economic activities (such as grazing sheep and growing corn) change too. At the top of many mountains, snow is found all year.

Populations change over time due to many factors, and these changes can have significant impact on cultures. When a population grows in size, it becomes necessary for it to either expand its geographic boundaries to make room for new people or to increase its density. Population density is simply the number of people in a population divided by the geographic area in which they live. Cultures with a high population density are likely to have different ways of interacting with one another than those with low density, as people in the former type of culture live in closer proximity to one another.

As a population grows, its **economic** needs change. More basic needs are required, and more workers are needed to produce them. If a population's production or purchasing power does not keep pace with its growth, its economy can be adversely affected. The age distribution of a population can affect the economy as well, if the number of young and old people who are not working is disproportionate to those who are employed.

Growth in some areas may spur migration to other parts of a population's geographic region that are less densely populated. This redistribution of population also places demands on the economy, as infrastructure is needed to connect these new areas to older population centers, and land is put to new use.

Populations can grow naturally, when the rate of birth is higher than the rate of death, or by adding new people from other populations through **immigration**. Immigration is often a source of societal change as people from other cultures bring their institutions and languages to a new area. Immigration also affects a population's educational and economic institutions as immigrants enter the workforce and place their children in schools.

Populations can also decline when the death rate exceeds the birth rate or when people migrate to another area. War, famine, disease and natural disasters can reduce population, causing various economic problems. In extreme cases, a population may decline to the point where it can no longer perpetuate itself and its members and their culture disappear or are absorbed into another population.

Social creatures by nature, people generally live in communities or settlements of some kind. **Settlements** are the cradles of culture, political structure, education, and resource management. The relative placement of these settlements is shaped by proximity to natural resources, movement of raw materials, production of finished products, availability of a workforce, and delivery of finished products. The composition of communities is largely determined by shared values, language, culture, religion, and subsistence.

Settlements begin in areas that offer the natural resources to support life – food and water. With the ability to manage the environment, one finds a concentration of populations. With the ability to transport raw materials and finished products comes mobility. With increasing technology and the rise of industrial centers comes a migration of the workforce.

Cities are the major hubs of human settlement. Almost half of the population of the world now lives in cities. The fastest growth, however, is occurring in developing areas. In some regions there are "metropolitan areas" made up of urban and suburban areas. In some places, cities and urban areas are interconnected into "megalopoli" (e.g., Tokyo-Kawasaki-Yokohama).

The concentrations of populations and the divisions of these areas among various groups that constitute the cities can differ significantly. North American cities are different from European cities in shape, size, population density, and modes of transportation. While in North America the wealthiest economic groups tend to live outside the cities, the opposite is true in Latin American cities.

There are significant differences among the cities of the world in terms of connectedness to other cities. While European and North American cities tend to be well linked both by transportation and communication connections, there are other places in the world in which communication between the cities of the country may be inferior to communication with the rest of the world.

Rural areas tend to be less densely populated due to the needs of agriculture. More land is needed to produce crops or for animal husbandry than for manufacturing. Yet, rural areas too must be connected via communication and transportation in order to provide food and raw materials to urban areas.

Learn more about:
Plate tectonics
http://www.platetectonics.com/
Landforms
http://www.edu.pe.ca/southernkings/landforms.htm

DOMAIN IV. SCIENCE AND TECHNOLOGY/ENGINEERING

COMPETENCY 14.0 UNDERSTAND AND APPLY BASIC CONCEPTS AND PRINCIPLES OF LIFE SCIENCE TO INTERPRET AND ANALYZE PHENOMENA

Skill 14.1 Basic characteristics and needs of living things

The organization of living systems builds by levels from small to increasingly larger and complex. All aspects, whether it is a cell or an ecosystem, have the same requirements to sustain life. Life is organized from simple to complex in the following way:

Organelles make up **cells** that make up **tissues** that make up **organs**. Groups of organs make up **organ systems**. Organ systems work together to provide life for the **organism.**

Several characteristics, such as the following, have been described to identify living versus non-living substances:

*   **Living things are made of cells**; they grow, are capable of reproduction and respond to stimuli.
*   **Living things must adapt to environmental changes or perish**.
*   **Living things carry on metabolic processes**. They use and make energy.

All organic life has a common element: carbon. Carbon is recycled through the ecosystem through both biotic and abiotic means. It is the link between biological processes and the chemical makeup of life.

Skill 14.2 Basic concepts and processes related to cells and organisms

Parts of Eukaryotic Cells

1. Nucleus - The brain of the cell. The nucleus contains:

*   **chromosomes**- DNA, RNA and proteins tightly coiled to conserve space while providing a large surface area.
*   **chromatin** - loose structure of chromosomes. Chromosomes are called chromatin when the cell is not dividing.
*   **nucleoli** - where ribosomes are made. These are seen as dark spots in the nucleus.
*   **nuclear membrane** - contains pores that let RNA out of the nucleus. The nuclear membrane is continuous with the endoplasmic reticulum, which allows the membrane to expand or shrink if needed.

2. Ribosomes - the site of protein synthesis. Ribosomes may be free floating in the cytoplasm or attached to the endoplasmic reticulum. There may be up to a half a million ribosomes in a cell, depending on how much protein is made by the cell.

3. Endoplasmic Reticulum - these are folded and provide a large surface area. They are the "roadway" of the cell and allow for transport of materials. The lumen of the endoplasmic reticulum helps to keep materials out of the cytoplasm and headed in the right direction. The endoplasmic reticulum is capable of building new membrane material. There are two types:

- **Smooth Endoplasmic Reticulum** - contains no ribosomes on its surface.
- **Rough Endoplasmic Reticulum** - contains ribosomes on its surface. This form of ER is abundant in cells that make many proteins, like in the pancreas, which produces many digestive enzymes.

4. Golgi Complex or Golgi Apparatus - This structure is stacked to increase surface area. The Golgi Complex functions to sort, modify and package molecules that are made in other parts of the cell. These molecules are either sent out of the cell or to other organelles within the cell.

5. Lysosomes - found mainly in animal cells. These contain digestive enzymes that break down food, substances not needed, viruses, damaged cell components, and eventually the cell itself. It is believed that lysosomes are responsible for the aging process.

6. Mitochondria - large organelles that make adenosine triphosphate (ATP) to supply energy to the cell. Muscle cells have many mitochondria because they use a great deal of energy. The folds inside the mitochondria are called cristae. They provide a large surface where the reactions of cellular respiration occur. Mitochondria have their own DNA and are capable of reproducing themselves if a greater demand is made for additional energy. Mitochondria are found only in animal cells.

7. Plastids - found in photosynthetic organisms only. They are similar to the mitochondria due to their double membrane structure. They also have their own DNA and can reproduce if increased capture of sunlight becomes necessary. There are several types of plastids:

- **Chloroplasts** - green; function in photosynthesis. They are capable of trapping sunlight.
- **Chromoplasts** - make and store yellow and orange pigments; they provide color to leaves, flowers and fruits.
- **Amyloplasts** - store starch and are used as a food reserve. They are abundant in roots like potatoes.

8. Cell Wall - found in plant cells only, it is composed of cellulose and fibers. It is thick enough for support and protection, yet porous enough to allow water and dissolved substances to enter. Cell walls are cemented to each other.

9. Vacuoles - hold stored food and pigments. Vacuoles are very large in plants. This allows them to fill with water to provide turgor pressure. Lack of turgor pressure causes a plant to wilt.

10. Cytoskeleton - composed of protein filaments attached to the plasma membrane and organelles. It provides a framework for the cell and aids in cell movement. It constantly changes shape and moves about. The cytoskeleton is made up of three types of fibers:

- **Microtubules** - largest of the three; makes up cilia and flagella for locomotion. Flagella grow from a basal body. Some examples are sperm cells and tracheal cilia. Centrioles are also composed of microtubules. They form the spindle fibers that pull the cell apart into two cells during cell division. Centrioles are not found in the cells of higher plants.
- **Intermediate Filaments** - they are smaller than microtubules but larger than microfilaments. They help the cell to keep its shape.
- **Microfilaments** - smallest of the three, they are made of actin and small amounts of myosin (like in muscle cells). They function in cell movement such as cytoplasmic streaming, endocytosis, and ameboid movement. This structure pinches the two cells apart after cell division, forming two cells.

Skill 14.3   Plant structures, functions, and processes (e.g., photosynthesis)

Plant Tissues - specialization of tissues enables plants to grow larger. Be familiar with the following tissues and their functions:

Xylem - transports water.

Phloem - transports food (glucose).

Cortex - storage of food and water.

Epidermis – protective covering.

Endodermis - controls movement between the cortex and the cell interior.

Pericycle - meristematic tissue that can divide when necessary.

Pith - storage in stems.

Sclerenchyma and collenchyma - support in stems.

Stomata - openings on the underside of leaves. They let carbon dioxide in and water out (transpiration).

Guard cells - control the size of the stomata. If the plant has to conserve water, the stomata will close.

Palisade mesophyll - contain chloroplasts in leaves. Site of photosynthesis.

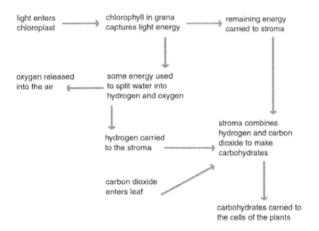

Spongy mesophyll - open spaces in the leaf that allows for gas circulation.

Seed coat - protective covering on a seed.

Cotyledon - small seed leaf that emerges when the seed germinates.

Endosperm - food supply in the seed.

Apical meristem - this is an area of cell division allowing for growth.

Flowers – these are the reproductive organs of the plant. Know the following functions and locations:

Pedicel - supports the weight of the flower.

Receptacle - holds the floral organs at the base of the flower.

Sepals - green leaf- like parts that cover the flower prior to blooming.

Petals - contain coloration by pigments; purpose is to attract insects to assist in pollination.

Anther - male part that produces pollen.

Filament - supports the anther; the filament and anther make up the **stamen**.

Stigma - female part that holds pollen grains that came from the male part.

Style - tube that leads to the ovary (female).

Ovary - contains the ovules; the stigma, style and ovary make up the **carpel**.

Skill 14.4   The systems of the human body

Skeletal System: The skeletal system functions to support the body. Vertebrates have an endoskeleton, with muscles attached to bones. Skeletal proportions are controlled by area-to-volume relationships. Body size and shape are limited due to the forces of gravity. Surface area is increased to improve efficiency in all organ systems.

The **axial skeleton** consists of the bones of the skull and vertebrae. The **appendicular skeleton** consists of the bones of the legs, arms, and shoulder girdle. Bone is a connective tissue. Parts of the bone include the compact bone, which gives strength; spongy bone, which contains red marrow to make blood cells; yellow marrow in the center of long bones to store fat cells; and the periosteum or the protective covering on the outside of the bone.

A **joint** is defined as a place where two bones meet. Joints enable movement. **Ligaments** attach bone to bone. **Tendons** attach bones to muscles.

Muscular System: This is responsible for functions of movement. There are three types of muscle tissue. Skeletal muscle is voluntary. It is attached to bones. Smooth muscle, which is involuntary, is found in organs and enables functions such as digestion and respiration. Cardiac muscle is a specialized type of smooth muscle and is found in the heart. Muscles can only contract; therefore they work in antagonistic pairs to allow back-and-forward movement. Muscle fibers are made of groups of myofibrils, which are made of groups of sarcomeres. Actin and myosin are proteins making up the sarcomere.

Physiology of muscle contraction: A nerve impulse strikes a muscle fiber. This causes calcium ions to flood the sarcomere. Calcium ions allow ATP to expend energy. The myosin fibers creep along the actin, causing the muscle to contract. Once the nerve impulse has passed, calcium is pumped out and the contraction ends.

Nervous System: The neuron is the basic unit of the nervous system. It consists of an axon, which carries impulses away from the cell body; the dendrite, which carries impulses toward the cell body; and the cell body, which contains the nucleus. Synapses are spaces between neurons. Chemicals called neurotransmitters are found close to the synapse. The myelin sheath, composed of Schwann cells, covers the neurons and provides insulation.

Physiology of the nerve impulse: Nerve action depends on depolarization and an imbalance of electrical charges across the neuron. A polarized nerve has a positive charge outside the neuron. A depolarized nerve has a negative charge outside the neuron. Neurotransmitters turn off the sodium pump, which results in depolarization of the membrane. This wave of depolarization (as it moves from neuron to neuron) carries an electrical impulse. This is actually a wave of opening and closing gates that allows for the flow of ions across the synapse. Nerves have an action potential. There is a threshold of the level of chemicals that must be met or exceeded for muscles to respond. This is called the "all or none" response.

The **reflex arc** is the simplest nerve response in which the brain is bypassed. When a stimulus (like touching a hot stove) occurs, sensors in the hand send the message directly to the spinal cord. This stimulates motor neurons that contract the muscles to move the hand.

Voluntary nerve responses involve the brain. Receptor cells send the message to sensory neurons that lead to association neurons. The message is taken to the brain. Motor neurons are stimulated and the message is transmitted to effector cells that cause the end effect.

Organization of the Nervous System: The somatic nervous system is controlled consciously. It consists of the central nervous system (brain and spinal cord) and the peripheral nervous system (nerves that extend from the spinal cord to the muscles). The autonomic nervous system is unconsciously controlled by the hypothalamus of the brain. Smooth muscles, the heart and digestion are some processes controlled by the autonomic nervous system. The sympathetic nervous system works opposite of the parasympathetic nervous system. For example, if the sympathetic nervous system stimulates an action, the parasympathetic nervous system would end that action.

Neurotransmitters: These are chemicals released by exocytosis. Some neurotransmitters stimulate, while others inhibit, action.

Acetylcholine: The most common neurotransmitter; it controls muscle contraction and heartbeat. The enzyme acetylcholinesterase breaks it down to end the transmission.

Epinephrine: –This is responsible for the "fight or flight" reaction. It causes an increase in heart rate and blood flow to prepare the body for action. It is also called adrenaline.

Endorphins and enkephalins: These are natural pain killers and are released during serious injury and childbirth.

Digestive System: The digestive system breaks food down and absorbs it into the blood stream where it can be delivered to all cells of the body for use in cellular respiration. The teeth and saliva begin digestion by breaking food down into smaller pieces and lubricating it so it can be swallowed. The lips, cheeks, and tongue form a bolus (ball) of food. It is carried down the pharynx by the process of peristalsis (wave-like contractions) and enters the stomach through the cardiac sphincter which closes to keep food from going back up. In the stomach, pepsinogen and hydrochloric acid form pepsin, the enzyme that breaks down proteins. The food is broken down further by this chemical action and is turned into chyme. The pyloric sphincter muscle opens to allow the food to enter the small intestine.

Most nutrient absorption occurs in the small intestine. Its large surface area, accompanied by its length and protrusions called villi and microvilli, allows for a great absorptive surface. Upon arrival into the small intestine, chyme is neutralized to allow the enzymes found there to function. Any food left after the trip through the small intestine enters the large intestine. The large intestine functions to reabsorb water and produce vitamin K. The feces, or remaining waste, are passed out through the anus.

Accessory organs: These produce necessary enzymes and bile. The pancreas makes many enzymes to break down food in the small intestine. The liver makes bile, which breaks down and emulsifies fatty acids.

Respiratory System: This functions in the gas exchange of oxygen (needed) and carbon dioxide (waste). It delivers oxygen to the bloodstream and releases carbon dioxide out of the body. Air enters the mouth and nose, where it is warmed, moistened and filtered of dust particles. Cilia in the trachea trap unwanted material in mucus, which can be expelled. The trachea splits into two bronchial tubes, which divide into smaller bronchioles in the lungs. The internal surface of the lung is composed of alveoli, thin-walled air sacs. These allow for a large surface area for gas exchange. The alveoli are lined with capillaries. Oxygen diffuses into the bloodstream and carbon dioxide diffuses out to be exhaled. The oxygenated blood is carried to the heart and delivered to all parts of the body.

The thoracic cavity holds the lungs. The diaphragm – a muscle below the lungs – makes inhalation possible. As the volume of the thoracic cavity increases, the diaphragm flattens for inhalation. When the diaphragm relaxes, exhalation occurs.

Circulatory System: The circulatory system carries oxygenated blood and nutrients to all cells of the body and returns carbon dioxide to be expelled from the lungs. Be familiar with the parts of the heart and the path blood takes from the heart to the lungs, through the body, and back to the heart. Unoxygenated blood enters the heart through the inferior and superior vena cava. The first chamber it encounters is the right atrium. It goes through the tricuspid valve to the right ventricle, on to the pulmonary arteries, and then to the lungs where it is oxygenated. It returns to the heart through the pulmonary vein into the left atrium. It travels through the bicuspid valve to the left ventricle where it is pumped to all parts of the body through the aorta.

Sinoatrial node (SA node): This is the pacemaker of the heart. Located on the right atrium, it is responsible for contraction of the right and left atrium.

Atrioventricular node (AV node): Located on the left ventricle, it is responsible for contraction of the ventricles.

Blood vessels include:
- **arteries** - lead away from the heart. All carry oxygenated blood, except the pulmonary artery going to the lungs. Arteries are under high pressure.
- **arterioles** - arteries branch off to form these smaller passages.
- **capillaries** - arterioles branch off to form tiny capillaries that reach every cell. Blood moves slowest here due to the small size; only one red blood cell may pass at a time to allow for diffusion of gases into and out of cells. Nutrients are also absorbed by the cells from the capillaries.
- **venules** - capillaries combine to form larger venules. The vessels carry waste products from the cells.
- **veins** - venules combine to form larger veins, leading back to the heart. Veins contain valves to prevent the backward flow of blood due to gravity.

Components of the blood include:
- **plasma** – 60% of the blood is plasma. It contains salts called electrolytes, nutrients, and waste. It is the liquid part of blood.
- **erythrocytes** - also called red blood cells; they contain hemoglobin which carries oxygen molecules.
- **leukocytes** - also called white blood cells. White blood cells are larger than red cells. They are phagocytic and can engulf invaders. White blood cells are not confined to the blood vessels and can enter the interstitial fluid between cells.
- **platelets** - assist in blood clotting. Platelets are made in the bone marrow.
- **Blood clotting** - the neurotransmitter that initiates blood vessel constriction following an injury is called serotonin. A material called prothrombin is converted to thrombin with the help of thromboplastin. The thrombin is then used to convert fibrinogen to fibrin, which traps red blood cells to form a scab and stop blood flow.

Lymphatic System (Immune System)

Nonspecific defense mechanisms – They do not target specific pathogens, but are a whole body response. Results of nonspecific mechanisms are seen as symptoms of an infection. These mechanisms include the skin, mucous membranes and cells of the blood and lymph (i.e.: white blood cells, macrophages). Fever is a result of an increase of white blood cells. Pyrogens are released by white blood cells, setting the body's thermostat to a higher temperature. This inhibits the growth of microorganisms. It also increases metabolism to increase phagocytosis and body repair.

Specific defense mechanisms - They recognize foreign material and respond by destroying the invader. These mechanisms are specific in purpose and diverse in type. They are able to recognize individual pathogens. They are able to differentiate between foreign material and self. Memory of the invaders provides immunity upon further exposure.

Antigen - any foreign particle that invades the body.

Antibody - manufactured by the body, they recognize and latch onto antigens, hopefully destroying them.

Immunity - this is the body's ability to recognize and destroy an antigen before it causes harm. Active immunity develops after recovery from an infectious disease (chicken pox) or after a vaccination (mumps, measles, rubella). Passive immunity may be passed from one individual to another. It is not permanent. A good example is the immunities passed from mother to nursing child.

Excretory System- The function of the excretory system is to rid the body of nitrogenous wastes in the form of urea. The functional units of excretion are the nephrons, which make up the kidneys. Antidiuretic hormone (ADH), which is made in the hypothalamus and stored in the pituitary, is released when differences in osmotic balance occur. This will cause more water to be reabsorbed. As the blood becomes more dilute, ADH release ceases.

The Bowman's capsule contains the glomerulus, a tightly packed group of capillaries. The glomerulus is under high pressure. Waste and fluids leak out due to pressure. Filtration is not selective in this area. Selective secretion by active and passive transport occur in the proximal convoluted tubule. Unwanted molecules are secreted into the filtrate. Selective secretion also occurs in the loop of Henle. Salt is actively pumped out of the tube and much water is lost due to the hyperosmosity of the inner part (medulla) of the kidney. As the fluid enters the distal convoluted tubule, more water is reabsorbed. Urine forms in the collecting duct which leads to the ureter and then to the bladder where the urine is stored. Urine is passed from the bladder through the urethra. The amount of water reabsorbed back into the body depends on how much water or fluids an individual has consumed. Urine can be very dilute or very concentrated if dehydration is present.

Endocrine System- The function of the endocrine system is to manufacture proteins called hormones. Hormones are released into the bloodstream and are carried to a target tissue where they stimulate an action. Hormones may build up over time to cause their effect, as in puberty or the menstrual cycle.

Hormone activation - Hormones are specific and fit receptors on the target tissue cell surface. The receptor activates an enzyme which converts ATP to cyclic AMP. Cyclic AMP (cAMP) is a second messenger from the cell membrane to the nucleus. The genes found in the nucleus turn on or off to cause a specific response.

There are two classes of hormones. **Steroid hormones** come from cholesterol. They produce sexual characteristics and affect mating behavior. Hormones include estrogen and progesterone in females and testosterone in males. **Peptide hormones** are made in the pituitary, adrenal glands (kidneys), and the pancreas. They include the following:

- **Follicle stimulating hormone (FSH)** - production of sperm or egg cells
- **Luteinizing hormone (LH)** - functions in ovulation
- **Luteotropic hormone (LTH)** - assists in production of progesterone
- **Growth hormone (GH)** - stimulates growth
- **Antidiuretic hormone (ADH)** - assists in retention of water
- **Oxytocin** - stimulates labor contractions at birth and let-down of milk
- **Melatonin** - regulates circadian rhythms and seasonal changes
- **Epinephrine (adrenaline)** - causes fight-or-flight reaction of the nervous system
- **Thyroxin** - increases metabolic rate
- **Calcitonin** - removes calcium from the blood
- **Insulin** - decreases glucose level in blood
- **Glucagon** - increases glucose level in blood

Hormones work on a feedback system. The increase or decrease in one hormone may cause the increase or decrease in another. Release of hormones causes a specific response.

Reproductive System- Sexual reproduction greatly increases diversity due to the many combinations possible through meiosis and fertilization. Gametogenesis is the production of the sperm and egg cells. Spermatogenesis begins at puberty in the male. One spermatozoa produces four sperms. The sperm mature in the seminiferous tubules located in the testes. Oogenesis, the production of egg cells, is usually complete by the birth of a female. Egg cells are not released until menstruation begins at puberty. Meiosis forms one ovum with all the cytoplasm and three polar bodies, which are reabsorbed by the body. The ovum are stored in the ovaries and released each month from puberty to menopause.

Path of the sperm - sperm are stored in the seminiferous tubules in the testes where they mature. Mature sperm are found in the epididymis located on top of the testes. After ejaculation, the sperm travel up the vas deferens where they mix with semen made in the prostate and seminal vesicles and travel out the urethra.

Path of the egg - eggs are stored in the ovaries. Ovulation releases the egg into the fallopian tubes which are ciliated to move the egg along. Fertilization normally occurs in the fallopian tube. If pregnancy does not occur, the egg passes through the uterus and is expelled through the vagina during menstruation. Levels of progesterone and estrogen stimulate menstruation. In the event of pregnancy, hormonal levels are affected by the implantation of a fertilized egg, so menstruation does not occur.

Pregnancy - if fertilization occurs, the zygote implants in about two to three days in the uterus. Implantation promotes secretion of human chorionic gonadotropin (HCG). This is what is detected in pregnancy tests. The HCG keeps the level of progesterone elevated to maintain the uterine lining in order to feed the developing embryo until the umbilical cord forms. Labor is initiated by oxytocin which causes labor contractions and dilation of the cervix. Prolactin and oxytocin cause the production of milk.

Skill 14.5   Basic principles of genetics and heredity

Some definitions to know:

Dominant - the stronger of two traits. If a dominant gene is present, it will be expressed. Shown by a capital letter.
Recessive - the weaker of the traits. In order for the recessive gene to be expressed, there must be two recessive genes present. Shown by a lower case letter.
Homozygous - purebred; having two of the same genes present. An organism may be homozygous dominant with two dominant genes or homozygous recessive with two recessive genes.
Heterozygous - hybrid; having one dominant gene and one recessive gene. The dominant gene will be expressed due to the Law of Dominance.
Genotype - the genes the organism possesses. Genes are represented with letters. AA, Bb, and tt are examples of genotypes.
Phenotype - how a trait is expressed in an organism. Blue eyes, brown hair, and red flowers are examples of phenotypes.
Incomplete dominance - neither gene masks the other; a new phenotype is formed. For example, red flowers and white flowers may have equal strength. A

heterozygote (Rr) would have pink flowers. If a problem occurs with a third phenotype, incomplete dominance is occurring.

Codominance - genes may form new phenotypes. The ABO blood grouping is an example of co-dominance. A and B are of equal strength and O is recessive. Therefore, type A blood may have the genotypes of AA or AO, type B blood may have the genotypes of BB or BO, type AB blood has the genotype A and B, and type O blood has two recessive O genes.

Linkage - genes that are found on the same chromosome usually appear together unless crossing over has occurred in meiosis. (Example: blue eyes and blonde hair)

Lethal alleles - these are usually recessive due to the early death of the offspring. If a 2:1 ratio of alleles is found in offspring, a lethal gene combination is usually the reason. Some examples of lethal alleles include sickle cell anemia, tay-sachs and cystic fibrosis. Usually the coding for an important protein is affected.

Inborn errors of metabolism - these occur when the protein affected is an enzyme. Examples include PKU (phenylketonuria) and albinism.

Polygenic characters - many alleles code for a phenotype. There may be as many as twenty genes that code for skin color. This is why there is such a variety of skin tones. Another example is height. A couple of medium height may have a very tall offspring.

Sex-linked traits - the Y chromosome found only in males (XY) carries very little genetic information, whereas the X chromosome found in females (XX) carries very important information. Since men have no second X chromosome to cover up a recessive gene, the recessive trait is expressed more often in men. Women need the recessive gene on both X chromosomes to show the trait. Examples of sex linked traits include hemophilia and color-blindness.

Sex-influenced traits – these traits are influenced by the sex hormones. Male pattern baldness is an example of a sex-influenced trait. Testosterone influences the expression of the gene. Mostly men lose their hair due to this trait.

Skill 14.6   How organisms interact with one another and their environments

Relationships among organisms in a community

There are many interactions that may occur between different species living together. Predation, parasitism, competition, commensalism, and mutualism are the different types of relationships populations have amongst each other.

Predation and **parasitism** result in a benefit for one species and a detriment for the other. Predation is when a predator eats its prey. The common conception of predation is of a carnivore consuming other animals. This is one form of predation. Although not always resulting in the death of the plant, herbivory is a form of predation. Some animals eat enough of a plant to cause death. Parasitism involves a predator that lives on or in their hosts, causing detrimental effects to the host. Insects and viruses living off and reproducing in their hosts is an example of parasitism. Many plants and animals have defenses against predators. Some plants have poisonous chemicals that will harm the predator if ingested, and some animals are camouflaged so they are harder to detect.

Competition is when two or more species in a community use the same resources. It is usually detrimental to both populations. Competition is often difficult to find in nature because competition between two populations is not continuous. Either the weaker population will no longer exist, or one population will evolve to utilize other available resources.

Symbiosis is when two species live close together. Parasitism, as described earlier, is one example of symbiosis. Another example is commensalism. Commensalism occurs when one species benefits from the other without harmful effects. Mutualism is when both species benefit from each other. Species involved in mutualistic relationships must co-evolve to survive. As one species evolves, the other must as well if it is to be successful in life. The grouper and a species of shrimp live in a mutualistic relationship. The shrimp feed off parasites living on the grouper; thus the shrimp are fed and the grouper stays healthy. Many microorganisms are in mutualistic relationships.

Effects of population density on the environment
Population density is the number of individuals per unit area or volume. The spacing pattern of individuals in an area is dispersion. Dispersion patterns can be clumped, with individuals grouped in patches; uniformed, where individuals are approximately equidistant from each other; or random.

Population densities are usually estimated based on a few representative plots. Aggregation of a population in a relatively small geographic area can have detrimental effects on the environment. Food, water, and other resources will be rapidly consumed, resulting in an unstable environment. A low population density is less harmful to the environment. The use of natural resources will be more widespread, allowing for the environment to recover and continue growth.

Learn more about:
Basic cell structure
http://staff.jccc.net/pdecell/cells/basiccell.html
Plant structure and functions
http://www.uic.edu/classes/bios/bios100/summer2002/lect15.htm
Human body and anatomy
http://www.innerbody.com/htm/body.html

COMPETENCY 15.0   UNDERSTAND AND APPLY BASIC CONCEPTS AND PRINCIPLES OF PHYSICAL AND EARTH SCIENCES TO INTERPRET AND ANALYZE PHENOMENA

Skill 15.1   The composition and structure of matter (e.g., atoms, molecules)

Atomic theory basically states that atoms are the basic, smallest building units of matter. The nucleus of the atom is very small in relationship to the atom, and much of the atom is actually empty space. Atoms, in turn, are made up of **protons, neutrons and electrons**. The proton is the positively charged component of the atom. The neutron has a zero or no charge. Electrons, which circle the nucleus, carry a negative charge. If you break an atom into its smaller parts, you lose the property of the element.

Atoms differ depending upon the elemental form they make. The simplest atom is hydrogen, which has one proton and one electron that are attracted to each other due to an electrical charge. The spinning force of the electron keeps the electron from crashing into the proton and keeps the electron always moving.

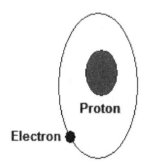

Proton

Electron

Hydrogen Atom

This is the hydrogen atom, abbreviated H. It has a single proton and single rotating electron.

Atoms are the smallest unit of any element. They retain the properties of the element. Sometimes, more than one atom must be present. The smallest stable unit of an element (pure substance) is called a molecule. The word "matter" describes everything that has physical existence, i.e. has mass and takes up space. However, the makeup of matter allows it to be separated into categories. The two main classes of matter are **pure substance** and **mixture.** Each of these classes can also be divided into smaller categories such as element, compound, homogeneous mixture or heterogeneous mixture based on composition.

A pure substance is a form of matter with a definite composition and distinct properties. This type of matter cannot be separated by ordinary processes like filtering, centrifuging, boiling or melting. Pure substances are divided into elements and compounds.

Elements: A single type of matter, called an atom, is present. Elements cannot be broken down any further by ordinary chemical processes. They are the smallest whole part of a substance that still represents that substance.

Compounds: Two or more elements chemically combined are present. A compound may be broken down into its elements by chemical processes such as heating or electric current. Compounds have a uniform composition regardless of the sample size or source of the sample.

Skill 15.2   Properties and states of matter; forms of energy (e.g., electrical, magnetic, sound, light)

The kinetic theory states that matter consists of molecules, possessing kinetic energies, in continual random motion. The state of matter (solid, liquid, or gas) depends on the speed of the molecules and the amount of kinetic energy the molecules possess. The molecules of solid matter merely vibrate, allowing strong intermolecular forces to hold the molecules in place. The molecules of liquid matter move freely and quickly throughout the body, and the molecules of gaseous matter move randomly and at high speeds.

Matter changes state when energy is added or taken away. The addition of energy, usually in the form of heat, increases the speed and kinetic energy of the component molecules. Faster moving molecules more readily overcome the intermolecular attractions that maintain the form of solids and liquids. So, as the speed of molecules increases, matter changes state from solid to liquid to gas (melting and evaporation).

As matter loses heat energy to the environment, the speed of the component molecules decreases. Intermolecular forces have greater impact on slower moving molecules. Thus, as the speed of molecules decreases, matter changes from gas to liquid to solid (condensation and freezing).

Forms of energy (e.g., electrical, magnetic, sound, light)

Technically, **energy is the ability to do work or supply heat.** Work is the transfer of energy to move an object a certain distance. It is motion against an opposing force. Lifting a chair into the air is work; the opposing force is gravity. Pushing a chair across the floor is work; the opposing force is friction.

Heat, on the other hand, is not a form of energy but a method of transferring energy.

This energy, according to the First Law of Thermodynamics, is conserved. That means energy is neither created nor destroyed in ordinary physical and chemical processes (non-nuclear). Energy is merely changed from one form to another. Energy in all of its forms must be conserved. In any system, $\Delta E = q + w$ (E = energy, q = heat and w = work).

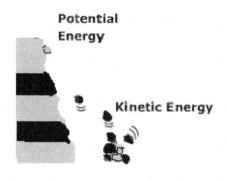

Potential Energy

Kinetic Energy

Energy exists in two basic forms, potential and kinetic. Kinetic energy is the energy of a moving object. Potential energy is the energy stored in matter due to position relative to other objects.

In any object, solid, liquid or gas, the atoms and molecules that make up the object are constantly moving (vibration, translation and rotational motion) and colliding with each other. They are not stationary.

Due to this motion, the object's particles have varying amounts of kinetic energy. A fast moving atom can push a slower moving atom during a collision, so it has energy. All moving objects have energy and that energy depends on the object's mass and velocity. Kinetic energy is calculated: $K.E. = \frac{1}{2} mv^2$.

The temperature exhibited by an object is proportional to the average kinetic energy of the particles in the substance. Increase the temperature of a substance, and its particles move faster so their average kinetic energies increase as well. But temperature is *not* an energy, it is not conserved.

The energy an object has due to its position or arrangement of its parts is called potential energy. Potential energy due to position is equal to the mass of the object times the gravitational pull on the object times the height of the object, or:

$$PE = mgh$$

Where PE = potential energy; m = mass of object; g = gravity; and h = height.

Heat is energy that is transferred between objects and caused by differences in their temperatures. Heat passes spontaneously from an object of higher temperature to one of lower temperature. This transfer continues until both objects reach the same temperature. Both kinetic energy and potential energy can be transformed into heat energy. When you step on the brakes in your car, the kinetic energy of the car is changed to heat energy by friction between the brake and the wheels. Other transformations can occur from kinetic to potential as well. Since most of the energy in our world is in a form that is not easily used, man and mother nature have developed some clever ways of changing one form of energy into another form that may be more useful.

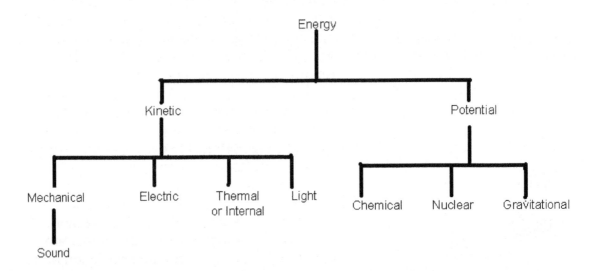

Skill 15.3   Basic concepts related to the motion of objects (e.g., inertia, momentum)

Dynamics is the study of the relationship between motion and the forces affecting motion. **Force** causes motion.

Mass and weight are not the same quantities. An object's **mass** gives it a reluctance to change its current state of motion. It is also the measure of an object's resistance to acceleration. The force that the earth's gravity exerts on an object with a specific mass is called the object's weight on earth. Weight is a force that is measured in Newtons. Weight (W) = mass times acceleration due to gravity (**W = mg**). To illustrate the difference between mass and weight, picture two rocks of equal mass on a balance scale. If the scale is balanced in one place, it will be balanced everywhere, regardless of the gravitational field.

However, the weight of the rocks would vary on a spring scale, depending upon the gravitational field. In other words, the rocks would be balanced both on earth and on the moon. However, the weight of the rocks would be greater on earth than on the moon.

Inertia is the continuation of an object at rest to remain at rest. Conversely, **momentum** is the likelihood that an object in motion will remain in motion.

Speed is a scalar quantity that refers to how fast an object is moving (ex. the car was traveling 60 mi./hr). **Velocity** is a vector quantity that refers to the rate at which an object changes its position. In other words, velocity is speed with direction (ex. the car was traveling 60 mi./hr east).

$$\text{Average speed} = \frac{\text{Distance traveled}}{\text{Time of travel}}$$

$$v = \frac{d}{t}$$

$$\text{Average velocity} = \frac{\Delta \text{position}}{\text{time}} = \frac{\text{displacement}}{\text{time}}$$

Instantaneous Speed - speed at any given instant in time

Average Speed - average of all instantaneous speeds, found simply by a distance/time ratio

Acceleration is a vector quantity defined as the rate at which an object changes its velocity.

$$a = \frac{\Delta velocity}{time} = \frac{v_f - v_i}{t}$$ where *f* represents the final velocity and

i represents the initial velocity

Since acceleration is a vector quantity, it always has a direction associated with it. The direction of the acceleration vector depends on

- whether the object is speeding up or slowing down
- whether the object is moving in the positive or negative direction

Skill 15.4   Components and structure of the solar system

There are eight established planets in our solar system; Mercury, Venus, Earth, Mars, Jupiter, Saturn, Uranus, and Neptune. Pluto was an established planet in our solar system, but as of summer 2006, its status is being reconsidered. The planets are divided into two groups based on distance from the sun. The inner planets include: Mercury, Venus, Earth, and Mars. The outer planets include: Jupiter, Saturn, Uranus, and Neptune.

Planets

Mercury:– This is the closest planet to the sun. Its surface has craters and rocks. The atmosphere is composed of hydrogen, helium and sodium. Mercury was named after the Roman messenger god.

Venus: This has a slow rotation when compared to Earth. Venus and Uranus rotate in opposite directions from the other planets. This opposite rotation is called retrograde rotation. The surface of Venus is not visible due to the extensive cloud cover. The atmosphere is composed mostly of carbon dioxide. Sulfuric acid droplets in the dense cloud cover give Venus a yellow appearance. Venus has a greater greenhouse effect than observed on Earth. The dense clouds combined with carbon dioxide trap heat. Venus was named after the Roman goddess of love.

Earth: This is considered a water planet, with 70% of its surface covered by water. Gravity holds the masses of water in place. The different temperatures observed on earth allow for the different states (solid. liquid, gas) of water to exist. The atmosphere is composed mainly of oxygen and nitrogen. Earth is the only planet that is known to support life.

Mars: The surface of Mars contains numerous craters, active and extinct volcanoes, ridges, and valleys with extremely deep fractures. Iron oxide found in the dusty soil makes the surface seem rust colored and the skies seem pink in color. The atmosphere is composed of carbon dioxide, nitrogen, argon, oxygen and water vapor. Mars has polar regions with ice caps composed of water. It has two satellites. Mars was named after the Roman war god.

Jupiter: This is the largest planet in the solar system. Jupiter has 16 moons. The atmosphere is composed of hydrogen, helium, methane and ammonia. There are white-colored bands of clouds indicating rising gas and dark-colored bands of clouds indicating descending gases. The gas movement is caused by heat resulting from the energy of Jupiter's core. Jupiter has a Great Red Spot that is thought to be a hurricane-type cloud. Jupiter has a strong magnetic field.

Saturn: This is the second largest planet in the solar system. Saturn has rings of ice, rock, and dust particles circling it. Its atmosphere is composed of hydrogen, helium, methane, and ammonia. Saturn has over 20 satellites and was named after the Roman god of agriculture.

Uranus: This is the third largest planet in the solar system (in diameter), with retrograde revolution. Uranus is a gaseous planet. It has 10 dark rings and 15 satellites. Its atmosphere is composed of hydrogen, helium, and methane. Uranus was named after the Greek god of the heavens.

Neptune: This is another gaseous planet, with an atmosphere consisting of hydrogen, helium, and methane. Neptune has three rings and two satellites.

Neptune was named after the Roman sea god because its atmosphere is the same color as the seas.

Pluto: Once considered the smallest planet in the solar system, its status as a planet is being reconsidered. Pluto's atmosphere probably contains methane, ammonia, and frozen water. It has one satellite and revolves around the sun every 250 years. Pluto was named after the Roman god of the underworld.

Comets, asteroids, and meteors

Astronomers believe that rocky fragments may have been the remains of the birth of the solar system that never formed into a planet. **Asteroids** are found in the region between Mars and Jupiter.

Comets are masses of frozen gases, cosmic dust, and small rocky particles. Astronomers think that most comets originate in a dense comet cloud beyond Pluto. Comets consist of a nucleus, a coma, and a tail. A comet's tail always points away from the sun. The most famous comet, **Halley's Comet,** is named after the person who first discovered it. It returns to the skies near earth every 75 to 76 years.

Meteoroids are composed of particles of rock and metal of various sizes. When a meteoroid travels through the earth's atmosphere, friction causes its surface to heat up and it begins to burn. The burning meteoroid falling through the earth's atmosphere is called a **meteor** (also known as a "shooting star").

Meteorites are meteors that strike the earth's surface. A physical example of a meteorite's impact on the earth's surface can be seen in Arizona. The Barringer Crater is a huge meteor crater. There are many other meteor craters throughout the world.

Oort cloud and Kuiper belt

The **Oort cloud** is a hypothetical spherical cloud surrounding our solar system. It extends approximately three light years or 30-trillion kilometers from the sun. The cloud is believed to be made up of materials ejected out of the inner solar system because of interaction with Uranus and Neptune, but still gravitationally bound to the sun. It is named the Oort cloud after Jan Oort who suggested its existence in 1950. Comets from the Oort cloud exhibit a wide range of sizes, inclinations and eccentricities and are often referred to as long-period comets because they have a period of more than 200 years.

It seems that the Oort cloud objects were formed closer to the Ssun than the Kuiper belt objects. Small objects formed near the giant planets would have been ejected from the solar system by gravitational encounters. Those that didn't escape entirely formed the distant Oort Cloud. Small objects formed farther out had no such interactions and remained as the Kuiper Belt objects.

The **Kuiper belt** is the name given to a vast population of small bodies orbiting the sun beyond Neptune. There are more than 70,000 of these small bodies with diameters larger than 100 km extending outwards from the orbit of Neptune to 50AU. They exist mostly within a ring or belt surrounding the sun. It is believed that the objects in the Kuiper belt are primitive remnants of the earliest phases of the solar system. It is also believed that the Kuiper belt is the source of many short-period comets (periods of less than 200 years). It is a reservoir for the comets in the same way that the Oort cloud is a reservoir for long-period comets.

Occasionally the orbit of a Kuiper belt object will be disturbed by the interactions of the giant planets in such a way as to cause the object to cross the orbit of Neptune. It will then very likely have a close encounter with Neptune, sending it out of the solar system or into an orbit crossing those of the other giant planets or even into the inner solar system. Prevailing theory states that scattered disk objects began as Kuiper belt objects, which were scattered through gravitational interactions with the giant planets.

Astronomers use groups or patterns of stars called **constellations** as reference points to locate other stars in the sky. Familiar constellations include: Ursa Major (also known as the big bear) and Ursa Minor (known as the little bear). Within the Ursa Major, the bigger constellation, the Big Dipper is found. Within the Ursa Minor, the smaller constellation, the Little Dipper is found.

Different constellations appear as the earth continues its revolution around the sun with the seasonal changes.

First magnitude stars are 21 of the brightest stars that can be seen from earth. These are the first stars noticed at night. In the Northern Hemisphere, there are 15 commonly observed first magnitude stars.

A vast collection of stars is defined as a **galaxy**. Galaxies are classified as irregular, elliptical, and spiral. Irregular galaxies have no real structured appearance; most are in their early stages of life. An elliptical galaxy consists of smooth ellipses containing little dust and gas, but composed of million or trillion stars. Spiral galaxies are disk-shaped and have extending arms that rotate around its dense center. Earth's galaxy is found in the Milky Way and is a spiral galaxy.

A **pulsar** is defined as a variable radio source that emits signals in very short, regular bursts; it is believed to be a rotating neutron star.

A **quasar** is defined as an object that photographs like a star but has an extremely large redshift and a variable energy output; it is believed to be the active core of a very distant galaxy.

Black holes are defined as objects that have collapsed to such a degree that light cannot escape from their surface; light is trapped by the intense gravitational field.

Origin of the Solar System

Two main hypotheses of the origin of the solar system are: (1) **the tidal hypothesis** and (2) **the condensation hypothesis**.

The tidal hypothesis proposes that the solar system began with a near collision of the sun and a large star. Some astronomers believe that as these two stars passed each other, the great gravitational pull of the large star extracted hot gases out of the sun. The mass from the hot gases started to orbit the sun and then began to cool and condense into the nine planets. (Few astronomers support this example).

The condensation hypothesis proposes that the solar system began with rotating clouds of dust and gas. Condensation occurred in the center forming the sun; the smaller parts of the cloud formed the nine planets. (This hypothesis is widely accepted by many astronomers.)

Two main theories to explain the origins of the universe include: (1) **the big bang theory** and (2) **the steady-state theory.**

The big bang theory has been widely accepted by many astronomers. It states that the universe originated from a magnificent explosion spreading mass, matter and energy into space. The galaxies formed from this material as it cooled during the next half-billion years.

The steady-state theory is the least accepted theory. It states that the universe is continuously being renewed. Galaxies move outward and new galaxies replace the older galaxies. Astronomers have not found any evidence to prove this theory.

The future of the universe is hypothesized with the **oscillating universe hypothesis**. It states that the universe will oscillate or expand and contract. Galaxies will move away from one another and will in time slow down and stop. Then a gradual moving toward each other will again activate the explosion or big bang.

The stages of life for a star start with a mass of gas and dust that becomes a nebula, then a main sequence star. Next it becomes a red giant, then a nova, and then finally a white dwarf (the dying core of a giant star), a neutron star or a black hole.

The forces of gravity acting on particles of gas and dust in a cloud in an area of space produce stars. This cloud is called a nebula. Particles in this cloud attract each other, and its temperature increases as it grows. With the increased temperature, the star begins to glow. Fusion occurs in the core of the star, releasing radiant energy at the star's surface.

When hydrogen becomes exhausted in a small, or even an average star, its core will collapse and cause its temperature to rise. This released heat causes nearby gases to heat, contract, carry out fusion, and produce helium. Stars at this stage are nearing the end of their life. These stars are called red giants or supergiants. A white dwarf is the dying core of a giant star. A nova is an ordinary star that experiences a sudden increase in brightness and then fades back to its original brightness. A supernova radiates even greater light energy. A neutron star is the result of mass left behind after a supernova collapses. A black hole is a star with condensed matter and gravity so intense that light cannot escape.

Skill 15.5   Climate and weather; forces that shape the earth's surface

Dry air has three basic components: dry gas, water vapor, and solid particles (dust from soil, etc.).

The most abundant dry gases in the atmosphere are:

- (N_2)   Nitrogen   78.09 %
- (O_2)   Oxygen   20.95 %
- (AR)   Argon   0.93 %
- (CO_2) Carbon Dioxide 0.03 %

The atmosphere is divided into four main layers based on temperature: troposphere, stratosphere, mesosphere, and thermosphere.

Troposphere - this layer is the closest to the earth's surface. All weather phenomena occurs here as it is the layer with the most water vapor and dust. Air temperature decreases with increasing altitude. The average thickness of the troposphere is 7 miles (11 km).

Stratosphere - this layer contains very little water; clouds within this layer are extremely rare. The ozone layer is located in the upper portions of the stratosphere. Air temperature is fairly constant but increases somewhat with height due to absorption of solar energy and ultraviolet rays from the ozone layer.

Mesosphere - air temperature again decreases with height in this layer. It is the coldest layer with temperatures in the range of -100^0 C at the top.

Thermosphere – this layer extends upward into space. Oxygen molecules in this layer absorb energy from the sun, causing temperatures to increase with height.

The lower part of the thermosphere is called the Ionosphere. Here, charged particles or ions and free electrons can be found. When gases in the Ionosphere are excited by solar radiation, the gases give off light and glow in the sky. These glowing lights are called the Aurora Borealis in the northern hemisphere and Aurora Australis in southern hemisphere. The upper portion of the thermosphere is called the exosphere. Gas molecules are very far apart in this layer. Layers of exosphere are also known as the Van Allen Belts and are held together by earth's magnetic field.

Cloud types:

- **Cirrus clouds** - white and feathery; high in the sky
- **Cumulus** – thick, white, fluffy
- **Stratus** – layers of clouds cover most of the sky
- **Nimbus** – heavy, dark clouds that represent thunderstorm clouds

Variations on the clouds mentioned above include cumulo-nimbus and strato-nimbus.

El Niño refers to a sequence of changes in the ocean and atmospheric circulation across the Pacific Ocean. The water around the equator is unusually hot every two to seven years. Trade winds normally blow east to west across the equatorial latitudes, piling warm water into the western Pacific. A huge mass of heavy thunderstorms usually forms in the area and produces vast currents of rising air that displace heat poleward. This helps create strong mid-latitude jet streams. The world's climate patterns are disrupted by this change in location of thunderstorm activity.

Air masses moving toward or away from the Earth's surface are called air currents. Air moving parallel to Earth's surface is called **wind**. Weather conditions are generated by winds and air currents carrying large amounts of heat and moisture from one part of the atmosphere to another. Wind speeds are measured by instruments called anemometers.

The wind belts in each hemisphere consist of convection cells that encircle Earth like belts. There are three major wind belts on Earth: trade winds, prevailing westerlies, and polar easterlies. Wind belt formation depends on the differences in air pressures that develop in the doldrums, the horse latitudes, and the polar regions. The Doldrums surround the equator. Within this belt heated air usually rises straight up into Earth's atmosphere. The Horse latitudes are regions of high barometric pressure with calm and light winds, and the Polar regions contain cold dense air that sinks to the Earth's surface.

Winds caused by local temperature changes include sea breezes and land breezes.

Sea breezes are caused by unequal heating of the land and an adjacent, large body of water. Land heats up faster than water. The movement of cool ocean air toward the land is called a sea breeze. Sea breezes usually begin blowing about mid-morning, ending about sunset.

A breeze that blows from the land to the ocean or a large lake is called a **land breeze.**

Monsoons are huge wind systems that cover large geographic areas and that reverse direction seasonally. The monsoons of India and other parts of Asia are examples of these seasonal winds. They alternate wet and dry seasons. As denser cooler air over the ocean moves inland, a steady seasonal wind called a summer or wet monsoon is produced.

The air temperature at which water vapor begins to condense is called the **dew point.**

Relative humidity is the actual amount of water vapor in a certain volume of air compared to the maximum amount of water vapor this air could hold at a given temperature.

Types of storms:

A **thunderstorm** is a brief, local storm produced by the rapid upward movement of warm, moist air within a cumulo-nimbus cloud. Thunderstorms always produce lightning and thunder, accompanied by strong wind gusts and heavy rain or hail.

A severe storm with swirling winds that may reach speeds of hundreds of kilometers per hour is called a **tornado**. Such a storm is also referred to as a "twister." The sky is covered by large cumulo-nimbus clouds and violent thunderstorms; a funnel-shaped swirling cloud may extend downward from a cumulo-nimbus cloud and reach the ground. Tornadoes are storms that leave a narrow path of destruction on the ground.

A swirling, funnel-shaped cloud that **extends** downward and touches a body of water is called a **waterspout.**

Hurricanes are storms that develop when warm, moist air carried by trade winds rotates around a low-pressure "eye." A large, rotating, low-pressure system accompanied by heavy precipitation and strong winds is called a tropical cyclone (better known as a hurricane). In the Pacific region, a hurricane is called a typhoon.

A **blizzard** is a storm with strong winds, blowing snow and producing frigid temperatures. An **ice storm** consists of falling rain that freezes when it strikes the ground, covering everything with a layer of ice.

The forces that shape the earth's surface:

A **mountain** is terrain that has been raised high above the surrounding landscape by volcanic action or some form of tectonic plate collisions. The plate collisions could be intercontinental or ocean-floor collisions with a continental crust (subduction). The physical composition of mountains includes igneous, metamorphic, or sedimentary rocks; some may have rock layers that are tilted or distorted by plate collision forces.

There are many different types of mountains. The physical attributes of a mountain range depends upon the angle at which plate movement thrust layers of rock to the surface. Many mountains (Adirondacks, Southern Rockies) were formed along high-angle faults.

Folded mountains (Alps, Himalayas) are produced by the folding of rock layers during their formation. The Himalayas – the highest mountains in the world – feature Mount Everest, which rises almost 9 km above sea level. The Himalayas were formed when India collided with Asia. The movement which created this collision is still in process at the rate of a few centimeters per year.

Fault-block mountains (Utah, Arizona, and New Mexico) are created when plate movement produces tension forces instead of compression forces. The area under tension produces normal faults, and rock along these faults is displaced upward.

Dome mountains are formed as magma tries to push up through the crust but fails to break the surface. Dome mountains resemble a huge blister on the earth's surface.

Upwarped mountains (Black Hills of South Dakota) are created in association with a broad arching of the crust. They can also be formed by rock thrust upward along high angle faults.

Volcanic mountains are often the end-result of volcanism – the movement of magma through the crust and its emergence as lava onto the earth's surface. Volcanic mountains are built up by successive deposits of volcanic materials. An active volcano is one that is presently erupting or building to an eruption. A dormant volcano is one that is between eruptions but still shows signs of internal activity that might lead to an eruption in the future. An extinct volcano is said to be no longer capable of erupting. Most of the world's active volcanoes are found along the rim of the Pacific Ocean, which is also a major earthquake zone. This curving belt of active faults and volcanoes is often called the Ring of Fire. The world's best known volcanic mountains include Mount Etna in Italy and Mount Kilimanjaro in Africa. The Hawaiian Islands are actually the tops of a chain of volcanic mountains that rise from the ocean floor.

There are three types of volcanic mountains: shield volcanoes, cinder cones and composite volcanoes.

Shield volcanoes are associated with quiet eruptions. Lava emerges from the vent or opening in the crater and flows freely out over the earth's surface until it cools and hardens into a layer of igneous rock. A repeated lava flow builds this type of volcano into the largest volcanic mountain. Mauna Loa found in Hawaii, is the largest volcano on earth.

Cinder cone volcanoes are associated with explosive eruptions as lava is hurled high into the air in a spray of droplets of various sizes. These droplets cool and harden into cinders and particles of ash before falling to the ground. The ash and cinder pile up around the vent to form a steep, cone-shaped hill called the cinder cone. Cinder cone volcanoes are relatively small but may form quite rapidly.

Composite volcanoes are described as being built by both lava flows and layers of ash and cinders. Mount Fuji in Japan, Mount St. Helens in Washington, USA, and Mount Vesuvius in Italy are all famous composite volcanoes.

Volcanic activity affects the earth's surface in numerous ways, resulting in many new formations.

As lava hardens and cools, for example, it forms into igneous rock either above ground or below ground.

Intrusive rock includes any igneous rock that was formed below the earth's surface. Batholiths are the largest structures of intrusive-type rock and are composed of near-granite materials; they are the core of the Sierra Nevada Mountains.

Extrusive rock includes any igneous rock that was formed at the earth's surface.

Among other formations resulting from volcanic activity, **dikes** are old lava tubes formed when magma entered a vertical fracture and hardened. Sometimes, magma squeezes between two rock layers and hardens into a thin horizontal sheet called a **sill**. A **laccolith** is formed in much the same way as a sill, but the magma that creates a laccolith is very thick and does not flow easily. It pulls and forces the overlying strata upward, creating an obvious surface dome.

A **caldera** is normally formed by the collapse of the top of a volcano. This collapse can be caused by a massive explosion that destroys the cone and empties most if not all of the magma chamber below the volcano. The cone collapses into the empty magma chamber, forming a caldera.

An inactive volcano may have magma solidified in its pipe. This structure, called a **volcanic neck**, is resistant to erosion and today may be the only visible evidence of the past presence of an active volcano.

How mountains are formed:

Mountains are produced as a result of various phenomena. Most major mountain ranges are formed by the processes of folding and faulting.

Folded mountains are produced by the folding of rock layers. Crustal movements may press horizontal layers of sedimentary rock together from the sides, squeezing them into wavelike folds. Up-folded sections of rock are called anticlines; down-folded sections of rock are called synclines. The Appalachian Mountains are an example of folded mountains with long ridges and valleys in a series of anticlines and synclines formed by folded rock layers.

Faults also contribute to mountain formation. Faults are fractures in the earth's crust, which have been created by either tension or compression forces transmitted through the crust. These forces are produced by the movement of separate blocks of crust. Faults are categorized on the basis of the relative movement between the blocks on both sides of the fault plane. The movement can be horizontal, vertical or oblique.

A dip-slip fault occurs when the movement of the plates is vertical and opposite. The displacement is in the direction of the inclination or dip of the fault. Dip-slip faults are classified as normal faults when the rock above the fault plane moves down relative to the rock below.

Reverse faults are created when the rock above the fault plane moves up relative to the rock below. Reverse faults having a very low angle to the horizontal are also referred to as thrust faults.

Strike-slip faults are faults in which the dominant displacement is horizontal movement along the trend or strike (length) of the fault. When a large strike-slip fault is associated with plate boundaries, it is called a **transform fault**. The San Andreas Fault in California is a well-known transform fault.

Oblique-slip faults are faults that have both vertical and horizontal movement.

Glaciation

A continental glacier covered a large part of North America during the most recent ice age. Evidence of this glacial coverage remains as abrasive grooves, large boulders from northern environments dropped in southerly locations, glacial troughs created by the rounding out of steep valleys by glacial scouring, and the remains of glacial sources called cirques that were created by frost wedging the rock at the bottom of the glacier. Remains of plants and animals found in warm climate have been discovered in the moraines, and outwash plains help to support the theory of periods of warmth during the past ice ages.

The ice age began about 2 -3 million years ago. This age saw the advancement and retreat of glacial ice over millions of years. Theories relating to the origin of glacial activity include plate tectonics, where it can be demonstrated that some continental masses, now in temperate climates, were at one time blanketed by ice and snow. Another theory involves changes in the earth's orbit around the sun, changes in the angle of the earth's axis, and the wobbling of the earth's axis. Support for the validity of this theory has come from deep ocean research that indicates a correlation between climatic sensitive microorganisms and the changes in the earth's orbital status.

About 12,000 years ago, a vast sheet of ice covered a large part of the northern United States. This huge, frozen mass had moved southward from the northern regions of Canada as several large bodies of slow-moving ice, or glaciers. A time period in which glaciers advance over a large portion of a continent is called an ice age. A glacier is a large mass of ice that moves or flows over the land in response to gravity. Glaciers form among high mountains and in other cold regions.

There are two main types of glaciers: valley glaciers and continental glaciers. Erosion by valley glaciers is characteristic of U-shaped erosion. They produce sharp peaked mountains such as the Matterhorn in Switzerland. Erosion by continental glaciers often rides over mountains in their paths leaving smoothed, rounded mountains and ridges.

Learn more about:
States of matter
http://www.grc.nasa.gov/WWW/K-12/airplane/state.html
Forms of energy
http://www.ftexploring.com/energy/enrg-types.htm
Solar system
http://starchild.gsfc.nasa.gov/docs/StarChild/solar_system_level1/solar_system.html
Forces that shape the earth's surface
http://www.enotes.com/earth-science/weather-climate

COMPETENCY 16.0 **UNDERSTAND THE FOUNDATIONS OF SCIENTIFIC THOUGHT, THE HISTORICAL DEVELOPMENT OF MAJOR SCIENTIFIC IDEAS AND TECHNOLOGICAL DISCOVERIES, AND THE PRINCIPLES AND PROCEDURES OF SCIENTIFIC INQUIRY AND EXPERIMENTATION**

Skill 16.1 **The development of scientific thinking (e.g., the process of observation, classification, and notation of evidence developed by the ancient Greeks, the scientific revolution of the seventeenth century, the concepts of uncertainty and relativity introduced in the early twentieth century)**

See Skill 16.4

Skill 16.2 **The history of major scientific and technological discoveries and inventions**

The history of biology follows man's understanding of the living world from the earliest recorded history to modern times. Though the concept of biology as a field of science arose only in the 19th century, its origins can be traced back to the ancient Greeks (Galen and Aristotle).

During the Renaissance and Age of Discovery, renewed interest in the rapidly increasing number of known organisms generated lot of interest in biology.

Andreas Vesalius (1514-1564) was a Belgian anatomist and physician whose dissections of the human body, along with the descriptions of his findings, helped to correct misconceptions of science. The books Vesalius wrote on anatomy were the most accurate and comprehensive anatomical texts of that time.

Anton van Leeuwenhoek is known as the father of microscopy. In the 1650s, Leeuwenhoek began making tiny lenses that gave magnifications up to 300x. He was the first to see and describe bacteria, yeast plants, and the microscopic life found in water. Over the years, light microscopes have advanced to produce greater clarity and magnification. The scanning electron microscope (SEM) was developed in the 1950s. Instead of light, a beam of electrons passes through the specimen. The SEM has a resolution about one thousand times greater than light microscopes. The disadvantage of the SEM is that the chemical and physical methods used to prepare the sample result in the death of the specimen.

Carl Von Linnaeus (1707-1778), a Swedish botanist, physician, and zoologist, is well known for his contributions in ecology and taxonomy. Linnaeus is famous for his binomial system of nomenclature in which each living organism has two names, a genus and a species name. He is considered the father of modern ecology and taxonomy.

In the late 1800s, French chemist Louis Pasteur emerged as a major contributor to the field of microbiology by discovering the role of microorganisms in the cause of disease. He also introduced the rabies vaccine and the process of pasteurization. German physician Robert Koch took Pasteur's observations one step further by postulating that specific diseases were caused by specific pathogens. **Koch's postulates** are still used as guidelines in microbiology. They state that the same pathogen must be found in every diseased person, the pathogen must be isolated and grown in culture, the disease must be induced in experimental animals from the culture, and the same pathogen must be isolated from the experimental animal.

In the 18th century, many fields of science like botany, zoology and geology began to evolve as scientific disciplines in the modern sense.

In the 20th century, American scientist Thomas Hunt Morgan and his students rediscovered and researched the works of Gregor Mendel – the Austrian "father of genetics." This led to the rapid development of the genetics field.

DNA structure became another key emphasis in biological study. In the 1950s, James Watson and Francis Crick discovered the structure of a DNA molecule as that of a double helix. This structure made it possible to explain DNA's ability to replicate and to control the synthesis of proteins.

Following the understanding of the genetic code, biology has largely split between organismal biology – consisting of ecology, ethology, systematics, paleontology, evolutionary biology, developmental biology, and other disciplines that deal with whole organisms or group of organisms – and the disciplines related to molecular biology, which include cell biology, biophysics, biochemistry, neuroscience, and immunology.

The use of animals in biological research has expedited many scientific discoveries. Animal research allows scientists to learn more about animal biological systems, including the circulatory and reproductive systems. One significant use of animals is for the testing of drugs, vaccines, and other products (such as perfumes and shampoos) before use or consumption by humans. There are both pros and cons of animal research. Debate over ethical treatment of animals has been ongoing since the introduction of animals to research. Many people believe the use of animals in research is cruel and unnecessary, and animal use is federally and locally regulated. The Institutional Animal Care and Use Committee (IACUC) oversees and evaluates all aspects of an institution's animal care and use program.

Skill 16.3   Cultural and historical factors that have promoted or discouraged scientific discovery and technological innovation

Humans have been engaging in science since prehistoric times. We have much documentation of scientific experiments and discoveries from classical times. Additionally, feats of engineering show that technology was highly developed in Ancient Greek, Roman, Egyptian, Chinese, and other civilizations. However, modern Western science is typically thought to have begun during the Scientific Revolution of the 16th and 17th century. This is when the more modern version of the scientific method began to be practiced. Since that time, several trends in science and technology have emerged.

First, science is increasingly used to serve the public good. Most early science was largely "pure research" science. That is, its only aim was to increase our knowledge of the natural world. As the Industrial Revolution dawned, more and more scientific discoveries were put to use in emerging technologies. This trend has continued and resulted in the development of modern conveniences and necessities, ranging from automobiles to computers to high-tech medicine. The continuation of this trend means that now nearly all science is application-driven; most research must at least have the potential to provide a practical advancement for humanity. Therefore, unfortunately, there is little funding for pure science in the present day.

Second, science has become increasingly specialized and expensive to perform. During the 16th and 17th century, most scientists were largely hobbyists who had trained under other scientists as apprentices. Additionally, they likely performed research in all scientific areas. As universities developed and people wished to investigate phenomena in more detail, scientists began to require more formal training. In modern times, most scientists have advanced degrees, work in high-tech labs with expensive equipment, and may spend entire careers focused on a single problem.

Finally, as communication and technology has improved, science is more and more a part of our everyday lives. Just a few hundred years ago, many people were unable to read and most knew little about current scientific discoveries. Now, it is easy for most of us to learn more about new science being performed and we've become accustomed to the constant emergence of new inventions. This has also had the effect of making people less reticent of accepting new technologies and ideas. Historically, individuals and organizations were often highly opposed to scientists' new findings. As the potential for these discoveries to improve our lives has increased, so has people's willingness to embrace them.

Skill 16.4 Basic concepts of scientific experimentation (e.g., hypothesis, control, variable, replication of results)

Science may be defined as a body of knowledge that is systematically derived from study, observations and experimentation. Its goal is to identify and establish principles and theories that may be applied to solve problems. Scientific inquiry starts with observation. Observation is a very important skill by itself, since it leads to experimentation and finally communicating the experimental findings to the public. After observing, a question is formed, which starts with "why" or "how." To answer these questions, experimentation is necessary. Between observation and experimentation, there are three more important steps. These are: gathering information (or researching about the problem), stating a hypothesis, and designing the experiment.

Designing an experiment is very important since it involves identifying control, constants, independent variables and dependent variables. A control is something to which results are compared at the end of the experiment. It is like a reference. Constants are the factors that must be kept constant in an experiment to get reliable results. Independent variables are factors that change in an experiment. It is very important to bear in mind that there should be more constants than variables to obtain reproducible results in an experiment.

Classifying is grouping items according to their similarities. It is important for students to realize relationships and similarities as well as differences to reach a reasonable conclusion in a lab experience.

After the experiment is done, it is repeated and results are graphically presented. The results are then analyzed and conclusions drawn.

It is the responsibility of the scientists to share the knowledge they obtain through their research.

After the conclusion is drawn, the final step is communication. In this age, much emphasis is put on the method of communication. The conclusions must be communicated by clearly describing the information using accurate data and visual presentations like graphs, tables, charts, diagrams, artwork, and other appropriate media. Modern technology must be used whenever it is necessary. The method of communication must be suitable to the audience.

Written communication is as important as oral communication. This is essential for submitting research papers to scientific journals, newspapers, magazines etc.

The **scientific method** is the basic process behind science. It involves several steps, beginning with hypothesis formulation and working through to the conclusion.

Posing a question

Although many discoveries happen by chance, the standard thought process of a scientist begins with forming a question to research. The more limited the question, the easier it is to set up an experiment to answer it.

Forming a hypothesis

Once the question is formulated, take an educated guess about the answer to the problem or question. This 'best guess' is your hypothesis.

Doing the test

To make a test fair, data from an experiment must have a **variable** or any condition that can be changed – such as temperature or mass. A good test will try to manipulate as few variables as possible so as to see which variable is responsible for the result. This requires a **control**. A control is an extra setup in which all the conditions are the same except for the variable being tested.

Observing and recording the data

Data reports must state specifics of how the measurements were calculated. For beginning students, technique must be part of the instructional process so as to give validity to the data.

Drawing a conclusion

After recording data, you compare your data with that of other groups. A conclusion is the judgment derived from the data results.

Graphing data

Graphing utilizes numbers to demonstrate patterns. The patterns offer a visual representation, making it easier to draw and explain the conclusions.

Applying knowledge of designing and performing investigations

Normally, knowledge is integrated in the form of a lab report. A report has many sections. It begins with a specific **title** that tells exactly what is being studied. The beginning of the paper has an **abstract**, a summary of the report. There's also a **purpose**, a well-written paragraph that clearly states and defines the problem. Included in the purpose is the **hypothesis** (educated guess) of what is expected to be the outcome of the experiment.

For the validity of a scientific experiment, it is important to describe exactly what was done to prove or disprove a hypothesis. A **control** is necessary to prove that the results occurred from the changed conditions and would not have happened normally. (Only one variable should be manipulated at a time.) **Observations** and **results** of the experiment should be recorded, including all results from data. Drawings, graphs and illustrations should be included to support information. Observations are objective, whereas analysis and interpretation are subjective. A **conclusion** should explain why the results of the experiment either proved or disproved the hypothesis.

While the scientific method is the basic process of inquiry and experimentation, a **scientific theory** is an explanation of a set of related observations based on a proven hypothesis. A **scientific law** usually lasts longer than a scientific theory and has more experimental data to support it.

Skill 16.5   Health and safety measures related to scientific inquiry and experimentation

Safety in the science classroom and laboratory is of paramount importance to the science educator. The following are general guidelines related to the types of safety equipment that should be available within a given school system, as well as general locations where the protective equipment or devices should be maintained and used. (Please note that this is only a partial list and that your school system should be reviewed for unique hazards and site-specific hazards at each facility.)

The key to a safe learning environment is proactive training and regular in-service updates for all staff and students who utilize the science laboratory. Proactive training should include how to **identify potential hazards**, **evaluate them**, and **prevent or respond to them.** The following types of training should be considered:

- Right to Know (OSHA training on the importance and benefits of properly recognizing and safely working with hazardous materials) along with some basic chemical hygiene as well as guidelines on reading and understanding a material safety data sheet
- Instruction in how to use a fire extinguisher
  Instruction in how to use a chemical fume hood; general guidance in when and how to use personal protective equipment (e.g. safety glasses or gloves)
- Instruction in how to monitor activities for potential negative effects on indoor air quality

It is also important for the instructor to utilize **Material Safety Data Sheets**. Maintain a copy of the material safety data sheet for every item in your chemical inventory. This information will outline the health and safety hazards posed by different substances and assist you in determining how to store and handle these materials. In most cases, the manufacturer will recommend the necessary protective equipment, ventilation and storage practices. This information should be your first guide when considering the use of a new material.

Frequent monitoring and in-service training on all equipment, materials, and procedures will help to ensure a safe and orderly laboratory environment. It will also provide everyone who uses the laboratory the safety fundamentals necessary to discern a safety hazard and to respond appropriately.

Maintain safe practices and procedures in all areas related to science instruction

In addition to requirements set forth by your place of employment, the NABT (National Association of Biology Teachers) and ISEF (International Science Education Foundation) have been instrumental in setting parameters for the science classroom. All science labs should contain the following items of **safety equipment**. Those marked with a number are required by state laws:

- Fire blankets that are visible and accessible.
- Ground Fault Circuit Interrupters (GCFI) within two feet of water supplies
- Signs designating room exits.
- Emergency shower providing a continuous flow of water.
- Emergency eye-wash station that can be activated by the foot or forearm.
- Eye protection for every student.
- A means of sanitizing equipment.
- Emergency exhaust fans providing ventilation to the outside of the building.
- Master cut-off switches for gas, electric and compressed air. Switches must have permanently attached handles. Cut-off switches must be clearly labeled.
- An ABC fire extinguisher
- Storage cabinets for flammable materials
    1. Chemical spill control kit
    2. Fume hood with a spark-proof motor
    3. Protective laboratory aprons made of flame-retardant material
    4. Signs that display warnings of potential hazardous conditions
    5. Properly labeled containers for broken glassware, flammables, corrosives, and waste

Students should wear safety goggles when performing dissections, heating, or using acids and bases. Hair should always be tied back, and objects should never be placed in the mouth. Food should not be consumed while in the laboratory. Hands should always be washed before and after laboratory experiments. In case of an accident, eye washes and showers should be used for eye contamination or a chemical spill that covers the student's body. Small chemical spills should only be contained and cleaned by the teacher. Kitty litter or a chemical spill kit should be used to clean spill. For large spills, the school administration and the local fire department should be notified. Biological spills should also be handled only by the teacher. Contamination with biological waste can be cleaned by using bleach when appropriate.

Accidents and injuries should always be reported to the school administration and local health facilities. The severity of the accident or injury will determine the course of action to pursue.

It is the responsibility of the teacher to provide a safe environment for their students. Proper supervision greatly reduces the risk of injury, so a teacher should never leave a class for any reason without providing alternate supervision. After an accident, two factors are considered; **foreseeability** and **negligence**. Foreseeability is the anticipation that an event may occur under certain circumstances. Negligence is the failure to exercise ordinary or reasonable care. Safety procedures should be a part of the science curriculum. A well-managed classroom is important to avoid potential lawsuits.

Apply first response procedures, including first aid, for responding to accidents

All students and staff should be trained in first aid in the science classroom and laboratory. Please remember to always report all accidents, however minor, to the lab instructor immediately. In most situations, 911 should immediately be called. Please refer to your school's specific safety plan for accidents in the classroom and laboratory. The classroom/laboratory should have a complete first-aid kit with supplies that are up-to-date and checked for expiration.

Know the location and use of fire extinguishers, eye-wash stations, and safety showers in the lab.

Do not attempt to smother a fire in a beaker or flask with a fire extinguisher. The force of the stream of material from it will turn over the vessel and result in a bigger fire. Just place a watch glass or a wet towel over the container to cut off the supply of oxygen.

If your clothing is on fire, **do not run** because this only increases the burning. It is normally best to fall on the floor and roll over to smother the fire. If a student whose clothing is on fire panics and begins to run, attempt to get the student on the floor and roll over to smother the flame. If necessary, use the fire blanket or safety shower in the lab to smother the fire.

Students with long hair should put their hair in a bun or a pony-tail to avoid their hair catching fire.

Below are common laboratory accidents and recommended responses:.

Burns (chemical or fire) – Use deluge shower for 15 minutes.

Burns (clothing on fire) – Use safety shower immediately. Keep victim immersed 15 minutes to wash away both heat and chemicals. All burns should be examined by medical personnel.

Chemical spills – Chemical spills on hands or arms should be washed immediately with soap and water. Washing hands should become an instinctive response to any chemical spilled on hands. Spills that cover clothing and other parts of the body should be drenched under the safety shower. If strong acids or bases are spilled on clothing, the clothing should be removed. If a large area is affected, remove clothing and immerse victim in the safety shower. If a small area is affected, remove article of clothing and use deluge shower for 15 minutes.

Eyes (chemical contamination) – Hold the eye wide open and flush with water from the eye wash for about 15 minutes. Seek medical attention.

Ingestion of chemicals or poisoning – See antidote chart on wall of lab for general first-aid directions. The victim should drink large amounts of water. All chemical poisonings should receive medical attention.

Learn more about:
Scientific method and experimentation
http://www.freeinquiry.com/intro-to-sci.html
Recognizing and evaluating hazards in the laboratory
http://www.osha.gov/SLTC/laboratories/index.html

DOMAIN V.   **CHILD DEVELOPMENT**

COMPETENCY 17.0   UNDERSTAND CHILD DEVELOPMENT FROM BIRTH THROUGH THE ELEMENTARY YEARS

Skill 17.1   Major theories of child development

There are many factors that affect student learning, including how students learn and how learning is presented and/or based on background knowledge or experiences. There are several educational learning theories that can be applied to classroom practices. One classic learning theory is Piaget's stages of development, which consist of four learning stages: sensory motor stage (from birth to age 2); pre-operation stage (ages 2 to 7 or early elementary); concrete operational stage (ages 7 to 11 or upper elementary); and formal operational stage (ages 7-15 or late elementary/high school). Piaget believed children pass through this series of stages to develop from the most basic forms of concrete thinking to sophisticated levels of abstract thinking.

The teacher of students in later childhood and early adolescence should have a broad knowledge and understanding of the phases of development that typically occur during this stage of life. The teacher must also be aware of how receptive children are to specific methods of instruction and learning during each period of development. A significant premise in the study of child development holds that all domains of development (physical, social, and academic) are integrated. Development in each dimension is influenced by development in the others. Equally important to the teacher's understanding of the process is the knowledge that developmental advances within the domains occur neither simultaneously nor necessarily parallel to one another.

It is important for the teacher to be aware of the physical stages of development and how changes to the child's physical attributes (internal developments, increased muscle capacity, improved coordination, hormonal imbalances, awakening sex drive, and other attributes) affect the child's ability to learn. Factors determined by the physical stage of development include: ability to sit and attend, the need for activity, the relationship between physical coordination and self-esteem, and the degree to which physical involvement in an activity (as opposed to being able to understand an abstract concept) affects learning and the child's sense of achievement.

Early adolescence is characterized by dramatic physical changes moving the individual from childhood toward physical maturity. Early, prepubescent changes are noted with the appearance of secondary sexual characteristics. Girls experience a concurrent rapid growth in height, which occurs between the ages of about 9.5 and 14.5 years and peaks somewhere around 12 years of age. Boys experience a concurrent rapid growth in height, which occurs between the ages of about 10.5 to 11 and 16 to 18, peaking around age 14.

The sudden and rapid physical changes that young adolescents experience typically cause this period of development to be one of self-consciousness, sensitivity and concern over one's own body changes, as well as sometimes hurtful comparisons between oneself and peers. Because physical changes may not occur in a smooth, regular schedule, adolescents may go through stages of awkwardness, both in terms of appearance and physical mobility and coordination.

The effect of these physical changes on individual students is that they often become more self-aware, self-conscious and self-absorbed. Constant comparison with peers developing at different rates will cause many individuals to feel inadequate or inferior, at least at times. While remaining sensitive to the genuine, emotional response of early adolescents to changes they cannot control and do not fully comprehend, the teacher will find it necessary to be more proactive in bringing students out of their shells so that they become interactive participants in the classroom learning experience.

Skill 17.2 Characteristics and processes of cognitive, language, physical, social, and emotional development during the elementary years

Cognitive (Academic) Development

Children go through patterns of learning beginning with pre-operational thought processes and move to concrete operational thoughts. Eventually, they begin to acquire the intellectual ability to contemplate and solve problems independently, when they mature enough to manipulate objects symbolically. Students in early childhood can use symbols such as words and numbers to represent objects and relations, but they need concrete reference points. Successful acquisition of the skills taught in early childhood, through the fourth grade, will progressively prepare the student for more advanced problem solving and abstract thinking in the later grades. The content of curriculum for younger students must be relevant for their stage of development (accessible and comprised of acquirable skills), engaging, and meaningful to the students.

Social Development

Children progress through a variety of social stages beginning with an awareness of self and self-concern. They soon develop an awareness of peers but demonstrate a lack of concern for their presence. For a time, young children engage in "parallel" activities, playing alongside their peers without directly interacting with one another.

During the primary years, children develop an intense interest in peers. They establish productive, positive, social and working relationships with one another. This area of social growth will continue to increase in significance throughout the child's academic career. The foundation for the students' successful development in this area is established through the efforts of the classroom teacher to plan and develop positive peer group relationships and to provide opportunities and support for cooperative small group projects that not only develop cognitive ability but promote peer interaction. The ability to work and relate effectively with peers contributes greatly to the child's sense of competence. In order to develop this sense of competence, children need to be successful in acquiring the information base and social skill sets that promote cooperative effort to achieve academic and social objectives.

High expectations for student achievement that are age-appropriate and focused provide the foundation for a teacher's positive relationship with young students, consistent with effective instructional strategies. It is equally important to determine what is appropriate for specific individuals in the classroom and approach classroom groups and individual students with an understanding and respect for their emerging capabilities.

Those who study childhood development recognize that young students grow and mature in common, recognizable patterns, but at different rates which cannot be effectively accelerated. This can result in variance in the academic performance of different children in the same classroom. With the establishment of inclusion as a standard in the classroom, it is necessary for all teachers to understand that variation in development among the student population is another aspect of diversity within the classroom. And this has implications for the ways in which instruction is planned and delivered and the ways in which students learn and are evaluated.

See also Skill 17.1.

Skill 17.3 Developmental progressions and ranges of individual and cultural variation in cognitive, language, physical, social, and emotional development

Teachers should have a toolkit of instructional strategies, materials and technologies to encourage and teach students how to problem solve and think critically about subject content. With each curriculum chosen by a district for school implementation, comes an expectation that students must master benchmarks and standards of learning skills. There is an established level of academic performance and proficiency in public schools that students are required to master in today's classrooms. Research of national and state standards indicate that there are specific benchmarks and learning objectives in the subject areas of science, foreign language, English language arts, history, art, health, civics, economics, geography, physical education, mathematics, and social studies that students are required to master in state assessments (Marzano & Kendall, 1996).

A critical thinking skill is a skill target that teachers help students develop to sustain learning in specific subject areas that can be applied within other subject areas. For example, when learning to understand algebraic concepts in solving a math word problem on how much fencing material is needed to build a fence around a backyard area that has a 8' x 12," a math student must understand the order of numerical expression in how to simplify algebraic expressions. Teachers can provide instructional strategies that show students how to group the fencing measurements into an algebraic word problem that with minor addition, subtraction and multiplication can produce a simple number equal to the amount of fencing materials needed to build the fence.

Students use basic skills to understand things that are read such as a reading passage or a math word problem or directions for a project. However, students apply additional thinking skills to fully comprehend how what was read could be applied to their own life or how to make comparatives or choices based on the factual information given. These higher-order thinking skills are called critical thinking skills as students think about thinking. Teachers are instrumental in helping students use these skills in everyday activities, such as:

- Analyzing bills for overcharges
- Comparing shopping ads or catalogue deals
- Finding the main idea from readings
- Applying what's been learned to new situations
- Gathering information/data from a diversity of sources to plan a project
- Following a sequence of directions
- Looking for cause and effect relationships
- Comparing and contrasting information in synthesizing information

Attention to learner needs during planning is foremost and includes identification of that which the students already know or need to know; the matching of learner needs with instructional elements such as content, materials, activities, and goals; and the determination of whether or not students have performed at an acceptable level, following instruction.

Since most teachers want their educational objectives to use higher level thinking skills, teachers need to direct students to these higher levels on the taxonomy. Questioning is an effective tool to build up students to these higher levels.

Low-order questions are useful to begin the process. They ensure the student is focused on the required information and understands what needs to be included in the thinking process. For example, if the objective is for students to be able to read and understand the story *Goldilocks and the Three Bears,* the teacher may wish to start with low-order questions (i.e., "what are some things Goldilocks did while in the bears home?" [knowledge] or "why didn't Goldilocks like the Papa Bear's chair?" [analysis]).

Through a series of questions, the teacher can move the students up the taxonomy. (For example, "if Goldilocks had come to your house, what are some things she may have used?" [application]; "how might the story differ if Goldilocks had visited the three fishes?" [synthesis]; "do you think Goldilocks was good or bad? Why?" [evaluation]). Through questioning, the teacher can control the thinking process of the class. As students become more involved in the discussion, they are systematically being lead to higher-level thinking.

Individualized student portfolios that contain performance-based assessments and a personal and professional chart of the student's academic and emotional growth are highly helpful tools for both student and teacher use. While students' attitudes toward themselves, school, and the world in general may constantly fluctuate, their portfolios become a reliable source for teachers to gauge student development and determine what is needed for further progress.

When a student studying a math concept is able to create a visual of the learning that transcends beyond the initial concept to a higher level of thinking and knowledge application, then the teacher can share a moment of enjoyable math comprehension with the student. Similarly, when students use art or imagery to help process reading and science concepts, they are essentially creating mental maps of what they are learning. Graphic organizers and web guides that center around a concept and its applications are all instructional tools that teachers can use to guide students into further inquiry of the subject. Imagine the research of the German chemist Fredrich August Kekule when he looked into a fire one night and solved the molecular structure of benzene, and you can imagine fostering that same creativity in students. Helping students understand the art of "visualization" and the power of discovery may impart a student visualizing a cure for AIDS or cancer or how to create more effective reading programs.

Helping students become effective note-takers and stimulating a diversity of perspectives for spatial techniques that can be applied to learning is a proactive teacher strategy in creating a visual learning environment where art and visualization become natural art forms for learning. In today's computer environment, students must understand that computers cannot replace the creative thinking and skill application of the human mind.

Skill 17.4 Factors that may facilitate or impede a child's development in various domains

Students often absorb the culture and social environment around them without deciphering the contextual meaning of their experiences. In the classrooms, teachers can help students derive appropriate meanings from their own experiences while also trying to understand the cultural cues contributed by students of other backgrounds.

Socio-cultural factors have a definite effect on students' psychological, emotional, affective, and physiological development, influencing the students' academic learning and future opportunities.

For most students, the experience of acquiring an education is a complicated and complex one – with a diversity of interlocking meanings and inferences. If one aspect of the complexity is altered, it affects other aspects, which may in turn determine how the student views an instructional or learning experience. Current school community demographics show a diverse population of students from varying backgrounds. Variations in cultural and socio-economic backgrounds, if not addressed effectively, could become significant roadblocks to learning for some students.

Teachers must create learning communities where every student is a valued member and contributor of the classroom. By incorporating the socio-cultural attributes of their student population into the learning process, teachers can foster dynamic interrelationships among students and teachers, personalize learning for individuals, and enhance the learning environment for all. Students can use academic and social opportunities to bond with students from other cultures, thereby enhancing multicultural understanding and enriching their worldview.

Researchers continue to show that personalized learning environments can improve students' willingness and ability to learn, decrease drop-out rates among marginalized students, and curb unproductive student behavior resulting from constant cultural misunderstandings and conflicts between students. Classrooms that promote diversity and cultural competency open up a world of multicultural learning opportunities for students and teachers alike. For example, when students are encouraged to step outside their comfort zones and share the world of a homeless student or empathize with an English Language Learner (ELL) who has just immigrated to the United States and is learning English while trying to keep up with the pace of the class, they enhance their social understanding and cultural connectedness.

As personalized learning communities support students' diverse academic and emotional needs, teachers may begin to realize the importance of understanding and teaching to the "whole child" – a child shaped by many social, cultural, and economic factors.

.Skill 17.5　Major learning theories

Some of the most prominent learning theories in education today include brain-based learning and the multiple intelligence theory. Supported by recent brain research, brain-based learning suggests that knowledge about the way the brain retains information enables educators to design the most effective learning environments. As a result, researchers have developed twelve principles that relate knowledge about the brain to teaching practices. These twelve principles are:

- The brain is a complex adaptive system

- The brain is social
- The search for meaning is innate
- We use patterns to learn more effectively
- Emotions are crucial to developing patterns
- Each brain perceives and creates parts and whole simultaneously
- Learning involves focused and peripheral attention
- Learning involves conscious and unconscious processes
- We have at least two ways of organizing memory
- Learning is developmental
- Complex learning is enhanced by challenge (and inhibited by threat)

- Every brain is unique

Educators can use these principles to help design methods and environments in their classrooms to maximize student learning.

The multiple intelligence theory, developed by Howard Gardner, suggests that students learn in (at least) seven different ways. These include: visually/spatially, musically, verbally, logically/mathematically, interpersonally, intrapersonally, and bodily/kinesthetically.

The most current learning theory of constructivist learning allows students to construct learning opportunities. Constructivist teachers believe that students create their own reality of knowledge and determine how to process and observe the world around them. Students are constantly constructing new ideas, which serve as frameworks for learning and teaching. Researchers have shown that the constructivist model is based on four ideas:

1. Learner creates knowledge.
2. Learner constructs and adds meaningful new knowledge to existing knowledge.
3. Learner shapes and constructs knowledge by life experiences and social interactions.
4. In constructivist learning communities, the student, teacher and classmates establish knowledge cooperatively on a daily basis.

Kelly (1969) states "human beings construct knowledge systems based on their observations." This parallels Piaget's theory that individuals construct knowledge systems as they work with others who share a common background of thought and processes. Constructivist learning for students is dynamic and ongoing. For constructivist teachers, the classroom becomes a place where students are encouraged to interact with the instructional process by asking questions and posing new ideas to old theories.

Skill 17.6 Processes by which children acquire knowledge and construct meaning; interrelationships between cognitive development and other developmental domains

The metacognition learning theory deals with "the study of how to help the learner gain understanding about how knowledge is constructed and about the conscious tools for constructing that knowledge" (Joyce and Weil 1996). The cognitive approach to learning involves the teacher's understanding that teaching the student to process his/her own learning and mastery of skill provides the greatest learning and retention opportunities in the classroom. Students are taught to develop concepts and teach themselves skills in problem solving and critical thinking. The student becomes an active participant in the learning process, and the teacher facilitates that conceptual and cognitive learning process.

Social and behavioral theories look at social interactions that affect students' learning opportunities in the classroom. The psychological approaches behind both theories are subject to individual variables that are learned and applied either proactively or negatively in the classroom. The stimulus of the classroom can promote constructive learning or evoke behavior that is counterproductive for both students and teachers. Students are social beings that normally gravitate to action in the classroom. Teachers must be cognizant of this when planning classroom environments that provide both focus and engagement in maximizing learning opportunities.

Skill 17.7 Principles and procedures for promoting students' cognitive, language, physical, social, and emotional development

Elementary age children face many changes during their early school years, and these changes may positively and/or negatively affect how learning occurs. Some cognitive developments (i.e., learning to read) may broaden their areas of interest as students realize the amount of information (i.e., novels, magazines, non-fiction books) that is out there. On the other hand, a young student's limited comprehension may inhibit some of their confidence (emotional) or conflict with values taught at home (moral). Joke telling (linguistic) becomes popular with children age six or seven, and children may use this newly discovered "talent" to gain friends or social "stature" in their class (social). Learning within one domain often spills over into other areas for young students.

Likewise, learning continues to affect all domains as a child grows. Adolescence is a complex stage of life. While many people joke about the awkwardness of adolescence, this is the life stage just before adulthood. While people may develop further in adulthood, the changes are not as quick or significant.

When we say that development takes place within domains, what we mean is simply that different aspects of a human change. These aspects may be physical (e.g., body growth, sexuality); cognitive (e.g., better ability to reason); linguistic (e.g., further development of a child's vocabulary); social (e.g., forming one's identity); emotional (e.g., developing feelings of concern and empathy for others); and moral (e.g., testing limits).

The important thing to remember about adolescent development within each of these domains is that they are not exclusive. For example, physical and emotional development are tied intricately, particularly when one feels awkward about his or her body; when emotional feelings are tied to sexuality; or when one feels that he or she does not look old enough (as rates of growth are obviously not similar). Moral and cognitive developments often go hand in hand when an adolescent reasons behavior or searches for role models.

What do educators need to know about adolescent development? First, it is important to be sensitive to changes in adolescents. Just because you see a change in one area does not mean that there aren't bigger changes in another area, hidden beneath the surface. Second, educators must realize that adolescents may be deeply hurt over certain issues that may or may not be directly related to the changes they are experiencing. It is particularly important for educators to be on the lookout for signs of depression, drug use, and other damaging activities, behaviors, or symptoms.

Learn more about:
Child development
http://psychology.about.com/od/developmentalpsychology/a/childdevtheory.htm
Learning theories
http://www.ncrel.org/sdrs/areas/issues/students/earlycld/ea7lk18.htm

COMPETENCY 18.0 UNDERSTAND CHILD DEVELOPMENT AND LEARNING IN STUDENTS WITH EXCEPTIONALITIES

Skill 18.1 Types of disabling conditions, developmental delays, indices of advanced academic or artistic talent

A diverse classroom should address the needs of not just children learning English as a second language, but also of children with disabilities and exceptionalities. There can be numerous types of disabilities in children. Some of these are entirely physical, while others are entirely related to the mind, mental process, and learning. Yet other disabilities involve a combination of both aspects. While it would be a disservice to say that all kids should display the same characteristics to be considered "normal," when a teacher notices "out-of-the-ordinary" characteristics – such as a student's ability to solve a math problem without working it out (a potential attribute of giftedness) or another student's extreme trouble with spelling (a potential attribute of dyslexia) – the teacher may assume that a disability or exceptional ability is present.

Common learning disabilities include attention deficit hyperactivity disorder (where concentration can be very tough), auditory processing disorders (where listening comprehension is very difficult), visual processing disorders (where reading can be tough and visual memory may be impaired), dyslexia (where reading can be confusing), and many others. Physical disabilities include Down's syndrome (where mental retardation may be a factor), cerebral palsy (where physical movement is impaired), and many others. Developmental disabilities might include the lack of ability to use fine motor skills.

When giftedness is observed, teachers should also concern themselves with ensuring that such children get the attention they need and deserve so that they can continue to learn and grow.

Below are some of the more common approaches used in today's K-12 classrooms for children still learning English. Cognitive approaches to language learning focus on concepts. While words and grammar are important, when teachers use the cognitive approach, they focus on using language for conceptual purposes – rather than learning words and grammar for the sake of simply learning new words and grammatical structures. This approach focuses heavily on students' learning styles, and it cannot necessarily be pinned down as having specific techniques. Rather, it is more of a philosophy of instruction.

Another very common motivational approach is Total Physical Response. This is a kinesthetic approach that combines language learning and physical movement. In essence, students learn new vocabulary and grammar by responding with physical motion to verbal commands. Some people say it is particularly effective because the physical actions create good brain connections with the words.

In general, the best methods do not treat students as if they have a language deficit. Rather, the best methods build upon what students already know. They help to instill the target language as a communicative process rather than a list of vocabulary words that have to be memorized.

To ensure the maximum education for all diverse learners, teachers must plan to meet the needs of all their students. To promote diversity, teachers must seek opportunities of interaction with students, staff, community members, and parents from culturally diverse backgrounds. These interactions can help teachers learn from others' experiences. They can also make it easier for the teachers to effectively promote cultural diversity and inclusion in the classroom. Teachers can engage and challenge their students to develop and incorporate their own diversity skills in building character and relationships with cultures beyond their own. By fostering multicultural understanding and inclusion in the classroom, teachers are laying the foundation for students to become effective participants in a global society.

Skill 18.2 Effects of exceptionalities on cognitive, physical, social, and emotional development and functioning

Students with exceptional abilities can be a great challenge for teachers. It is very unfair to assume that since these students already "get it," they can be ignored. These students need to continue to learn, even if it is above and beyond the rest of the class. Gifted students often resent being smarter than the rest of the class because they are "called on" more often or treated as if they do not need any attention. While these students are a fantastic resource for the rest of the class, being a resource is not their role in the classroom. They are there to learn, just like the rest of the class. They occasionally need different work to engage them and stimulate their minds. They do *not* simply need *more* work; this is unfair and insulting to them.

Skill 18.3 Significance of various exceptionalities for learning

No two students are alike. It follows, then, that no two students *learn* alike. To apply a one-dimensional instructional approach and a strict tunnel vision perspective on testing is to impose learning limits on students. All students have the right to an education, but there cannot be a singular path to that education. Teachers must acknowledge the variety of learning styles and abilities among the students in their class (and, indeed, the varieties from class to class) and apply multiple instructional and assessment processes to ensure that every child has appropriate opportunities to master the subject matter, demonstrate such mastery, and improve and enhance learning skills with each lesson.

Students' attitudes and perceptions about learning are the most powerful factors influencing academic focus and success. When instructional objectives center on students' interests and are relevant to their lives, effective learning occurs.

Learners must believe that the tasks that they are asked to perform have some value and that they have the ability and resources to perform them. If students think a task is unimportant, they will not put much effort into it. If they think they lack the ability or resources to successfully complete a task, even attempting the task becomes too great a risk. Not only must teachers understand the students' abilities and interests, they must also help students develop positive attitudes and perceptions about tasks and learning.

Skill 18.4   identification of students with exceptionalities

Individuals with Disabilities Act and Child Study Teams

Collaborative teams play a crucial role in ensuring that the needs of *all* students are met; they also help identify students with special needs. Under the Individuals with Disabilities Act (IDEA), which federally mandates special education services in every state, it is the responsibility of public schools to provide consultative, evaluative and, if necessary, prescriptive services to children with special needs. In most school districts, this responsibility is handled by a collaborative group called the Child Study Team (CST). If a teacher or parent believes a child has academic, social or emotional problems, they are referred to the CST – a team of educational professionals (including teachers, specialists, the school psychologist, guidance, and other support staff) that reviews the student's case through meetings with the teacher and/or parents/guardians. The CST will determine what evaluations or tests are necessary, if any, and will also assess the results. Based on these results, the CST will suggest a plan of action if one is needed.

Inclusion, mainstreaming, and least-restrictive environment

Inclusion, mainstreaming and least-restrictive environment are interrelated policies under the IDEA, with varying degrees of statutory imperatives.

1. Inclusion is the right of students with disabilities to be placed in the regular classroom.
2. Least-restrictive environment is the mandate that children be educated to the maximum extent appropriate with their non-disabled peers.
3. Mainstreaming is a policy where disabled students can be placed in the regular classroom, as long as such placement does not interfere with the student's educational plan.

One plan of action is an Academic Intervention Plan (AIP). An AIP consists of additional instructional services that are provided to the student in order to help them better achieve academically if the student has met certain criteria (such as scoring below the state reference point on standardized tests or performing more than two levels below grade-level).

Another plan of action is a 504 plan. A 504 plan is a legal document based on the provisions of the Rehabilitation Act of 1973 (which preceded IDEA). A 504 plan is a plan for instructional services to assist students with special needs in a regular classroom setting. When a student's physical, emotional, or other impairments (such as attention deficit disorder) affect their ability to learn in a regular education classroom setting, that student can be referred for a 504 meeting. Typically, the CST and perhaps even the student's physician or therapist will participate in the 504 meeting and review to determine if a 504 plan will be written.

Finally, a child referred to CST may qualify for an Individualized Education Plan (IEP). An IEP is a legal document that determines the specific, adapted services a student with disabilities will receive. An IEP differs from a 504 plan in that the child must be identified for special education services to qualify for an IEP, and *all* students who receive special education services must have an IEP. Each IEP must contain statements pertaining to the student's present performance level, annual goals, related services and supplementary aids, testing modifications, a projected date of services, and assessment methods for monitoring progress. Each year, the CST and guardians meet to review and update a student's IEP.

See also Skill 18.7.

Skill 18.5 Criteria and procedures for selecting, creating, and modifying materials and equipment to address students' exceptionalities

Differentiated instruction
The effective teacher will seek to connect all students to the subject matter through multiple techniques, with the goal that each student, through their own abilities, will relate to one or more techniques and excel in the learning process. Differentiated instruction encompasses several areas:
1. Content: What is the teacher going to teach? Or, perhaps better put, what does the teacher want the students to learn? Differentiating content means that students will have access to content that piques their interest about a topic, with a complexity that provides an appropriate challenge to their intellectual development.
2. Process: A classroom management technique where instructional organization and delivery is maximized for the diverse student group. These techniques should include dynamic, flexible grouping activities, where instruction and learning occurs both as whole-class, teacher-led activities, as well as peer learning and teaching (while teacher observes and coaches) within small groups or pairs.
3. Product: The expectations and requirements placed on students to demonstrate their knowledge or understanding. The type of product expected from each student should reflect each student's own capabilities.

Alternative assessments
Alternative assessment is an assessment where students create an answer or a response to a question or task, as opposed to traditional, inflexible assessments

where students choose a prepared response from among a selection of responses, such as matching, multiple-choice or true/false.

When implemented effectively, an alternative assessment approach will exhibit these characteristics, among others:
- Requires higher-order thinking and problem-solving
- Provides opportunities for student self-reflection and self-assessment
- Uses real-world applications to connect students to the subject
- Provides opportunities for students to learn and examine subjects on their own, as well as to collaborate with their peers
- Encourages students to continue learning beyond the requirements of the assignment
- Clearly defines objective and performance goals

Testing modifications

The intent of testing modifications is to minimize the effect of a student's disability or learning challenge and to provide an equal opportunity to participate in assessments to demonstrate and express knowledge and ability.

Testing modifications should be identified in the student's IEP, consistently implemented, and used to the least extent possible. Types of testing modifications include:
- Flexible scheduling: providing time extensions or altering testing duration (e.g., by inserting appropriate breaks)
- Flexible setting: using special lighting or acoustics, minimizing distractions (e.g., testing the student in a separate location), using adaptive equipment
- Alternate test format: using large print or Braille, increasing the space allocated for student response, realigning the format of question and answer selections (e.g., vertically rather than horizontally)
- Use of mechanical aids: tape recorders, word processors, visual and auditory magnification devices, calculators, spell check and grammar check software (where spelling and grammar are not the focus of assessment)

Most classrooms contain a mixture of the following:
- Varying learning styles, classroom settings and academic outcomes
- Differences in biological, sociological, ethnic, socioeconomic, and psychological makeup of students
- Different settings and learning opportunities, such as collaborative, participatory, and individualized learning
- Expected learning outcomes that are theoretical, affective and cognitive for students

Students generally do not realize their own abilities and frequently lack self-confidence. Teachers should provide the kind of feedback that can instill positive self-concepts in children and thereby enhance their innate abilities. Such feedback includes attributing students' successes to their effort and specifying what the student did that produced the success. Qualitative comments influence attitudes more than quantitative feedback such as grades.

Instead of teaching tasks that fit their own plan and goals, teachers must design activities that address the students' concerns. To do this, they must collect information on and have a sense of their students' interests. Student surveys and friendly discussions can help teachers better understand their students and effectively link student interests with classroom tasks. This will help make students more responsive and productive in class.

Teachers are learning the value of giving assignments that meet the individual abilities and needs of students. After instruction, discussion, questioning, and practice have been provided, rather than assigning one task to all students, teachers are asking students to generate tasks that will show their knowledge of the information presented. Students are given choices and thereby have the opportunity to demonstrate more effectively the skills, concepts, or topics that they as individuals have learned. It has been established that student choice increases student originality, intrinsic motivation, and higher mental processes.

Skill 18.6 Legal requirements for providing education to students with disabling conditions

Per federal law, students with disabilities should be included as much as possible in the general education curriculum of their schools. While this may be difficult for new teachers (likewise, it may be difficult for new teachers to include gifted students in the general education curriculum), it is extremely important to do so.

Flexible grouping is a unique strategy to ensure that students with special needs are fully accommodated. While flexible grouping does indeed mean that groups for various learning activities will change (depending on the activity, or just depending on the need to rotate groups), when teachers consistently build in various group structures in order to accommodate various learning needs, their students will get varied and multiple opportunities to talk about, reflect upon, and question new learning. In some cases, teachers may wish to pair students with special needs with other students who are proficient in particular subjects; at other times, they may desire to pair students with others who have similar levels of proficiency.

Behavior issues often cause students with special needs to be excluded from full class participation. It is important for teachers to note that often, students with special needs do not want to be excluded, and often, they do not want to be "bad." Rather, they are seeking attention, or they are bored. In either case, classroom activities must be developed with these concerns in mind. All students, in fact, will be more engaged with hands-on, real-world learning activities. Often, when teachers give students even small amounts of choice, such as letting them choose one of three topics to write about, students feel empowered. Students with special needs are no different.

Finally, many students with special needs want to stay "caught up" with the rest of the class, but occasionally, they cannot. In such cases, it is imperative that teachers find ways that will allow these students to know that they are on the same page as the rest of the class. Reducing the amount of work for students with special needs is often productive; pairing such students with more proficient students can also be assistive.

Skill 18.7 Purposes and procedures for developing and implementing Individualized Education Plans (IEPs) or 504 Accommodation Plans

Strategies and Resources

Special education teachers, resource specialists, school psychologists, and other special education staff are present on school campuses to be resources for students who have special educational needs. Occasionally, new teachers fear that when a resource specialist seeks to work with them, it means that the resource specialist does not think they are doing an adequate job in dealing with students with IEPs. Quite the contrary; many IEPs require that resource specialists work in students' general education classrooms. Indeed, the law for special education ("IDEA") states that students should receive education in the "least restrictive environment." What this means is that if a student can function in a regular education classroom, even if the assistance of a specialist is required, the student should be in that regular education classroom. Considering that school is more than just about the learning of content standards – that it is often about socialization and the development of citizens for a democratic society – it is counterproductive and unfair to exclude students from regular classrooms.

First and foremost, teachers must be familiar with what is stated in their students' IEPs. For example, some IEPs have explicit strategies that teachers should use to help the students learn effectively. Teachers may want to provide additional attention to these students to ensure that they are progressing effectively. Sometimes, it may be necessary to reduce or modify assignments for students with disabilities. For example, if a teacher is assigning 15 math problems to the class, they might want to assign only five to students with disabilities to make the work of these particular students more effective. Teachers can use multiple strategies, group students in flexible situations, and pair them with others who can be of assistance.

Special education services are offered in many ways, and a student's IEP and CST will determine their least restrictive environment. Inclusion refers to the situation where a student with special needs remains in the regular education classroom with the support of special education support staff (usually in the form of a personal or class aid). Sometimes, a student requires some resource room, or pull out, services. In these cases, students are taken into smaller class settings where personalized services are delivered in their greatest area(s) of difficulty. Students who have difficulty functioning in a regular education classroom are placed in smaller classrooms for the full school day. These are sometimes referred to as LD or learning disabled classrooms.

Finally, welcome and include the suggestions and assistance of the special education staff. Most resource specialists are trained particularly to work with general education teachers, and most want to be able to do that in the most effective, non-threatening way.

See also Skill 1

Learn more about:
National Association for Gifted Children
http://www.nagc.org/
Learning disabilities and ADHD
http://www.ldonline.org/indepth/gifted
Benefits of an all-inclusive classroom
http://www.uni.edu/coe/inclusion/philosophy/benefits.html

Sample Test 1

Subarea I. Child Development and Learning

1. **What developmental patterns should a professional teacher assess to meet the needs of each student?**

   A. Academic, regional, and family background

   B. Social, physical, and academic

   C. Academic, physical, and family background

   D. Physical, family, and ethnic background

2. **The various domains of development are best described as:**

   A. Integrated

   B. Independent

   C. Simultaneous

   D. Parallel

3. **Which of the following best describes how different areas of development impact each other?**

   A. Development in other areas cannot occur until cognitive development is complete.

   B. Areas of development are inter-related and impact each other.

   C. Development in each area is independent of development in other areas.

   D. Development in one area leads to a decline in other areas.

4. **A student has developed and improved in vocabulary. However, the student is not confident enough to use the improved vocabulary, and the teacher is not aware of the improvement. What is this an example of?**

   A. Latent development

   B. Dormant development

   C. Random development

   D. Delayed development

5. **Which of the following has been shown to have the greatest impact on a student's academic performance?**

    A.   The teacher's expectations

    B.   Strict discipline

    C.   The student's social skills

    D.   Measurable objectives

6. **According to Piaget, when does the development of symbolic functioning and language first take place?**

    A.   Concrete operations stage

    B.   Formal operations stage

    C.   Sensory-motor stage

    D.   Pre-operational stage

7. **Playing team sports at young ages should be done for the following purpose:**

    A.   To develop the child's motor skills

    B.   To prepare children for competition in high school

    C.   To develop the child's interests

    D.   Both A and C

8. **The stages of play development from infancy stages to early childhood includes a move from:**

    A.   Cooperative to solitary

    B.   Solitary to cooperative

    C.   Competitive to collaborative

    D.   Collaborative to competitive

9. **Which of the following is NOT an economic factor that may influence the health of a child?**

    A.   Pollution

    B.   Malnutrition

    C.   Neglect

    D.   Poor medical care

10. **Which of the following is the main source of energy in the diet?**

    A.   Vitamins

    B.   Minerals

    C.   Water

    D.   Carbohydrates

11. **Which of the following would be likely to influence a student's learning and academic progress?**

    A.   Relocation

    B.   Emotional abuse

    C.   Bullying

    D.   All of the above

12. **Which of the following best explains why emotional upset and emotional abuse can reduce a child's classroom performance?**

    A.   They reduce the energy that students put towards schoolwork.

    B.   They lead to a reduction in cognitive ability.

    C.   They contribute to learning disorders such as dyslexia.

    D.   They result in the development of behavioral problems.

13. **A teacher has a class with several students from low income families in it. What would it be most important for a teacher to consider when planning homework assignments to ensure that all students have equal opportunity for academic success?**

    A.   Access to technology

    B.   Ethnicity

    C.   Language difficulties

    D.   Gender

14. **Family members with high levels of education often have high expectations for student success. This shows how students are influenced by their family's:**

    A.   Attitude

    B.   Resources

    C.   Income

    D.   Culture

15. **Why is it most important for teachers to ensure that students from different economic backgrounds have access to the resources they need to acquire the academic skills being taught?**

A. All students must work together on set tasks.

B. All students must achieve the same results in performance tasks.

C. All students must have equal opportunity for academic success.

D. All students must be fully included in classroom activities.

16. **A teacher attempting to create a differentiated classroom should focus on incorporating activities that:**

A. Favor academically advanced students

B. Challenge special education students to achieve more

C. Are suitable for whichever group of students is the majority

D. Meet the needs of all the students in the class

17. **When developing lessons, it is important that teachers provide equity in pedagogy so that:**

A. Unfair labeling of students will not occur

B. Student experiences will be positive

C. Students will achieve academic success

D. All of the above

18. **Which of the following is NOT a communication issue related to diversity within the classroom?**

A. Learning disorders

B. Sensitive terminology

C. Body language

D. Discussing differing viewpoints and opinions

19. **One common factor for students with all types of disabilities is that they are also likely to demonstrate difficulty with:**

A. Social skills

B. Cognitive skills

C. Problem-solving skills

D. Decision-making skills

20. A student does not respond to any signs of affection and responds to other children by repeating back what they have said. What condition is the student most likely to have?

A.   Mental retardation

B.   Autism

C.   Giftedness

D.   Hyperactivity

21. Which of the following conditions is more common for girls than boys?

A.   Attention deficit disorder

B.   Aggression

C.   Phobias

D.   Autism

22. In successful inclusion of students with disabilities:

A.   A variety of instructional arrangements are available

B.   School personnel shift the responsibility for learning outcomes to the student

C.   The physical facilities are used as they are

D.   Regular classroom teachers have sole responsibility for evaluating student progress

23. Mr. Gorman has taught a concept to his class. All of the students have grasped the concept except for Sam. Mr. Gorman should:

A.   Reteach the concept to the whole class in exactly the same way

B.   Reteach the concept to Sam in exactly the same way

C.   Reteach the concept to Sam in a different way

D.   Reteach the concept to the whole class in a different way

24. **Mrs. Gomez has a fully integrated early childhood curriculum. This is beneficial to students because it:**

    A. Is easier to plan for and maintain

    B. Allows students to apply their unique skills

    C. Helps the students see the relationships between subjects and concepts

    D. Provides opportunities for social interaction

Subarea II. Communication, Language and Literacy Development

25. **The relationship between oral language and reading skills is best described as:**

    A. Reciprocal

    B. Inverse

    C. Opposite

    D. There is no relationship.

26. **A teacher is showing students how to construct grammatically correct sentences. What is the teacher focusing on?**

    A. Morphology

    B. Syntax

    C. Semantics

    D. Pragmatics

27. **A teacher writes the following words on the board: cot, cotton, and cottage. What is the teacher most likely teaching the students about?**

    A. Morphology

    B. Syntax

    C. Semantics

    D. Pragmatics

28. **While standing in line at the grocery store, three-year-old Megan says to her mother in a regular tone of voice, "Mom, why is that woman so fat?" What does this indicate a lack of understanding of?**

    A. Syntax

    B. Semantics

    C. Morphology

    D. Pragmatics

29. **Which of the following is the first component of the constructivist model?**

    A. There are at least seven different types of learning.

    B. Learning depends on the social environment.

    C. Learner creates knowledge

    D. Learning progresses through set stages.

30. **Students are about to read a text that contains words that will need to be understood for the students to understand the text. When should the vocabulary be introduced to students?**

    A. Before reading

    B. During reading

    C. After reading

    D. It should not be introduced.

31. **Which of the following are examples of temporal words?**

    A. Beside and behind

    B. Hotter and colder

    C. In and on

    D. Before and after

32. **Which principle of Stephen Krashen's research suggests that the learning of grammatical structures is predictable?**

    A. The affective filter hypothesis

    B. The input hypothesis

    C. The natural order hypothesis

    D. The monitor hypothesis

33. **Above what age does learning a language become increasingly difficult?**

    A. 3

    B. 5

    C. 7

    D. 10

34. Ms. Chomski is presenting a new story to her class of first graders. In the story, a family visits their grandparents where they all gather around a record player and listen to music. Many students do not understand what a record player is, especially some children for whom English is not their first language. Which of the following would Ms. Chomski be best to do?

A. Discuss what a record player is with her students

B. Compare a record player with a CD player

C. Have students look up record player in a dictionary

D. Show the students a picture of a record player

35. Jose moved to the United States last month. He speaks little to no English at this time. His teacher is teaching the class about habitats in science and has chosen to read a story about various habitats to the class. The vocabulary is difficult. What should Jose's teacher do with Jose? (Skill 5.3; Average rigor)

A. Provide Jose with additional opportunities to learn about habitats

B. Read the story to Jose multiple times

C. Show Jose pictures of habitats from his native country

D. Excuse Jose from the assignment

36. In the early childhood classroom, it is important to limit teacher talk. What is the main problem with teacher talk?

A. It is often one sided and limited.

B. The vocabulary is too difficult for children.

C. It promotes misbehavior.

D. It only creates gains in receptive language.

37. **Which of the following is a convention of print that children learn during reading activities?**

    A.   The meaning of words

    B.   The left to right motion

    C.   The purpose of print

    D.   The identification of letters

38. **In her kindergarten class, Mrs. Thomas has been watching the students in the drama center. She has watched the children pretend to complete a variety of magic tricks. Mrs. Thomas decides to use stories about magic to share with her class. Her decision to incorporate their interests into the reading shows that Mrs. Thomas understands that:**

    A.   Including student interests is important at all times

    B.   Teaching by themes is crucial for young children

    C.   Young children respond to literature that reflects their lives

    D.   Science fiction and fantasy are the most popular genres

39. **Which of the following is NOT a characteristic of a fable?**

    A.   Have animal characters that act like humans

    B.   Considered to be true

    C.   Teaches a moral

    D.   Reveals human foibles

40. **Alphabet books are classified as:**

    A.   Concept books

    B.   Easy-to-read books

    C.   Board books

    D.   Pictures books

41. **The works of Paul Bunyan, John Henry, and Pecos Bill are all exaggerated accounts of individuals with superhuman strength. What type of literature are these works?**

    A.   Fables

    B.   Fairytales

    C.   Tall tales

    D.   Myths

42. **Which of the following is NOT a motivation behind providing reading activities, including reading aloud, to young children?**

    A. Developing word consciousness skills

    B. Developing functions of print skills

    C. Developing phonics skills

    D. Developing language skills

43. **Which of the following is an appropriate way for students to respond to literature?**

    A. Art

    B. Drama

    C. Writing

    D. All of the above

44. **John is having difficulty reading the word reach. In isolation, he pronounces each sound as /r/ /ee/ /sh/. Which of the following is a possible instructional technique which could help solve John's reading difficulty?**

    A. Additional phonemic awareness instruction

    B. Additional phonics instruction

    C. Additional skill and drill practice

    D. Additional minimal pair practice

45. **According to Marilyn Jager Adams, which skill would a student demonstrate by identifying that cat does not belong in the group of words containing dog, deer, and dress?**

    A. Recognize the odd member in a group

    B. Replace sounds in words

    C. Count the sounds in a word

    D. Count syllables in a word

46. **Which of the following is NOT true about phonological awareness?**

    A. It may involve print.

    B. It is a prerequisite for spelling and phonics.

    C. Activities can be done by the children with their eyes closed.

    D. It starts before letter recognition is taught.

47. **Which of the following explains a significant difference between phonics and phonemic awareness?**

    A. Phonics involves print, while phonemic awareness involves language.

    B. Phonics is harder than phonemic awareness.

    C. Phonics involves sounds, while phonemic awareness involves letters.

    D. Phonics is the application of sounds to print, while phonemic awareness is oral.

48. **To decode is to:**

    A. Construct meaning

    B. Sound out a printed sequence of letters

    C. Use a special code to decipher a message

    D. Revise for errors in grammar

49. **Ms. Walker's lesson objective is to teach her first graders the concept of morphology in order to improve their reading skills. Which group of words would be most appropriate for her to use in this lesson?**

    A. Far, farm, farmer

    B. Far, feather, fever

    C. Far, fear, fare

    D. Far, fare, farce

50. **Which stage of reading skill development occurs first?**

    A. Schema stage

    B. Early semantic stage

    C. Orthographic stage

    D. Simultaneous stage

51. **Which of the following is an important feature of vocabulary instruction according to the National Reading Panel?**

   A. Repetition of vocabulary items

   B. Keeping a consistent task structure at all times

   C. Teaching vocabulary in more than one language

   D. Isolation vocabulary instruction from other subjects

52. **The attitude an author takes toward his or her subject is the:**

   A. Style

   B. Tone

   C. Point of view

   D. Theme

53. **George has read his second graders three formats of the story "The Three Little Pigs." One is the traditional version, one is written from the wolf's point of view, and the third is written from the first pig's point of view. As George leads a discussion on the three texts with his students, he is trying to help his students develop their ability to:**

   A. Compare and contrast texts

   B. Understand point of view

   C. Recognize metaphors

   D. Rewrite fictional stories

54. **What is the first step in developing writing skills?**

   A. Early writing

   B. Experimental writing

   C Role play writing

   D. Conventional writing

55. **Which of the following is NOT a prewriting strategy?**

   A. Analyzing sentences for variety

   B. Keeping an idea book

   C. Writing in a daily journal

   D. Writing down whatever comes to mind

56. **Which of the following is probably the most important step for the writer in the writing process?**

    A. Revision

    B. Discovery

    C. Conclusion

    D. Organization

57. **The students in Tina's classroom are working together in pairs. Each student is reading another student's paper and asking who, what, when, where, why, and who questions. What is this activity helping the students to do?**

    A. Draft their writing

    B. Paraphrase their writing

    C. Revise their writing

    D. Outline their writing

58. **Young children learning to write commonly grip the pencil:**

    A. Too far from the point

    B. With the wrong hand

    C. With too many fingers

    D. Too tightly

59. **Which of the following approaches to student writing assignments is most likely to lead to students becoming disinterested?**

    A. Designing assignments where students write for a variety of audiences.

    B. Designing assignments where the teacher is the audience.

    C. Designing assignments where students write to friends and family.

    D. Designing assignments where students write to real people such as mayors, the principle, or companies.

60. **As a part of prewriting, students should identify their audience. Which of the following questions will help students to identify their audience?**

    A. Why is the audience reading my writing?

    B. What does my audience already know about my topic?

    C. Both A and B

    D. None of the above

61. **Which of these describes the best way to teach spelling?**

    A. At the same time that grammar and sentence structure is taught.

    B. Within the context of meaningful language experiences.

    C. Independently so that students can concentrate on spelling.

    D. In short lessons as students pick up spelling almost immediately.

62. **When editing, teachers should direct students to:**

    A. Edit for general understanding, while ignoring grammar and spelling.

    B. Edit for one specific purpose at a time.

    C. Identify all spelling, capitalization, and punctuation errors.

    D. Be critical of their work and that of others.

Subarea III. Learning in the Content Areas

63. **Kindergarten students are participating in a calendar time activity. One student adds a straw to the "ones can" to represent that day of school. What math principle is being reinforced?**

    A. Properties of a base ten number system

    B. Sorting

    C. Counting by twos

    D. Even and odd numbers

64. **First grade students are arranging four small squares of identical size to form a larger square. Each small square represents what part of the larger square?**

    A. One half

    B. One whole

    C. One fourth

    D. One fifth

65. What is the answer to this problem?

    25 ÷ 5 =

    A. 5

    B. 30

    C. 125

    D. 20

66. Third grade students are studying percents. When looking at a circle graph divided into three sections, they see that one section is worth 80% and one section is worth 5%. What will the remaining section be worth?

    A. 100%

    B. 85%

    C. 75%

    D. 15%

67. Which of the following letters does NOT have a line of symmetry?

    A. O

    B. D

    C. M

    D. J

68. Kindergarten students are doing a butterfly art project. They fold paper in half. On one half, they paint a design. Then they fold the paper closed and reopen. The resulting picture is a butterfly with matching sides. What math principle does this demonstrate?

    A. Slide

    B. Rotate

    C. Symmetry

    D. Transformation

69. What number comes next in this pattern?

    3, 8, 13, 18, _____

    A. 21

    B. 26

    C. 23

    D. 5

70. What is the main purpose of having kindergarten students count by twos?

    A. To hear a rhythm

    B. To recognize patterns in numbers

    C. To practice addition

    D. To become familiar with equations

71. The term *millimeters* indicates which kind of measurement?

    A. Volume

    B. Weight

    C. Length

    D. Temperature

72. What type of graph would be best to use to show changes in the height of a plant over the course of a month?

    A. Circle graph

    B. Bar graph

    C. Line graph

    D. Pictograph

73. A teacher completes a survey of student eye color. The teacher then creates a graph so students can compare how many students have each eye color. What type of graph should be used?

    A. Bar graph

    B. Pictograph

    C. Circle graph

    D. Line graph

74. Which of the following skills would a student develop first?

    A. Understanding place value

    B. Recognizing number patterns

    C. Counting objects

    D. Solving number problems

75. Maddie is a first grade teacher who understands the importance of including the family when providing instruction. She wants to take several steps to provide families with a connection to what the students are doing in her math class. Which of the following is NOT a strategy she could incorporate?

    A. Including a math portion in her regular newsletter

    B. Incorporating manipulatives into her math lessons

    C. Translating math homework into the native language of the students in her classroom

    D. Having a family math night at school

76. George has successfully mastered his basic addition facts. However, as his teacher presents more complex addition problems, it is obvious to him that George is lacking a basic understanding of the concept of addition. What would George's teacher be best to do to increase his basic understanding?

   A. Provide additional instruction with hands on materials

   B. Have George practice his addition facts more frequently

   C. Have George complete more challenging addition problems

   D. Provide George with remediation

77. Carrie approaches her teacher after class and expresses her personal frustration with math and her feeling that she will never get it. Which of the following is NOT a suitable method Carrie's teacher can utilize to improve Carrie's feelings about math?

   A. Incorporating some of Carrie's specific interests into math lessons

   B. Holding Carrie to high expectations

   C. Sharing with Carrie her own struggles and dislike for math

   D. Providing Carrie with extra positive reinforcement and encouragement

78. **The principal walks into your classroom during math class. He sees your students making cake mixtures. Later, the principal questions your lesson. What would be the best explanation for your lesson?**

   A.   The students earned a reward time and it was free choice.

   B.   You were teaching the students how math is used in real-life situations.

   C.   You had paperwork to complete and needed the time to complete it.

   D.   It kept the students interested in math and prevented boredom.

79. **What is a large, rotating, low-pressure system accompanied by heavy precipitation and strong winds known as?**

   A.   A hurricane

   B.   A tornado

   C.   A thunderstorm

   D.   A tsunami

80. **What does a primary consumer most commonly refer to?**

   A.   Herbivore

   B.   Autotroph

   C.   Carnivore

   D.   Decomposer

81. **Airplanes generate pressure and remain balanced by:**

   A.   Fast air movement over wings and slow movement under wings

   B.   Slow air movement over wings and fast movement under wings

   C.   Air movement that is equal above and below wings

   D.   Air movement that only occurs over the wings

82. **The breakdown of rock due to acid rain is an example of:**

   A.   Physical weathering

   B.   Frost wedging

   C.   Chemical weathering

   D.   Deposition

83. **What is the last step in the scientific method?**

    A. Pose a question

    B. Draw a conclusion

    C. Conduct a test

    D. Record data

84. **Which term best describes Newton's universal gravitation?**

    A. Theory

    B. Hypothesis

    C. Inference

    D. Law

85. **When teaching science, which of the following is a method of focusing on students' intrinsic motivation?**

    A. Adapting the lessons to students' interests

    B. Providing regular feedback

    C. Supplying rewards for the highest achievers

    D. Having regular science tests

86. **What does geography include the study of?**

    A. Location

    B. Distribution of living things

    C. Distribution of the earth's features

    D. All of the above

87. **Economics is the study of how a society allocates its scarce resources to satisfy:**

    A. Unlimited and competing wants

    B. Limited and competing wants

    C. Unlimited and cooperative wants

    D. Limited and cooperative wants

88. **The two elements of a market economy are:**

    A. Inflation and deflation

    B. Supply and demand

    C. Cost and price

    D. Wants and needs

89. Who has the power to veto a bill that has passed the House of Representatives and the Senate?

   A.   The President

   B.   The Vice President

   C.   The Speaker of the House

   D.   Any member of Congress

90. Which part of a map shows the relationship between a unit of measurement on the map versus the real world measure on the Earth?

   A.   Scale

   B.   Title

   C.   Legend

   D.   Grid

91. What is the most important focus in developing social studies skills during the early years?

   A.   Recalling facts

   B.   Understanding statistics

   C.   Discussing ideas

   D.   Memorizing rights and responsibilities

92. What is one of the ten essential themes identified by the National Council for Social Studies?

   A.   Culture

   B.   Lifestyle

   C.   Population

   D.   Democracy

93. Which subject would a color wheel most likely be used for?

   A.   Visual arts

   B.   Music

   C.   Movement

   D.   Drama

94. A student art sample book would include cotton balls and sand paper to represent:

   A.   Color

   B.   Lines

   C.   Texture

   D.   Shape

95. **Which terms refers to the arrangement of one or more items so that they appear symmetrical or asymmetrical?**

    A. Balance

    B. Contrast

    C. Emphasis

    D. Unity

96. **The four principles of modern dance are substance, form, metakinesis, and:**

    A. Dynamism

    B. Function

    C. Space

    D. Performance

97. **What should the arts curriculum for early childhood avoid?**

    A. Judgment

    B. Open expression

    C. Experimentation

    D. Discovery

98. **What would the viewing of a dance company performance be most likely to promote?**

    A. Critical-thinking skills

    B. Appreciation of the arts

    C. Improvisation skills

    D. Music vocabulary

99. **In which subject is it most important for students to work with costumes and props?**

    A. Visual arts

    B. Music

    C. Movement

    D. Drama

100. **According to Charles Fowler, why is it important for arts to be incorporated into the teaching of other subject areas?**

    A. It reduces loss of interest in the subject.

    B. It enhances the likelihood that students will retain the information.

    C. It provides a three dimensional view of the subject.

    D. It encourages the development of personal connections with the subject.

Answer Key: Sample Test 1

1.	B	45.	A	89.	A
2.	A	46.	A	90.	A
3.	B	47.	D	91.	C
4.	A	48.	B	92.	A
5.	A	49.	A	93.	A
6.	D	50.	A	94.	C
7.	D	51.	A	95.	A
8.	B	52.	B	96.	A
9.	A	53.	A	97.	A
10.	D	54.	C	98.	B
11.	D	55.	A	99.	D
12.	A	56.	A	100.	C
13.	A	57.	C		
14.	A	58.	D		
15.	C	59.	B		
16.	D	60.	C		
17.	D	61.	B		
18.	A	62.	B		
19.	A	63.	A		
20.	B	64.	C		
21.	C	65.	A		
22.	A	66.	D		
23.	C	67.	D		
24.	C	68.	C		
25.	A	69.	C		
26.	B	70.	B		
27.	A	71.	C		
28.	D	72.	C		
29.	C	73.	A		
30.	A	74.	C		
31.	D	75.	B		
32.	C	76.	A		
33.	C	77.	C		
34.	D	78.	B		
35.	A	79.	A		
36.	A	80.	A		
37.	B	81.	A		
38.	C	82.	C		
39.	B	83.	B		
40.	A	84.	D		
41.	C	85.	A		
42.	C	86.	D		
43.	D	87.	A		
44.	A	88.	B		

Sample Test 1 Rationales

Subarea I. Child Development and Learning

1. **What developmental patterns should a professional teacher assess to meet the needs of each student?**

    A. Academic, regional, and family background

    B. Social, physical, and academic

    C. Academic, physical, and family background

    D. Physical, family, and ethnic background

Answer B: Social, physical, and academic
The effective teacher applies knowledge of physical, social, and academic developmental patterns and of individual differences, to meet the instructional needs of all students in the classroom.

2. **The various domains of development are best described as:**

    A. Integrated

    B. Independent

    C. Simultaneous

    D. Parallel

Answer A: Integrated
The most important premise of child development is that all domains of development (physical, social, and academic) are integrated.

3. **Which of the following best describes how different areas of development impact each other?**

    A. Development in other areas cannot occur until cognitive development is complete.

    B. Areas of development are inter-related and impact each other.

    C. Development in each area is independent of development in other areas.

    D. Development in one area leads to a decline in other areas.

Answer B: Areas of development are inter-related and impact each other. Child development does not occur in a vacuum. Each element of development impacts other elements of development. For example, as cognitive development progresses, social development often follows. The reason for this is that all areas of development are fairly inter-related.

4. **A student has developed and improved in vocabulary. However, the student is not confident enough to use the improved vocabulary, and the teacher is not aware of the improvement. What is this an example of?**

    A. Latent development

    B. Dormant development

    C. Random development

    D. Delayed development

Answer A: Latent development
Latent development refers to the way that development in students may not always be observable. A student that has developed and improved in the area of vocabulary, but lacks the confidence to use the vocabulary would not show any outward signs of the development, and so the change may remain hidden. Teachers should be aware of this in order to identify a child's future or near-future capabilities.

5. **Which of the following has been shown to have the greatest impact on a student's academic performance?**

    A. The teacher's expectations

    B. Strict discipline

    C. The student's social skills

    D. Measurable objectives

Answer A: The teacher's expectations
Considerable research has been done, over several decades, regarding student performance. Time and again, a direct correlation has been demonstrated between the teacher's expectations for a particular student and that student's academic performance. This may be unintended and subtle, but the effects are manifest and measurable.

6. **According to Piaget, when does the development of symbolic functioning and language first take place?**

    A. Concrete operations stage

    B. Formal operations stage

    C. Sensory-motor stage

    D. Pre-operational stage

Answer D: Pre-operational stage
The pre-operational stage is where children begin to understand symbols. For example, as they learn language, they begin to realize that words are symbols of thoughts, actions, items, and other elements in the world. This stage lasts into early elementary school.

7. **Playing team sports at young ages should be done for the following purpose:**

    A. To develop the child's motor skills

    B. To prepare children for competition in high school

    C. To develop the child's interests

    D. Both A and C

Answer D: Both A and C

Sports, for both boys and girls, can be very valuable. Parents and teachers, though, need to remember that sports at young ages should only be for the purpose of development of interests and motor skills—not competition. Many children will learn that they do not enjoy sports, and parents and teachers should be respectful of these decisions.

8. **The stages of play development from infancy stages to early childhood includes a move from:**

    A. Cooperative to solitary

    B. Solitary to cooperative

    C. Competitive to collaborative

    D. Collaborative to competitive

Answer B: Solitary to cooperative

The stages of play development move from mainly solitary in the infancy stages to cooperative in early childhood. However, even in early childhood, children should be able to play on their own and entertain themselves from time to time.

9. **Which of the following is NOT an economic factor that may influence the health of a child?**

    A. Pollution

    B. Malnutrition

    C. Neglect

    D. Poor medical care

Answer A: Pollution

Malnutrition, neglect, and poor medical care are economic factors that may influence the health of a child. Pollution could influence the health of a child, but it is not an economic factor.

10. **Which of the following is the main source of energy in the diet?**

    A.   Vitamins

    B.   Minerals

    C.   Water

    D.   Carbohydrates

Answer D: Carbohydrates
The components of nutrition are carbohydrates, proteins, fats, vitamins, minerals, and water. Carbohydrates are the main source of energy (glucose) in the human diet. Common sources of carbohydrates are fruits, vegetables, grains, dairy products, and legumes.

11. **Which of the following would be likely to influence a student's learning and academic progress?**

    A.   Relocation

    B.   Emotional abuse

    C.   Bullying

    D.   All of the above

Answer D: All of the above
 Children can be influenced by social and emotional factors. Relocation, emotional, abuse, and bullying can all have a negative impact on a student's learning and academic progress.

12. **Which of the following best explains why emotional upset and emotional abuse can reduce a child's classroom performance?**

    A.   They reduce the energy that students put towards schoolwork.

    B.   They lead to a reduction in cognitive ability.

    C.   They contribute to learning disorders such as dyslexia.

    D.   They result in the development of behavioral problems.

Answer A: They reduce the energy that students put towards schoolwork. Although cognitive ability is not lost due to abuse, neglect, emotional upset, or lack of verbal interaction, the child will most likely not be able to provide as much intellectual energy as the child would if none of these things were present. This explains why classroom performance is often negatively impacted.

13. A teacher has a class containing several students from low income families. What would be the most important factor for a teacher to consider when planning homework assignments to ensure that all students have equal opportunity for academic success?

    A.   Access to technology

    B.   Ethnicity

    C.   Language difficulties

    D.   Gender

Answer A: Access to technology
Families with higher incomes are able to provide increased opportunities for students. Students from lower income families will need to depend on the resources available from the school system and the community. To ensure that all students have equal opportunity for academic success, teachers should plan assessments so that not having access to technology does not disadvantage students from low income families.

14. Family members with high levels of education often have high expectations for student success. This shows how students are influenced by their family's:

    A.   Attitude

    B.   Resources

    C.   Income

    D.   Culture

Answer A: Attitude
Parental/family influences on students include the influence of attitude. Family members with high levels of education often have high expectations for student success and this can have a positive impact on the student. The opposite can occur for some students from families with low levels of education. However, some families have high expectations for student success based on aspirations for their children regardless of their own status.

15. **Why is it most important for teachers to ensure that students from different economic backgrounds have access to the resources they need to acquire the academic skills being taught?**

    A.   All students must work together on set tasks.

    B.   All students must achieve the same results in performance tasks.

    C.   All students must have equal opportunity for academic success.

    D.   All students must be fully included in classroom activities.

Answer C: All students must have equal opportunity for academic success. The economic backgrounds of students can impact the resources they have. Regardless of the positive or negative impacts on the students' education from outside sources, it is the teacher's responsibility to ensure that all students in the classroom have an equal opportunity for academic success. This includes ensuring that all students have equal access to the resources needed to acquire the skills being taught.

16. **A teacher attempting to create a differentiated classroom should focus on incorporating activities that:**

    A.   Favor academically advanced students

    B.   Challenge special education students to achieve more

    C.   Are suitable for whichever group of students is the majority

    D.   Meet the needs of all the students in the class

Answer D: Meet the needs of all the students in the class
A differentiated classroom is one that meets the needs of special education students, the regular mainstream students, and those that are academically advanced. The purpose of the differentiated classroom is to provide appropriate activities for students at all levels.

17. **When developing lessons, it is important that teachers provide equity in pedagogy so that:**

    A. Unfair labeling of students will not occur

    B. Student experiences will be positive

    C. Students will achieve academic success

    D. All of the above

Answer D: All of the above
When there is equity pedagogy, teachers can use a variety of instructional styles to facilitate diversity in cooperative learning and individualized instruction that will provide more opportunities for positive student experiences and academic success. Empowering the school culture and climate by establishing an anti-bias learning environment and promoting multicultural learning inclusion will also discourage unfair labeling of certain students.

18. **Which of the following is NOT a communication issue related to diversity within the classroom?**

    A. Learning disorders

    B. Sensitive terminology

    C. Body language

    D. Discussing differing viewpoints and opinions

Answer A: Learning disorders
There are several communication issues that the teacher in a diverse classroom should be aware of. These include being sensitive to terminology, being aware of body language, and emphasizing the discussion of differing viewpoints and opinions.

19. **One common factor for students with all types of disabilities is that they are also likely to demonstrate difficulty with:**

    A.   Social skills

    B.   Cognitive skills

    C.   Problem-solving skills

    D.   Decision-making skills

Answer A: Social skills

Students with disabilities (in all areas) may demonstrate difficulty in social skills. For a student with a hearing impairment, social skills may be difficult because of not hearing social language. However, the emotionally disturbed student may have difficulty because of a special type of psychological disturbance. An autistic student, as a third example, would be unaware of the social cues given with voice, facial expression, and body language. Each of these students would need social skill instruction but in a different way.

20. **A student does not respond to any signs of affection and responds to other children by repeating back what they have said. What condition is the student most likely to have?**

    A.   Mental retardation

    B.   Autism

    C.   Giftedness

    D.   Hyperactivity

Answer B: Autism

There are six common features of autism. They are:
- Apparent sensory deficit – lack of reaction to or overreaction to a stimulus.
- Severe affect isolation – lack of response to affection, such as smiles and hugs.
- Self-stimulation – repeated or ritualistic actions that make no sense to others.
- Tantrums and self-injurious behavior (SIB) – throwing tantrums, injuring oneself, or aggression.
- Echolalia (also known as "parrot talk") – repetition of sounds or responding to others by repeating what was said to him.
- Severe deficits in behavior and self-care skills – behaving like children much younger than themselves.

21. **Which of the following conditions is more common for girls than boys?**

    A.   Attention deficit disorder

    B.   Aggression

    C.   Phobias

    D.   Autism

Answer C: Phobias
Many more boys than girls are identified as having emotional and behavioral problems, especially hyperactivity, attention deficit disorder, autism, childhood psychosis, and problems with self control such as aggression and socialized aggression. Girls have more problems with over control, such as withdrawal and phobias.

22. **In successful inclusion of students with disabilities:**

    A.   A variety of instructional arrangements are available

    B.   School personnel shift the responsibility for learning outcomes to the student

    C.   The physical facilities are used as they are

    D.   Regular classroom teachers have sole responsibility for evaluating student progress

Answer A: A variety of instructional arrangements are available
All students have the right to an education, but there cannot be a singular path to that education. A teacher must acknowledge the variety of learning styles and abilities among students within a class apply multiple instructional and assessment processes to ensure that every child has appropriate opportunities to master the subject matter, demonstrate such mastery, and improve and enhance learning skills with each lesson.

23. **Mr. Gorman has taught a concept to his class. All of the students have grasped the concept except for Sam. Mr. Gorman should:**

    A.   Reteach the concept to the whole class in exactly the same way

    B.   Reteach the concept to Sam in exactly the same way

    C.   Reteach the concept to Sam in a different way

    D.   Reteach the concept to the whole class in a different way

Answer C: Reteach the concept to Sam in a different way
There is always more than one way to approach a problem, an example, a process, fact or event, or any learning situation. Varying approaches for instruction helps to maintain the students' interest in the material and enables the teacher to address the diverse needs of individuals to comprehend the material.

24. **Mrs. Gomez has a fully integrated early childhood curriculum. This is beneficial to students because it:**

    A.   Is easier to plan for and maintain

    B.   Allows students to apply their unique skills

    C.   Helps the students see the relationships between subjects and concepts

    D.   Provides opportunities for social interaction

Answer C: Helps the students see the relationships between subjects and concepts
An integrated curriculum is a curriculum in which lessons are taught in several different subject areas according to the outcomes that deal with the same concepts. It may also be known as thematic teaching or interdisciplinary teaching.

Subarea II. Communication, Language and Literacy Development

25. **The relationship between oral language and reading skills is best described as:**

    A. Reciprocal

    B. Inverse

    C. Opposite

    D. There is no relationship.

Answer A: Reciprocal
A highly developed oral language vocabulary helps to build reading skills comprehension. The inverse is true as well, with highly developed reading and comprehension skills helping to develop oral language skills.

26. **A teacher is showing students how to construct grammatically correct sentences. What is the teacher focusing on?**

    A. Morphology

    B. Syntax

    C. Semantics

    D. Pragmatics

Answer B: Syntax
Syntax refers to the rules or patterned relationships that correctly create phrases and sentences from words. When readers develop an understanding of syntax, they begin to understand the structure of how sentences are built, and eventually the beginning of grammar.

27. **A teacher writes the following words on the board: cot, cotton, and cottage. What is the teacher most likely teaching the students about?**

    A. Morphology

    B. Syntax

    C. Semantics

    D. Pragmatics

Answer A: Morphology

Morphology is the study of word structure. When readers develop morphemic skills, they are developing an understanding of patterns they see in words. For example, English speakers realize that cat, cats, and caterpillar share some similarities in structure. This understanding helps readers to recognize words at a faster and easier rate, since each word doesn't need individual decoding.

28. **While standing in line at the grocery store, three-year-old Megan says to her mother in a regular tone of voice, "Mom, why is that woman so fat?" What does this indicate a lack of understanding of?**

    A. Syntax

    B. Semantics

    C. Morphology

    D. Pragmatics

Answer D: Pragmatics

Pragmatics is the development and understanding of social relevance to conversations and topics. It develops as children age. In this situation, Megan simply does not understand to the same level of an adult how that question could be viewed as offensive to certain members of society.

29. **Which of the following is the first component of the constructivist model?**

   A.   There are at least seven different types of learning.

   B.   Learning depends on the social environment.

   C.   Learner creates knowledge

   D.   Learning progresses through set stages.

Answer C: Learner creates knowledge
Researchers have shown that the constructivist model is comprised of the four components:
1. Learner creates knowledge
2. Learner constructs and makes meaningful new knowledge from existing knowledge
3. Learner shapes and constructs knowledge by life experiences and social interactions
4. In constructivist learning communities, the student, teacher and classmates establish knowledge cooperatively on a daily basis.

30. **Students are about to read a text that contains words that will need to be understood for the students to understand the text. When should the vocabulary be introduced to students?**

   A.   Before reading

   B.   During reading

   C.   After reading

   D.   It should not be introduced.

Answer A: Before reading
Vocabulary should be introduced before reading if there are words within the text that are definitely keys necessary for reading comprehension.

31. **Which of the following are examples of temporal words?**

    A. Beside and behind

    B. Hotter and colder

    C. In and on

    D. Before and after

Answer D: Before and after
Temporal words are words that indicate time. Before and after are two examples of temporal words.

32. **Which principle of Stephen Krashen's research suggests that the learning of grammatical structures is predictable?**

    A. The affective filter hypothesis

    B. The input hypothesis

    C. The natural order hypothesis

    D. The monitor hypothesis

Answer C: The natural order hypothesis
Stephen Krashen's natural order hypothesis suggests that the learning of grammatical structures is predictable and follows a natural order.

33. **Above what age does learning a language become increasingly difficult?**

    A. 3

    B. 5

    C. 7

    D. 10

Answer C: 7
The most important concept to remember regarding the difference between learning a first language and a second one is that if the learner is approximately age seven or older, learning a second language will occur very differently in the learner's brain than it would had the learner been younger. The reason for this is that there is a language-learning function that exists in young children that appears to go away as they mature. Learning a language prior to age seven is almost guaranteed, with relatively little effort.

34. **Ms. Chomski is presenting a new story to her class of first graders. In the story, a family visits their grandparents where they all gather around a record player and listen to music. Many students do not understand what a record player is, especially some children for whom English is not their first language. Which of the following would Ms. Chomski be best to do?**

    A.   Discuss what a record player is with her students

    B.   Compare a record player with a CD player

    C.   Have students look up record player in a dictionary

    D.   Show the students a picture of a record player

Answer D: Show the students a picture of a record player
The most effective method for ensuring adequate comprehension is through direct experience. Sometimes this cannot be completed and therefore it is necessary to utilize pictures or other visual aids to provide the students with experience in another mode besides oral language.

35. **Jose moved to the United States last month. He speaks little or no English at this time. His teacher is teaching the class about habitats in science and has chosen to read a story about various habitats to the class. The vocabulary is difficult. What should Jose's teacher do with Jose?**

    A.   Provide Jose with additional opportunities to learn about habitats

    B.   Read the story to Jose multiple times

    C.   Show Jose pictures of habitats from his native country

    D.   Excuse Jose from the assignment

Answer A: Provide Jose with additional opportunities to learn about habitats
Students who are learning English should be exposed to a variety of opportunities to learn the same concepts as native speakers. Content should not be changed, but the manner in which it is presented and reinforced should be changed.

36. **In the early childhood classroom, it is important to limit teacher talk. What is the main problem with teacher talk?**

    A. It is often one sided and limited.

    B. The vocabulary is too difficult for children.

    C. It promotes misbehavior.

    D. It only creates gains in receptive language.

Answer A: It is often one sided and limited.

While it is important to expose children to numerous opportunities throughout the day to read and interact with print, it is equally important for students to have the opportunity to express themselves and communicate with each other. Teacher-talk, is often one sided and limited. Instead, teachers should provide opportunities for students to develop and expand their vocabularies.

37. **Which of the following is a convention of print that children learn during reading activities?**

    A. The meaning of words

    B. The left to right motion

    C. The purpose of print

    D. The identification of letters

Answer B: The left to right motion

During reading activities, children learn conventions of print. Children learn the way to hold a book, where to begin to read, the left to right motion, and how to continue from one line to another.

38. **In her kindergarten class, Mrs. Thomas has been watching the students in the drama center. She has watched the children pretend to complete a variety of magic tricks. Mrs. Thomas decides to use stories about magic to share with her class. Her decision to incorporate their interests into the reading shows that Mrs. Thomas understands that:**

   A. Including student interests is important at all times

   B. Teaching by themes is crucial for young children

   C. Young children respond to literature that reflects their lives

   D. Science fiction and fantasy are the most popular genres

Answer C: Young children respond to literature that reflects their lives
Children's literature is intended to instruct students through entertaining stories, while also promoting an interest in the very act of reading, itself. Young readers respond best to themes that reflect their lives.

39. **Which of the following is NOT a characteristic of a fable?**

   A. Have animal characters that act like humans

   B. Considered to be true

   C. Teaches a moral

   D. Reveals human foibles

Answer B: Considered to be true
The common characteristics of fables are animals that act like humans, a focus on revealing human foibles, and teaching a moral or lesson. Fables are not considered to be true.

40. **Alphabet books are classified as:**

   A. Concept books

   B. Easy-to-read books

   C. Board books

   D. Pictures books

Answer A: Concept books
Concept books are books that combine language and pictures to show concrete examples of concepts. One category of concept books is alphabet books, which are popular with children from preschool through to grade 2.

41. **The stories of Paul Bunyan, John Henry, and Pecos Bill are all exaggerated accounts of individuals with superhuman strength. What type of literature are these works?**

    A. Fables

    B. Fairytales

    C. Tall tales

    D. Myths

Answer C: Tall tales

Tall tales are purposely exaggerated accounts of individuals with superhuman strength. The stories of Paul Bunyan, John Henry, and Pecos Bill are all examples of tall tales. Fables are usually stories about animals with human features that often teach a lesson. Fairytales usually focus on good versus evil, reward and punishment. Myths are stories about events from the earliest times.

42. **Which of the following is NOT a motivation behind providing reading activities, including reading aloud, to young children?**

    A. Developing word consciousness skills

    B. Developing functions of print skills

    C. Developing phonics skills

    D. Developing language skills

Answer C: Developing phonics skills

There are almost unlimited positive reasons for encouraging adults to provide reading activities for young children. While it can be true that reading aloud may improve the phonics skills for some students, it is not a motivation for providing such activities to students.

43. **Which of the following is an appropriate way for students to respond to literature?**

    A. Art

    B. Drama

    C. Writing

    D. All of the above

Answer D: All of the above

Responding to literature through art, writing, and drama helps children to reflect on the books they have read and make them a part of their lives.

44. **John is having difficulty reading the word reach. In isolation, he pronounces each sound as /r/ /ee/ /sh/. Which of the following is a possible instructional technique which could help solve John's reading difficulty?**

    A.   Additional phonemic awareness instruction

    B.   Additional phonics instruction

    C.   Additional skill and drill practice

    D.   Additional minimal pair practice

Answer A: Additional phonemic awareness instruction
John is having difficulty with the sound symbol relationship between the /ch/ and /sh/. While it may appear at first that this is a phonics problem, in fact, it is important to begin with the earlier skill of phonemic awareness to ensure the student has a solid foundational understanding of the oral portions before moving totally into the sound symbol arena. If John is able to distinguish between the two sounds orally, it is obvious more phonics instruction is needed. However, proceeding directly to phonics instruction may be pointless and frustrating for John if he is unable to hear the distinctions.

45. **According to Marilyn Jager Adams, which skill would a student demonstrate by identifying that cat does not belong in the group of words containing dog, deer, and dress?**

    A.   Recognize the odd member in a group

    B.   Replace sounds in words

    C.   Count the sounds in a word

    D.   Count syllables in a word

Answer A: Recognize the odd member in a group
One of Marilyn Jager Adams' basic types of phonemic awareness tasks involves the ability to do oddity tasks, which involves recognizing the member of a set that is different among the group. In this example, the word cat is the odd member because it starts with a different sound.

46. **Which of the following is NOT true about phonological awareness? (Skill 7.2; Average rigor)**

    A. It may involve print.

    B. It is a prerequisite for spelling and phonics.

    C. Activities can be done by the children with their eyes closed.

    D. It starts before letter recognition is taught.

Answer A: It may involve print.
All of the options are correct aspects of phonological awareness except the first one, because phonological awareness does not involve print.

47. **Which of the following explains a significant difference between phonics and phonemic awareness?**

    A. Phonics involves print, while phonemic awareness involves language.

    B. Phonics is harder than phonemic awareness.

    C. Phonics involves sounds, while phonemic awareness involves letters.

    D. Phonics is the application of sounds to print, while phonemic awareness is oral.

Answer D: Phonics is the application of sounds to print, while phonemic awareness is oral.
Both phonics and phonemic awareness activities involve sounds, but it is with phonics that the application of these sounds is applied to print. Phonemic awareness is an oral activity.

48. **To decode is to:**

    A. Construct meaning

    B. Sound out a printed sequence of letters

    C. Use a special code to decipher a message

    D. Revise for errors in grammar

Answer B: Sound out a printed sequence of letters
Decoding is the process students use to figure out unknown words when reading.

49. **Ms. Walker's lesson objective is to teach her first graders the concept of morphology in order to improve their reading skills. Which group of words would be most appropriate for her to use in this lesson?**

    A. Far, farm, farmer

    B. Far, feather, fever

    C. Far, fear, fare

    D. Far, fare, farce

Answer A: Far, farm, farmer
The concept of morphology is to understand how words relate to each other and can be built upon to increase reading skills. In the correct answer, the student can utilize the information they learned from learning to read far to help them decode the other words.

50. **Which stage of reading skill development occurs first?**

    A. Schema stage

    B. Early semantic stage

    C. Orthographic stage

    D. Simultaneous stage

Answer A: Schema stage
Reading develops in sequential skills levels. The first stage is the schema stage. This stage is a pre-reading level involving page turning and telling story from memory.

51. **Which of the following is an important feature of vocabulary instruction according to the National Reading Panel?**

    A. Repetition of vocabulary items

    B. Keeping a consistent task structure at all times

    C. Teaching vocabulary in more than one language

    D. Isolation vocabulary instruction from other subjects

Answer A: Repetition of vocabulary items
According to the National Reading Panel, repetition and multiple exposures to vocabulary items are important. Students should be given items that will be likely to appear in many contexts.

52. **The attitude an author takes toward his or her subject is the:**

    A. Style

    B. Tone

    C. Point of view

    D. Theme

Answer B: Tone
Tone is the attitude an author takes toward his or her subject. That tone is exemplified in the language of the text.

53. **George has read his second graders three formats of the story "The Three Little Pigs." One is the traditional version, one is written from the wolf's point of view, and the third is written from the first pig's point of view. As George leads a discussion on the three texts with his students, he is trying to help his students develop their ability to:**

    A. Compare and contrast texts

    B. Understand point of view

    C. Recognize metaphors

    D. Rewrite fictional stories

Answer A: Compare and contrast texts
George understands the importance of developing critical thinking skills in young children. He has read three different formats of the same story in order to help his students develop their ability to compare texts.

54. **What is the first step in developing writing skills?**

    A.   Early writing

    B.   Experimental writing

    C   Role play writing

    D.   Conventional writing

Answer C: Role play writing
Children develop writing skills through a series of steps. These steps are: role play writing, experimental writing, early writing, and then conventional writing. In the role play writing stage, the child writes in scribbles and assigns a message to the symbols. Even though an adult would not be able to read the writing, the child can read what is written although it may not be the same each time the child reads it. S/he will be able to read back the writing because of prior knowledge that print carries a meaning.

55. **Which of the following is NOT a prewriting strategy?**

    A.   Analyzing sentences for variety

    B.   Keeping an idea book

    C.   Writing in a daily journal

    D.   Writing down whatever comes to mind

Answer A: Analyzing sentences for variety
Prewriting strategies assist students in a variety of ways. Common prewriting strategies include keeping an idea book for jotting down ideas, writing in a daily journal, and writing down whatever comes to mind, which is also called "free writing." Analyzing sentences for variety is a revising strategy.

56. **Which of the following is probably the most important step for the writer in the writing process?**

    A. Revision

    B. Discovery

    C. Conclusion

    D. Organization

Answer A: Revision

Revision is probably the most important step for the writer in the writing process. Here, students examine their work and make changes in wording, details, and ideas. So many times, students write a draft and then feel they're done. Students must be encouraged to develop, change, and enhance their writing as they go, as well as once they've completed a draft.

57. **The students in Tina's classroom are working together in pairs. Each student is reading another student's paper and asking who, what, when, where, why, and who questions. What is this activity helping the students to do?**

    A. Draft their writing

    B. Paraphrase their writing

    C. Revise their writing

    D. Outline their writing

Answer C: Revise their writing

Students need to be trained to become effective at proofreading, revising and editing strategies. One way to do this is to have the students read their partners' papers and ask at least three who, what, when, why, how questions. The students answer the questions and use them as a place to begin discussing the piece.

58. Young children learning to write commonly grip the pencil:

A.   Too far from the point

B.   With the wrong hand

C.   With too many fingers

D.   Too tightly

Answer D: Too tightly
A common problem for all young children learning to write is gripping the pencil too tightly, which makes writing tiresome. Usually the student learns to relax their grip as writing skill develops, but teachers can remind students to hold the instrument gently.

59. Which of the following approaches to student writing assignments is most likely to lead to students becoming disinterested?

A.   Designing assignments where students write for a variety of audiences.

B.   Designing assignments where the teacher is the audience.

C.   Designing assignments where students write to friends and family.

D.   Designing assignments where students write to real people such as mayors, the principle, or companies.

Answer B: Designing assignments where the teacher is the audience
In the past, teachers have assigned reports, paragraphs and essays that focused on the teacher as the audience with the purpose of explaining information. However, for students to be meaningfully engaged in their writing, they must write for a variety of reasons. Writing for different audiences and aims allows students to be more involved in their writing. If they write for the same audience and purpose, they will continue to see writing as just another assignment

60. As a part of prewriting, students should identify their audience. Which of the following questions will help students to identify their audience?

    A.   Why is the audience reading my writing?

    B.   What does my audience already know about my topic?

    C.   Both A and B

    D.   None of the above

Answer C: Both A and B
As part of prewriting, students should identify the audience. Make sure students consider the following when analyzing the needs of their audience: why the audience is reading the writing; what the audience already knows about the topic; what the audience needs or wants to know; what will interest the reader; and what type of language will suit the reader.

61. Which of these describes the best way to teach spelling?

    A.   At the same time that grammar and sentence structure is taught.

    B.   Within the context of meaningful language experiences.

    C.   Independently so that students can concentrate on spelling.

    D.   In short lessons as students pick up spelling almost immediately.

Answer B: Within the context of meaningful language experiences.
Spelling should be taught within the context of meaningful language experiences. Giving a child a list of words to learn to spell and then testing the child on the words every Friday will not aid in the development of spelling. The child must be able to use the words in context and they must have some meaning for the child. The assessment of how well a child can spell or where there are problems also has to be done within a meaningful environment.

62. **When editing, teachers should direct students to:**

    A. Edit for general understanding, while ignoring grammar and spelling.

    B. Edit for one specific purpose at a time.

    C. Identify all spelling, capitalization, and punctuation errors.

    D. Be critical of their work and that of others.

Answer B: Edit for one specific purpose at a time.
Editing is a time-consuming task and it would be unreasonable to expect students to pick up on all the mistakes in a piece of writing. Therefore, teachers should ask students to edit for specific purposes at one time, such as correct spelling, capitalization or punctuation.

Subarea III. Learning in the Content Areas

63. **Kindergarten students are participating in a calendar time activity. One student adds a straw to the "ones can" to represent that day of school. What math principle is being reinforced?**

    A. Properties of a base ten number system

    B. Sorting

    C. Counting by twos

    D. Even and odd numbers

Answer A: Properties of a base ten number system
As the students group craft sticks into groups of tens to represent the days of school, they are learning the properties of our base ten number system.

64. **First grade students are arranging four small squares of identical size to form a larger square. Each small square represents what part of the larger square?**

    A. One half

    B. One whole

    C. One fourth

    D. One fifth

Answer C: One fourth
Four of the small squares make up the area of the large square. Each small square is one fourth of the larger square.

65. **What is the answer to this problem?**

    25 ÷ 5 =

    A. 5
    B. 30
    C. 125
    D. 20

Answer A: 5
Twenty-five can be divided into five equal groups of five.

66. **Third grade students are studying percents. When looking at a circle graph divided into three sections, they see that one section is worth 80% and one section is worth 5%. What will the remaining section be worth?**

    A. 100%
    B. 85%
    C. 75%
    D. 15%

Answer D: 15%
Percentages use the base ten number system. Percentages of a total amount will always add up to 100%. Since the two sections add to 85%, the third section must be 15%.

67. **Which of the following letters does NOT have a line of symmetry?**

    A. O
    B. D
    C. M
    D. J

Answer D: J
For an object to show symmetry, it must be able to be divided into identical halves. The letter O has an unlimited number of lines of symmetry. The letter D has a horizontal line of symmetry. The letter M has a vertical line of symmetry. The letter J does not have a line of symmetry.

68. **Kindergarten students are doing a butterfly art project. They fold paper in half. On one half, they paint a design. Then they fold the paper closed and reopen. The resulting picture is a butterfly with matching sides. What math principle does this demonstrate?**

   A.   Slide

   B.   Rotate

   C.   Symmetry

   D.   Transformation

Answer C: Symmetry
By folding the painted paper in half, the design is mirrored on the other side, creating symmetry and reflection. The butterfly design is symmetrical about the center.

69. **What number comes next in this pattern?**

   3, 8, 13, 18, _____

   A.   21

   B.   26

   C.   23

   D.   5

Answer C: 23
This pattern is made by adding five to the preceding number. The next number is found by adding 5 to 18, which gives the answer 23.

70. **What is the main purpose of having kindergarten students count by twos?**

   A.   To hear a rhythm

   B.   To recognize patterns in numbers

   C.   To practice addition

   D.   To become familiar with equations

Answer B: To recognize patterns in numbers
Recognizing patterns in numbers is an early skill for multiplication. It will also help children recognize patterns in word families such as *bit, hit, fit.*

71. **The term *millimeters* indicates which kind of measurement?**

    A. Volume
    B. Weight
    C. Length
    D. Temperature

Answer C: Length
The term *millimeters* is a reference to length in the metric system.

72. **What type of graph would be best to use to show changes in the height of a plant over the course of a month?**

    A. Circle graph
    B. Bar graph
    C. Line graph
    D. Pictograph

Answer C: Line graph
A line graph shows trends over time. A line graph would show how the plant's height changed over time.

73. **A teacher completes a survey of student eye color. The teacher then creates a graph so students can compare how many students have each eye color. What type of graph should be used?**

    A. Bar graph
    B. Pictograph
    C. Circle graph
    D. Line Graph

Answer A: Bar graph
Bar graphs are used to compare various quantities. In this case, the bar graph would show the number of students with each eye color. By looking at the graph, students would be able to compare how many students have each eye color. While a pictograph is also possible, if there are many different eye colors in the class, it would take up a lot of space to graph it this way.

74. **Which of the following skills would a student develop first?**

    A.   Understanding place value

    B.   Recognizing number patterns

    C.   Counting objects

    D.   Solving number problems

Answer C: Counting objects
As with the phonemic awareness skills in reading, number sense is the foundation upon which all future math topics will be built. While in this beginning stage, children will be able to identify how many objects are in a group.

75. **Maddie is a first grade teacher who understands the importance of including the family when providing instruction. She wants to take several steps to provide families with a connection to what the students are doing in her math class. Which of the following is NOT a strategy she could incorporate?**

    A.   Including a math portion in her regular newsletter

    B.   Incorporating manipulatives into her math lessons

    C.   Translating math homework into the native language of the students in her classroom

    D.   Having a family math night at school

Answer B: Incorporating manipulatives into her math lessons
While incorporating manipulatives into her curriculum is an excellent strategy, which should take place in every math classroom, it does not promote the inclusion of family into the curriculum.

76. **George has successfully mastered his basic addition facts. However, as his teacher presents more complex addition problems, it is obvious to him that George is lacking a basic understanding of the concept of addition. What would George's teacher be best to do to increase his basic understanding?**

    A. Provide additional instruction with hands on materials

    B. Have George practice his addition facts more frequently

    C. Have George complete more challenging addition problems

    D. Provide George with remediation

Answer A: Provide additional instruction with hands on materials
When students have the time to explore and build their own constructs using concrete objects, they are able to make more generalizations. Students may be able to memorize pieces of rote information, but without the foundational exposure to hands on materials they may not be able to demonstrate these generalizations. It is the role of the teacher to take the time to provide these opportunities.

77. **Carrie approaches her teacher after class and expresses her personal frustration with math and her feeling that she will never get it. Which of the following is NOT a suitable method Carrie's teacher can utilize to improve Carrie's feelings about math?**

    A. Incorporating some of Carrie's specific interests into math lessons

    B. Holding Carrie to high expectations

    C. Sharing with Carrie her own struggles and dislike for math

    D. Providing Carrie with extra positive reinforcement and encouragement

Answer C: Sharing with Carrie her own struggles and dislike for math
While it may seem to be a bonding experience to share your own personal struggles and dislike for the subject with a student who feels the same way, it is important for the teacher to maintain excitement and enthusiasm for the subject. Carrie's teacher would be better to share positive aspects about how math as affected her life, than to share any negative feelings. Building a positive excitement and interest in the subject is an important part of teaching.

78. **The principal walks into your classroom during math class. He sees your students making cake mixtures. Later, the principal questions your lesson. What would be the best explanation for your lesson?**

    A.   The students earned a reward time and it was free choice.

    B.   You were teaching the students how math is used in real-life situations.

    C.   You had paperwork to complete and needed the time to complete it.

    D.   It kept the students interested in math and prevented boredom.

Answer B: You were teaching the students how math is used in real-life situations.
Providing the students with the opportunity to explore how math is around them and how it is utilized in everyday experiences is important. As students identify and realize the importance of the skills being learned to their lives at home, they will become more involved in the learning, as it has new and better value for them.

79. **What is a large, rotating, low-pressure system accompanied by heavy precipitation and strong winds known as?**

    A.   A hurricane

    B.   A tornado

    C.   A thunderstorm

    D.   A tsunami

Answer A: A hurricane
Hurricanes are storms that develop when warm, moist air carried by trade winds rotates around a low-pressure "eye". These form a large, rotating, low-pressure system and are accompanied by heavy precipitation and strong winds. They are also known as tropical cyclones or typhoons.

80. **What does a primary consumer most commonly refer to?**

   A.   Herbivore

   B.   Autotroph

   C.   Carnivore

   D.   Decomposer

Answer A: Herbivore
Autotrophs are the primary producers of the ecosystem. Producers mainly consist of plants. Primary consumers are the next trophic level. The primary consumers are the herbivores that eat plants or algae. Secondary consumers are the carnivores that eat the primary consumers. Tertiary consumers eat the secondary consumer. These trophic levels may go higher depending on the ecosystem.

81. **Airplanes generate pressure and remain balanced by:**

   A.   Fast air movement over wings and slow movement under wings

   B.   Slow air movement over wings and fast movement under wings

   C.   Air movement that is equal above and below wings

   D.   Air movement that only occurs over the wings

Answer A: Fast air movement over wings and slow movement under wings
Airplanes or fixed-wing aircraft are heavier than aircraft that utilize the laws of physics to achieve flight. As the aircraft is propelled forward by thrust from the engines, air moves faster over the top of the wings and slower under the bottom. The slower airflow beneath the wing generates more pressure, while the faster airflow above generates less. This difference in pressure results in upward lift.

82. **The breakdown of rock due to acid rain is an example of:**

   A.   Physical weathering

   B.   Frost wedging

   C.   Chemical weathering

   D.   Deposition

Answer C: Chemical weathering
The breaking down of rocks at or near to the Earth's surface is known as weathering. Chemical weathering is the breaking down of rocks through changes in their chemical composition. The breakdown of rock due to acid rain is an example of chemical weathering.

83. **What is the last step in the scientific method?**

    A. Pose a question

    B. Draw a conclusion

    C. Conduct a test

    D. Record data

Answer B: Draw a conclusion
The steps in the scientific method, in order, are: pose a question, form a hypothesis, conduct a test, observe and record data, and draw a conclusion.

84. **Which term best describes Newton's universal gravitation?**

    A. Theory

    B. Hypothesis

    C. Inference

    D. Law

Answer D: Law
A hypothesis is an unproved theory or educated guess followed by research to best explain a phenomenon. A theory is the formation of principles or relationships, which have been verified and accepted. It is a proven hypothesis. A law is an explanation of events that occur with uniformity under the same conditions, such as laws of nature or laws of gravitation.

85. **When teaching science, which of the following is a method of focusing on students' intrinsic motivation?**

    A. Adapting the lessons to students' interests

    B. Providing regular feedback

    C. Supplying rewards for the highest achievers

    D. Having regular science tests

Answer A: Adapting the lessons to students' interests
Teachers can focus on students' intrinsic motivation through adapting the tasks to students' interests, providing opportunities for active response, including a variety of tasks, providing rapid feedback, incorporating games into the lesson, and allowing students the opportunity to make choices, create, and interact with peers.

86. **What does geography include the study of?**

   A.   Location

   B.   Distribution of living things

   C.   Distribution of the earth's features

   D.   All of the above

Answer D: All of the above
Geography involves studying location and how living things and earth's features are distributed throughout the earth. It includes where animals, people, and plants live and the effects of their relationship with earth's physical features.

87. **Economics is the study of how a society allocates its scarce resources to satisfy:**

   A.   Unlimited and competing wants

   B.   Limited and competing wants

   C.   Unlimited and cooperative wants

   D.   Limited and cooperative wants

Answer A: Unlimited and competing wants
Economics is the study of how a society allocates its scarce resources to satisfy what are basically unlimited and competing wants. A fundamental fact of economics is that resources are scarce and that wants are infinite.

88. **The two elements of a market economy are:**

   A.   Inflation and deflation

   B.   Supply and demand

   C.   Cost and price

   D.   Wants and needs

Answer B: Supply and demand
A market economy is based on supply and demand. Demand is based on consumer preferences and satisfaction and refers to the quantities of a good or service that buyers are willing and able to buy at different prices during a given period of time. Supply is based on costs of production and refers to the quantities that sellers are willing and able to sell at different prices during a given period of time.

89. **Who has the power to veto a bill that has passed the House of Representatives and the Senate?**

   A.   The President

   B.   The Vice President

   C.   The Speaker of the House

   D.   Any member of Congress

Answer A: The President
Once a bill receives final approval by a conference committee, it is signed by the Speaker of the House and the Vice President, who is also the President of the Senate, and sent to the President for consideration. The President may either sign the bill or veto it. If he vetoes the bill, his veto may be overruled if two-thirds of both the Senate and the House vote to do so. Once the President signs it the bill becomes a law.

90. **Which part of a map shows the relationship between a unit of measurement on the map versus the real world measure on the Earth?**

   A.   Scale

   B.   Title

   C.   Legend

   D.   Grid

Answer A: Scale
The scale of a map is used to show the relationship between a unit of measurement on the map versus the real world measure on the Earth.

91. **What is the most important focus in developing social studies skills during the early years?**

      A.   Recalling facts

      B.   Understanding statistics

      C.   Discussing ideas

      D.   Memorizing rights and responsibilities

Answer C: Discussing ideas

The early years of childhood education is important in shaping the values of a democracy and preparing students for citizenship in later life. Social studies begin the exploration of the processes, rights and freedoms of a democracy. Early in a child's education they begin to learn cooperation, tolerance, and sharing. During the early years, the recalling of factual information is not as important as encouraging discussion and exploration of different perspectives.

92. **What is one of the ten essential themes identified by the National Council for Social Studies?**

    A.   Culture

    B.   Lifestyle

    C.   Population

    D.   Democracy

Answer A: Culture

The National Council for Social Studies identifies 10 themes essential to social science instruction. These are:

1. Culture
2. Time, Continuity and Change
3. People, Places and Environments
4. Individual development and identity
5. Individuals, Groups and Institutions
6. Power, Authority and Governance
7. Production, Distribution and Consumption
8. Science, Technology and Society
9. Global Connections
10. Civic Ideals and Practices

93. **Which subject would a color wheel most likely be used for?**

    A.   Visual arts

    B.   Music

    C.   Movement

    D.   Drama

Answer A: Visual arts

A color wheel is an important tool in teaching students visual arts. It is used to teach students about primary colors and secondary colors. It is also used to help students learn about mixing colors.

94. **A student art sample book would include cotton balls and sand paper to represent:**

    A.   Color

    B.   Lines

    C.   Texture

    D.   Shape

Answer C: Texture

Texture refers to the way something feels because of the tactile quality of its surface. An art sample book can include materials such as cotton balls and sand paper as examples of different textures.

95. **Which terms refers to the arrangement of one or more items so that they appear symmetrical or asymmetrical?**

    A.   Balance

    B.   Contrast

    C.   Emphasis

    D.   Unity

Answer A: Balance

The principles of visual are that students should be introduced to include abstract, background, balance, contrast, emphasis, sketch, texture, and unity. Balance refers to the arrangement of one or more elements in a work of art so that they appear symmetrical or asymmetrical in design and proportion.

96. **The four principles of modern dance are substance, form, metakinesis, and:**

    A.   Dynamism

    B.   Function

    C.   Space

    D.   Performance

Answer A: Dynamism

Modern dance is a type of dance where the focus is on expressing opposites, such as fast-slow or contract-release. Modern dance is based on four principles. These are substance, form, metakinesis, and dynamism.

97. **What should the arts curriculum for early childhood avoid?**

    A.   Judgment

    B.   Open expression

    C.   Experimentation

    D.   Discovery

Answer A: Judgment
The arts curriculum for early childhood should focus on the experimental and discovery aspects of the arts. The emphasis should be on creative processes with little judgment and criticism should be minimal.

98. **What would the viewing of a dance company performance be most likely to promote?**

    A.   Critical-thinking skills

    B.   Appreciation of the arts

    C.   Improvisation skills

    D.   Music vocabulary

Answer B: Appreciation of the arts
Live performances are an important part of learning arts and help to develop aesthetic appreciation of the arts. A dance company performance is one example of a live performance that students could attend.

99. **In which subject is it most important for students to work with costumes and props?**

    A.   Visual arts

    B.   Music

    C.   Movement

    D.   Drama

Answer D: Drama
When studying drama, students should experience working with props and performing in costume. These can both help students act out experiences and tend to increase creativity.

100. According to Charles Fowler, why is it important for arts to be incorporated into the teaching of other subject areas?

      A.   It reduces loss of interest in the subject.

      B.   It enhances the likelihood that students will retain the information.

      C.   It provides a three dimensional view of the subject.

      D.   It encourages the development of personal connections with the subject.

Answer C: It provides a three dimensional view of the subject.
Charles Fowler has argued that the best schools also have the best arts programs. According to Fowler, integrating arts with other subject areas gives a more complete view of the subject. Students then gain a more three dimensional understanding of the subject.

Sample Test 2

Reading, Language & Literature

1. **The main core of the English language is based on:**
    (Rigorous) (Skill 1.2)

    A. Latin

    B. Anglo-Saxon

    C. Greek

    D. None of the above

2. **Generally, oral language is differentiated from written language by accent, tone, and:**
    (Easy) (Skill 1.4)

    A. Word choice.

    B. Feeling.

    C. Topic.

    D. Content.

3. **All of the following are true about phonological awareness EXCEPT:**
    (Average Rigor) (Skill 1.5)

    A. It may involve print.

    B. It is a prerequisite for spelling and phonics.

    C. Activities can be done by the children with their eyes closed.

    D. It starts before letter recognition is taught.

4. **The arrangement and relationship of words in sentences or sentence structure best describes:**
    (Average Rigor) (Skill 1.5)

    A. Style

    B. Discourse

    C. Thesis

    D. Syntax

5. **Which of the following indicates that a student is a fluent reader?**
    (Easy) (Skill 1.5)

    A. Reads texts with expression or prosody

    B. Reads word-to-word and haltingly

    C. Must intentionally decode a majority of the words

    D. In a writing assignment, sentence structure and organization are poor

6. **Which of the following contains an error in possessive inflection?** *(Rigorous) (Skill 1.6)*

    A. Doris's shawl

    B. Mother's-in-law frown

    C. Children's lunches

    D. Ambassador's briefcase

7. **Which of the following is a complex sentence?** *(Easy) (Skill 1.7)*

    A. Anna and Margaret read a total of fifty-four books during summer vacation.

    B. The youngest boy on the team had the best earned run average, which mystified the coaching staff.

    C. Earl decided to attend Princeton; his twin brother Roy, who aced the ASVAB test, will be going to Annapolis.

    D. "Easy come, easy go," Marcia moaned.

8. **Which of the following is not a characteristic of a fable?** *(Easy) (Skill 3.2)*

    A. Animals that feel and talk like humans

    B. Happy solutions to human dilemmas

    C. Teaches a standard or moral for behavior

    D. Illustrates specific people or groups without directly naming them

9. **Which of the following is an epic?** *(Average Rigor) (Skill 3.2)*

    A. On the Choice of Books

    B. The Faerie Queene

    C. Northanger Abbey

    D. A Doll's House

10. **Which is an untrue statement about a theme in literature?**
(Rigorous) (Skill 3.3)

A. The theme is always stated directly somewhere in the text..

B. The theme is the central idea in a literary work..

C. All parts of the work (plot, setting, mood. should contribute to the theme in some way..

D. By analyzing the various elements of the work, the reader should be able to arrive at an indirectly stated theme..

11. **Which of the following is an example of alliteration?**
(Average Rigor) (Skill 3.5)

A. "The City's voice itself is soft like Solitude."

B. "Both in one faith unanimous; though sad"

C. "By all their country's wishes blest!"

D. "In earliest Greece to thee with partial choice"

12. **Which is not a true statement concerning an author's literary tone?**
(Rigorous) (Skill 4.4)

A. Tone is partly revealed through the selection of details.

B. Tone is the expression of the author's attitude toward his/her subject.

C. Tone in literature is usually satiric or angry.

D. Tone in literature corresponds to the tone of voice a speaker uses.

13. **Which definition below is the best for defining diction?**
(Easy) (Skill 4.4)

A. The specific word choices of an author to create a particular mood or feeling in the reader

B. writing which explains something thoroughly

C. the background, or exposition, for a short story or drama

D. word choices which help teach a truth or moral

14. **Which of the following is not a technique of prewriting?**
(Average Rigor) (Skill 5.1)

   A. Clustering

   B. Listing

   C. Brainstorming

   D. Proofreading

15. **Middle and high school students are more receptive to studying grammar and syntax:**
(Average Rigor) (Skill 5.3)

   A. Through worksheets and end -of-lesson practices in textbooks.

   B. Through independent homework assignments.

   C. Through analytical examination of the writings of famous authors.

   D. Though application to their own writing.

16. **Which of the following mostly addresses grammatical and technical errors?**
(Easy) (Skill 5.3)

   A. Revising

   B. Editing

   C. Proofreading

   D. Rough draft writing

17. **Which of the following should not be included in the opening paragraph of an informative essay?**
(Rigorous) (Skill 5.5)

   A. Thesis sentence

   B. Details and examples supporting the main idea

   C. A broad general introduction to the topic

   D. A style and tone that grabs the reader's attention

18. **A student has written a paper with the following characteristics: written in first person; characters, setting, and plot; some dialogue; events organized in chronological sequence with some flashbacks. In what genre has the student written?**
(Easy) (Skill 5.5)

   A. Expository writing

   B. Narrative writing

   C. Persuasive writing

   D. Technical writing

19. Which of the following is not an approach to keep students ever conscious of the need to write for audience appeal? *(Average Rigor) (Skill 5.6)*

    A. Pairing students during the writing process

    B. Reading all rough drafts before the students write the final copies

    C. Having students compose stories or articles for publication in school literary magazines or newspapers

    D. Writing letters to friends or relatives

20. What is the best place for students to find appropriate synonyms, antonyms, and other related words to enhance their writing? *(Average Rigor) (Skill 5.6)*

    A. Dictionary

    B. Spell check

    C. Encyclopedia

    D. Thesaurus

Math

21. Which of the following is an irrational number? *(Rigorous)(Skill 6.1)*

    A. .362626262...

    B. $4\frac{1}{3}$

    C. $\sqrt{5}$

    D. $-\sqrt{16}$

22. An item that sells for $375 is put on sale at $120. What is the percent of decrease? *(Average Rigor) (Skill 6.7, 7.1)*

    A. 25%

    B. 28%

    C. 68%

    D. 34%

23. A sofa sells for $520. If the retailer makes a 30% profit, what was the wholesale price? *(Average Rigor) (Skill 7.1)*

    A. $400

    B. $676

    C. $490

    D. $364

24. Two mathematics classes have a total of 410 students. The 8:00 am class has 40 more than the 10:00 am class. How many students are in the 10:00 am class?
(Average Rigor) (Skill 7.1)

A. 123.3

B. 370

C. 185

D. 330

25. The following chart shows the yearly average number of international tourists visiting Palm Beach for 1990-1994. How many more International tourists visited Palm Beach in 1994 than in 1991?
(Easy) (Skill 7.7)

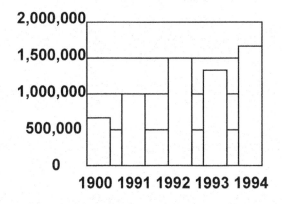

A. 100,000

B. 600,000

C. 1,600,000

D. 8,000,000

26. $\left(\dfrac{^{-}4}{9}\right) + \left(\dfrac{^{-}7}{10}\right) =$
(Easy) (Skill 8.2)

A. $\dfrac{23}{90}$

B. $\dfrac{^{-}23}{90}$

C. $\dfrac{103}{90}$

D. $\dfrac{^{-}103}{90}$

27. Solve for x:
$|2x + 3| > 4$
(Rigorous) (Skill 8.4)

A. $-\frac{7}{2} > x > \frac{1}{2}$

B. $-\frac{1}{2} > x > \frac{7}{2}$

C. $x < \frac{7}{2}$ or $x < -\frac{1}{2}$

D. $x < -\frac{7}{2}$ or $x > \frac{1}{2}$

28. Graph the solution:
$|x| + 7 < 13$
(Rigorous) (Skill 8.4)

A. ![number line with open circles at -6 and 6]
   -6   0   6

B. ![number line with filled circles at -6 and 6]
   -6   0   6

C. ![number line with open circles at -6 and 6]
   -6   0   6

D. ![number line with filled circles at -6 and 6]
   -6   0   6

29. 3x + 2y = 12
    12x + 8y = 15
    (Average Rigor) (Skill 8.6)

    A. All real numbers

    B. x = 4, y = 4

    C. x = 2, y = -1

    D. ∅

30. If $4x - (3 - x) = 7(x - 3) + 10$,

    then x = ?

    (Rigorous) (Skill 8.6)

    A. x = 8

    B. x = -8

    C. x = 4

    D. x = -4

31. _____ lines do not
    intersect.
    (Rigorous) (Skill 8.7)

    A. Perpendicular

    B. Parallel

    C. Intersecting

    D. Skew

32. Which angle would measure
    less than 90 degrees?
    (Average Rigor) (Skill 8.7)

    A. Acute

    B. Obtuse

    C. Right

    D. Straight

33. What is the area of a square
    whose side is 13 feet?
    (Rigorous) (Skill 8.9)

    A. 169 feet

    B. 169 square feet

    C. 52 feet

    D. 52 square feet

34. In similar polygons, if the
    perimeters are in a ratio of
    x:y, the sides are in a ratio of
    (Average Rigor) (Skill 8.9)

    A. x : y

    B. x2: y^2

    C. 2x: y

    D. 1/2 x: y

35. **What measure could be used to report the distance traveled in walking around a track?**
(*Easy*) (*Skill 9.3*)

   A. Degrees

   B. Square meters

   C. Kilometers

   D. Cubic feet

36. **The mass of a cookie is closest to:**
(*Easy*) (*Skill 9.3*)

   A. 0.5 kg

   B. 0.5 grams

   C. 15 grams

   D. 1.5 grams

37. **3 km is equivalent to**
(*Easy*) (*Skill 9.3*)

   A. 300 cm

   B. 300 m

   C. 3000 cm

   D. 3000 m

38. **Corporate salaries are listed for several employees. Which would be the best measure of central tendency?**
(*Average Rigor*) (*Skill 9.5*)

   $24,000 $24,000 $26,000
   $28,000 $30,000 $120,000

   A. Mean

   B. Median

   C. Mode

   D. No difference

39. **Given a drawer with 5 black socks, 3 blue socks, and 2 red socks, what is the probability that you will draw two black socks in two draws in a dark room?**
(*Rigorous*) (*Skill 9.5*)

   A. 2/9

   B. 1/4

   C. 17/18

   D. 1/18

40. **What is the probability of drawing 2 consecutive aces from a standard deck of cards?**
(Rigorous) (Skill 9.5)

A. $\dfrac{3}{51}$

B. $\dfrac{1}{221}$

C. $\dfrac{2}{104}$

D. $\dfrac{2}{52}$

History & Social Science

41. **What was the long-term importance of the Mayflower Compact?**
(Average Rigor) (Skill 2.1)

A. It established the foundation of all later agreements with the Native Peoples.

B. It established freedom of religion in the original English colonies.

C. It ended the war in Europe between Spain, France and England.

D. It established a model of small, town-based government that was adopted throughout the New England colonies.

42. **An economist might engage in which of the following activities?**
(Average Rigor) (Skill 9.6)

A. An observation of the historical effects of a nation's banking practices

B. The application of a statistical test to a series of data

C. Introduction of an experimental factor into a specified population to measure the effect of the factor

D. An economist might engage in all of these

43. **Which two Native American nations or tribes inhabited the Mid-Atlantic and Northeastern regions at the time of the first European contact?**
(Average Rigor) (Skill 10.1)

A. Pueblo and Inuit

B. Algonquian and Cherokee

C. Seminoles and Sioux

D. Algonquian and Iroquois

44. Which of the following were results of the Age of Exploration?
(Easy) (Skill 10.2)

A. More complete and accurate maps and charts

B. New and more accurate navigational instruments

C. Proof that the earth is round

D. All of the above

45. The "divine right" of kings was the key political characteristic of:
(Rigorous) (Skill 10.2)

A. The Age of Absolutism

B. The Age of Reason

C. The Age of Feudalism

D. The Age of Despotism

46. During the period of Spanish colonialism, which of the following was not a key to the goal of exploiting, transforming and including the native people?
(Average Rigor) (Skill 10.2)

A. Missions

B. Ranchos

C. Presidios

D. Pueblos

47. Which one of the following is not a reason why Europeans came to the New World?
(Rigorous) (Skill 10.2)

A. To find resources in order to increase wealth

B. To establish trade.

C. To increase a ruler's power and importance.

D. To spread Christianity

48. The year 1619 was a notable time for the colony of Virginia. Three important events occurred resulting in lasting effects on US history. Which one of the following is not one of those events?
(Rigorous) (Skill 10.3)

A. Twenty African slaves arrived in Virginia.

B. The London Company granted the colony a charter making it independent..

C. The colonists were given the right by the London Company to govern themselves through representative government in the Virginia House of Burgesses.

D. The London Company sent to the colony 60 women who were quickly married, establishing families and stability in the colony.

49. What was "triangular trade"?
(Rigorous) (Skill 10.3)

A. It was regulated trade between the colonies, England and France.

B. It was an approach to trade that transported finished goods from the mother country to the African colonies, slaves and goods from Africa to the North American Colonies, and raw materials and tobacco or rum back to the mother country.

C. It was an approach to trade that resulted in colonists obtaining crops and goods from the Native tribes in exchange for finished goods from England.

D. It was trade between the colonists of the three regions (Southern, mid-Atlantic, and New England).

50. What event sparked a great migration of people from all over the world to California?
(Average Rigor) (Skill 10.5)

A. The birth of Labor Unions

B. California statehood

C. The invention of the automobile

D. The Gold Rush

51. How did the United States gain Florida from Spain?
(Average Rigor) (Skill 10.5)

A. It was captured from Spain after the Spanish-American War.

B. It was given to the British and became part of the original thirteen colonies.

C. America bought it from Spain.

D. America acquired it after the First World War.

52. The belief that the United States should control all of North America was called:
(Easy) (Skill 10.5)

A. Westward Expansion

B. Pan Americanism

C. Manifest Destiny

D. Nationalism

53. The Unites States' concern about the possible spread of communism is most closely associated with:
(Rigorous) (Skill 10.7)

A. The Vietnam War.

B. The Civil War.

C. The Korean War.

D. World War I.

54. Which one of the following would NOT be considered a result of World War II?
(Average Rigor) (Skill 10.7)

A. Economic depressions and slow resumption of trade and financial aid

B. Western Europe was no longer the center of world power.

C. The beginnings of new power struggles not only in Europe but in Asia as well

D. Territorial and boundary changes for many nations, especially in Europe

55. In 1957, the formation of the Southern Christian Leadership Conference was started by:
(Rigorous) (Skill 10.8)

A. Martin Luther King, Jr

B. Rev. T. J. Jemison

C. Ella Baker

D. All of the above

56. The advancement of understanding in dealing with human beings has led to a number of interdisciplinary areas. Which of the following interdisciplinary studies would NOT be considered under the social sciences?
(Average Rigor) (Skills 10.8, 10.12, 13.2)

A. Molecular biophysics.

B. Peace studies.

C. African-American studies.

D. Cartographic information systems.

57. What are the three branches of the United States government?
(Easy) (Skill 11.2)

A. Legislative, judicial, international affairs

B. Legislative, executive, foreign trade

C. Legislative, executive, judicial

D. Executive, judicial, state governments

58. Which document includes the freedom of religion and right to trial by jury?
(Rigorous) (Skill 11.8)

A. Bill of Rights

B. Gettysburg Address

C. Articles of Confederation

D. The Amendments

59. For the historian studying ancient Egypt, which of the following would be least useful?
(Average Rigor) (Skill 12.1)

A. The record of an ancient Greek historian on Greek-Egyptian interaction

B. Letters from an Egyptian ruler to his/her regional governors

C. Inscriptions on stele of the Fourteenth Egyptian Dynasty

D. Letters from a nineteenth century Egyptologist to his wife

60. What intellectual movement during the period of North American colonization contributed to the development of public education and the founding of the first colleges and universities?
(Average Rigor) (Skill 12.2)

A. Enlightenment

B. Great Awakening

C. Libertarianism

D. The Scientific Revolution

Science

61. All of the following are considered Newton's Laws except for:
(Easy) (Skills 12.2)

A. An object in motion will continue in motion unless acted upon by an outside force.

B. For every action force, there is an equal and opposite reaction force.

C. Nature abhors a vacuum.

D. Mass can be considered the ratio of force to acceleration.

62. **Which is a form of precipitation?**
(Rigorous) (Skill 13.5)

A. Snow

B. Frost

C. Fog

D. All of the above

63. **Identify the correct sequence of organization of living things from lower to higher order:**
(Rigorous) (Skill 14.1)

A. Cell, Organelle, Organ, Tissue, System, Organism

B. Cell, Tissue, Organ, Organelle, System, Organism

C. Organelle, Cell, Tissue, Organ, System, Organism

D. Organelle, Tissue, Cell, Organ, System, Organism

64. **What cell organelle contains the cell's stored food?**
(Rigorous) (Skill 14.2)

A. Vacuoles

B. Golgi Apparatus

C. Ribosomes

D. Lysosomes

65. **Enzymes speed up reactions by _____.** *(Rigorous)*
(Skill 14.4)

A. Utilizing ATP

B. Lowering pH, allowing reaction speed to increase.

C. Increasing volume of substrate

D. Lowering energy of activation

66. **Which parts of an atom are located inside the nucleus?**
(Average Rigor) (Skill 15.1)

A. Electrons and neutrons

B. Protons and neutrons

C. Protons only

D. Neutrons only

67. **Energy is:**
(Rigorous) (Skill 15.2)

A. The combination of power and work.

B. The ability to cause change in matter.

C. The transfer of power when force is applied to a body.

D. Physical force.

68. The measure of the pull of the earth's gravity on an object is called _____.
(Average Rigor) (Skill 15.3)

   A. Mass number.

   B. Atomic number.

   C. Mass.

   D. Weight

69. Which of the following is the best definition for 'meteorite'?
(Rigorous) (Skill 15.4)

   A. A meteorite is a mineral composed of mica and feldspar.

   B. A meteorite is material from outer space that has struck the earth's surface.

   C. A meteorite is an element that has properties of both metals and nonmetals.

   D. A meteorite is a very small unit of length measurement.

70. Which of the following types of rock are made from magma?
(Average Rigor) (Skill 15.5)

   A. Fossils

   B. Sedimentary

   C. Metamorphic

   D. Igneous

71. The calm point at the center of a storm such as a hurricane is often called the "eye" of the storm. This "eye" is caused by:
(Average Rigor) (Skill 15.5)

   A. Centripetal force.

   B. A high-pressure air mass.

   C. A low-pressure air mass.

   D. Heavier precipitation in the area.

72. Air masses moving toward or away form the Earth's surface is called _____.
(Average Rigor) (Skill 15.5)

   A. Wind.

   B. Breeze.

   C. Air currents.

   D. Doldrums.

73. Which type of cloud is most likely to produce precipitation?
(Average Rigor) (Skill 15.5)

   A. Cirrus

   B. Cumulus

   C. Stratus

   D. Nimbus

74. **Which of the following instruments measures wind speed?**
(Easy) (Skill 15.5)

A. A barometer

B. An anemometer

C. A thermometer

D. A weather vane

75. **By discovering the structure of DNA, Watson and Crick made it possible to:**
(Rigorous) (Skill 16.2)

A. Clone DNA.

B. Explain DNA's ability to replicate and control the synthesis of proteins.

C. Sequence human DNA.

D. Predict genetic mutations.

76. **In an experiment measuring the growth of bacteria at different temperatures, what is the independent variable?**
(Rigorous) (Skill 16.4)

A. Number of bacteria

B. Growth rate of bacteria

C. Temperature

D. Size of bacteria

77. **A scientific law_____.**
(Average Rigor) (Skill 16.4)

A. Proves scientific accuracy.

B. May never be broken.

C. Is the current most accuracte explanation for natural phemonon, and experimental data.

D. Is the result of one excellent experiment.

78. **The control group of an experiment is:**
(Average Rigor) (Skill 16.4)

A. An extra group in which all experimental conditions are the same and the variable being tested is unchanged.

B. A group of authorities in charge of an experiment.

C. The group of experimental participants who are given experimental drugs.

D. A group of subjects that is isolated from all aspects of the experiment.

79. **What is the scientific method?**
(Average Rigor) (Skill 16.4)

A. It is the process of doing an experiment and writing a laboratory report.

B. It is the process of using open inquiry and repeatable results to establish theories.

C. It is the process of reinforcing scientific principles by confirming results.

D. It is the process of recording data and observations.

80. **Which is the correct order of methodology?**
(Average Rigor) (Skill 16.4)

1. Collecting data
2. Planning a controlled experiment
3. Drawing a conclusion
4. Hypothesizing a result
5. Revisiting a hypothesis to answer a question

A. 1,2,3,4,5

B. 4,2,1,3,5

C. 4,5,1,3,2

D. 1,3,4,5,2

Human Development

81. **Followers of Piaget's learning theory believe that adolescents in the formal operations period:**
(Average Rigor) (Skill 17.1)

A. Behave properly from fear of punishment rather than from a conscious decision to take a certain action

B. See the past more realistically and can relate to people from the past more than preadolescents

C. Are less self-conscious and thus more willing to project their own identities into those of fictional characters

D. Have not yet developed a symbolic imagination

82. **According to Piaget, what stage is characterized by the ability to think abstractly and to use logic?**
(Average Rigor) (Skill 17.1)

A. Concrete operational

B. Pre-operational

C. Formal operational

D. Sensory Motor

83. **At approximately what age is the average child able to define abstract terms such as honesty and justice?**
(Rigorous) (Skill 17.1)

   A. 10-12 years old

   B. 4-6 years old

   C. 14-16 years old

   D. 6-8 years old

84. **How can the teacher establish a positive climate in the classroom?**
(Average Rigor) (Skill 17.2)

   A. Help students see the unique contributions of individual differences.

   B. Use whole-group instruction for all content areas.

   C. Help students divide into cooperative groups based on ability.

   D. Eliminate teaching strategies that allow students to make choices.

85. **When are students more likely to understand complex ideas?**
(Rigorous) (Skill 17.3)

   A. When they do outside research before coming to class

   B. When they write out the definitions of complex words

   C. When they attend a lecture on the subject

   D. When the ideas are clearly defined by the teacher and the students are given examples of the concept

86. **What should a teacher do when students have not responded well to an instructional activity?**
(Rigorous) (Skill 17.3)

   A. Reevaluate learner needs

   B. Request administrative help

   C. Continue with the activity another day

   D. Assign homework on the concept

87. What developmental patterns should a professional teacher assess to meet the needs of the student?
(Rigorous) (Skill 17.4)

A. Academic, regional, and family background

B. Social, physical, academic

C. Academic, physical, and family background

D. Physical, family, ethnic background

88. Who developed the theory of multiple intelligences?
(Easy) (Skill 17.5)

A. Bruner

B. Gardner

C. Kagan

D. Cooper

89. Johnny, a middle-schooler, comes to class uncharacteristically tired, distracted, withdrawn, sullen, and cries easily. What should be the teacher's first response?
(Average Rigor) (Skill 17.7)

A. Send him to the office to sit

B. Call his parents

C. Ask him what is wrong

D. Ignore his behavior

90. A six-year-old student in Mrs. Brack's first grade class has exhibited a noticeable change in behavior over the last month. The child was usually outgoing and alert, but she has become quiet, withdrawn, and unable to concentrate on her work. Yesterday, bruises were evident on the child's arm and right eye. Mrs. Brack should:
(Rigorous) (Skill 17.7)

A. Ignore the situation

B. Provide remedial work

C. Immediately report the suspected abuse to the authorities

D. Call the girl's parents

91. If a student has a poor vocabulary, the teacher should ensure that:
(Rigorous) (Skill 18.1)

A. The student learns vocabulary through communication.

B. The student enroll in a Latin Class.

C. The student write the words repetitively after looking them up in the dictionary.

D. The student use a thesaurus to locate synonyms and incorporate them into his/her vocabulary.

92. What is a good strategy for teaching ethnically diverse students?
(Average Rigor) (Skill 18.1)

A. Don't focus on the students' culture

B. Expect them to assimilate easily into your classroom

C. Imitate their speech patterns

D. Include ethnic studies in the curriculum

93. Why do gifted students often resent being smarter?
(Rigorous) (Skill 18.2)

A. Their work is harder.

B. They are called on more often.

C. They are treated as if they do not need any attention.

D. Answers B & C

94. Because students have different abilities, teachers should:
(Easy) (Skill 18.3)

A. Apply multiple instruction processes.

B. Vary assessment methods.

C. Use differentiated materials.

D. All of the above

95. "Inclusion" refers to:
(Rigorous) (Skill 18.4)

A. 504 plans only.

B. IEPs only.

C. The right of students with disabilities to be placed in the regular classroom.

D. Reading intervention services.

96. Alternative assessment in math may include:
(Rigorous) (Skill 18.5)

A. Student explanation of reasoning behind their answer.

B. Analysis of data.

C. Multimedia.

D. All of the above.

97. Which best describes differentiated instruction in reading?
(Rigorous) (Skill 18.5)

A. Whole group instruction

B. Instruction based on student strengths

C. Novel study

D. Student workbooks

98. **What are critical elements of instructional process?**
(Rigorous) (Skill 18.6)

   A. Content, goals, teacher needs

   B. Means of getting money to regulate instruction

   C. Content, materials, activities, goals, learner needs

   D. Materials, definitions, assignments

99. **What would improve planning for instruction?**
(Rigorous) (Skill 18.6)

   A. Describe the role of the teacher and student.

   B. Evaluate the outcomes of instruction.

   C. Rearrange the order of activities.

   D. Give outside assignments.

100. **What is a reason that a teacher would give fewer math problems to a student with a disability?**
(Easy) (Skill 18.7)

   A. The teacher is using a modification that takes the student's unique learning needs into account.
   B. The student's parents asked for less homework.
   C. The teacher feels sorry for the student.
   D. Special education students should never be in the regular classroom.

Answer Key

1.	B	26.	D	51.	C	76.	C
2.	A	27.	D	52.	C	77.	C
3.	A	28.	A	53.	C	78.	A
4.	D	29.	D	54.	A	79.	B
5.	A	30.	C	55.	D	80.	B
6.	B	31.	B	56.	A	81.	B
7.	B	32.	A	57.	C	82.	C
8.	D	33.	B	58.	A	83.	A
9.	B	34.	A	59.	D	84.	A
10.	A	35.	C	60.	A	85.	D
11.	A	36.	C	61.	C	86.	A
12.	D	37.	D	62.	A	87.	B
13.	A	38.	B	63.	C	88.	B
14.	D	39.	A	64.	A	89.	C
15.	D	40.	B	65.	D	90.	C
16.	C	41.	D	66.	B	91.	A
17.	B	42.	D	67.	B	92.	D
18.	B	43.	D	68.	D	93.	D
19.	B	44.	D	69.	B	94.	D
20.	D	45.	A	70.	D	95.	C
21.	C	46.	B	71.	C	96.	D
22.	C	47.	B	72.	C	97.	B
23.	A	48.	B	73.	D	98.	C
24.	C	49.	B	74.	B	99.	B
25.	B	50.	D	75.	B	100.	A

Sample Test 2 Rationales

Reading, Language & Literature

1. The main core of the English language is based on:
   (Rigorous) (Skill 1.2)

   A. Latin

   B. Anglo-Saxon

   C. Greek

   D. None of the above

Answer B: Anglo-Saxon
Although the English language has many words borrowed or derived from Latin and Greek, the core of the language is attributed to Anglo-Saxon.

2. **Generally, oral language is differentiated from written language by accent, tone, and:**
   (Easy) (Skill 1.4)

   A. Word choice.

   B. Feeling.

   C. Topic.

   D. Content.

Answer A: Word choice
Oral language is different from written language in the selection of words. Regional slang and dialect is evident in oral language while feeling, topic, and content can be communicated by either oral or written language.

3. **All of the following are true about phonological awareness EXCEPT:**
    (Average Rigor) (Skill 1.5)

    A. It may involve print.

    B. It is a prerequisite for spelling and phonics.

    C. Activities can be done by the children with their eyes closed.

    D. It starts before letter recognition is taught.

Answer A: It may involve print.
The key word here is EXCEPT which will be highlighted in upper case on the test as well. All of the options are correct aspects of phonological awareness except the first one, A, because phonological awareness DOES NOT involve print.

4. **The arrangement and relationship of words in sentences or sentence structure best describes:**
    (Average Rigor) (Skill 1.5)

    A. Style

    B. Discourse

    C. Thesis

    D. Syntax

Answer D: Syntax
Syntax is the grammatical structure of sentences.

5. **Which of the following indicates that a student is a fluent reader?**
    (Easy) (Skill 1.5)

    A. Reads texts with expression or prosody

    B. Reads word-to-word and haltingly

    C. Must intentionally decode a majority of the words

    D. In a writing assignment, sentence structure and organization are poor

Answer A: Reads texts with expression or prosody
The teacher should listen to the children read aloud, but there are also clues to reading levels in their writing

6.   **Which of the following contains an error in possessive inflection?**
     (Rigorous) (Skill 1.6)

     A. Doris's shawl

     B. Mother's-in-law frown

     C. Children's lunches

     D. Ambassador's briefcase

Answer B: Mother's-in-law frown
Mother-in-Law is a compound common noun and the inflection should be at the
end of the word, according to the rule.

7.   **Which of the following is a complex sentence?**
     (Easy) (Skill 1.7)

     A. Anna and Margaret read a total of fifty-four books during summer
         vacation.

     B. The youngest boy on the team had the best earned run average, which
         mystified the coaching staff.

     C. Earl decided to attend Princeton; his twin brother Roy, who aced the
         ASVAB test, will be going to Annapolis.

     D. "Easy come, easy go," Marcia moaned.

Answer B: The youngest boy on the team had the best earned run average
which mystifies the coaching staff.
Here, the use of the relative pronoun "which", whose antecedent is "the best run
average, introduces a clause that is dependent on the independent clause "The
youngest boy on the team had the best run average". The idea expressed in the
subordinate clause is subordinate to the one expressed in the independent
clause.

8. **Which of the following is not a characteristic of a fable?**
   (Easy) (Skill 3.2)

   A. Animals that feel and talk like humans

   B. Happy solutions to human dilemmas

   C. Teaches a standard or moral for behavior

   D. Illustrates specific people or groups without directly naming them

Answer D: Illustrates specific people or groups without directly naming them. A fable is a short tale with animals, humans, gods, or even inanimate objects as characters. Fables often conclude with a moral, delivered in the form of an epigram (a short, witty, and ingenious statement in verse). Fables are among the oldest forms of writing in human history: it appears in Egyptian papyri of c1,500 BC. The most famous fables are those of Aesop, a Greek slave living in about 600 BC. In India, the Pantchatantra appeared in the third century. The most famous modern fables are those of seventeenth century French poet Jean de La Fontaine.

9. **Which of the following is an epic?**
   (Average Rigor) (Skill 3.2)

   A. On the Choice of Books

   B. The Faerie Queene

   C. Northanger Abbey

   D. A Doll's House

Answer B: The Faerie Queene
An epic is a long poem, usually of book length, reflecting the values of the society in which it was produced. *On the Choice of Books* is an essay by Thomas Carlyle. *Northanger Abbey* is a novel written by Jane Austen, and *A Doll's House* is a play written by Henrik Ibsen.

10. **Which is an untrue statement about a theme in literature?**
    (Rigorous) (Skill 3.3)

    A. The theme is always stated directly somewhere in the text.

    B. The theme is the central idea in a literary work.

    C. All parts of the work (plot, setting, mood. Should contribute to the theme in some way.

    D. By analyzing the various elements of the work, the reader should be able to arrive at an indirectly stated theme.

Answer A: The theme is always stated directly somewhere in the text
The theme may be stated directly, but it can also be implicit in various aspects of the work, such as the interaction between characters, symbolism, or description

11. **Which of the following is an example of alliteration?**
    (Average Rigor) (Skill 3.5)

    A. "The City's voice itself is soft like Solitude."

    B. "Both in one faith unanimous; though sad"

    C. "By all their country's wishes blest!"

    D. "In earliest Greece to thee with partial choice"

Answer A: "The City's voice itself is soft like Solitude"
Alliteration is the repetition of consonant sounds in two or more neighboring words or syllables, usually the beginning sound but not always. This line from Shelley's *Stanzas Written in Dejection Near Naples* is an especially effective use of alliteration using the sybillant *s* not only at the beginning of words but also within words. Alliteration usually appears in prosody; however, effective use of alliteration can be found in other genres.

12. **Which is not a true statement concerning an author's literary tone?**
    (Rigorous) (Skill 4.4)

    A. Tone is partly revealed through the selection of details.

    B. Tone is the expression of the author's attitude toward his/her subject.

    C. Tone in literature is usually satiric or angry.

    D. Tone in literature corresponds to the tone of voice a speaker uses.

Answer D: Tone in literature corresponds to the tone of voice a speaker uses. Tone in literature conveys a mood and can be as varied as the tone of voice of a speaker (e.g., sad, nostalgic, whimsical, angry, formal, intimate, satirical, sentimental, etc).

13. **Which definition below is the best for defining diction?**
    (Easy) (Skill 4.4)

    A. The specific word choices of an author to create a particular mood or feeling in the reader

    B. Writing which explains something thoroughly

    C. The background, or exposition, for a short story or drama

    D. Word choices which help teach a truth or moral

Answer A: The specific word choices of an author to create a particular mood or feeling in the reader
Diction refers to an author's choice of words, expressions and style to convey his/her meaning.

14. **Which of the following is not a technique of prewriting?**
    (Average Rigor) (Skill 5.1)

    A. Clustering

    B. Listing

    C. Brainstorming

    D. Proofreading

Answer D: Proofreading
Proofreading cannot be a method of prewriting, since it is done on already written texts only.

15. **Middle and high school students are more receptive to studying grammar and syntax:**
    (Average Rigor) (Skill 5.3)

    A. Through worksheets and end-of-lesson practices in textbooks.

    B. Through independent homework assignments.

    C. Through analytical examination of the writings of famous authors.

    D. Though application to their own writing.

Answer D: Though application to their own writing.
The answer is D. At this age, students learn grammatical concepts best through practical application in their own writing.

16. **Which of the following mostly addresses grammatical and technical errors?**
    (Easy) (Skill 5.3)

    A. Revising

    B. Editing

    C. Proofreading

    D. Rough draft writing

Answer C: Proofreading
During the proofreading process grammatical and technical errors are addressed. The other choices indicate times when writing or rewriting is taking place.

17. **Which of the following should not be included in the opening paragraph of an informative essay? (Rigorous) (Skill 5.5)**

    A. Thesis sentence

    B. Details and examples supporting the main idea

    C. A broad general introduction to the topic

    D. A style and tone that grabs the reader's attention

Answer B: Details and examples supporting the main idea
The introductory paragraph should introduce the topic, capture the reader's interest, state the thesis and prepare the reader for the main points in the essay. Details and examples, however, should be given in the second part of the essay, so as to help develop the thesis presented at the end of the introductory paragraph, following the inverted triangle method consisting of a broad general statement followed by some information, and then the thesis at the end of the paragraph.

18. **A student has written a paper with the following characteristics: written in first person; characters, setting, and plot; some dialogue; events organized in chronological sequence with some flashbacks. In what genre has the student written?**
(Easy) (Skill 5.5)

A. Expository writing

B. Narrative writing

C. Persuasive writing

D. Technical writing

Answer B: Narrative writing
These are all characteristics of narrative writing. Expository writing is intended to give information, such as an explanation or directions, and the information is logically organized. Persuasive writing gives an opinion in an attempt to convince the reader that this point of view is valid or tries to persuade the reader to take a specific action. The goal of technical writing is to clearly communicate a select piece of information to a targeted reader or group of readers for a particular purpose in such a way that the subject can readily be understood. It is persuasive writing that anticipates a response from the reader.

19. **Which of the following is not an approach to keep students ever conscious of the need to write for audience appeal?**
(Average Rigor) (Skill 5.6)

A. Pairing students during the writing process

B. Reading all rough drafts before the students write the final copies

C. Having students compose stories or articles for publication in school literary magazines or newspapers

D. Writing letters to friends or relatives

Answer B: Reading all rough drafts before the students write the final copies
Reading all rough drafts will not encourage the students to take control of their text and might even inhibit their creativity. On the contrary, pairing students will foster their sense of responsibility, and having them compose stories for literary magazines will boost their self esteem as well as their organization skills. As far as writing letters is concerned, the work of authors such as Madame de Sevigne in the seventeenth century are good examples of epistolary literary work.

20. **What is the best place for students to find appropriate synonyms, antonyms, and other related words to enhance their writing?** *(Average Rigor) (Skill 5.6)*

    A. Dictionary

    B. Spell check

    C. Encyclopedia

    D. Thesaurus

Answer D: Thesaurus
Students need plenty of exposure to the new words. A thesaurus is an excellent resource to use when writing. Students can use a thesaurus to find appropriate synonyms, antonyms, and other related words to enhance their writing

Math

21. **Which of the following is an irrational number?** *(Rigorous)(Skill 6.1)*

    A. .362626262...

    B. $4\frac{1}{3}$

    C. $\sqrt{5}$

    D. $-\sqrt{16}$

Answer C: $\sqrt{5}$
Irrational numbers are real numbers that cannot be written as the ratio of two integers, such as infinite non-repeating decimals. $\sqrt{5}$ fits this description; the others do not.

22. An item that sells for $375 is put on sale at $120. What is the percent of decrease?
    (Average Rigor) (Skill 6.7, 7.1)

    A. 25%

    B. 28%

    C. 68%

    D. 34%

Answer C: 68%
Use $(1 - x)$ as the discount.
$375(1 - x) = 120 \rightarrow 375 - 375x = 120 \rightarrow 375x = 255 \rightarrow x = 0.68 = 68\%$

23. A sofa sells for $520. If the retailer makes a 30% profit, what was the wholesale price?
    (Average Rigor) (Skill 7.1)

    A. $400

    B. $676

    C. $490

    D. $364

Answer A: $400
Let x be the wholesale price, then x + .30x = 520, 1.30x = 520. Divide both sides by 1.30.

24. **Two mathematics classes have a total of 410 students. The 8:00 am class has 40 more than the 10:00 am class. How many students are in the 10:00 am class?**
(Average Rigor) (Skill 7.1)

A. 123.3

B. 370

C. 185

D. 330

Answer C: 185
Let x = # of students in the 8 am class and $x - 40$ = # of student in the 10 am class.
So there are 225 students in the 8 am class, and $225 - 40 = 185$ in the 10 am class.

25. **The following chart shows the yearly average number of international tourists visiting Palm Beach for 1990-1994. How may more international tourists visited Palm Beach in 1994 than in 1991?**
(Easy) (Skill 7.7)

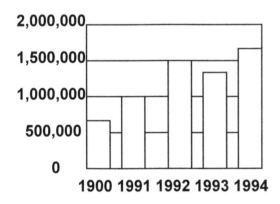

A. 100,000

B. 600,000

C. 1,600,000

D. 8,000,000

Answer B: 600,000
The number of tourists in 1991 was 1,000,000 and the number in 1994 was 1,600,000. Subtract to get a difference of 600,000.

26. $\left(\dfrac{^-4}{9}\right) + \left(\dfrac{^-7}{10}\right) =$

(Easy) (Skill 8.2)

A. $\dfrac{23}{90}$

B. $\dfrac{^-23}{90}$

C. $\dfrac{103}{90}$

D. $\dfrac{^-103}{90}$

Answer D: $\dfrac{^-103}{90}$

Find the LCD of $\dfrac{^-4}{9}$ and $\dfrac{^-7}{10}$. The LCD is 90, so you get $\dfrac{^-40}{90} + \dfrac{^-63}{90} = \dfrac{^-103}{90}$

27. Solve for x:
$|2x+3| > 4$
(Rigorous) (Skill 8.4)

A. $-\frac{7}{2} > x > \frac{1}{2}$

B. $-\frac{1}{2} > x > \frac{7}{2}$

C. $x < \frac{7}{2}$ or $x < -\frac{1}{2}$

D. $x < -\frac{7}{2}$ or $x > \frac{1}{2}$

Answer D: $x < -\frac{7}{2}$ or $x > \frac{1}{2}$

The quantity within the absolute value symbols must be either > 4 or < -4. Solve the two inequalities 2x + 3 > 4 or 2x + 3 < -4.

28. **Graph the solution:**
    $|x| + 7 < 13$
    (Rigorous) (Skill 8.4)

A.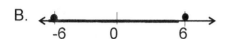
   -6   0   6

B.
   -6   0   6

C.
   -6   0   6

D.
   -6   0   6

Answer A.
   -6   0   6

Solve by adding -7 to each side of the inequality. Since the absolute value of x is less than 6, x must be between -6 and 6. The end points are not included, so the circles on the graph are hollow.

29. $3x + 2y = 12$
    $12x + 8y = 15$
    (Average Rigor) (Skill 8.6)

    A. All real numbers

    B. $x = 4, y = 4$

    C. $x = 2, y = -1$

    D. $\varnothing$

Answer D. $\varnothing$
Multiplying the top equation by -4 and adding results in the equation 0 = -33. Since this is a false statement, the correct choice is the null set.

30. If $4x - (3 - x) = 7(x - 3) + 10$, solve for x.

   (Rigorous) (Skill 8.6)

   A. $x = 8$

   B. $x = -8$

   C. $x = 4$

   D. $x = -4$

Answer C: $x = 4$
Solve for x.
$$4x - (3 - x) = 7(x - 3) + 10$$
$$4x - 3 + x = 7x - 21 + 10$$
$$5x - 3 = 7x - 11$$
$$5x = 7x - 11 + 3$$
$$5x - 7x = {}^- 8$$
$${}^- 2x = {}^- 8$$
$$x = 4$$

31. _____ lines do not intersect.
   (Rigorous) (Skill 8.7)

   A. Perpendicular

   B. Parallel

   C. Intersecting

   D. Skew

Answer B: Parallel
Parallel lines continue at equal distance apart indefinitely. The other choices all intersect at some point.

32. **Which angle would measure less than 90 degrees?**
    (Average Rigor) (Skill 8.7)

    A. Acute

    B. Obtuse

    C. Right

    D. Straight

Answer A: Acute
Acute angles measure less than 90 degrees. Obtuse angles measure greater than 90 and less than 180 degrees. Right angles measure 90 degrees, and straight angles measure 180 degrees.

33. **What is the area of a square whose side is 13 feet?**
    (Rigorous) (Skill 8.9)

    A. 169 feet

    B. 169 square feet

    C. 52 feet

    D. 52 square feet

Answer B: 169 square feet
Area = length times width (*lw*).
Length = 13 feet
Width = 13 feet (square, so length and width are the same).
Area = $13 \times 13 = 169$ square feet.
Area is measured in square feet.

34. **In similar polygons, if the perimeters are in a ratio of x:y, the sides are in a ratio of _____.**
    (Average Rigor) (Skill 8.9)

    A. $x : y$

    B. $x^2 : y^2$

    C. $2x : y$

    D. $1/2\ x : y$

Answer: A. $x : y$
The sides are in the same ratio.

35. **What measure could be used to report the distance traveled in walking around a track?**
    (Easy) (Skill 9.3)

    A. Degrees

    B. Square meters

    C. Kilometers

    D. Cubic feet

Answer C: Kilometers
Degrees measure angles, square meters measure area, cubic feet measure volume, and kilometers measure length. Kilometers is the only reasonable answer.

36. **The mass of a cookie is closest to:**
(Easy) (Skill 9.3)

   A. 0.5 kg

   B. 0.5 grams

   C. 15 grams

   D. 1.5 grams

Answer C: 15 grams
Science utilizes the metric system, and the unit of grams is used when measuring mass (the amount of matter in an object). A common estimation of mass used in elementary schools is that a paperclip has a mass of approximately one gram, which eliminates choices B and D as they are very close to 1 gram. A common estimation of one kilogram is equal to one liter of water. Half of one liter of water is still much more than one cookie, eliminating choice A. Therefore, the best estimation for one cookie is narrowed to 15 grams.

37. **3 km is equivalent to**
(Easy) (Skill 9.3)

   A. 300 cm

   B. 300 m

   C. 3000 cm

   D. 3000 m

Answer D: 3000 m
To change kilometers to meters, move the decimal 3 places to the right.

38. Corporate salaries are listed for several employees. Which would be the best measure of central tendency?
    (Average Rigor) (Skill 9.5)

    $24,000 $24,000 $26,000 $28,000 $30,000 $120,000

    A. Mean

    B. Median

    C. Mode

    D. No difference

Answer B: Median
The median provides the best measure of central tendency in this case where the mode is the lowest number and the mean would be disproportionately skewed by the outlier $120,000.

39. Given a drawer with 5 black socks, 3 blue socks, and 2 red socks, what is the probability that you will draw two black socks in two draws in a dark room?
    (Rigorous) (Skill 9.5)

    A. 2/9

    B. 1/4

    C. 17/18

    D. 1/18

Answer A: 2/9
In this example of conditional probability, the probability of drawing a black sock on the first draw is 5/10. It is implied in the problem that there is no replacement, therefore the probability of obtaining a black sock in the second draw is 4/9. Multiply the two probabilities and reduce to lowest terms.

40. **What is the probability of drawing 2 consecutive aces from a standard deck of cards?**
    (Rigorous) (Skill 9.5)

    A. $\dfrac{3}{51}$

    B. $\dfrac{1}{221}$

    C. $\dfrac{2}{104}$

    D. $\dfrac{2}{52}$

Answer B: $\dfrac{1}{221}$

P(first ace) = $\dfrac{4}{52}$. P(second ace) = $\dfrac{3}{51}$.

P(first ace and second ace) = P(one ace)xP(second ace| first ace)

= $\dfrac{4}{52} \times \dfrac{3}{51} = \dfrac{1}{221}$.

History & Social Science

41. **What was the long-term importance of the Mayflower Compact?**
    (Average Rigor) (Skill 2.1)

    A. It established the foundation of all later agreements with the Native Peoples.

    B. It established freedom of religion in the original English colonies.

    C. It ended the war in Europe between Spain, France and England.

    D. It established a model of small, town-based government that was adopted throughout the New England colonies.

Answer D: Established a model of small, town-based government
Before setting foot on land in 1620, the Pilgrims aboard the Mayflower agreed to a form of self-government by signing the Mayflower Compact. The Compact served as the basis for governing the Plymouth colony for many years and set an example of small, town-based government that would proliferate throughout New England. The present day New England town meeting is an extension of this tradition. This republican ideal was later to clash with the policies of British colonial government.

42. **An economist might engage in which of the following activities?**
    (Average Rigor) (Skill 9.6)

    A. An observation of the historical effects of a nation's banking practices

    B. The application of a statistical test to a series of data

    C. Introduction of an experimental factor into a specified population to measure the effect of the factor

    D. An economist might engage in all of these

Answer D: An economist might engage in all of these
Economists use statistical analysis of economic data, controlled experimentation, and historical research in their field of social science.

43. **Which two Native American nations or tribes inhabited the Mid-Atlantic and Northeastern regions at the time of the first European contact?** *(Average Rigor) (Skill 10.1)*

    A. Pueblo and Inuit

    B. Algonquian and Cherokee

    C. Seminoles and Sioux

    D. Algonquian and Iroquois

Answer D: Algonquian and Iroquois

The Algonquian and Iroquois nations inhabited the Mid-Atlantic and Northeastern regions of the U.S. These Native Americans are classified among the Woods Peoples. Some of the most famous of these nations are Squanto, Pocahontas, Chief Powhatan, Tecumseh, and Black Hawk. These two nations were frequently at odds over territory. The people of these nations taught early settlers about the land and survival in the new world. They introduced the settlers to maize and tobacco. The settlers and the Native Americans gradually developed respect and opened trade and cultural sharing.

44. **Which of the following were results of the Age of Exploration?** *(Easy) (Skill 10.2)*

    A. More complete and accurate maps and charts

    B. New and more accurate navigational instruments

    C. Proof that the earth is round

    D. All of the above

Answer D: All of the above

The importance of the Age of Exploration was not only the discovery and colonization of the New World, but also better maps and charts; new accurate navigational instruments; increased knowledge; great wealth; new and different foods and items not known in Europe; a new hemisphere as a refuge from poverty, persecution, a place to start a new and better life; and proof that Asia could be reached by sea and that the earth was round; ships and sailors would not sail off the edge of a flat earth and disappear forever into nothingness.

45. **The "divine right" of kings was the key political characteristic of:**
   (Rigorous) (Skill 10.2)

   A. The Age of Absolutism

   B. The Age of Reason

   C. The Age of Feudalism

   D. The Age of Despotism

Answer A: The Age of Absolutism.
The "divine right" of kings was the key political characteristic of The Age of Absolutism and was most visible in the reign of King Louis XIV of France, as well as during the times of King James I and his son, Charles I. The divine right doctrine claims that kings and absolute leaders derive their right to rule by virtue of their birth alone. They see this both as a law of God and of nature.

46. **During the period of Spanish colonialism, which of the following was not a key to the goal of exploiting, transforming and including the native people?**
   (Average Rigor) (Skill 10.2)

   A. missions

   B. ranchos

   C. presidios

   D. pueblos

Answer B: Ranchos.
The goal of Spanish colonialism was to exploit, transform and include the native people of California. The Spanish empire sought to do this first by gathering the native people into communities where they could both be taught Spanish culture and be converted to Roman Catholicism and its value system. The social institutions by which this was accomplished was the encouragement of the Mission System, which established a number of Catholic missions a day's journey apart. Once the native people were brought to the missions, they were incorporated into a mission society and indoctrinated in the teachings of Catholicism. The Presidios were fortresses that were constructed to protect Spanish interests and the communities from invaders. The Pueblos were small civilian communities that attracted settlers with the gift of land, seed, and farming equipment. The function of the Pueblos was to produce food for the missions and for the presidios.

47. **Which one of the following is not a reason why Europeans came to the New World?**
   (Rigorous) (Skill 10.2)

   A. To find resources in order to increase wealth

   B. To establish trade

   C. To increase a ruler's power and importance

   D. To spread Christianity

Answer B: To establish trade
The Europeans came to the New World for a number of reasons; often, they came to find new natural resources to extract for manufacturing. The Portuguese, Spanish and English were sent over to increase the monarch's power and spread influences such as religion (Christianity) and culture. Therefore, the only reason given that Europeans didn't come to the New World for was to establish trade.

48. **The year 1619 was a notable time for the colony of Virginia. Three important events occurred resulting in lasting effects on US history. Which one of the following is not one of those events?**
   (Rigorous) (Skill 10.3)

   A. Twenty African slaves arrived in Virginia.

   B. The London Company granted the colony a charter making it independent.

   C. The colonists were given the right by the London Company to govern themselves through representative government in the Virginia House of Burgesses.

   D. The London Company sent to the colony 60 women who were quickly married, establishing families and stability in the colony.

Answer B: The London Company granted the colony a charter making it independent.
In the year 1619, the Southern colony of Virginia had an eventful year including the first arrival of twenty African slaves, the right to self-governance through representative government in the Virginia House of Burgesses (their own legislative body), and the arrival of sixty women sent to marry and establish families in the colony. The London Company did not, however, grant the colony a charter in 1619.

49. **What was "triangular trade"?**
    (Rigorous) (Skill 10.3)

    A. It was regulated trade between the colonies, England and France.

    B. It was an approach to trade that transported finished goods from the mother country to the African colonies, slaves and goods from Africa to the North American Colonies, and raw materials and tobacco or rum back to the mother country.

    C. It was an approach to trade that resulted in colonists obtaining crops and goods from the Native tribes in exchange for finished goods from England.

    D. It was trade between the colonists of the three regions (Southern, mid-Atlantic, and New England).

Answer B: It was an approach to trade that transported finished goods from the mother country to the African colonies, slaves and goods from Africa to the North American Colonies, and raw materials and tobacco or rum back to the mother country.

The New England and Middle Atlantic colonies at first felt threatened by these laws as they had started producing many of the same products being produced in Britain. But they soon found new markets for their goods and began what was known as a **"triangular trade."** Colonial vessels started the first part of the triangle by sailing for Africa loaded with kegs of rum from colonial distilleries. On Africa's West Coast, the rum was traded for either gold or slaves. The second part of the triangle was from Africa to the West Indies where slaves were traded for molasses, sugar, or money. The third part of the triangle was home, bringing sugar or molasses (to make more rum), gold, and silver.

50. **What event sparked a great migration of people from all over the world to California?**
(Average Rigor) (Skill 10.5)

   A. The birth of Labor Unions

   B. California statehood

   C. The invention of the automobile

   D. The Gold Rush

Answer D: The Gold Rush
The discovery of gold in California created a lust for gold that quickly brought immigrants from the eastern United States and many parts of the world. Yet this vast migration of people from all parts of the world began the process that has created California's uniquely diverse culture.

51. **How did the United States gain Florida from Spain?**
(Average Rigor) (Skill 10.5)

   A. It was captured from Spain after the Spanish-American War

   B. It was given to the British and became part of the original thirteen colonies

   C. America bought it from Spain

   D. America acquired it after the First World War

Answer C: America bought it from Spain
Spain received $5 million dollars for Florida, mostly to pay for damages incurred during the war. Following the War of 1812, Spain actually ceded Florida to the United States as part of the treaty. Florida, while under Spanish control, had been a difficult issue for the United States. Runaway slaves would often seek refuge there and the Seminole Indians of Florida would attack Georgia from the South. Therefore, in 1819, the Spanish agreed to put Florida into U.S. hands as part of a treaty to stop the fighting between the two nations. Andrew Jackson, the hero of the War of 1812 became the first governor of Florida.

52. **The belief that the United States should control all of North America was called:**
(Easy) (Skill 10.5)

   A. Westward Expansion

   B. Pan Americanism

   C. Manifest Destiny

   D. Nationalism

Answer C: Manifest Destiny
The belief that the United States should control all of North America was called (C) Manifest Destiny. This idea fueled much of the violence and aggression towards those already occupying the lands, such as the Native Americans. Manifest Destiny was certainly driven by sentiments of (D) nationalism and gave rise to (A) westward expansion.

53. **The Unites States' concern about the possible spread of communism is most closely associated with:**
(Rigorous) (Skill 10.7)

   A. The Vietnam War

   B. The Civil War

   C. The Korean War

   D. World War I

Answer C: The Korean War
The rise of Soviet power and communism was most greatly feared during the time of the Korean War

54. **Which one of the following would NOT be considered a result of World War II?**
    (Average Rigor) (Skill 10.7)

    A. Economic depressions and slow resumption of trade and financial aid

    B. Western Europe was no longer the center of world power.

    C. The beginnings of new power struggles not only in Europe but in Asia as well

    D. Territorial and boundary changes for many nations, especially in Europe

Answer A: Economic depressions and slow resumption of trade and financial aid.
Following World War II, the economy was vibrant and flourished from the stimulant of war and an increased dependence of the world on United States' industries. Therefore, World War II didn't result in economic depressions and slow resumption of trade and financial aid. Western Europe was no longer the center of world power. New power struggles arose in Europe and Asia and many European nations underwent changing territories and boundaries.

55. **In 1957, the formation of the Southern Christian Leadership Conference was started by:**
    (Rigorous) (Skill 10.8)

    A. Martin Luther King, Jr

    B. Rev. T. J. Jemison

    C. Ella Baker

    D. All of the above

Answer: D: All of the above
In 1957, the formation of the Southern Christian Leadership Conference by Martin Luther King, Jr., John Duffy, Rev. C. D. Steele, Rev. T. J. Jemison, Rev. Fred Shuttlesworth, Ella Baker, A. Philip Randolph, Bayard Rustin and Stanley Levison provided training and assistance to local efforts to fight segregation.

56. The advancement of understanding in dealing with human beings has led to a number of interdisciplinary areas. Which of the following interdisciplinary studies would NOT be considered under the social sciences?
(Average Rigor) (Skills 10.8, 10.12, 13.2)

   A. Molecular biophysics

   B. Peace studies

   C. African-American studies

   D. Cartographic information systems

Answer A: Molecular biophysics
Molecular biophysics is an interdisciplinary field combining the fields of biology, chemistry and physics. These are all natural sciences, and not social sciences.

57. What are the three branches of the United States government?
(Easy) (Skill 11.2)

   A. Legislative, judicial, international affairs

   B. Legislative, executive, foreign trade

   C. Legislative, executive, judicial

   D. Executive, judicial, state governments

Answer C: Legislative, executive, judicial
There are three parts of the federal United Sates government: legislative, executive, and judicial.

58. **Which document includes the freedom of religion and right to trial by jury?**
    (Rigorous) (Skill 11.8)

    A. Bill of Rights

    B. Gettysburg Address

    C. Articles of Confederation

    D. The Amendments

Answer A: Bill of Rights
The Bill of Rights includes ten basic rights of individuals including freedom of religion and right to trial by jury.

59. **For the historian studying ancient Egypt, which of the following would be least useful?**
    (Average Rigor) (Skill 12.1)

    A. The record of an ancient Greek historian on Greek-Egyptian interaction

    B. Letters from an Egyptian ruler to his/her regional governors

    C. Inscriptions on stele of the Fourteenth Egyptian Dynasty

    D. Letters from a nineteenth century Egyptologist to his wife

Answer D: Letters from a nineteenth century Egyptologist to his wife.
Historians use primary sources from the actual time they are studying whenever possible. (A) Ancient Greek records of interaction with Egypt, (B) letters from an Egyptian ruler to regional governors, and (C) inscriptions from the Fourteenth Egyptian Dynasty are all primary sources created at or near the actual time being studied. (D) Letters from a nineteenth century Egyptologist would not be considered primary sources, as they were created thousands of years after the fact and may not actually be about the subject being studied.

60. **What intellectual movement during the period of North American colonization contributed to the development of public education and the founding of the first colleges and universities?**
(Average Rigor) (Skill 12.2)

   A. Enlightenment

   B. Great Awakening

   C. Libertarianism

   D. The Scientific Revolution

Answer A: Enlightenment
Enlightenment thinking quickly made the voyage across the Atlantic Ocean. It valued human reason and the importance of education, knowledge, and scholarly research. Education in the middle colonies was influenced largely by the Enlightenment movement, which emphasized scholarly research and public service. Benjamin Franklin embodied these principles in Philadelphia, which became a center of learning and culture, owing largely to its economic success and ease of access to European books and tracts.

Science

61. **All of the following are considered Newton's Laws except for:**
(Easy) (Skills 12.2)

   A. An object in motion will continue in motion unless acted upon by an outside force

   B. For every action force, there is an equal and opposite reaction force

   C. Nature abhors a vacuum

   D. Mass can be considered the ratio of force to acceleration

Answer C: Nature abhors a vacuum
Newton's Laws include his law of inertia (an object in motion (or at rest) will stay in motion (or at rest) until acted upon by an outside force) (A), his law that (Force)=(Mass)(Acceleration) (D), and his equal and opposite reaction force law (B). Therefore, the answer to this question is (C), because "Nature abhors a vacuum" is not one of these.

62. **Which is a form of precipitation?**
    (Rigorous) (Skill 13.5)

    A. Snow

    B. Frost

    C. Fog

    D. All of the above

Answer A: Snow

Snow is a form of precipitation. Precipitation is the product of the condensation of atmospheric water vapor that falls to the Earth's surface. It occurs when the atmosphere becomes saturated with water vapor and the water condenses and falls out of solution. Frost and fog do not qualify as precipitates.

63. **Identify the correct sequence of organization of living things from lower to higher order:**
    (Rigorous) (Skill 14.1)

    A. Cell, Organelle, Organ, Tissue, System, Organism

    B. Cell, Tissue, Organ, Organelle, System, Organism

    C. Organelle, Cell, Tissue, Organ, System, Organism

    D. Organelle, Tissue, Cell, Organ, System, Organism

Answer C: Organelle, Cell, Tissue, Organ, System, Organism

Organelles are parts of the cell; cells make up tissue, which makes up organs. Organs work together in systems (e.g. the respiratory system), and the organism is the living thing as a whole. Therefore, the answer must be (C).

64. What cell organelle contains the cell's stored food?
(Rigorous) (Skill 14.2)

A. Vacuoles

B. Golgi Apparatus

C. Ribosomes

D. Lysosomes

Answer A: Vacuoles
In a cell, the sub-parts are called organelles. Of these, the vacuoles hold stored food (and water and pigments). The Golgi Apparatus sorts molecules from other parts of the cell; the ribosomes are sites of protein synthesis; the lysosomes contain digestive enzymes. This is consistent only with answer (A).

65. Enzymes speed up reactions by _____ .
(Rigorous) (Skill 14.4)

A. Utilizing ATP

B. Lowering pH, allowing reaction speed to increase.

C. Increasing volume of substrate

D. Lowering energy of activation

Answer D: Lowering energy of activation
Because enzymes are catalysts, they work the same way—they cause the formation of activated chemical complexes, which require a lower activation energy. Therefore, the answer is (D). ATP is an energy source for cells, and pH or volume changes may or may not affect reaction rate, so these answers can be eliminated.

66. **Which parts of an atom are located inside the nucleus?**
    (Average Rigor) (Skill 15.1)

    A. Electrons and neutrons

    B. Protons and neutrons

    C. Protons only

    D. Neutrons only

Answer B: Protons and neutrons
Protons and neutrons are located in the nucleus, while electrons move around outside the nucleus. This is consistent only with answer (B).

67. **Energy is:**
    (Rigorous) (Skill 15.2)

    A. The combination of power and work

    B. The ability to cause change in matter

    C. The transfer of power when force is applied to a body

    D. Physical force

Answer B: The ability to cause change in matter
Physical force is one form of power. The transfer of power when force is applied to a body is work. The combination of power and work is not energy. Energy is simply the ability to cause change in matter.

68. The measure of the pull of the earth's gravity on an object is called

_____.

(Average Rigor) (Skill 15.3)

A. Mass number

B. Atomic number

C. Mass.

D. Weight

Answer D: Weight

To answer this question, recall that mass number is the total number of protons and neutrons in an atom, atomic number is the number of protons in an atom, and mass is the amount of matter in an object. The only remaining choice is (D), weight, which is correct because weight is the force of gravity on an object.

69. **Which of the following is the best definition for 'meteorite'?**
    (Rigorous) (Skill 15.4)

A. A meteorite is a mineral composed of mica and feldspar.

B. A meteorite is material from outer space that has struck the earth's surface.

C. A meteorite is an element that has properties of both metals and nonmetals.

D. A meteorite is a very small unit of length measurement.

Answer B: A meteorite is material from outer space that has struck the earth's surface.

Meteoroids are pieces of matter in space, composed of particles of rock and metal. If a meteoroid travels through the earth's atmosphere, friction causes burning and a "shooting star"—i.e. a meteor. If the meteor strikes the earth's surface, it is known as a meteorite. Note that although the suffix –ite often means a mineral, answer (A) is incorrect. Answer (C) refers to a 'metalloid' rather than a 'meteorite', and answer (D) is simply a misleading pun on 'meter'. Therefore, the answer is (B).

70. **Which of the following types of rock are made from magma?**
    (Average Rigor) (Skill 15.5)

    A. Fossils

    B. Sedimentary

    C. Metamorphic

    D. Igneous

Answer D: Igneous

Few fossils are found in metamorphic rock and virtually none found in igneous rocks. Igneous rocks are formed from magma and magma is so hot that any organisms trapped by it are destroyed. Metamorphic rocks are formed by high temperatures and great pressures. When fluid sediments are transformed into solid sedimentary rocks, the process is known as lithification.

71. **The calm point at the center of a storm such as a hurricane is often called the "eye" of the storm. This "eye" is caused by:**
    (Average Rigor) (Skill 15.5)

    A. Centrepidal force

    B. A high-pressure air mass

    C. A low-pressure air mass

    D. Heavier precipitation in the area

Answer C: A low-pressure air mass

A large, low-pressure system accompanied by heavy precipitation and strong winds is called a hurricane. Heavier precipitation is not considered a characteristic of the eye of the storm. Centrepidal force would cause the low-pressure eye to expand outwards, dispersing the storm.

72. **Air masses moving toward or away form the Earth's surface is called**
_____.
   (Average Rigor) (Skill 15.5)

   A. Wind

   B. Breeze

   C. Air currents

   D. Doldrums

Answer C: Air currents
The doldrums, answer (D), describe the air masses near the equator. A breeze, answer (B), is a term used to describe winds created by local tempature changes. Wind, (answer (A), occurs when air masses move across the surface of the planet. Air currents, answer (C), is the term used to the vertical movement of air masses.

73. **Which type of cloud is most likely to produce precipitation?**
   (Average Rigor) (Skill 15.5)

   A. Cirrus

   B. Cumulus

   C. Stratus

   D. Nimbus

Answer D: Nimbus
Cirrus and Stratus clouds (answers (A) and (C)) occur at the highest levels of cloud formation, and are thin veil like or small patches, respectively. Cumulus clouds (answer (B)), occur low in the atmosphere, and are usually large irregular shaped puffs with large amounts of blue sky, these are the clouds that are usually used when looking for shapes in clouds. Leaving nimbus clouds (answer (D)) to be correct. These clouds are most often associated with thunderstorms, these large, puffy, clouds have smooth or flattened tops, and can produce heavy rain and thunder.

74. **Which of the following instruments measures wind speed?**
    (Easy) (Skill 15.5)

    A. A barometer

    B. An anemometer

    C. A thermometer

    D. A weather vane

Answer B: An anemometer

An anemometer is a device to measure wind speed, while a barometer measures pressure, a thermometer measures temperature, and a weather vane indicates wind direction. This is consistent only with answer (B).

If you chose "barometer," here is an old physics joke to console you:

A physics teacher asks a student the following question:

> "Suppose you want to find out the height of a
> building, and the only tool you have is a barometer.
> How could you find out the height?"

(The teacher hopes that the student will remember that pressure is inversely proportional to height, and will measure the pressure at the top of the building and then use the data to calculate the height of the building.)

"Well," says the student, "I could tie a string to the barometer and lower it from the top of the building, and then measure the amount of string required." "You could," answers the teacher, "but try to think of a method that uses your physics knowledge from our class.""All right," replies the student, "I could drop the barometer from the roof and measure the time it takes to fall, and then use free-fall equations to calculate the height from which it fell." "Yes," says the teacher, "but what about using the barometer per se?" "Oh," answers the student, "I could find the building superintendent, and offer to exchange the barometer for a set of blueprints, and look up the height!"

75. **By discovering the structure of DNA, Watson and Crick made it possible to:**
    (Rigorous) (Skill 16.2)

    A. Clone DNA

    B. Explain DNA's ability to replicate and control the synthesis of proteins

    C. Sequence human DNA

    D. Predict genetic mutations

Answer B: Explain DNA's ability to replicate and control the synthesis of proteins
While more recent discoveries have made it possible to sequence the human genome, clone DNA, and predict genetic mutations, it was Watson and Crick's discovery of DNA's structure that made it possible for scientists to understand and therefore explain DNA's ability to replicate and control the synthesis of proteins. Thus, the correct answer is (B).

76. **In an experiment measuring the growth of bacteria at different temperatures, what is the independent variable?**
    (Rigorous) (Skill 16.4)

    A. Number of bacteria

    B. Growth rate of bacteria

    C. Temperature

    D. Size of bacteria

Answer C: Temperature
To answer this question, recall that the independent variable in an experiment is the entity that is changed by the scientist, in order to observe the effects (the dependent variable(s). In this experiment, temperature is changed in order to measure growth of bacteria, so (C) is the answer. Note that answer (A) is the dependent variable, and neither (B) nor (D) is directly relevant to the question.

77. A scientific law_____.
(Average Rigor) (Skill 16.4)

A. Proves scientific accuracy.

B. May never be broken.

C. Is the current most accuracte explanation for natural phemonon, and experimental data.

D. Is the result of one excellent experiment.

Answer C: Is the current most accuracte explanation for natural Phemonon, and experimental data
A scientific law is a tool that is used for making predications about the natural occurances and experimental data. A scientific law is always the result of many experiments, and never 'proves' anything but rather is implied or supported by various results. Therefore, such a law may be revised in light of new data, and may be replaced by a new law that is a more accuracte tool. For example Newton's Laws have been Replaced by Einstiens's Laws of Relativity, because the Laws of realitivity can explain natural occurances that Newton's laws can not. Therefore, the answer must be (C).

78. The control group of an experiment is:
(Average Rigor) (Skill 16.4)

A. An extra group in which all experimental conditions are the same and the variable being tested is unchanged.

B. A group of authorities in charge of an experiment.

C. The group of experimental participants who are given experimental drugs.

D. A group of subjects that is isolated from all aspects of the experiment.

Answer A: An extra group in which all experimental conditions are the same and the variable being tested is unchanged
A group of authorities in charge of an experiment, while they might be in control, they are not a control group. The group of experimental participants given the experimental drugs would be the experimental group, and a group of subjects isolated from all aspects of the experiment would not be part of the experiment at all. Thus, the answer is (A).

79. What is the scientific method?
(Average Rigor) (Skill 16.4)

A. It is the process of doing an experiment and writing a laboratory report.

B. It is the process of using open inquiry and repeatable results to establish theories.

C. It is the process of reinforcing scientific principles by confirming results.

D. It is the process of recording data and observations.

Answer B: It is the process of using open inquiry and repeatable results to establish theories.
Scientific research often includes elements from answers (A), (C), and (D), but the basic underlying principle of the scientific method is that people ask questions and do repeatable experiments to answer those questions and develop informed theories of why and how things happen. Therefore, the best answer is (B).

80. Which is the correct order of methodology?
(Average Rigor) (Skill 16.4)

1. Collecting data
2. Planning a controlled experiment
3. Drawing a conclusion
4. Hypothesizing a result
5. Revisiting a hypothesis to answer a question

A. 1,2,3,4,5

B. 4,2,1,3,5

C. 4,5,1,3,2

D. 1,3,4,5,2

Answer B: 4,2,1,3,5
The correct methodology for the scientific method is first to make a meaningful hypothesis (educated guess), then to plan and execute a controlled experiment to test that hypothesis. Using the data collected in that experiment, the scientist then draws conclusions and attempts to answer the original question related to the hypothesis. This is consistent only with answer (B).

Human Development

81. **Followers of Piaget's learning theory believe that adolescents in the formal operations period:**
    (Average Rigor) (Skill 17.1)

    A. Behave properly from fear of punishment rather than from a conscious decision to take a certain action.

    B. See the past more realistically and can relate to people from the past more than preadolescents.

    C. Are less self-conscious and thus more willing to project their own identities into those of fictional characters.

    D. Have not yet developed a symbolic imagination.

Answer B: See the past more realistically and can relate to people from the past more than preadolescents.
According to Piaget, since adolescents 12-15 years old begin thinking beyond the immediate and obvious, their assessment of events shifts from considering an action as "right" or "wrong" to considering the intent and behavior in which the action was performed. Fairy tale or other kinds of unreal characters have ceased to satisfy them and they are able to recognize the difference between pure history and historical fiction.

82. **According to Piaget, what stage is characterized by the ability to think abstractly and to use logic?**
(Average Rigor) (Skill 17.1)

A. Concrete operational

B. Pre-operational

C. Formal operational

D. Sensory Motor

Answer C: Formal operational

The four development stages are described in Piaget's theory as follows:

1. Sensorimotor stage: from birth to age 2 years (children experience the world through movement and senses).
2. Preoperational stage: from ages 2 to 7 (acquisition of motor skills).
3. Concrete operational stage: from ages 7 to 11 (children begin to think logically about concrete events).
4. Formal operational stage: after age 11 (development of abstract reasoning).

These chronological periods are approximate and, in light of the fact that studies have demonstrated great variation between children, cannot be seen as rigid norms. Furthermore, these stages occur at different ages, depending upon the domain of knowledge under consideration. The ages normally given for the stages reflect when each stage tends to predominate even though one might elicit examples of two, three, or even all four stages of thinking at the same time from one individual, depending upon the domain of knowledge and the means used to elicit it.

83. **At approximately what age is the average child able to define abstract terms such as honesty and justice?**
(Rigorous) (Skill 17.1)

A. 10-12 years old

B. 4-6 years old

C. 14-16 years old

D. 6-8 years old

Answer A: 10-12 years old
The usual age for the fourth stage (the formal operational stage) as described by Piaget is from 10 to 12 years old. It is in this stage that children begin to be able to define abstract terms.

84. **How can the teacher establish a positive climate in the classroom?**
(Average Rigor) (Skill 17.2)

A. Help students see the unique contributions of individual differences.

B. Use whole-group instruction for all content areas.

C. Help students divide into cooperative groups based on ability.

D. Eliminate teaching strategies that allow students to make choices.

Answer A: Help students see the unique contributions of individual differences. During the primary years, children develop an intense interest in peers. They establish productive, positive, social and working relationships with one another. This area of social growth will continue to increase in significance throughout the child's academic career. The foundation for the students' successful development in this area is established through the efforts of the classroom teacher to plan and develop positive peer group relationships and to provide opportunities and support for cooperative small group projects that not only develop cognitive ability but promote peer interaction. The ability to work and relate effectively with peers contributes greatly to the child's sense of competence.

85. **When are students more likely to understand complex ideas?**
   (Rigorous) (Skill 17.3)

   A. When they do outside research before coming to class.

   B. When they write out the definitions of complex words.

   C. When they attend a lecture on the subject.

   D. When the ideas are clearly defined by the teacher and the students are given examples of the concept.

Answer D: When they are clearly defined by the teacher and are given examples and non-examples of the concept.
Several studies have been carried out to determine the effectiveness of giving examples as well as the difference in effectiveness of various types of examples. It was found conclusively that the most effective method of concept presentation included giving a definition along with examples and non-examples and also providing an explanation of them. These same studies indicate that boring examples were just as effective as interesting examples in promoting learning. Additional studies have been conducted to determine the most effective number of examples that will result in maximum student learning. These studies concluded that a few thoughtfully selected examples are just as effective as many examples. It was determined that the actual number of examples necessary to promote student learning was relative to the learning characteristics of the learners. It was again ascertained that learning is facilitated when examples are provided along with the definition.

86. **What should a teacher do when students have not responded well to an instructional activity?**
(Rigorous) (Skill 17.3)

   A. Reevaluate learner needs

   B. Request administrative help

   C. Continue with the activity another day

   D. Assign homework on the concept

Answer A: Reevaluate learner needs
The value of teacher observations cannot be underestimated. It is through the use of observations that the teacher is able to informally assess the needs of the students during instruction. These observations will drive the lesson and determine the direction that the lesson will take based on student activity and behavior. After a lesson is carefully planned, teacher observation is the single most important component of an instructional presentation. If it is observed that a particular student is not on-task, the teacher will change the method of instruction accordingly. The teacher may change from a teacher-directed approach to a more interactive approach. Questioning will increase in order to increase the participation of the students. If appropriate, the teacher will introduce manipulative materials to the lesson. In addition, the teacher may switch to a cooperative group activity, thereby removing the responsibility of instruction from the teacher and putting it on the students.

87. **What developmental patterns should a professional teacher assess to meet the needs of the student?**
(Rigorous) (Skill 17.4)

   A. Academic, regional, and family background

   B. Social, physical, academic

   C. Academic, physical, and family background

   D. Physical, family, ethnic background

Answer B: Social, physical, academic
The effective teacher applies knowledge of physical, social, and academic developmental patterns and of variations in these areas from student to student to meet the instructional needs of *all* students in the classroom. The most important premise of child development is that all domains of development (physical, social, and academic) are integrated. The teacher has a broad knowledge and thorough understanding of the development that typically occurs during the students' current period of life. More importantly, the teacher understands how children learn best during each period of development. An examination of the student's file, coupled with ongoing evaluation, assures a successful educational experience for both teacher and students.

88. **Who developed the theory of multiple intelligences?**
(Easy) (Skill 17.5)

   A. Bruner

   B. Gardner

   C. Kagan

   D. Cooper

Answer B: Gardner
Howard Gardner's most famous work is probably *Frames of Mind*, which details seven dimensions of intelligence (visual/spatial intelligence, musical intelligence, verbal intelligence, logical/mathematical intelligence, interpersonal intelligence, intrapersonal intelligence, and bodily/kinesthetic intelligence). Gardner's claim that pencil and paper IQ tests do not capture the full range of human intelligences has garnered much praise within the field of education but has also met criticism, largely from psychometricians. Since the publication of *Frames of Mind*, Gardner has additionally identified the eighth dimension of intelligence – naturalist intelligence – and is considering a possible ninth one called existentialist intelligence.

89. Johnny, a middle-schooler, comes to class uncharacteristically tired, distracted, withdrawn, sullen, and cries easily. What should be the teacher's first response?
 (Average Rigor) (Skill 17.7)

   A. Send him to the office to sit

   B. Call his parents

   C. Ask him what is wrong

   D. Ignore his behavior

Answer C: Ask him what is wrong
If the teacher has developed a trusting relationship with the child, the reasons for the child's behavior may come out. It might be that the child needs a teacher they trust to intervene and help with something. If the child is unwilling to talk to the teacher about what is going on, the next step is to contact the parents, who may or may not be willing to cooperate. If they simply do not know what's troubling their child, then it's time to add a professional physician or counselor to the mix.

90. A six-year-old student in Mrs. Brack's first grade class has exhibited a noticeable change in behavior over the last month. The child was usually outgoing and alert, but she has become quiet, withdrawn, and unable to concentrate on her work. Yesterday, bruises were evident on the child's arm and right eye. Mrs. Brack should:
 (Rigorous) (Skill 17.7)

   A. Ignore the situation

   B. Provide remedial work

   C. Immediately report the suspected abuse to the authorities

   D. Call the girl's parents

Answer C: Immediately report the suspected abuse to the authorities.
Immediate reporting is important to minimize chances of any further abuse and to provide immediate protection to the child. It is a moral and legal obligation.

91. **If a student has a poor vocabulary, the teacher should ensure that:**
(Rigorous) (Skill 18.1)

   A. The student learns vocabulary through communication.

   B. The student enrolls in a Latin Class.

   C. The student write the words repetitively after looking them up in the dictionary.

   D. The student use a thesaurus to locate synonyms and incorporate them into his/her vocabulary.

Answer A: The student learns vocabulary through communication.
Students should engage in classroom lessons and activities to build vocabulary. They should be familiar with using the dictionary and thesaurus. However, the most effective way to learn new words is to practice using them in communication.

92. **What is a good strategy for teaching ethnically diverse students?**
(Average Rigor) (Skill 18.1)

   A. Don't focus on the students' culture

   B. Expect them to assimilate easily into your classroom

   C. Imitate their speech patterns

   D. Include ethnic studies in the curriculum

Answer D: Include ethnic studies in the curriculum
Exploring their own cultures increases students' confidence levels in the group. It is also a very useful tool when students are struggling to develop identities with which they may be comfortable and feel accepted...

93. Why do gifted students often resent being smarter?
(Rigorous) (Skill 18.2)

    A. Their work is harder.

    B. They are called on more often.

    C. They are treated as if they do not need any attention.

    D. Answers B & C

Answer D: Answers B & C
In a classroom with differentiated instruction (including assignments) the work of the gifted student may be more difficult. However, the difficulty will be aligned with the student's abilities and is usually welcomed as challenging, interesting, and not boring. Often, however, gifted students resent being called on more often. They often feel that they are expected to understanding everything and do not get the same attention from the teacher. Answers B & C are both correct for this question.

94. Because students have different abilities, teachers should:
(Easy) (Skill 18.3)

    A. Apply multiple instruction processes.

    B. Vary assessment methods.

    C. Use differentiated materials.

    D. All of the above

Answer D: All of the above
The effective teacher will address different abilities of her students in all of the areas listed. While some students are auditory learners, others will learn better from hands-on activities. The learning strengths and differences of the students will influence the methods and materials used by the teacher. Additionally, some students' knowledge can be fairly assessed with the traditional paper-pencil method; others will require alternate assessment. The answer is D.

95. "Inclusion" refers to:
    (Rigorous) (Skill 18.4)

    A. 504 plans only.

    B. IEPs only.

    C. The right of students with disabilities to be placed in the regular classroom.

    D. Reading intervention services.

Answer C: The right of students with disabilities to be placed in the regular classroom.
A student with a 504 plan has a documented disability but can be served throughout the school day in the regular classroom with modifications and accommodations. A student with an IEP may also be in the regular education classroom with modifications and accommodations as well as special education instruction. Some of this student's special education instruction may come in the special education classroom. The term "inclusion" refers to the right of a student with a disability to be placed in the regular classroom for instruction. It can apply to a student with a 504 plan or an IEP. Students who receive reading intervention services are not special education students, but rather those who have been identified through testing as needing additional reading instruction to be successful across the curriculum.

96. Alternative assessment in math may include:
    (Rigorous) (Skill 18.5)

    A. Student explanation of reasoning behind their answer

    B. Analysis of data

    C. Multimedia

    D. All of the above

Answer D: All of the above
The question asks about *alternative* assessment so any of the choices might be used instead of a tradition paper and pencil test.

97. **Which best describes differentiated instruction in reading?**
    (Rigorous) (Skill 18.5)

    A. Whole group instruction

    B. Instruction based on student strengths

    C. Novel study

    D. Student workbooks

Answer B: Instruction based on student strengths
Differentiated instruction looks at the individual student's strengths in learning and addresses those. There may be several groups (or individuals) working on different material in a classroom that uses differentiated instruction.

98. **What are critical elements of instructional process?**
    (Rigorous) (Skill 18.6)

    A. Content, goals, teacher needs

    B. Means of getting money to regulate instruction

    C. Content, materials, activities, goals, learner needs

    D. Materials, definitions, assignments

Answer C: Content, materials, activities, goals, learner needs
Goal-setting is a vital component of the instructional process. Although teachers have overall short- and long-term goals for their class, they pay special attention to setting goals that take into account the individual learners' needs, background, and stage of development. Forming a child-centered educational program involves building on the natural curiosity children bring to school and asking children what they want to learn. Student-centered classrooms contain not only textbooks, workbooks, and literature, but also a variety of audiovisual equipment and computers. There are tape recorders, language masters, filmstrip projectors, and laser disc players to help meet the diverse learning styles of the students. Planning for instructional activities entails identification or selection of the activities the teacher and students will engage in during a period of instruction

99. **What would improve planning for instruction?**
(Rigorous) (Skill 18.6)

   A. Describe the role of the teacher and student.

   B. Evaluate the outcomes of instruction.

   C. Rearrange the order of activities.

   D. Give outside assignments.

Answer B: Evaluate the outcomes of **instruction**
No matter how carefully teachers plan their classroom agenda, determine content, select materials, and set goals based on learner needs, all of their hard work makes no difference if students are not able to demonstrate improvement in the skills being taught. An important part of the planning process is for the teacher to constantly adapt all aspects of the curriculum to what is actually happening in the classroom. Planning often fails to allow for unexpected factors. Evaluating the outcomes of instruction regularly and making adjustments accordingly will have a positive effect on the overall success of a teaching methodology.

100. **What is a reason that a teacher would give fewer math problems to a student with a disability?**
(Average Rigor) (Skill 18.7)

   A. The teacher is using a modification that takes the student's unique learning needs into account.

   B. The student's parents asked for less homework.

   C. The teacher feels sorry for the student.

   D. Special education students should never be in the regular classroom.

Answer A: The teacher is using a modification that takes the student's unique learning needs into account.
Many learning disabled students, for example, can grasp the math concept of a particular lesson but may become overwhelmed when asked to complete an entire page of practice problems. Completing a section or only the even problems may be a more realistic expectation.

Sample Constructed Response Questions

Directions: In the next few pages, you will see eleven constructed response prompts. You will need to prepare a short essay for each one. Each assignment will be to write a response of about 300 words on the assigned topic. Your score will be based on these following factors:

- Purpose: You will be assessed on the extent to which you answer the question on each prompt. You must write your response so that it directly addresses what the prompt asks you to do.
- Subject-Matter Knowledge: You will be assessed on the extent to which you demonstrate content knowledge.
- Support: You will be assessed on the extent to which you provide a coherent, fully supported response. Your response should provide evidence for any assertions you make.

Although your writing ability will not be directly assessed, please take care to write an essay that is as free of grammatical errors as possible.

Reading, Language & Literature

The Writing Process

Using your knowledge of teaching English Composition at the middle school level, write a response in which you:

- Instruct students as to effective strategies for selecting an appropriate topic for a 400-word essay; and
- relate this to three stages of composition: pre-writing, drafting, and revision

Sample Strong Response

For this assignment, my first question to students is: What is an experience, person, value or interest in your life so important to you that you want others to know about it? This question dovetails with the writer's commandment: Write about what you know. Of course I will emphasize this, but I will also try to inspire students by insisting that writing can be more than an academic exercise. It is also a part of self-expression.

Before choosing a topic, however, one must tailor it to the length requirement of the assignment. For a 400-word personal experience essay, the general rule is: The more narrowly focused the topic, the better. This sounds quite vague, which is why the rule will be backed up with readings of brief personal essays appearing in our course textbook. In particular, essays that cover only a very short period of time will be read. Furthermore, students will be asked to judge the likely appropriateness of sample titles that indicate how much time an essay covers: "My Year as an Exchange Student in Germany" vs. "My Most Memorable Day in Berlin" are but two possible examples intended to drive home the point: In a 400-word essay, less is more.

In-class discussions and brief written assignments will follow from this, giving students the opportunity to study how experienced writers introduce and develop topics. When techniques, structures and strategies are recognized and subsequently described, students will be encouraged to imitate them—in their own words.

Much has been made, and rightly so, about the process of writing—especially regarding the stages of pre-writing, drafting, and revision. Textbook material related to this will be introduced and thoroughly explained in class. However, I must take care to avoid making these processes seem too iron-clad or programmatic; indeed, "going too far" on this point can make writing seem terribly mechanical and boring. If a student wishes to stand on her head, speak into a tape recorder, transcribe the words, then turn them into a clear, concise, and grammatically correct essay, this would be—as far as I'm concerned—perfectly acceptable. Sometimes even revision isn't necessary, if only rarely. What counts is the final product.

Math

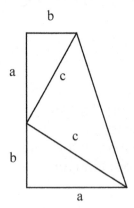

Using your knowledge of algebra and geometry:

- write an expression for the area of the trapezoid base using the formula: area = half the sum of the bases times the altitude
- write an expression for the area of the trapezoid in terms of the area of its component parts (the three triangles); and
- set these two expressions as equal and show that this leads to a proof of the Pythagorean theorem.

Response:
The expression for the area of the trapezoid would be:

$$A = \frac{1}{2}(b_1 + b_2)(h) = \frac{1}{2}(a+b)(a+b) = \frac{1}{2}(a^2 + 2ab + b^2) = \frac{1}{2}a^2 + ab + \frac{1}{2}b^2$$

To determine the area of the trapezoid by adding the sum of the areas of each triangle, we use the formula $A = \frac{1}{2}bh$:

$$A = \frac{1}{2}ab + \frac{1}{2}ab + \frac{1}{2}c^2$$

By setting the two expressions equal to each other, we prove the Pythagorean Theorem:

$$\frac{1}{2}a^2 + ab + \frac{1}{2}b^2 = \frac{1}{2}ab + \frac{1}{2}ab + \frac{1}{2}c^2$$

$$\frac{1}{2}a^2 + ab + \frac{1}{2}b^2 = ab + \frac{1}{2}c^2$$

$$\frac{1}{2}a^2 + \frac{1}{2}b^2 = \frac{1}{2}c^2$$

$$a^2 + b^2 = c^2$$

Rationale

The response is considered to be good because it demonstrates the respondent's knowledge of the subject matter (algebra and geometry) and addresses the specific questions asked by the test. The thinking behind the process and the derivation of the answers are fully explained in a clear and concise manner. All areas of the calculations and proof are covered.

Sample Test 3

READING

1. **To make a prediction a reader must:**
   (Average)

   A. Use text clues to evaluate the text at an inferential level

   B. Find a line of reasoning on which to rely

   C. Make a decision based on an observation

   D. Use prior knowledge and apply it to the current situation

2. **Which of the following is NOT a characteristic of a good reader?**
   (Rigorous)

   A. When faced with unfamiliar words, they skip over them unless meaning is lost

   B. They formulate questions that they predict will be answered in the text

   C. They establish a purpose before reading

   D. They go back to reread when something doesn't make sense

3. **All of the following are true about schemata EXCEPT:**
   (Rigorous)

   A. Used as a basis for literary response

   B. Structures that represent concepts stored in our memories

   C. A generalization that is proven with facts

   D. Used together with prior knowledge for effective reading comprehension.

4. **Children are taught phonological awareness when they are taught all but which concept?**
   (Average)

   A. The sounds made by the letters

   B. The correct spelling of words

   C. The sounds made by various combinations of letters

   D. The ability to recognize individual sounds in words

5. **Which of the following is true about semantics?**
   (Average)

   A. Semantics will sharpen the effect and meaning of a text

   B. Semantics refers to the meaning expressed when words are arranged in a specific way.

   C. Semantics is a vocabulary instruction technique.

   D. Semantics is representing spoken language through the use of symbols.

6. **Spelling instruction should include:**
   (Average)

   A. Breaking down sentences

   B. Developing a sense of correct and incorrect spellings

   C. Identifying every word in a given text

   D. Spelling words the way that they sound

7. **Answering questions, monitoring comprehension, and interacting with a text are common methods of:**
   (Average)

   A. Whole-class instruction

   B. Comprehension instruction

   C. Research-based instruction

   D. Evidence-based instruction

8. **Mrs. Young is a first grade teacher trying to select a books that are "just right" for her students to read independently. She needs to consider which of the following:**
   (Rigorous)

   A. Illustrations should support the meaning of the text

   B. Content that relates to student interest and experiences

   C. Predictable text structures and language patterns

   D. All of the above

9. Which of the following is NOT characteristic of a folktale? *(Average)*

A. Considered true among various societies

B. A hero on a quest

C. Good versus evil

D. Adventures of animals

10. Which of the following did NOT contribute to a separate literature genre for adolescents? *(Rigorous)*

A. The social changes of post–World War II

B. The Civil Rights movement

C. An interest in fantasy and science fiction

D. Issues surrounding teen pregnancy

11. Which of the following is important in understanding fiction? *(Rigorous)*

I. Realizing the artistry in telling a story to convey a point.
II. Knowing fiction is imaginary.
III. Seeing what is truth and what is perspective.
IV. Acknowledging the difference between opinion and truth.

A. I and II only

B. II and IV only

C. III and IV only

D. IV only

12. Assonance is a poetic device where: *(Average)*

A. The vowel sound in a word matches the same sound in a nearby word, but the surrounding consonant sounds are different

B. The initial sounds of a word, beginning either with a consonant or a vowel, are repeated in close succession

C. The words used evoke meaning by their sounds

D. The final consonant sounds are the same, but the vowels are different

13. Which of the following is true of the visible shape of poetry?
(Rigorous)

    I. Forced sound repetition may underscore the meaning.
    II. It was a new rule of poetry after poets began to feel constricted by rhyming conventions.
    III. The shaped reflected the poem's theme.
    IV. It was viewed as a demonstration of ingenuity.

    A. I and II only

    B. II and IV only

    C. III and IV only

    D. IV only

14. "Reading maketh a full man, conference a ready man, and writing an exact man" is an example of which type of figurative language?
(Average)

    A. Euphemism

    B. Bathos

    C. Parallelism

    D. Irony

15. Which of the following is NOT a strategy of teaching reading comprehension?
(Rigorous)

    A. Summarization

    B. Utilizing graphic organizers

    C. Manipulating sounds

    D. Having students generate questions

16. Which of the following sentences contains a subject-verb agreement error?
(Average)

    A. Both mother and her two sisters were married in a triple ceremony

    B. Neither the hen nor the rooster is likely to be served for dinner

    C. My boss, as well as the company's two personnel directors, have been to Spain

    D. Amanda and the twins are late again

17. Which of the following are punctuated correctly?
(Rigorous)

I. The teacher directed us to compare Faulkner's three symbolic novels *Absalom, Absalom*; *As I Lay Dying*; and *Light in August*.

II. Three of Faulkner's symbolic novels are: *Absalom, Absalom*; *As I Lay Dying*; and *Light in August*.

III. The teacher directed us to compare Faulkner's three symbolic novels: *Absalom, Absalom*; *As I Lay Dying*; and *Light in August*.

IV. Three of Faulkner's symbolic novels are *Absalom, Absalom*; *As I Lay Dying*; and *Light in August*.

A. I and II only

B. II and III only

C. III and IV only

D. IV only

18. All of the following are true about verb tense EXCEPT:
(Rigorous)

A. Present perfect tense is used to express action or a condition that started in the past and is continued to or completed in the present

B. Future tense is used to express a condition of future time

C. Past perfect tense expresses action or a condition that occurred as a precedent to some other action or condition

D. Future participial tense expresses action that started in the past or present and will conclude at some time in the future

19. Which sentence is NOT correct?
(Rigorous)

A. He ought not to get so angry.

B. I should of gone to bed.

C. I had set the table before dinner.

D. I have lain down.

20. All of the following are true about a descriptive essay EXCEPT:
(Average)

  A. Its purpose is to make an experience available through one of the five senses

  B. Its words make it possible for the reader to see with their mind's eye

  C. Its language will move people because of the emotion involved

  D. It is not trying to get anyone to take a certain action

21. A student has written a paper with the following characteristics: written in first person; characters, setting, and plot; some dialogue; events organized in chronological sequence with some flashbacks. In what genre has the student written?
(Rigorous)

  A. Expository writing

  B. Narrative writing

  C. Persuasive writing

  D. Descriptive writing

22. All of the following are stages of the writing process EXCEPT:
(Average)

  A. Prewriting

  B. Revising

  C. Organizing

  D. Presenting

23. Which of the following should not be included in the opening paragraph of an informative essay?
(Average)

  A. Thesis sentence

  B. Details and examples supporting the main idea

  C. Broad general introduction to the topic

  D. A style and tone that grabs the reader's attention

24. A sentence that contains one independent clause and three dependent clauses best describes a:
(Average)

  A. Simple sentence

  B. Compound sentence

  C. Complex sentence

  D. Compound-complex sentence

25. **The main idea of a paragraph or story:**
(Average)

   A. Is what the paragraph or story is about.

   B. Indicates what the passage is about.

   C. Gives more information about the topic.

   D. States the important ideas that the author wants the reader to know about a topic.

26. **A strong topic sentence will:**
(Rigorous)

   A. Be phrased as a question

   B. Always be the first sentence in a paragraph

   C. Both A and B

   D. Neither A nor B

27. **Which of the following is a great way to keep a natural atmosphere when speaking publicly?**
(Average)

   A. Speak slowly

   B. Maintain a straight, but not stiff, posture

   C. Use friendly gestures

   D. Take a step to the side every once in a while

28. **Students returning from a field trip to the local newspaper want to thank their hosts for the guided tour. As their teacher, what form of communication should you encourage them to use?**
(Rigorous)

   A. Each student will send an e-mail expressing his or her appreciation

   B. As a class, students will create a blog, and each student will write about what they learned

   C. Each student will write a thank you letter that the teacher will fax to the newspaper

   D. Each student will write a thank you note that the teacher will mail to the newspaper

29. Which of the following skills can help students improve their listening comprehension?
(Rigorous)

I.   Tap into prior knowledge.
II. Look for transitions between ideas.
III. Ask questions of the speaker.
IV. Discuss the topic being presented.

A. I and II only

B. II and IV only

C. II and IV only

D. IV only

30. As Ms. Wolmark looks at the mandated vocabulary curriculum for the 5th grade, she notes that she can opt to teach foreign words and abbreviations which have become part of the English language. She decides:
(Rigorous)

A. To forego that since she is not a teacher of foreign language.

B. To teach only foreign words from the native language of her four ELL students.

C. To use the ELL students' native languages as a start for an extensive study of foreign language words.

C. To teach 2-3 foreign language words that are now in English and let it go at that.

MATH

31. A truck rental company charges $40 per day plus $2.50 per mile. The odometer reading is *M* miles when a customer rents a truck and *m* miles when it is returned *d* days later. Which expression represents the total charge for the rental?
(Rigorous)

A. $40d + 2.5M - m$

B. $40d + 2.5m - M$

C. $40d + 2.5(M - m)$

D. $40d + 2.5(m - M)$

32. Using a pattern is an appropriate strategy for which of the following:

I   Skip counting
II Counting backward
III Finding doubles
(Easy)

A. I and II

B. I and III

C. II and III

D. I, II, and III

33. The following set of numbers is not closed under addition:
(Rigorous)

A. Set of all real numbers

B. Set of all even numbers

C. Set of all odd numbers

D. Set of all rational numbers

34. What is the value of the following expression?

$$\frac{25 - 2(6 - 2 \bullet 3)}{{}^-5(2 + 2 \bullet 4)}$$

(Rigorous)

A. 0.5

B. 5.0

C. -0.5

D. 3.4

35. Which of the following expressions are equivalent to $28 - 4 \cdot 6 + 12$?

    I. $(28 - 4) \cdot 6 + 12$
    II. $28 - (4 \cdot 6) + 12$
    III. $(28 - 4) \cdot (6 + 12)$
    IV. $(28 + 12) - (4 \cdot 6)$
    V. $28 - 4 \cdot 12 + 6$

(Average)

A. I and V

B. II and IV

C. III and V

D. IV and V

36. If *n* represents an odd number, which of the following does not represent an even number?
(Average)

A. $2n$

B. $2(n + 1)$

C. n^2

D. $10n - 2$

37. Based upon the following examples, can you conclude that the sum of two prime numbers is also a prime number? Why or why not?

$$2 + 3 = 5$$
$$2 + 5 = 7$$
$$11 + 2 = 13$$

(Rigorous)

A. Yes, there is a pattern.

B. Yes, there are many more examples, such as $17 + 2 = 19$ and $29 + 2 = 31$.

C. No, there are many counterexamples

D. No, the sums are not prime numbers

38. If *x* is a whole number, what is the best description of the number $4x + 1$?
(Rigorous)

A. Prime number

B. Composite number

C. Odd number

D. Even number

39. The plot for a proposed new city hall plaza is 120 feet long by 90 feet wide. A scale model for the plaza must fit in an area that is 10 feet square. If the largest possible model is built in that area, what will be the maximum possible width for the scale model?

(Rigorous)

A. $\frac{2}{15}$ ft.

B. $1\frac{1}{3}$ ft.

C. $7\frac{1}{2}$ ft.

D. $13\frac{1}{3}$ ft.

40. Jocelyn wants create a magnetic board in the back of her classroom by covering part of the wall with a special magnetic paint. Each can of paint will cover 15 square feet. If the area is 12 feet wide and 8 feet high, how many cans of paint should she buy?

(Average)

A. 5 cans

B. 6 cans

C. 7 cans

D. 8 cans

41. A recipe makes 6 servings and calls for $1\frac{1}{2}$ cups of rice. How much rice is needed to make 10 servings?

(Average)

A. 2 cups

B. $2\frac{1}{4}$ cups

C. $2\frac{1}{2}$ cups

D. $2\frac{3}{4}$ cups

42. Which table(s) represents solutions of the following equation?

$$2x - 5y = 50$$

I
x	‾5	0	5	10
y	‾12	‾10	‾8	‾6

II
x	‾5	0	5	‾10
y	‾12	‾10	‾12	‾10

III
x	20	25	30	35
y	‾2	0	2	4

(Rigorous)

A. I

B. II

C. II and III

D. I and III

43. The relations given below demonstrate the following addition and multiplication property of real numbers:

$a + b = b + a$
$ab = ba$

(Average)

A. Commutative

B. Associative

C. Identity

D. Inverse

44. Which property (or properties) is applied below?

$$^-8x + 5x = (^-8 + 5)x$$
$$= ^-3x$$

I. Associative Property of Addition

II. Zero Property of Addition

III. Additive Inverses

IV. Identity Property of Multiplication

V. Distributive Property

(Rigorous)

A. I

B. V

C. I and III

D. II and IV

45. For which of the following is the additive inverse equal to the multiplicative inverse? *(Rigorous)*

A. $\dfrac{2}{3} + \dfrac{3}{2}$

B. $\sqrt{-1}$

C. $\dfrac{1 - \sqrt{2}}{1 + \sqrt{2}}$

D. $(a + b) / (b - a)$

46. Which of the statements below explain the error(s), if any, in the following calculation?

$$\dfrac{18}{18} + 23 = 23$$

I   A number divided by itself is 1, not 0.
II The sum of 1 and 23 is 24, not 23.
III The 18s are "cancelled" and replaced by 0.

(Rigorous)

A. I and II

B. II and III

C. I, II, and III

D. There is no error

47. Which statement is a model for the following problem?

   27 less than 5 times a number is 193.

   (Average)

   A. $27 < 5x + 193$

   B. $27 - 5x < 193$

   C. $5x - 27 < 193$

   D. $5x - 27 = 193$

48. What is the solution set of the following inequality?

   $$4x + 9 \geq 11(x - 3)$$

   (Average)

   A. $x \leq 0$

   B. $x \geq 0$

   C. $x \leq 6$

   D. $x \geq 6$

49. A car is rented in Quebec. The outside temperature shown on the dashboard reads 17°C. What is the temperature in degrees Fahrenheit? (Use the formula $F = \frac{9}{5}C + 32$.)

   (Average)

   A. $27.2°F$

   B. $41.4°F$

   C. $62.6°F$

   D. $88.2°F$

50. The two solutions of the quadratic equation $ax^2 + bx + c = 0$ are given by the formula

   $$x = \frac{-b \pm \sqrt{b^2 - 4ac}}{2a}$$

   What are the solutions of the equation $x^2 - 18x + 32$?
   (Rigorous)

   A. ¯5 and 23

   B. 2 and 16

   C. $9 \pm \sqrt{113}$

   D. $9 \pm 2\sqrt{113}$

51. Triangle *ABC* is rotated 90° clockwise about the origin and translated 6 units left.

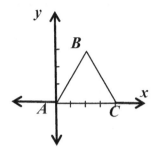

What are the coordinates of *B* after the transformations?
(Rigorous)

A. (2, ⁻3)

B. (3, ⁻2)

C. (⁻2, ⁻3)

D. (⁻3, ⁻2)

52. The following represents the net of a

(Average)

A. Cube

B. Tetrahedron

C. Octahedron

D. Dodecahedron

53. Ginny and Nick head back to their respective colleges after being home for the weekend. They leave their house at the same time and drive for 4 hours. Ginny drives due south at the average rate of 60 miles per hour and Nick drives due east at the average rate of 0 miles per hour. What is the straight-line distance between them, in miles, at the end of the 4 hours?
(Rigorous)

A. 169.7 miles

B. 240 miles

C. 288 miles

D. 339.4 miles

54. What is the surface area of the prism shown below?

(Rigorous)

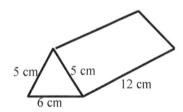

A. 204 cm²

B. 216 cm²

C. 360 cm²

D. 180 cm²

55. Which of the following is not equivalent to 3 km?

   I. 3.0×10^3 m
   II. 3.0×10^4 cm
   III. 3.0×10^6 mm

   (Average)

   A. I

   B. II

   C. III

   D. None of the above

56. A school band has 200 members. Looking at the pie chart below, determine which statement is true about the band.
   (Average)

   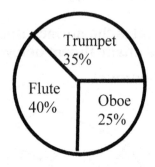

   A. There are more trumpet players than flute players

   B. There are fifty oboe players in the band

   C. There are forty flute players in the band

   D. One-third of all band members play the trumpet

57. A restaurant offers the following menu choices.

Green Vegetable	Yellow Vegetable
Asparagus	Carrots
Broccoli	Corn
Peas	Squash
Spinach	

   If a customer chooses a green vegetable and a yellow vegetable at random, what is the probability that the customer will order neither asparagus nor corn?
   (Rigorous)

   A. $\dfrac{1}{12}$

   B. $\dfrac{1}{6}$

   C. $\dfrac{1}{3}$

   D. $\dfrac{1}{2}$

58. A school has 15 male teachers and 35 female teachers. In how many ways can they form a committee with 2 male teachers and 4 female teachers on it?
   (Average)

   A. 525

   B. 5497800

   C. 88

   D. 263894400

59. A music store owner wants to change the window display every week. Only 4 out of 6 instruments can be displayed in the window at the same time. How many weeks will it be before the owner must repeat the same arrangement (in the same order) of instruments in the window display?

(Rigorous)

A. 24 weeks

B. 36 weeks

C. 120 weeks

D. 360 weeks

60. Half the students in a class scored 80% on an exam; one student scored 10%; and the rest of the class scored 85%. Which would be the best measure of central tendency for the test scores?

(Rigorous)

A. Mean

B. Median

C. Mode

D. Either the median or the mode because they are equal

SOCIAL SCIENCES

61. The Great Plains in the United States are an excellent place to grow corn and wheat for all of the following reasons EXCEPT:
(Average)

A. Rainfall is abundant and the soil is rich

B. The land is mostly flat and easy to cultivate

C. The human population is modest in size, so there is plenty of space for large farms

D. The climate is semitropical

62. What is characteristic of areas of the world with high populations?
(Rigorous)

A. These areas tend to have heavy pollution

B. These areas are almost always surrounded by suburbs

C. Populations are rarely located near one another

D. Most populated places in the world also tend to be close to agricultural lands

63. Meridians, or lines of longitude, not only help in pinpointing locations but are also used for:
(Average)

   A. Measuring distance from the Poles

   B. Determining direction of ocean currents

   C. Determining the time around the world

   D. Measuring distance on the equator

64. The Western Hemisphere contains all of which of the following continents?
(Rigorous)

   A. Russia

   B. Europe

   C. North America

   D. Asia

65. Mr. Allen is discussing the earthquake in Chile and explains the aftershocks and tsunamis that threatened Pacific islands thousands of miles away. What aspect of geographical studies was he emphasizing?
(Rigorous)

   A. Regional

   B. Topical

   C. Physical

   D. Human

66. Which of the following are non-renewable resources?
(Average)

   A. Fish, coffee, and forests

   B. Fruit, water, and solar energy

   C. Wind power, alcohol, and sugar

   D. Coal, natural gas, and oil

67. What people perfected the preservation of dead bodies?
(Average)

   A. Sumerians

   B. Phoenicians

   C. Egyptians

   D. Assyrians

68. **Which of these is NOT a true statement about the Roman civilization?**
(Rigorous)

   A. Its period of Pax Romana provided long periods of peace during which travel and trade increased, enabling the spread of culture, goods, and ideas over the known world

   B. It borrowed the concept of democracy from the Greeks and developed it into a complex representative government

   C. It flourished in the arts with a realistic approach to art and a dramatic use of architecture

   D. It developed agricultural innovations such as crop rotation and terrace farming

69. **The major force in eighteenth and nineteenth century politics was:**
(Average)

   A. Nationalism

   B. Revolution

   C. War

   D. Diplomacy

70. **The identification of individuals or groups as they are influenced by their own group or culture is called:**
(Average)

   A. Cross-cultural exchanges

   B. Cultural diffusion

   C. Cultural identity

   D. Cosmopolitanism

71. **The New England colonies included:**
(Average)

   A. South Carolina

   B. Georgia

   C. Massachusetts

   D. New York

72. **Which major economic activity of the Southern colonies led to the growth of slavery?**
(Rigorous)

   A. Manufacturing

   B. Fishing

   C. Farming

   D. Coal mining

73. **Which was the first instance of an internal tax on the American colonies?**
(Average)

A. The Proclamation Act

B. The Sugar Act

C. The Currency Act

D. The Stamp Act

74. **The Lewis and Clark expedition advanced knowledge in each of the following areas EXCEPT:**
(Average)

A. Geography

B. Modern warfare

C. Botany

D. Animal life

75. **Populism arises out of a feeling:**
(Average)

A. Of intense happiness

B. Of satisfaction with the activities of large corporations

C. That women should not be allowed to vote

D. Perceived oppression

76. **At the end of the Twentieth Century, the United States was:**
(Average)

A. A central leader in international affairs

B. A reluctant participant in international affairs

C. One of two superpowers

D. Lacking a large consumer culture

77. **How did manufacturing change in the early 1800s?**
(Rigorous)

A. The electronics industry was born

B. Production moved from small shops or homes into factories

C. Industry benefited from the Federal Reserve Act

D. The timber industry was hurt when Theodore Roosevelt set aside 238 million acres of federal lands to be protected from development

78. **The early ancient civilizations developed systems of government:**
    (Rigorous)

    A. To provide for defense against attack

    B. To regulate trade

    C. To regulate and direct the economic activities of the people as they worked together in groups

    D. To decide on the boundaries of the different fields during planting seasons

79. **What is another name for dictatorship?**
    (Rigorous)

    A. Oligarchy

    B. Monarchy

    C. Anarchism

    D. Communism

80. **Which of the following documents described and defined the system and structure of the United States government?**
    (Average)

    A. The Bill of Rights

    B. The Declaration of Independence

    C. The Constitution

    D. The Articles of Confederation

81. **How did the ideology of John Locke influence Thomas Jefferson in writing the Declaration of Independence?**
    (Rigorous)

    A. Locke emphasized human rights and believed that people should rebel against governments who violated those rights

    B. Locke emphasized the rights of government to protect its people and to levy taxes

    C. Locke believed in the British system of monarchy and the rights of Parliament to make laws

    D. Locke advocated individual rights over the collective whole

82. **Which of the following is not a right declared by the U.S. Constitution?**
(Average)

   A. The right to speak out in public

   B. The right to use cruel and unusual punishment

   C. The right to a speedy trial

   D. The right not to be forced to testify against yourself

83. **The cold weather froze orange crops in Florida and the price of orange juice increased. This is an example of what economic concept?**
(Rigorous)

   A. Output market

   B. Input market

   C. Supply and demand

   D. Entrepreneurship

84. **What type of production process must producers choose?**
(Average)

   A. One that is inefficient

   B. One that often produces goods that consumers don't want

   C. One that is efficient

   D. One that is sometimes efficient and sometimes inefficient

85. **The existence of economics is based on:**
(Rigorous)

   A. The scarcity of resources

   B. The abundance of resources

   C. Little or nothing that is related to resources

   D. Entrepreneurship

86. In the fictional country of Nacirema, the government controls the means of production and directs resources. It alone decides what will be produced; as a result, there is an abundance of capital and military goods but a scarcity of consumer goods. What type of economy is this?
(Rigorous)

   A. Market economy

   B. Centrally planned economy

   C. Market socialism

   D. Capitalism

87. Which of the following are secondary research materials?
(Average)

   A. The conclusions and inferences of other historians

   B. Literature and nonverbal materials, novels, stories, poetry, and essays from the period, as well as coins, archaeological artifacts, and art produced during the period

   C. Interviews and surveys conducted by the researcher

   D. Statistics gathered as the result of the research's experiments

88. For their research paper on the effects of the Civil War on American literature, students have brainstormed a list of potential online sources and are seeking your authorization. Which of these represent the strongest source?
(Rigorous)

   A. http://www.wikipedia.org/

   B. http://www.google.com

   C. http://www.nytimes.com

   D. http://docsouth.unc.edu /southlit/civilwar.html

89. For the historian studying ancient Egypt, which of the following would be least useful?
(Rigorous)

   A. The record of an ancient Greek historian on Greek-Egyptian interaction

   B. Letters from an Egyptian ruler to his/her regional governors

   C. Inscriptions on stele of the Fourteenth Egyptian Dynasty

   D. Letters from a nineteenth century Egyptologist to his wife

90. **Which of the following can be considered the primary goal of social studies?**
    (Rigorous)

    A. Recalling specific dates and places

    B. Identifying and analyzing social links

    C. Using contextual clues to identify eras

    D. Linking experiments with history

SCIENCE

91. **Which is the correct order for the layers of Earth's atmosphere?**
    (Easy)

    A. Troposphere, stratosphere, mesosphere, and thermosphere

    B. Mesosphere, stratosphere, troposphere, and thermosphere

    C. Troposphere, stratosphere, thermosphere, and mesosphere

    D. Thermosphere, troposphere, stratosphere, mesosphere

92. **Which statement correctly describes the theory of plate tectonics?**
    (Easy)

    A. There eight major plates and many small plates that move at a rate of 10 to 50 millimeters per year

    B. There is one plate for each continent and they move at a speed too small to measure

    C. There are thousands of plates that move 1 to 5 meters per year

    D. Earthquakes are caused by the collision of plates

93. **What type of rock can be classified by the size of the crystals in the rock?**
    (Easy)

    A. Metamorphic

    B. Igneous

    C. Minerals

    D. Sedimentary

94. **What are solids with a definite chemical composition and a tendency to split along planes of weakness?**
(Easy)

 A. Ores

 B. Rocks

 C. Minerals

 D. Salts

95. **In which of the following eras did life appear?**
(Easy)

 A. Paleozoic

 B. Mesozoic

 C. Cenozoic

 D. Precambrian

96. **The use of radioactivity to determine the age of rocks and fossils is called which of the following?**
(Easy)

 A. Carbon dating

 B. Absolute dating

 C. Stratigraphy

 D. Geological dating

97. **Which of the following astronomical entities is not part of the galaxy the Sun is located in?**
(Easy)

 A. Nebulae

 B. Quasars

 C. Pulsars

 D. Neutron stars

98. **Why is the winter in the southern hemisphere colder than winter in the northern hemisphere?**
(Average)

 A. Earth's axis of 24-hour rotation tilts at an angle of 23½°

 B. The elliptical orbit of Earth around the Sun changes the distance of the Sun from Earth

 C. The southern hemisphere has more water than the northern hemisphere

 D. The green house effect is greater for the northern hemisphere

99. **Which of the following facts of physics best explains the cause of tides? (Rigorous)**

   A. The density of water is less than the density of rock

   B. The force of gravity follows the inverse square law

   C. Centripetal acceleration causes water on Earth to bulge

   D. The gravitational force of the Moon on Earth's oceans

100. **Which of the following is not a property that eukaryotes have and prokaryotes do not have? (Average)**

   A. Nucleus

   B. Ribosomes

   C. Chromosomes

   D. Mitochondria

101. **Which of the following processes and packages macromolecules? (Easy)**

   A. Lysosomes

   B. Cytosol

   C. Golgi apparatus

   D. Plastids

102. **Which is not a characteristic of living organisms? (Easy)**

   A. Sexual reproduction

   B. Ingestion

   C. Synthesis

   D. Respiration

103. **At what stage in mitosis does the chromatin become chromosomes? (Average)**

   A. Telophase

   B. Anaphase

   C. Prophase

   D. Metaphase

104. **Meiosis starts with a single cell and ends with which of the following? (Average)**

   A. Two diploid cells.

   B. Two haploid cells.

   C. Four diploid cells

   D. Four haploid cells

105. How many autosomes are in somatic cells of human beings?
(Easy)

A. 22

B. 23

C. 44

D. 46

106. Which of the following is not part of Darwinian evolution?
(Average)

A. Survival of the fittest

B. Random mutations

C. Heritability of acquired traits

D. Natural selection

107. Taxonomy classifies species into genera (plural of genus) based on similarities. Species are subordinate to genera. The most general or highest taxonomical group is the kingdom. Which of the following is the correct order of the other groups from highest to lowest?
(Easy)

A. Class $\Rightarrow$ order $\Rightarrow$ family $\Rightarrow$ phylum

B. Phylum $\Rightarrow$ class $\Rightarrow$ family $\Rightarrow$ order

C. Phylum $\Rightarrow$ class $\Rightarrow$ order $\Rightarrow$ family

D. Order $\Rightarrow$ phylum $\Rightarrow$ class $\Rightarrow$ family

108. Which of the following describes the interaction between community members when one species feeds of another species but does not kill it immediately?
(Easy)

A. Parasitism

B. Predation

C. Commensalism

D. Mutualism

109. Which of the following statements about the density of a substance is true?
(Easy)

A. It is a chemical property

B. It is a physical property

C. It does not depend on the temperature of the substance

D. It is a property only of liquids and solids

110. The electrons in a neutral atom that is not in an excited energy state are in various energy shells. For example, there are two electrons in the lowest energy shell and eight in the next shell if the atom contains more than 10 electrons. How many electrons are in the shell with the maximum number of electrons?
(Easy)

A. 8

B. 18

C. 32

D. 44

111. Which statement best explains why a balance scale is used to measure both weight and mass?
(Rigorous)

A. The weight and mass of an object are identical concepts

B. The force of gravity between two objects depends on the mass of the two objects

C. Inertial mass and gravitational mass are identical

D. A balance scale compares the weight of two objects

112. Which of the following does not determine the frictional force between a box sliding down a ramp?
(Average)

A. The weight of the box

B. The area of the box

C. The angle the ramp makes with the horizontal

D. The chemical properties of the two surfaces.

113. **Which statement is true about temperature?**
   (Easy)

   A. Temperature is a measurement of heat

   B. Temperature is how hot or cold an object is

   C. The coldest temperature ever measured is zero degrees Kelvin

   D. The temperature of a molecule is its kinetic energy

114. **When glass is heated, it becomes softer and softer until it becomes a liquid. Which of the following statements best describes this phenomenon?**
   (Rigorous)

   A. Glass has no heat of vaporization

   B. Glass has no heat of fusion

   C. The latent heat of glass is zero calories per gram

   D. Glass is made up of crystals

115. **Which statement could be described as the first law of thermodynamics?**
   (Average)

   A. No machine can convert heat energy to work with 100 percent efficiency

   B. Energy is neither created nor destroyed

   C. Thermometers can be used to measure temperatures

   D. Heat flows from hot objects to cold objects

116. **What kind of chemical reaction is the burning of coal?**
   (Average)

   A. Exothermic and composition

   B. Exothermic and decomposition

   C. Endothermic and composition

   D. Exothermic and decomposition

117. Which of the following is a result of a nuclear reaction called fission?
(Easy)

A. Sunlight

B. Cosmic radiation

C. Supernova

D. Existence of the elements in the periodic table

118. What is technology?
(Easy)

A. The application of science to satisfy human needs

B. Knowledge of complex machines, computer systems, and manufacturing processes

C. The study of engineering

D. A branch of science

119. An experiment is performed to determine how the surface area of a liquid affects how long it takes for the liquid to evaporate. One hundred milliliters of water is put in containers with surface areas of 10 cm^2, 30 cm^2, 50 cm^2, 70 cm^2, and 90 cm^2. The time it took for each container to evaporate is recorded. Which of the following is a controlled variable?
(Average)

A. The time required for each evaporation

B. The area of the surfaces

C. The amount of water

D. The temperature of the water

120. Stars near Earth can be seen to move relative to fixed stars. In observing the motion of a nearby star over a period of decades, an astronomer notices that the path is not a straight line but wobbles about a straight line. The astronomer reports in a peer-reviewed journal that a planet is rotating around the star, causing it to wobble. Which of the following statements best describes the proposition that the star has a planet?
(Rigorous)

A. Observation

B. Hypothesis

C. Theory

D. Inference

Answer Key: Reading

1. A	16. C
2. A	17. C
3. C	18. D
4. B	19. B
5. B	20. D
6. B	21. B
7. B	22. D
8. D	23. B
9. A	24. C
10. C	25. D
11. A	26. D
12. A	27. C
13. C	28. D
14. C	29. A
15. C	30. C

Answer Key: Math

31. D	46. C
32. A	47. D
33. C	48. C
34. C	49. C
35. B	50. B
36. C	51. D
37. C	52. C
38. C	53. D
39. C	54. B
40. C	55. B
41. C	56. B
42. D	57. D
43. A	58. B
44. B	59. D
45. B	60. B

Answer Key: Social Sciences

61. D	76. A
62. D	77. B
63. C	78. C
64. C	79. A
65. C	80. C
66. D	81. A
67. C	82. B
68. D	83. C
69. A	84. C
70. C	85. A
71. C	86. B
72. C	87. A
73. D	88. D
74. B	89. D
75. D	90. B

Answer Key: Science

91. A	106. C
92. A	107. C
93. B	108. A
94. C	109. B
95. D	110. C
96. B	111. C
97. B	112. B
98. B	113. B
99. B	114. B
100. B	115. B
101. C	116. A
102. A	117. D
103. C	118. A
104. D	119. C
105. C	120. D

Sample Test 3 Rationales

READING

1. **To make a prediction a reader must:**
   (Average)

   A. Use text clues to evaluate the text at an inferential level

   B. Find a line of reasoning on which to rely

   C. Make a decision based on an observation

   D. Use prior knowledge and apply it to the current situation

Answer: A. Use text clues to evaluate the text at an inferential level
Making a prediction requires the reader to evaluate a text by going beyond the literal level of what is stated to an inferential level by using text clues to make predictions as to what will happen next in the text. Because choices B–D do not involve evaluating a text on an inferential level, they are not correct ways to make a prediction.

2. **Which of the following is NOT a characteristic of a good reader?**
   (Rigorous)

   A. When faced with unfamiliar words, they skip over them unless meaning is lost

   B. They formulate questions that they predict will be answered in the text

   C. They establish a purpose before reading

   D. They go back to reread when something doesn't make sense

Answer: A. When faced with unfamiliar words, they skip over them unless meaning is lost
While skipping over an unknown word may not compromise the meaning of the text, a good reader will attempt to pronounce the word by using analogies to familiar words. They also formulate questions, establish a purpose, and go back to reread if meaning is lost.

3. **All of the following are true about schemata EXCEPT:**
   (Rigorous)

   A. Used as a basis for literary response

   B. Structures that represent concepts stored in our memories

   C. A generalization that is proven with facts

   D. Used together with prior knowledge for effective reading comprehension

Answer: C. A generalization that is proven with facts
Schemata are structures that represent concepts stored in the memory. When used together with prior knowledge and ideas from the printed text while reading, comprehension takes place. Schemata have nothing to do with making a generalization and proving it with facts.

4. **Children are taught phonological awareness when they are taught all but which concept?**
   (Average)

   A. The sounds made by the letters

   B. The correct spelling of words

   C. The sounds made by various combinations of letters

   D. The ability to recognize individual sounds in words

Answer: B. The correct spelling of words
Phonological awareness happens during the pre-K years or even earlier and involves connecting letters to sounds. Children begin to develop a sense of correct and incorrect spellings of words in a transitional spelling phase that is traditionally entered in elementary school.

5. **Which of the following is true about semantics?**
   (Average)

   A. Semantics will sharpen the effect and meaning of a text

   B. Semantics refers to the meaning expressed when words are arranged in a specific way

   C. Semantics is a vocabulary instruction technique

   D. Semantics is representing spoken language through the use of symbols

Answer: B. Semantics refers to the meaning expressed when words are arranged in a specific way
Understanding semantics means understanding that meaning is imbedded in the order of words in a sentence. Changing the order of the words would change the meaning of a sentence. The other three choices do not involve finding meaning through the order of words.

6. **Spelling instruction should include:**
   (Average)

   A. Breaking down sentences

   B. Developing a sense of correct and incorrect spellings

   C. Identifying every word in a given text

   D. Spelling words the way that they sound

Answer: B. Developing a sense of correct and incorrect spellings
Developing a sense of correct and incorrect spellings is part of the developmental stages of spelling and is a phase that is typically entered later in elementary school. Breaking down sentences involves paragraph analysis, identifying every word in a given text is not necessary to construct meaning from that text, and spelling words the way that they sound is not an effective way to teach spelling.

7. **Answering questions, monitoring comprehension, and interacting with a text are common methods of:**
   (Average)

   A. Whole-class instruction

   B. Comprehension instruction

   C. Research-based instruction

   D. Evidence-based instruction

Answer: B. Comprehension instruction
Comprehension instruction helps students learn strategies that they can use independently with any text. Answering questions, monitoring comprehension, and interacting with a text are a few strategies that teachers can teach to their students to help increase their comprehension. Research-based, evidence-based, and whole-class instruction relate to specific reading programs available.

8. **Mrs. Young is a first grade teacher trying to select a books that are "just right" for her students to read independently. She needs to consider which of the following:**
   (Rigorous)

   A. Illustrations should support the meaning of the text.

   B. Content that relates to student interest and experiences

   C. Predictable text structures and language patterns

   D. All of the above

Answer: D. All of the above
It is important that all of the above factors be considered when selecting books for young children.

9. **Which of the following is NOT characteristic of a folktale?**
(Average)

A. Considered true among various societies

B. A hero on a quest

C. Good versus evil

D. Adventures of animals

Answer: A. Considered true among various societies
There are few societies that would consider folktales to be true as folktale is another name for fairy tale, and elements such as heroes on a quest, good versus evil, and adventures of animals are popular, fictional, themes in fairy tales.

10. **Which of the following did NOT contribute to a separate literature genre for adolescents?**
(Rigorous)

A. The social changes of post–World War II

B. The Civil Rights movement

C. An interest in fantasy and science fiction

D. Issues surrounding teen pregnancy

Answer: C. An interest in fantasy and science fiction
Social changes after World War II, the Civil Rights movement, and personal issues like teen pregnancy all contributed to authors writing a new breed of contemporary fiction to help adolescents understand and cope with the world they live in. Adolescents may be interested in fantasy and science fiction topics but that interest did not cause the creation of an entire genre.

11. Which of the following is important in understanding fiction?
    (Rigorous)

    I.   Realizing the artistry in telling a story to convey a point.
    II. Knowing fiction is imaginary.
    III. Seeing what is truth and what is perspective.
    IV. Acknowledging the difference between opinion and truth.

    A. I and II only

    B. II and IV only

    C. III and IV only

    D. IV only

Answer: A. I and II only
In order to understand a piece of fiction, it is important that readers realize that an author's choice in a work of fiction is for the sole purpose of conveying a viewpoint. It is also important to understand that fiction is imaginary. Seeing what is truth and what is perspective and acknowledging the difference between opinion and truth are important in understanding nonfiction.

12. Assonance is a poetic device where:
    (Average)

    A. The vowel sound in a word matches the same sound in a nearby word, but the surrounding consonant sounds are different

    B. The initial sounds of a word, beginning either with a consonant or a vowel, are repeated in close succession

    C. The words used evoke meaning by their sounds

    D. The final consonant sounds are the same, but the vowels are different

Answer: A. The vowel sound in a word matches the same sound in a nearby word, but the surrounding consonant sounds are different
Assonance takes the middle territory of rhyming so that the vowel sounds are similar, but the consonant sounds are different: "tune" and "food" are assonant. Repeating words in close succession that have the same initial sound ("puppies who pant pathetically") is alliteration. Using the sounds of words to evoke meaning ("zip, pow, pop") is onomatopoeia. When final consonant sounds are the same and the vowels are different, and author has used a different kind of alliteration.

13. Which of the following is true of the visible shape of poetry?
   (Rigorous)

   I. Forced sound repetition may underscore the meaning.
   II. It was a new rule of poetry after poets began to feel constricted by rhyming conventions.
   III. The shaped reflected the poem's theme.
   IV. It was viewed as a demonstration of ingenuity.

   A. I and II only

   B. II and IV only

   C. III and IV only

   D. IV only

Answer: C. III and IV only
During the seventeenth century, some poets shaped their poems on the page. The shape would reflect the poem's theme. While an interesting device, the skill was viewed as a demonstration of ingenuity but did not add to the effect or meaning of the poem. Sound repetition has no effect on the visible shape of a poem. Shaping a poem was never a rule all poets deemed to follow.

14. "Reading maketh a full man, conference a ready man, and writing an exact man" is an example of which type of figurative language?
   (Average)

   A. Euphemism

   B. Bathos

   C. Parallelism

   D. Irony

Answer: C. Parallelism
Parallelism is the arrangement of ideas into phrases, sentences, and paragraphs that balance one element with another of equal importance and similar wording. In the example given, reading, conference, and writing are balanced in importance and wording. A euphemism substitutes an agreeable term for one that might offend. Bathos is a ludicrous attempt to evoke pity, sympathy, or sorrow. Irony is using an expression that is the opposite to the literal meaning.

15. Which of the following is NOT a strategy of teaching reading comprehension? (*Rigorous*)

    A. Summarization

    B. Utilizing graphic organizers

    C. Manipulating sounds

    D. Having students generate questions

Answer: C. Manipulating sounds
Comprehension simply means that the reader can ascribe meaning to text. Teachers can use many strategies to teach comprehension, including questioning, asking students to paraphrase or summarize, utilizing graphic organizers, and focusing on mental images.

16. Which of the following sentences contains a subject-verb agreement error? (*Average*)

    A. Both mother and her two sisters were married in a triple ceremony

    B. Neither the hen nor the rooster is likely to be served for dinner

    C. My boss, as well as the company's two personnel directors, have been to Spain

    D. Amanda and the twins are late again

Answer: C. My boss, as well as the company's two personnel directors, have been to Spain
In choice C, the true subject of the verb is "My boss," not "two personnel directors." Because the subject is singular, the verb form must be singular, "has." In choices A and D, the compound subjects are joined by "and" and take the plural form of the verb. In choice B, the compound subject is joined by "nor" so the verb must agree with the subject closer to the verb. "Rooster" is singular so the correct verb is "is."

17. Which of the following are punctuated correctly?
    (Rigorous)

    I.   The teacher directed us to compare Faulkner's three symbolic novels *Absalom, Absalom*; *As I Lay Dying*; and *Light in August*.
    II. Three of Faulkner's symbolic novels are: *Absalom, Absalom*; *As I Lay Dying*; and *Light in August*.
    III. The teacher directed us to compare Faulkner's three symbolic novels: *Absalom, Absalom*; *As I Lay Dying*; and *Light in August*.
    IV. Three of Faulkner's symbolic novels are *Absalom, Absalom*; *As I Lay Dying*; and *Light in August*.

    A. I and II only

    B. II and III only

    C. III and IV only

    D. IV only

Answer: C. III and IV only
These sentences are focusing on the use of a colon. The rule is to place a colon at the beginning of a list of items except when the list is preceded by a verb. Sentences I and III do not have a verb before the list and therefore need a colon. Sentences II and IV have a verb before the list and therefore do not need a colon.

18. All of the following are true about verb tense EXCEPT:
    (Rigorous)

    A. Present perfect tense is used to express action or a condition that started in the past and is continued to or completed in the present

    B. Future tense is used to express a condition of future time

    C. Past perfect tense expresses action or a condition that occurred as a precedent to some other action or condition

    D. Future participial tense expresses action that started in the past or present and will conclude at some time in the future

Answer: D. Future participial tense expresses action that started in the past or present and will conclude at some time in the future
Choices A–C are correct statements about each type of verb tense. D is incorrect because there is no such thing as future participial tense.

19. Which sentence is NOT correct?
    (Rigorous)

    A. He ought not to get so angry.

    B. I should of gone to bed.

    C. I had set the table before dinner.

    D. I have lain down.

Answer: B. I should of gone to bed.
The most frequent problems in verb use come from the improper formation of the past and past participial forms. Choices A, C, and D may sound awkward but are actually correct uses of the participial tense. "I should of gone to bed" is incorrect because "of" is not a verb. A correct sentence would be, "I should have gone to bed."

20. All of the following are true about a descriptive essay EXCEPT:
    (Average)

    A. Its purpose is to make an experience available through one of the five senses

    B. Its words make it possible for the reader to see with their mind's eye

    C. Its language will move people because of the emotion involved

    D. It is not trying to get anyone to take a certain action

Answer: D. It is not trying to get anyone to take a certain action
The descriptive essay uses language to make an experience available to readers. It uses descriptive words so the reader can see with their mind's eye, smell with their mind's nose, etc. Descriptive writing will involve the emotions of both the reader and writer. Poems are excellent examples of descriptive writing. An exposition is the type of essay that is not interested in getting anyone to take a certain action.

21. A student has written a paper with the following characteristics: written in first person; characters, setting, and plot; some dialogue; events organized in chronological sequence with some flashbacks. In what genre has the student written?
(Rigorous)

    A. Expository writing

    B. Narrative writing

    C. Persuasive writing

    D. Descriptive writing

Answer: B. Narrative writing
These are all characteristics of narrative writing. Expository writing is intended to give information such as an explanation or directions, and the information is logically organized. Persuasive writing gives an opinion in an attempt to convince the reader that this point of view is valid or tries to persuade the reader to take a specific action. The goal of technical writing is to clearly communicate a select piece of information to a targeted reader or group of readers for a particular purpose in such a way that the subject can readily be understood. It is persuasive writing that anticipates a response from the reader.

22. All of the following are stages of the writing process EXCEPT:
(Average)

    A. Prewriting

    B. Revising

    C. Organizing

    D. Presenting

Answer: D. Presenting
Writing is a process that can be clearly defined. First, students must prewrite to discover ideas, materials, experiences, sources, etc. Next, they must organize and determine their purpose, thesis, and supporting details. Last, they must edit and revise to polish the paper. While presenting is a nice finale to the writing process, it is not necessary for a complete and polished work.

23. Which of the following should not be included in the opening paragraph of an informative essay?
(*Average*)

A. Thesis sentence

B. Details and examples supporting the main idea

C. Broad general introduction to the topic

D. A style and tone that grabs the reader's attention

Answer B. Details and examples supporting the main idea
The introductory paragraph should introduce the topic, capture the reader's interest, state the thesis, and prepare the reader for the main points in the essay. Details and examples, however, should be given in the second part of the essay, so as to help develop the thesis presented at the end of the introductory paragraph, following the inverted triangle method consisting of a broad general statement followed by some information, and then the thesis at the end of the paragraph.

24. A sentence that contains one independent clause and three dependent clauses best describes a:
(*Average*)

A. Simple sentence

B. Compound sentence

C. Complex sentence

D. Compound-complex sentence

Answer: C. Complex Sentence
A complex sentence is made up of one independent clause and at least one dependent clause. This type of sentence can have multiple dependent clauses in it. Simple and compound sentences will not have any dependent clauses, and a compound-complex sentence will have more than one independent clause as well as one or more dependent clauses.

25. The main idea of a paragraph or story:
(Average)

   A. Is what the paragraph or story is about

   B. Indicates what the passage is about

   C. Gives more information about the topic

   D. States the important ideas that the author wants the reader to know about a topic

Answer: D. States the important ideas that the author wants the reader to know about a topic.

The main idea of a paragraph or story states the important ideas that the author wants the reader to know about his/her topic. The main idea can be directly stated or simply implied. The topic is what the paragraph or story is about. A topic sentence will indicate what a specific passage is about. And supporting details will give more information about a topic.

26. A strong topic sentence will:
(Rigorous)

   A. Be phrased as a question.

   B. Always be the first sentence in a paragraph.

   C. Both A and B

   D. Neither A nor B

Answer: D. Neither A nor B

A topic sentence will tell what the passage is about. A tip for finding a topic sentence is to phrase the possible topic sentence as a question and see if the other sentences answer the question, but the topic sentence doesn't need to be in question form. A topic sentence is usually the first sentence in a paragraph but could also be in any other position. Therefore neither choices A nor B are correct choices.

27. Which of the following is a great way to keep a natural atmosphere when speaking publicly?
(*Average*)

A. Speak slowly

B. Maintain a straight, but not stiff, posture

C. Use friendly gestures

D. Take a step to the side every once in a while

Answer: C. Use friendly gestures
Gestures are a great way to keep a natural atmosphere when speaking publicly. Gestures that are common in friendly conversation will make the audience feel at ease. Gestures that are exaggerated, stiff, or awkward will only distract from a speech. Speaking slowly, monitoring posture, and taking a step to the side are great speaking skills but not skills that will create a natural atmosphere.

28. Students returning from a field trip to the local newspaper want to thank their hosts for the guided tour. As their teacher, what form of communication should you encourage them to use?
(*Rigorous*)

A. Each student will send an e-mail expressing his or her appreciation

B. As a class, students will create a blog, and each student will write about what they learned

C. Each student will write a thank you letter that the teacher will fax to the newspaper

D. Each student will write a thank you note that the teacher will mail to the newspaper.

Answer: D. Each student will write a thank you note that the teacher will mail to the newspaper
Courtesy requires a hand-written message that is brief and specific. While using technology such as e-mails, blogs, and faxes are quicker, they are less personal. Communication channels and language styles vary; teachers should model correct behavior and appropriate uses of communication.

29. Which of the following skills can help students improve their listening comprehension?
   (Rigorous)

   I.   Tap into prior knowledge.
   II. Look for transitions between ideas.
   III. Ask questions of the speaker.
   IV. Discuss the topic being presented.

   A. I and II only

   B. II and IV only

   C. II and IV only

   D. IV only

Answer: A. I and II only
Many strategies that are effective in improving reading comprehension are also effective in improving listening comprehension. Tapping into prior knowledge and looking for transitions between ideas are excellent listening and reading comprehension strategies. Asking questions of the speaker may help clarify ideas and discussing the topic may help organize the thoughts being presented, but both are difficult to do during the actual act of listening.

30. As Ms. Wolmark looks at the mandated vocabulary curriculum for the 5th grade, she notes that she can opt to teach foreign words and abbreviations which have become part of the English language. She decides: *(Rigorous)*

    A. To forego that since she is not a teacher of foreign language

    B. To teach only foreign words from the native language of her four ELL students

    C. To use the ELL students' native languages as a start for an extensive study of foreign language words

    D. To teach 2-3 foreign language words that are now in English and let it go at that

Answer: C. To use the ELL students' native languages as a start for an extensive study of foreign language words
Incorporating the native language of ELL students into instruction helps to form a bond between their native language and English. It also serves as a point of confidence that connects that student with the other students in the class.

MATH

31. A truck rental company charges $40 per day plus $2.50 per mile. The odometer reading is *M* miles when a customer rents a truck and *m* miles when it is returned *d* days later. Which expression represents the total charge for the rental?
(Rigorous)

   A. $40d + 2.5M - m$

   B. $40d + 2.5m - M$

   C. $40d + 2.5(M - m)$

   D. $40d + 2.5(m - M)$

Answer: D. $40d + 2.5(m - M)$
Rental for *d* days is 40*d*. The number of miles driven is *m* − *M*. The charge for miles driven is 2.50(*m* − *M*). Beginning mileage must be subtracted from ending mileage and the *difference* multiplied by 2.5.

32. Using a pattern is an appropriate strategy for which of the following:

   I.   Skip counting
   II. Counting backward
   III. Finding doubles

   (Easy)

   A. I and II

   B. I and III

   C. II and III

   D. I, II, and III

Answer: A. I and II
The skip-counting pattern adds the same number repeatedly. Counting backward subtracts 1 repeatedly.

33. **The following set of numbers is not closed under addition:**
    (Rigorous)

    A. Set of all real numbers

    B. Set of all even numbers

    C. Set of all odd numbers

    D. Set of all rational numbers

Answer: C. Set of all odd numbers

Adding two real numbers will result in a real number. The same is true for even or rational numbers. Adding two odd numbers, however, will not always produce an odd number.

34. **What is the value of the following expression?**

$$\frac{25 - 2(6 - 2 \bullet 3)}{^-5(2 + 2 \bullet 4)}$$

(Rigorous)

    A. 0.5

    B. 5.0

    C. -0.5

    D. 3.4

Answer: C. –0.5

The fraction line is equivalent to parentheses and indicates that the numerator is to be simplified first. Then use the standard order of operations.

$$\frac{25 - 2(6 - 2 \bullet 3)}{^-5(2 + 2 \bullet 4)} = \frac{25 - 2(6 - 6)}{-5(2 + 8)} = \frac{25 - 0}{-5(10)} = \frac{25}{-50} = -0.5$$

35. Which of the following expressions are equivalent to 28 – 4 • 6 +12?

    I. (28 – 4) • 6 +12

    II. 28 – (4 • 6) +12

    III. (28 – 4) • (6 +12)

    IV. (28 + 12) – (4 • 6)

    V. 28 – 4 • 12 + 6

(Average)

    A. I and V

    B. II and IV

    C. III and V

    D. IV and V

Answer: B. II and IV
The parentheses in expression II indicate that the multiplication is to be done first. Using the standard order of operations: multiply and divide from left to right, then add and subtract from left to right.

36. If *n* represents an odd number, which of the following does not represent an even number?
(Average)

    A. $2n$

    B. $2(n + 1)$

    C. n^2

    D. $10n - 2$

Answer: C. n^2
n^2 represents an odd number times an odd number, which will be an odd number. Choices A, B, and D are multiples of 2 and represent even numbers.

37. Based upon the following examples, can you conclude that the sum of two prime numbers is also a prime number? Why or why not?

2 + 3 = 5
2 + 5 = 7
11 + 2 = 13

(Rigorous)

A. Yes; there is a pattern

B. Yes; there are many more examples, such as 17 + 2 = 19 and 29 + 2 = 31

C. No; there are many counterexamples

D. No; the sums are not prime numbers

Answer: C. No; there are many counterexamples
Only one counterexample is needed to disprove a statement. For example, in 3 + 5 = 8 the sum is a composite number. Care must be taken not to generalize a perceived pattern based upon too few examples. Additional examples are not sufficient to establish a pattern. In choice D, 5, 7, and 13 are prime numbers.

38. If x is a whole number, what is the best description of the number $4x + 1$? *(Rigorous)*

A. Prime number

B. Composite number

C. Odd number

D. Even number

Answer: C. Odd number
Since $4x$ is a multiple of 4, it is an even number. One more than an even number is an odd number. The prime numbers do not follow a pattern. $4x + 1$ may be either prime, for example 13, or composite, for example 9.

39. The plot for a proposed new city hall plaza is 120 feet long by 90 feet wide. A scale model for the plaza must fit in an area that is 10 feet square. If the largest possible model is built in that area, what will be the maximum possible width for the scale model?
(*Rigorous*)

A. $\dfrac{2}{15}$ ft

B. $1\dfrac{1}{3}$ ft

C. $7\dfrac{1}{2}$ ft

D. $13\dfrac{1}{3}$ ft

Answer: C $7\dfrac{1}{2}$ ft

Use a proportion to find the maximum width:

$$\dfrac{120}{10} = \dfrac{90}{x} \rightarrow x = 7\dfrac{1}{2}$$

The maximum width is $7\dfrac{1}{2}$ ft. Be sure to set up the proportion with equivalent ratios to find the maximum width. Check for reasonableness of results. The width cannot exceed 10 ft.

40. Jocelyn wants create a magnetic board in the back of her classroom by covering part of the wall with a special magnetic paint. Each can of paint will cover 15 square feet. If the area is 12 feet wide and 8 feet high, how many cans of paint should she buy?
  (Average)

   A. 5 cans

   B. 6 cans

   C. 7 cans

   D. 8 cans

Answer: C. 7 cans
First, find the area of the magnetic board. Then divide by 15.

$12 \times 8 = 96$
$96 \div 15 = 6.4$

Jocelyn cannot buy 6.4 cans. She must buy 7 cans. Consider the meaning of any remainder in the context of the problem.

41. A recipe makes 6 servings and calls for $1\frac{1}{2}$ cups of rice. How much rice is needed to make 10 servings?
   (Average)

   A. 2 cups

   B. $2\frac{1}{4}$ cups

   C. $2\frac{1}{2}$ cups

   D. $2\frac{3}{4}$ cups

Answer: C. $2\frac{1}{2}$ cups

Write and solve a proportion.

$$\frac{1.5}{6} = \frac{x}{10}$$
$$1.5(10) = 6x$$
$$x = 2.5$$

When writing a proportion, check that the ratios are equivalent:

$$\frac{\text{cups of rice}}{\text{servings}} = \frac{\text{cups of rice}}{\text{servings}}$$

42. Which table(s) represents solutions of the following equation?

$$2x - 5y = 50$$

I

x	ˉ5	0	5	10
y	ˉ12	ˉ10	ˉ8	ˉ6

II

x	ˉ5	0	5	ˉ10
y	ˉ12	ˉ10	ˉ12	ˉ10

III

x	20	25	30	35
y	ˉ2	0	2	4

(Rigorous)

A. I

B. II

C. II and III

D. I and III

Answer: D. I and III
Substitute values for *x* and *y* into the equation. For example, if *x* = ˉ5 and *y* = ˉ12, then

$$2(\bar{5}) - 5(\bar{1}2) = 50$$
$$\bar{1}0 - (\bar{6}0) = 50$$
$$\bar{1}0 + 60 = 50$$

Since the equation is true, the values *x* = ˉ5 and *y* = ˉ12 are solutions of the equation. In table II, substituting the values *x* = 5 and *y* = ˉ12, gives a false statement since

$$2(5) - 5(\bar{1}2) = 50$$
$$10 - (\bar{6}0) = 50$$
$$10 + 60 = 50$$

43. **The relations given below demonstrate the following addition and multiplication property of real numbers:**

$a + b = b + a$
$ab = ba$

(Average)

A. Commutative

B. Associative

C. Identity

D. Inverse

Answer: A. Commutative
Both addition and multiplication of real numbers satisfy the commutative property, according to which changing the order of the operands does not change the result of the operation.

44. **Which property (or properties) is applied below?**

$^-8x + 5x = (^-8 + 5)x$

$= ^-3x$

I. Associative Property of Addition
II. Zero Property of Addition
III. Additive Inverses
IV. Identity Property of Multiplication
V. Distributive Property

(Rigorous)

A. I

B. V

C. I and III

D. II and IV

Answer: B. V
The variable x is distributed over the sum of $^-8$ and 5. Check definitions of properties.

45. For which of the following is the additive inverse equal to the multiplicative inverse?
(*Rigorous*)

A. $\dfrac{2}{3} + \dfrac{3}{2}$

B. $\sqrt{-1}$

C. $\dfrac{1 - \sqrt{2}}{1 + \sqrt{2}}$

D. $(a + b) / (b - a)$

Answer: B. $\sqrt{-1}$
Let the number for which the additive inverse is equal to the multiplicative inverse be x.
Then $-x = \dfrac{1}{x}; \Rightarrow x^2 = -1; x = \sqrt{-1}$

46. Which of the statements below explain the error(s), if any, in the following calculation?

$$\dfrac{18}{18} + 23 = 23$$

I.   A number divided by itself is 1, not 0.

II. The sum of 1 and 23 is 24, not 23.

III. The 18s are "cancelled" and replaced by 0.

(*Rigorous*)

A. I and II

B. II and III

C. I, II, and III

D. There is no error.

Answer: C. I, II, and III
$\dfrac{18}{18} = 1$ and 1 + 23 = 24

47. Which statement is a model for the following problem?
27 less than 5 times a number is 193.
(Average)

    A. $27 < 5x + 193$

    B. $27 - 5x < 193$

    C. $5x - 27 < 193$

    D. $5x - 27 = 193$

Answer: D. $5x - 27 = 193$
5 times a number is represented by $5x$; 27 less than $5x$ by $5x - 27$; the difference *is* (equals) 193, not *is less than* 193. Avoid confusing *is less than* with *less than*.

48. What is the solution set of the following inequality?

    $4x + 9 \geq 11(x - 3)$

    (Average)

    A. $x \leq 0$

    B. $x \geq 0$

    C. $x \leq 6$

    D. $x \geq 6$

Answer: C. $x \leq 6$
Apply the distributive property on the right.

$$4x + 9 \geq 11(x - 3)$$
$$4x + 9 \geq 11x - 33$$
$$11x - 4x \leq 9 + 33$$
$$7x \leq 42$$
$$x \leq 6$$

49. A car is rented in Quebec. The outside temperature shown on the dashboard reads 17°C. What is the temperature in degrees Fahrenheit? (Use the formula $F = \frac{9}{5}C + 32$.)
(Average)

   A. 27.2°F

   B. 41.4°F

   C. 62.6°F

   D. 88.2°F

Answer: C. 62.6°F

Use the order of operations. First multiply $\frac{9}{5}$ and 17. Then add 32 to the result.

$$F = (\frac{9}{5} \cdot 17) + 32$$
$$= 30.6 + 32$$
$$= 62.6$$

50. The two solutions of the quadratic equation $ax^2 + bx + c = 0$ are given by the formula $x = \frac{-b \pm \sqrt{b^2 - 4ac}}{2a}$. What are the solutions of the equation $x^2 - 18x + 32$?
(Rigorous)

   A. ⁻5 and 23

   B. 2 and 16

   C. $9 \pm \sqrt{113}$

   D. $9 \pm 2\sqrt{113}$

Answer: B. 2 and 16

Substitute in the formula: $a = 1$, $b = $ ⁻18, $c = 32$: $x = \frac{18 \pm \sqrt{18^2 - 4(32)}}{2}$. Then apply the standard order of operations: $x = \frac{18 + 14}{2}$ and $x = \frac{18 - 14}{2}$, or $x = 16$ and $x = 2$. Be sure to apply the standard order of operations after substituting in the formula.

51. Triangle *ABC* is rotated 90° clockwise about the origin and translated 6 units left.

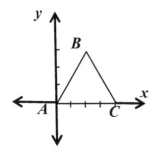

What are the coordinates of *B* after the transformations?
(*Rigorous*)

A. (2, ⁻3)

B. (3, ⁻2)

C. (⁻2, ⁻3)

D. (⁻3, ⁻2)

Answer: D. (⁻3, ⁻2)
Under the rotation, (2, 3) → (3, ⁻2). Sliding 6 units left, (3, ⁻2) → (⁻3, ⁻2). Work with one transformation at a time, rather than trying to do both at the same time.

52. The following represents the net of a

(*Average*)

A. Cube

B. Tetrahedron

C. Octahedron

D. Dodecahedron

Answer: C. Octahedron
The eight equilateral triangles make up the eight faces of an octahedron.

53. **Ginny and Nick head back to their respective colleges after being home for the weekend. They leave their house at the same time and drive for 4 hours. Ginny drives due south at the average rate of 60 miles per hour and Nick drives due east at the average rate of 60 miles per hour. What is the straight-line distance between them, in miles, at the end of the 4 hours?**
(Rigorous)

A. 169.7 miles

B. 240 miles

C. 288 miles

D. 339.4 miles

Answer: D. 339.4 miles
Ginny and Nick each drive a distance of 4 × 60, or 240 miles. Draw a diagram.

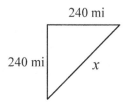

240 mi

240 mi

x

Then apply the Pythagorean Theorem: $c^2 = a^2 + b^2$.

$$x^2 = 240^2 + 240^2$$
$$= 115,200$$
$$x = \sqrt{115,200}$$
$$x = 339.4$$

So x is about 339.4 miles. Be sure to use the standard order of operations when solving for x.

54. **What is the surface area of the prism shown below?**
(Rigorous)

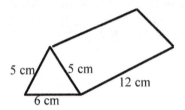

A. 204 cm^2

B. 216 cm^2

C. 360 cm^2

D. 180 cm^2

Answer: B. 216 cm^2
Find the area of each face. Each triangular face has an altitude of 4 cm and area of 12 cm^2. Surface area = 5(12) + 5(12) + 6(12) + 12 + 12, which equals 216. Check that the areas of all the faces are included in the sum, especially the bottom and the back of the prism.

55. **Which of the following is not equivalent to 3 km?**

I.   3.0 × 10^3 m

II. 3.0 × 10^4 cm

III. 3.0 × 10^6 mm

(Average)

A. I

B. II

C. III

D. None of the above

Answer: B. II
There are 1000, or 103 meters in each kilometer; 100, or 10^2 cm, in each meter; and 10 millimeters in each centimeter. Remember to add exponents when multiplying: for example, 3.0 × 10^3 m = 3.0 × 10^3 × 10^2 cm, or 3.0 × 10^5 cm.

56. A school band has 200 members. Looking at the pie chart below, determine which statement is true about the band.

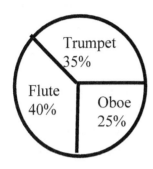

(Average)

A. There are more trumpet players than flute players

B. There are fifty oboe players in the band

C. There are forty flute players in the band

D. One-third of all band members play the trumpet

Answer: B. There are fifty oboe players in the band
There are fifty oboe players in the band since 25% of 200 is 50.

57. A restaurant offers the following menu choices.

Green Vegetable	Yellow Vegetable
Asparagus	Carrots
Broccoli	Corn
Peas	Squash
Spinach	

If a customer chooses a green vegetable and a yellow vegetable at random, what is the probability that the customer will order neither asparagus nor corn?
(Rigorous)

A. $\dfrac{1}{12}$

B. $\dfrac{1}{6}$

C. $\dfrac{1}{3}$

D. $\dfrac{1}{2}$

Answer: D. $\dfrac{1}{2}$

There are 4 × 3, or 12 possible combinations of choices. Of those, 6 include either asparagus or corn or both (1 asparagus and corn, 2 asparagus and not corn, and 3 corn but not asparagus). Since 6 out of the 12 choices are favorable, the probability is $\dfrac{6}{12}$, or $\dfrac{1}{2}$. Be careful not to count any choice (asparagus and corn) more than once.

58. **A school has 15 male teachers and 35 female teachers. In how many ways can they form a committee with 2 male teachers and 4 female teachers on it? (Average)**

   A. 525

   B. 5497800

   C. 88

   D. 263894400

Answer: B. 5497800
The number of ways one can pick 2 male teachers out of 15 =
$$_2^{15}C = \frac{15!}{13!2!} = \frac{14 \times 15}{2} = 105$$

The number of ways one can pick 4 female teachers out of 35 =
$$_4^{35}C = \frac{35!}{31!4!} = \frac{32 \times 33 \times 34 \times 35}{2 \times 3 \times 4} = 52360$$

Hence, the total number of ways the committee can be chosen =
105 x 52360 = 5497800.

59. **A music store owner wants to change the window display every week. Only 4 out of 6 instruments can be displayed in the window at the same time. How many weeks will it be before the owner must repeat the same arrangement (in the same order) of instruments in the window display? (Rigorous)**

   A. 24 weeks

   B. 36 weeks

   C. 120 weeks

   D. 360 weeks

Answer: D. 360 weeks
There are 6 choices for the first position. For each of those choices, there are 5 choices for the second position and 6 × 5 choices for the first two positions. For each of those there are 3 choices for the third position and 2 for the fourth position: 6 × 5 × 4 × 3 = 360.

60. **Half the students in a class scored 80% on an exam; one student scored 10%; and the rest of the class scored 85%. Which would be the best measure of central tendency for the test scores?**
   (Rigorous)

   A. Mean

   B. Median

   C. Mode

   D. Either the median or the mode because they are equal

Answer: B. Median

The median is the least sensitive to extreme values. The mode reports only one score and is not a reflection of the entire data set. The mean will be skewed by the outlier of 10%.

SOCIAL SCIENCES

61. **The Great Plains in the United States are an excellent place to grow corn and wheat for all of the following reasons EXCEPT:**
    (Average)

    A. Rainfall is abundant and the soil is rich

    B. The land is mostly flat and easy to cultivate

    C. The human population is modest in size, so there is plenty of space for large farms

    D. The climate is semitropical

Answer: D. The climate is semitropical
The climate on the Great Plains is not semitropical. It is temperate, with harsh winters. Rainfall and soil conditions are good. The land is flat. The human population is not overcrowded; there is room for large farms.

62. **What is characteristic of areas of the world with high populations?**
    (Rigorous)

    A. These areas tend to have heavy pollution

    B. These areas are almost always surrounded by suburbs

    C. Populations are rarely located near one another

    D. Most populated places in the world also tend to be close to agricultural lands

Answer: D. Most populated places in the world also tend to be close to agricultural lands
Pollution (choice A) and suburbs (choice B) are often found in populated areas, but they are not always present and are not mentioned in the text. The text says that population centers are often, not rarely (choice C), located near each other.

63. **Meridians, or lines of longitude, not only help in pinpointing locations but are also used for:**
    (Average)

    A. Measuring distance from the Poles

    B. Determining direction of ocean currents

    C. Determining the time around the world

    D. Measuring distance on the equator

Answer: C. Determining the time around the world
Meridians, or lines of longitude, are the determining factor in separating time zones and determining time around the world.

64. **The Western Hemisphere contains all of which of the following continents?**
    (Rigorous)

    A. Russia

    B. Europe

    C. North America

    D. Asia

Answer: C. North America
The Western Hemisphere, located between the North and South Poles and between the Prime Meridian (0 degrees longitude) west to the International Date Line at 180 degrees longitude, consists of all of North and South America, a tiny part of the easternmost part of Russia that extends east of 180 degrees longitude, and a part of Europe that extends west of the Prime Meridian (0 degrees longitude).

65. **Mr. Allen is discussing the earthquake in Chile and explains the aftershocks and tsunamis that threatened Pacific islands thousands of miles away. What aspect of geographical studies was he emphasizing?**
    (Rigorous)

    A. Regional

    B. Topical

    C. Physical

    D. Human

Answer: C. Physical
Earthquakes, aftershocks, and tsunamis are physical features on the earth. Regional studies would focus on the elements or characteristics of a particular region, such as in Chile itself. Topical studies focus on an earth feature or human activity occurring throughout the entire world, such as talking about earthquakes in Italy, Haiti, Chile, Mexico and other countries. Human studies would focus on human activity patterns and how they relate to the environment including political, cultural, historical, urban, and social geographical fields of study.

66. **Which of the following are non-renewable resources?**
    (Average)

    A. Fish, coffee, and forests

    B. Fruit, water, and solar energy

    C. Wind power, alcohol, and sugar

    D. Coal, natural gas, and oil

Answer: D. Coal, natural gas, and oil
Coal, natural gas, and oil are fossil fuels, which cannot be renewed. Nonrenewable resources are natural resources that cannot be remade or regenerated in the same proportion that they are used. Renewable resources are generally living resources (fish, coffee, and forests, for example), which can restock (renew) themselves if they are not over harvested. Renewable resources can restock themselves and be used indefinitely if they are sustained.

67. **What people perfected the preservation of dead bodies?**
    (Average)

    A. Sumerians

    B. Phoenicians

    C. Egyptians

    D. Assyrians

Answer: C. Egyptians
The Sumerians (choice A), Phoenicians (choice B), and Assyrians (choice D) all made contributions to ancient civilization but preserving dead bodies was not among their respective contributions.

68. **Which of these is NOT a true statement about the Roman civilization?**
    (Rigorous)

    A. Its period of Pax Romana provided long periods of peace during which travel and trade increased, enabling the spread of culture, goods, and ideas over the known world

    B. It borrowed the concept of democracy from the Greeks and developed it into a complex representative government

    C. It flourished in the arts with realistic approach to art and a dramatic use of architecture

    D. It developed agricultural innovations such as crop rotation and terrace farming

Answer: D. It developed agricultural innovations such as crop rotation and terrace farming
China had developed crop rotation and terrace farming.

69. **The major force in eighteenth and nineteenth century politics was:**
    (Average)

    A. Nationalism

    B. Revolution

    C. War

    D. Diplomacy

Answer: A. Nationalism
Nationalism was the driving force in politics in the eighteenth and nineteenth century. Groups of people that shared common traits and characteristics wanted their own government and countries. This led to some revolution, war, and the failure of diplomacy.

70. **The identification of individuals or groups as they are influenced by their own group or culture is called:**
    (Average)

    A. Cross-cultural exchanges

    B. Cultural diffusion

    C. Cultural identity

    D. Cosmopolitanism

Answer: C. Cultural identity
Cross-cultural exchanges involved the discovery of shared values and needs as well as an appreciation of differences. Cultural diffusion is the movement of cultural ideas or materials between populations independent of the movement of those populations. Cosmopolitanism blurs cultural differences in the creation of a shared new culture.

71. **The New England colonies included:**
(Average)

A. South Carolina

B. Georgia

C. Massachusetts

D. New York

Answer: C. Massachusetts
South Carolina (choice A) and Georgia (choice B) were southern colonies. New York (choice D) was a middle Atlantic colony.

72. **Which major economic activity of the Southern colonies led to the growth of slavery?**
(Rigorous)

A. Manufacturing

B. Fishing

C. Farming

D. Coal mining

Answer: C. Farming
The major economic activity in this region was farming. Here the soil was very fertile, and the climate was very mild with an even longer growing season than farther north. The large plantations, eventually requiring large numbers of slaves, were found in the coastal or tidewater areas. Although the wealthy slave-owning planters set the pattern of life in this region, most of the people lived inland away from coastal areas. They were small farmers and very few, if any, owned slaves.

73. **Which was the first instance of an internal tax on the American colonies?**
   (Average)

   A. The Proclamation Act

   B. The Sugar Act

   C. The Currency Act

   D. The Stamp Act

Answer: D. The Stamp Act
The Proclamation Act prohibited English settlement beyond the Appalachian Mountains to appease the Native Americans. The Sugar Act imposed a tax on foreign molasses, sugar, and other goods imported into the colonies. The Currency Act prohibited colonial governments from issuing paper money. The Stamp Act placed a tax on newspapers, legal documents, licenses, almanacs, and playing cards which made it the first instance of an "internal" tax on the colonies.

74. **The Lewis and Clark expedition advanced knowledge in each of the following areas except:**
   (Average)

   A. Geography

   B. Modern warfare

   C. Botany

   D. Animal life

Answer: B. Modern warfare
The Lewis and Clark expedition was peaceful. Lewis and Clark learned a great deal about geography, botany, and animal life.

75. **Populism arises out of a feeling:**
    (Average)

    A. Of intense happiness

    B. Of satisfaction with the activities of large corporations

    C. That women should not be allowed to vote

    D. Perceived oppression

Answer: D. Perceived oppression
Perceived oppression felt by average people toward the wealthy elite gave rise to Populism. Populists do not become prominent when people are happy (choice A), or when people are satisfied with the activities of large corporations (choice B). Populists and other progressives fought for, not against (choice C), voting rights for women.

76. **At the end of the Twentieth Century, the United States was:**
    (Average)

    A. A central leader in international affairs

    B. A reluctant participant in international affairs

    C. One of two superpowers

    D. Lacking a large consumer culture

Answer: A. A central leader in international affairs
It was a reluctant participant (choice B) in international affairs at the beginning of the twentieth century. The United States was the only superpower (choice C) left at the end of the twentieth century. The United States developed a large consumer culture (choice D) in the 1950s and still has it today.

77. **How did manufacturing change in the early 1800s?**
(*Rigorous*)

   A. The electronics industry was born

   B. Production moved from small shops or homes into factories

   C. Industry benefited from the Federal Reserve Act

   D. The timber industry was hurt when Theodore Roosevelt set aside 238 million acres of federal lands to be protected from development

Answer: B. Production moved from small shops or homes into factories
Factories had modern machinery in them that could produce goods efficiently. The electronics industry (choice A) did not exist in the early 1800s. The Federal Reserve Act (choice C) came much later, in the Twentieth Century. Theodore Roosevelt's protection of federal lands from development (choice D) also took place in the Twentieth Century.

78. **The early ancient civilizations developed systems of government:**
(*Rigorous*)

   A. To provide for defense against attack

   B. To regulate trade

   C. To regulate and direct the economic activities of the people as they worked together in groups

   D. To decide on the boundaries of the different fields during planting seasons

Answer: C. To regulate and direct the economic activities of the people as they worked together in groups
Although ancient civilizations were concerned with defense, trade regulation, and the maintenance of boundaries in their fields, they could not have done any of them without first regulating and directing the economic activities of the people as they worked in groups. This provided for a stable economic base from which they could trade and actually had something worth providing defense for.

79. **What is another name for dictatorship?**
 (Rigorous)

 A. Oligarchy

 B. Monarchy

 C. Anarchism

 D. Communism

Answer: A. Oligarchy
Monarchy (choice B) features a king or a queen, not a dictator. Anarchism (choice C) favors the elimination of all government and its replacement by a cooperative community of individuals. Dictatorship is not about cooperating between individuals. Communism (choice D) is decentralized, while dictatorship is highly centralized.

80. **Which of the following documents described and defined the system and structure of the United States government?**
 (Average)

 A. The Bill of Rights

 B. The Declaration of Independence

 C. The Constitution

 D. The Articles of Confederation

Answer: C. The Constitution
The United States Constitution is the written document that describes and defines the system and structure of the United States government. The first ten Amendments to the Constitution are called the Bill of Rights. The Declaration of Independence, written in 1776 by Thomas Jefferson, was a call to the colonies to unite against the King, detailing the grievances of the colonies and articulating the philosophical framework upon which the United States is founded. The Articles of Confederation were the first attempt of the newly independent states to reach a new understanding among themselves.

81. **How did the ideology of John Locke influence Thomas Jefferson in writing the Declaration of Independence?**
(*Rigorous*)

    A. Locke emphasized human rights and believed that people should rebel against governments who violated those rights

    B. Locke emphasized the rights of government to protect its people and to levy taxes

    C. Locke believed in the British system of monarchy and the rights of Parliament to make laws

    D. Locke advocated individual rights over the collective whole

Answer: A. Locke emphasized human rights and believed that people should rebel against governments who violated those rights
The Declaration of Independence is an outgrowth of both ancient Greek ideas of democracy and individual rights and the ideas of the European Enlightenment and the Renaissance, especially the ideology of the political thinker John Locke. Thomas Jefferson (1743–1826) the principle author of the Declaration borrowed much from Locke's theories and writings. John Locke was one of the most influential political writers of the seventeenth century who put great emphasis on human rights and put forth the belief that when governments violate those rights people should rebel. He wrote the book *Two Treatises of Government* in 1690, which had tremendous influence on political thought in the American colonies and helped shape the U.S. Constitution and Declaration of Independence.

82. **Which of the following is not a right declared by the U.S. Constitution?** *(Average)*

   A. The right to speak out in public

   B. The right to use cruel and unusual punishment

   C. The right to a speedy trial

   D. The right not to be forced to testify against yourself

Answer: B. The right to use cruel and unusual punishment
A person who lives in a democratic society legally has a comprehensive list of rights guaranteed to him or her by the government. In the United States, this is the Constitution and its Amendments. Among these very important rights are:

*   the right to speak out in public;
*   the right to pursue any religion;
*   the right for a group of people to gather in public for any reason that doesn't fall under a national security cloud;
*   the right not to have soldiers stationed in your home;
*   the right not to be forced to testify against yourself in a court of law;
*   the right to a speedy and public trial by a jury of your peers;
*   the right not to be the victim of cruel and unusual punishment; and
*   the right to avoid unreasonable search and seizure of your person, your house, and your vehicle.

83. The cold weather froze orange crops in Florida and the price of orange juice increased. This is an example of what economic concept?
(Rigorous)

   A. Output market

   B. Input market

   C. Supply and demand

   D. Entrepreneurship

Answer: C. Supply and demand
Output markets refer to the market in which goods and services are sold. The input market is the market in which factors of production, or resources, are bought and sold.

84. What type of production process must producers choose?
(Average)

   A. One that is inefficient

   B. One that often produces goods that consumers don't want

   C. One that is efficient

   D. One that is sometimes efficient and sometimes inefficient

Answer: C. One that is efficient
Producers cannot stay in business if they operate inefficiently (choice A). Producers cannot afford to produce goods that consumers don't want (choice B). Producers will suffer if their efficiency is inconsistent (choice D).

85. **The existence of economics is based on:**
    (Rigorous)

    A. The scarcity of resources

    B. The abundance of resources

    C. Little or nothing that is related to resources

    D. Entrepreneurship

Answer: A. The scarcity of resources
If resources were always abundant (choice B), economics would be unnecessary. Economics is closely, not loosely (choice C) related to resources. Entrepreneurship (choice D) is part of economics, but is not the primary basis of economics.

86. **In the fictional country of Nacirema, the government controls the means of production and directs resources. It alone decides what will be produced; as a result, there is an abundance of capital and military goods but a scarcity of consumer goods. What type of economy is this?**
    (Rigorous)

    A. Market economy

    B. Centrally planned economy

    C. Market socialism

    D. Capitalism

Answer: B. Centrally planned economy
In a planned economy, the means of production are publicly owned, with little, if any private ownership. Instead of the "three questions" being solved by markets, there is a planning authority that makes the decisions. The planning authority decides what will be produced and how. Since most planned economies direct resources into the production of capital and military goods, there is little remaining for consumer goods; the result is often chronic shortages.

87. **Which of the following are secondary research materials?**
    (Average)

    A. The conclusions and inferences of other historians

    B. Literature and nonverbal materials, novels, stories, poetry, and essays from the period, as well as coins, archaeological artifacts, and art produced during the period

    C. Interviews and surveys conducted by the researcher

    D. Statistics gathered as the result of the research's experiments

Answer: A. The conclusions and inferences of other historians
Secondary sources are works written significantly after the period being studied and based upon primary sources. In this case, historians have studied artifacts of the time and drawn their conclusion and inferences. Primary sources are the basic materials that provide raw data and information. Students or researchers may use literature and other data they have collected to draw their own conclusions or inferences.

88. **For their research paper on the effects of the Civil War on American literature, students have brainstormed a list of potential online sources and are seeking your authorization. Which of these represent the strongest source?**
    (Rigorous)

    A. http://www.wikipedia.org/

    B. http://www.google.com

    C. http://www.nytimes.com

    D. http://docsouth.unc.edu/southlit/civilwar.html

Answer: D. http://docsouth.unc.edu/southlit/civilwar.html
Sites with an "edu" domain are associated with educational institutions and tend to be more trustworthy for research information. Wikipedia has an "org" domain, which means it is a nonprofit. While Wikipedia may be appropriate for background reading, its credibility as a research site is questionable. Both Google and the New York Times are "com" sites, which are for profit. Even though this does not discredit their information, each site is problematic for researchers. With Google, students will get overwhelmed with hits and may not choose the most reputable sites for their information. As a newspaper, the New York Times would not be a strong source for historical information.

89. **For the historian studying ancient Egypt, which of the following would be least useful?**
(Rigorous)

    A. The record of an ancient Greek historian on Greek-Egyptian interaction

    B. Letters from an Egyptian ruler to his/her regional governors

    C. Inscriptions on stele of the Fourteenth Egyptian Dynasty

    D. Letters from a nineteenth century Egyptologist to his wife

Answer: D. Letters from a nineteenth century Egyptologist to his wife
Historians use primary sources from the actual time they are studying whenever possible. Ancient Greek records of interaction with Egypt (choice A), letters from an Egyptian ruler to regional governors (choice B), and inscriptions from the Fourteenth Egyptian Dynasty (choice C) are all primary sources created at or near the actual time being studied. Choice D, letters from a nineteenth century Egyptologist, would not be considered primary sources, as they were created thousands of years after the fact and may not actually be about the subject being studied.

90. **Which of the following can be considered the primary goal of social studies?**
(Rigorous)

    A. Recalling specific dates and places

    B. Identifying and analyzing social links

    C. Using contextual clues to identify eras

    D. Linking experiments with history

Answer: B. Identifying and analyzing social links
Historic events and social issues cannot be considered only in isolation. People and their actions are connected in many ways, and events are linked through cause and effect over time. Identifying and analyzing these social and historic links is a primary goal of the social sciences. The methods used to analyze social phenomena borrow from several of the social sciences. Interviews, statistical evaluation, observation, and experimentation are just some of the ways that people's opinions and motivations can be measured. From these opinions, larger social beliefs and movements can be interpreted, and events, issues and social problems can be placed in context to provide a fuller view of their importance.

SCIENCE

91. **Which is the correct order for the layers of Earth's atmosphere? (Easy)**

    A. Troposphere, stratosphere, mesosphere, and thermosphere

    B. Mesosphere, stratosphere, troposphere, and thermosphere

    C. Troposphere, stratosphere, thermosphere, and mesosphere

    D. Thermosphere, troposphere, stratosphere, mesosphere

Answer: A. Troposphere, stratosphere, mesosphere, and thermosphere
All weather occurs in the troposphere. There are few clouds in the stratosphere, but weather balloons can float in this region. Air temperatures start to drop in the mesosphere. The coldest spot on Earth is where the mesosphere meets the thermosphere. The thermosphere extends into outer space.

92. **Which statement correctly describes the theory of plate tectonics? (Easy)**

    A. There eight major plates and many small plates that move at a rate of 10 to 50 millimeters per year

    B. There is one plate for each continent and they move at a speed too small to measure

    C. There are thousands of plates that move 1 to 5 meters per year

    D. Earthquakes are caused by the collision of plates

Answer: A. There eight major plates and many small plates that move at a rate of 10 to 50 millimeters meters per year
The motion of plates explains, not only earthquakes, but also mountain building, and the creation of volcanoes. The speed is measureable because there are ways to determine the time it took the plates to move from one position on Earth's surface to another.

93. **What type of rock can be classified by the size of the crystals in the rock?**
(Easy)

    A. Metamorphic

    B. Igneous

    C. Minerals

    D. Sedimentary

Answer: B. Igneous
Igneous rock is formed when molten rock material cools. It is characterized by its grain size and mineral content. Metamorphic rocks are formed from other rocks as a result of heat and pressure. Sedimentary rocks come from weathering and erosion of pre existing rocks.

94. *What are solids with a definite chemical composition and a tendency to split along planes of weakness?*
(Easy)

    A. Ores

    B. Rocks

    C. Minerals

    D. Salts

Answer: C. Minerals
Rocks are made up of minerals, and ores are rocks than can be processed for a commercial use. Salts are ionic compounds formed from acids and bases.

95. **In which of the following eras did life appear?**
    (Easy)

    A. Paleozoic

    B. Mesozoic

    C. Cenozoic

    D. Precambrian

Answer: D. Precambrian

The Cambrian explosion, the rapid appearance of most groups of complex organisms, took place in the Cambrian period, which is part of the Paleozoic era. Humans evolved in the Cenozoic era, dinosaurs in the Mesozoic era, and fish in the Paleozoic era.

96. **The use of radioactivity to determine the age of rocks and fossils is called which of the following?**
    (Easy)

    A. Carbon dating

    B. Absolute dating

    C. Stratigraphy

    D. Geological dating

Answer: B. Absolute dating

Carbon dating measures the relative amount of carbon-14, which is radioactive, with the amount of carbon-12. The ratio of carbon-12 and carbon-14 in an organic substance at different points in time is known. Stratigraphy is the study or rock layers.

97. Which of the following astronomical entities is not part of the galaxy the Sun is located in?
(Easy)

   A. Nebulae

   B. Quasars

   C. Pulsars

   D. Neutron stars

Answer: B. Quasars
Nebulae are visible in the night sky and are glowing clouds of dust, hydrogen, and plasma. Neutron stars are the remnants of super novae, and pulsars are neutron stars that emit radio waves on a periodic basis. A quasar is a distant galaxy that emits large amounts of visible light and radio waves.

98. Why is the winter in the southern hemisphere colder than winter in the northern hemisphere?
(Average)

   A. Earth's axis of 24-hour rotation tilts at an angle of 23½°

   B. The elliptical orbit of Earth around the Sun changes the distance of the Sun from Earth

   C. The southern hemisphere has more water than the northern hemisphere

   D. The green house effect is greater for the northern hemisphere

Answer: B. The elliptical orbit of Earth around the Sun changes the distance of the Sun from Earth
The tilt of Earth's axis causes the seasons. The Earth is close to the Sun during winter in the northern hemisphere. Winter in the southern hemisphere occurs six months later when Earth is farther from the Sun. The presence of water explains why winters are harsher inland than by the coast.

99. **Which of the following facts of physics best explains the cause of tides?**
    (Rigorous)

    A. The density of water is less than the density of rock

    B. The force of gravity follows the inverse square law

    C. Centripetal acceleration causes water on Earth to bulge

    D. The gravitational force of the Moon on Earth's oceans

Answer: B. The force of gravity follows the inverse square law
The main cause of lunar tides is that the Moon's gravitational force is greater on water near the Moon than on the other side of Earth. This causes the bulge of water. Earth's rotation causes the location of the bulge to change. Centripetal acceleration causes Earth's water to bulge and affects tides caused by the Sun's gravity, however, the effect is minor.

100. **Which of the following is not a property that eukaryotes have and prokaryotes do not have?**
    (Average)

    A. Nucleus

    B. Ribosomes

    C. Chromosomes

    D. Mitochondria

Answer: B. Ribosomes
Prokaryotes do not have a nuclear membrane, and the DNA is not packed into chromosomes. Mitochondria are organelles that produce power are not in the smaller, simpler cell. Ribosomes are the sites where cells assemble proteins.

101. Which of the following processes and packages macromolecules?
(Easy)

    A. Lysosomes

    B. Cytosol

    C. Golgi apparatus

    D. Plastids

Answer: C. Golgi apparatus
Lysosomes contain digestive enzymes. Cytosol is the liquid inside cells. Plastids manufacture chemicals used in plant cells.

102. Which is not a characteristic of living organisms?
(Easy)

    A. Sexual reproduction

    B. Ingestion

    C. Synthesis

    D. Respiration

Answer: A. Sexual reproduction
Only certain organisms reproduce sexually, that is by mixing DNA. Single-celled organisms generally reproduce by cell division. Ingestion means taking nutrients from outside the cell wall. Synthesis means creating new cellular material. Respiration means generating energy by combining oxygen or some other gas with material in the cell.

103. At what stage in mitosis does the chromatin become chromosomes? (Average)

    A. Telophase

    B. Anaphase

    C. Prophase

    D. Metaphase

Answer: C. Prophase
Prophase is the beginning of mitosis. In metaphase, fibers attach to chromosomes, and in anaphase, the chromosomes separate. In telophase, the cells divide.

104. Meiosis starts with a single cell and ends with which of the following? (Average)

    A. Two diploid cells

    B. Two haploid cells

    C. Four diploid cells

    D. Four haploid cells

Answer: D. Four haploid cells
The single cell that begins the creation of a gamete has a full set of chromosomes in matched pairs. This is called a diploid cell. After the first division there are two haploid cells. After the second division, there are four haploid cells.

105. **How many autosomes are in a somatic cells of human beings?**
    (Easy)

    A. 22

    B. 23

    C. 44

    D. 46

Answer: C. 44
The total number of chromosomes is 46, but two of them are the sex chromosomes. Autosomes refer to the chromosomes that are not X or Y chromosomes.

106. **Which of the following is not part of Darwinian evolution?**
    (Average)

    A. Survival of the fittest

    B. Random mutations

    C. Heritability of acquired traits

    D. Natural selection

Answer: C. Heritability of acquired traits
Acquired traits change somatic cells but not gametes. So they are not passed on to succeeding generations. Natural selection occurs because offspring through random mutations are more fit than others to survive. The idea that acquired traits can be passed on to offspring is called Lamarkism.

107. Taxonomy classifies species into genera (plural of genus) based on similarities. Species are subordinate to genera. The most general or highest taxonomical group is the kingdom. Which of the following is the correct order of the other groups from highest to lowest?
(Easy)

  A. Class ⇒ order⇒ family ⇒ phylum

  B. Phylum ⇒ class ⇒ family ⇒ order

  C. Phylum ⇒ class ⇒ order ⇒ family

  D. Order ⇒ phylum ⇒ class ⇒ family

Answer: C. Phylum ⇒ class ⇒ order ⇒ family
In the case of the domestic dog, the genus (Canis) includes wolves, the family (Canidae) includes jackals and coyotes, the order (Carnivore) includes lions, the class (Mammals) includes mice, and the phylum (Chordata) includes fish.

108. Which of the following describes the interaction between community members when one species feeds of another species but does not kill it immediately?
(Easy)

  A. Parasitism

  B. Predation

  C. Commensalism

  D. Mutualism

Answer: A. Parasitism
Predation occurs when one species kills another species. In mutualism, both species benefit. In commensalisms, one species benefits without the other being harmed.

109. Which of the following statements about the density of a substance is true?
(Easy)

    A. It is a chemical property

    B. It is a physical property

    C. It does not depend on the temperature of the substance

    D. It is a property only of liquids and solids

Answer: B. It is a physical property
The density of a substance is the mass of an object made of the substance divided by the object's volume. Chemical properties involve chemical reactions. Densities of substances generally decrease with higher temperatures.

110. The electrons in a neutral atom that is not in an excited energy state are in various energy shells. For example, there are two electrons in the lowest energy shell and eight in the next shell if the atom contains more than 10 electrons. How many electrons are in the shell with the maximum number of electrons?
(Easy)

    A. 8

    B. 18

    C. 32

    D. 44

Answer: C. 32
There is no energy level with 44 electrons. There is however, a shell with 18 electrons. The number of electrons in an atom's outer shell determines how the atom chemically interacts with other atoms.

111. **Which statement best explains why a balance scale is used to measure both weight and mass?**
(Rigorous)

    A. The weight and mass of an object are identical concepts

    B. The force of gravity between two objects depends on the mass of the two objects

    C. Inertial mass and gravitational mass are identical

    D. A balance scale compares the weight of two objects

Answer: C. Inertial mass and gravitational mass are identical
The mass of an object is a fundamental property of matter and is measured in kilograms. The weight is the force of gravity between Earth and an object near Earth's surface and is measured in newtons or pounds. Newton's second law ($F = ma$) and the universal law of gravity ($F = G\dfrac{m_{earth}m}{d^2}$) determine the weight of an object. The mass in Newton's second law is called the inertial mass and the mass in the universal law of gravity is called the gravitational mass. The two kinds of masses are identical.

112. **Which of the following does not determine the frictional force between a box sliding down a ramp?**
(Average)

    A. The weight of the box

    B. The area of the box

    C. The angle the ramp makes with the horizontal

    D. The chemical properties of the two surfaces

Answer: B. The area of the box
The frictional force is caused by bonding between the molecules of the box with the molecules of the ramp. At a small number of points, there is contact between the molecules. While there may be a small increase in the frictional force as the area increases, it is not noticeable. The main determinant of the frictional force is the weight of the box and the nature of the two surfaces.

113. Which statement is true about temperature?
   (Easy)

   A. Temperature is a measurement of heat

   B. Temperature is how hot or cold an object is

   C. The coldest temperature ever measured is zero degrees Kelvin

   D. The temperature of a molecule is its kinetic energy

Answer: B. Temperature is how hot or cold an object is
Temperature is a physical property of objects relating to how they feel when touched.
For example, 0 degrees Celsius or 32 degrees Fahrenheit is defined as the temperature
of ice water. Heat is a form of energy that flows from hot objects in thermal contact with
cold objects. The greater the temperature of an object, the greater the kinetic energy of
the molecules making up the object, but a single molecule does not have a temperature.
The third law of thermodynamics is that absolute zero can never be achieved in a
laboratory.

**114. When glass is heated, it becomes softer and softer until it becomes a liquid.
   Which of the following statements best describes this phenomenon?**
   (Rigorous)

   A. Glass has no heat of vaporization

   B. Glass has no heat of fusion

   C. The latent heat of glass is zero calories per gram

   D. Glass is made up of crystals

Answer: B. Glass has no heat of fusion
When a substance goes from the solid state to the liquid state as heat is added at the
melting point, the temperature is constant. All the heat energy goes into changing the
forces between the atoms, ions, or molecules so that the substance becomes a liquid.
The heat of vaporization is the calories of heat needed to change one gram of the liquid
into a gas.

115. **Which statement could be described as the first law of thermodynamics?**
    (Average)

    A. No machine can convert heat energy to work with 100 percent efficiency

    B. Energy is neither created nor destroyed

    C. Thermometers can be used to measure temperatures

    D. Heat flows from hot objects to cold objects

Answer: B. Energy is neither created nor destroyed
The first law of thermodynamics is considered to be a statement of the conservation of energy. Choices B and D are statements of the second law of thermodynamics. Answer C is the zeroth law of thermodynamics.

116. **What kind of chemical reaction is the burning of coal?**
    (Average)

    A. Exothermic and composition

    B. Exothermic and decomposition

    C. Endothermic and composition

    D. Exothermic and decomposition

Answer: A. Exothermic and composition
Burning coal means oxygen is combining with carbon to produce carbon dioxide. Since heat is released, the reaction is exothermic. Since elements are combining to for a compound, the reaction is a composition.

117. Which of the following is a result of a nuclear reaction called fission? (Easy)

A. Sunlight

B. Cosmic radiation

C. Supernova

D. Existence of the elements in the periodic table

Answer: D. Existence of the elements in the periodic table
Sunlight comes from fusion. Cosmic radiation has many sources. Inside stars, hydrogen and helium combine to form the higher elements on the periodic table.

118. What is technology? (Easy)

A. The application of science to satisfy human needs

B. Knowledge of complex machines, computer systems, and manufacturing processes

C. The study of engineering

D. A branch of science

Answer: A. The application of science to satisfy human needs
Science is knowledge of the universe gained by observations and experiments. Technology is the use of this knowledge to help human beings.

119. An experiment is performed to determine how the surface area of a liquid affects how long it takes for the liquid to evaporate. One hundred milliliters of water is put in containers with surface areas of 10 cm^2, 30 cm^2, 50 cm^2, 70 cm^2, and 90 cm^2. The time it took for each container to evaporate is recorded. Which of the following is a controlled variable?
(Average)

   A. The time required for each evaporation

   B. The area of the surfaces

   C. The amount of water

   D. The temperature of the water

Answer: C. The amount of water
The surface area is the independent variable and the time is the dependent variable. The temperature of the water should have been controlled in this experiment.

120. Stars near Earth can be seen to move relative to fixed stars. In observing the motion of a nearby star over a period of decades, an astronomer notices that the path is not a straight line but wobbles about a straight line. The astronomer reports in a peer-reviewed journal that a planet is rotating around the star, causing it to wobble. Which of the following statements best describes the proposition that the star has a planet?
(Rigorous)

   A. Observation

   B. Hypothesis

   C. Theory

   D. Inference

Answer: D. Inference
The observation in the report was the wobbly path of the star. It would be a hypothesis if this was the basis of a further experiment or observation about the existence of the planet. A theory would be more speculative. The astronomer didn't just suggest that the planet was there; the report stated that the star has a planet.

GENERAL CURRICULUM

CPSIA information can be obtained
at www.ICGtesting.com
Printed in the USA
BVOW09s1058210217
476767BV00008B/43/P

9 781607 874034